AMERICA'S NEWCOMERS AND THE DYNAMICS OF DIVERSITY

AMERICA'S NEWCOMERS AND THE DYNAMICS OF DIVERSITY

FRANK D. BEAN AND GILLIAN STEVENS

A Volume in the American Sociological Association's
Rose Series in Sociology

Russell Sage Foundation • New York

Library of Congress Cataloging-in-Publication Data

Bean, Frank D.

America's newcomers and the dynamics of diversity / Frank D. Bean and Gillian Stevens.

p. cm. — (The American Sociological Association's Rose series in sociology)
Includes bibliographical references and index.
ISBN 0-87154-124-6 (cloth)   ISBN 0-87154-128-9 (paperback)
1. Immigrants—United States. 2. United States—Emigration and immigration.
3. United States—Emigration and immigration—Government policy.
4. Americanization.   I. Stevens, Gillian.   II. Title.   III. Rose series in sociology.

JV6455 .B42 2003
304.8'73—dc21   2002036744

The paper used in this publication meets the minimum requirements of American National Standard for Information Sciences—Permanence of Paper for Printed Library Materials. ANSI Z39.48-1992.

Text design by Suzanne Nichols

RUSSELL SAGE FOUNDATION
112 East 64th Street, New York, New York 10021
10 9 8 7 6 5 4 3 2 1

Previous Volumes in the Series

Forthcoming Titles

The Rose Series in Sociology

THE AMERICAN Sociological Association's Rose Series in Sociology publishes books that integrate knowledge and address controversies from a sociological perspective. Books in the Rose Series are at the forefront of sociological knowledge. They are lively and often involve timely and fundamental issues on significant social concerns. The series is intended for broad dissemination throughout sociology, across social science and other professional communities, and to policy audiences. The series was established in 1967 by a bequest to ASA from Arnold and Caroline Rose to support innovations in scholarly publishing.

DOUGLAS L. ANDERTON
DAN CLAWSON
NAOMI GERSTEL
JOYA MISRA
RANDALL STOKES
ROBERT ZUSSMAN

EDITORS

= Contents =

About the Authors

Frank D. Bean is professor of sociology and codirector of the Center for Research on Immigration, Population and Public Policy at the University of California, Irvine.

Gillian Stevens is associate professor of sociology and advertising at the University of Illinois, Champaign-Urbana.

Jennifer Lee is assistant professor of sociology at the University of California, Irvine.

Jennifer Van Hook is assistant professor of sociology at Bowling Green State University.

Susan Wierzbicki is assistant professor of sociology at the University of California, Irvine.

═ Acknowledgments ═

T HIS book represents the culmination of several years of research and thinking about a number of social science research
questions that have occupied center stage in the longstanding
(but never more salient than now) debate in the United States over
the issue of immigration reform. Whether and how U.S. admissions
policies should be modified in order to try to achieve a stronger
American society and economy is a subject with many facets. Thus,
researching and writing this book has constituted a long project with
a large number of sub-topics. As a result, many people and institutions have contributed in one way or another, in some form or fashion, to the furtherance and no doubt the betterment of the endeavor.
In acknowledging these contributions, it is perhaps appropriate to
start at the beginning. In this regard, special thanks are owed first to
Harley Browning for encouraging and providing an opportunity
when the first author was an assistant professor at the University of
Texas to become involved in the field of what now might be called
Latino population studies, an involvement that eventually led to the
development of substantial interests in the economic sociology and
demography of immigration. A particular note of thanks is also ac-
corded Sidney Weintraub, now the William Simon Chair in Political
Economy at the Center for Strategic and International Studies in
Washington, D.C., whose collaboration with the first author some
years ago in a project on Mexican migration and U.S. policy led to the
development of a program of research, many of whose results have
been included in this volume.

The investigations on which the book is based have received support from several institutions. Some of the work incorporated into
several of the chapters occurred when the first author was still affiliated with the University of Texas at Austin, working at the Population Research Center as a faculty member in the Department of Sociology and the Lyndon Baines Johnson School of Public Affairs. A
word of appreciation is in order to both the Population Research Cen-

ter (and its then director, Myron Gutmann) and the LBJ School (and
its then dean, Max Sherman) for providing in ways both large and
small the kind of stimulating intellectual environment and the sort of
research infrastructure that makes possible policy-relevant social science research. The University Research Institute of the University of
Texas also supported some of the projects out of which this book developed, as did the Department of Sociology through its granting of a
leave to the senior investigator. The University of Texas at Austin also
welcomed Stevens as a visiting scholar from 1998 to 1999 when she
had a sabbatical leave from the University of Illinois, a time that enabled the collaborative nature of this effort to begin to flourish. We
would particularly like to acknowledge the help of a number of persons at the Texas Population Research Center for their assistance: Ce-
cilia Dean, Diane Fisher, Jenny Frary, Eve Kleinman, and Starling
Pullum.

We also extend a very special note of thanks to the Department of
Sociology, the School of Social Sciences, and the Office of Research
and Graduate Studies at the University of California, Irvine, for contributing in important ways to the project, especially through the es-
tablishment of the Center for Research on Immigration, Population,
and Public Policy (codirected by the first author), which has also supported some of the book's research. We are extremely grateful for the
research or other assistance provided by Jeanne Batalova, Carolynn
Bramlett, Andrea Dinesh, Charles Morgan, Christine Oh, Ping Ren,
and MaryAnn Zovak, all at the University of California, Irvine. We
also appreciate very much the research assistance provided by Xavier
Escandell and Hiromi Ishizawa, both at the University of Illinois.

We also express our deepest appreciation to several foundations
and funding agencies that have generously furnished financial support for some of the research on which the book is based. These include the Andrew W. Mellon Foundation, the Russell Sage Foundation, the William P. and Flora Hewlett Foundation, the Tomás Rivera
Policy Institute, the National Institute of Aging, and the National Institute of Child Health and Development. A Guggenheim Fellowship
to the first author during 2002 was particularly helpful in allowing
relatively unencumbered time that could be devoted to writing, and a
Visiting Scholar award at the Russell Sage Foundation to the first author during the academic year 2002 to 2003 provided an opportunity
to undertake final revisions and put finishing touches on the manuscript. We should emphasize, however, that the ideas and points of
view expressed in the work are our own and not those of any of the
foundations, funding agencies, or institutions with which we have
been affiliated.

We also wish to acknowledge the stimulating and helpful nature of our intellectual interactions with the many colleagues with whom we have worked in recent years. A number of persons have talked and collaborated with us on various research endeavors in ways that have contributed to the development of some of the ideas in the book. These persons include: Stephanie Bell-Rose, Randy Capps, Philip Cohen, Rodolfo Corona, Robert Cushing, John Dinardo, Rodolfo de la Garza, Michael Fix, Gary Freeman, Parker Frisbie, Jennifer Glick, Susan Gonzalez Baker, Daniel Hamermesh, Charles Haynes, Augustin Escobar Latapi, Magnus Lofstrom, Lindsay Lowell, Jeffrey Passel, Bryan Roberts, David Spener, Roberto Suro, Steven Trejo, Rodolfo Tuiràn, Michael Tyler, Robert Warren, and Karen Woodrow-Lafield. And we particularly want to acknowledge the significant contributions of three colleagues—Jennifer Lee, Susan Wierzbicki, and Jennifer Van Hook—each of whom is a coauthor of one of the chapters in the volume.

Some parts of some chapters are based on revised sections from the following previous publications of the first author: "Assessing Immigrant Policy Options: Labor Market Conditions and Declining Immigrant Welfare Receipt," (with Magnus Lofstrom), *Demography* 39, 2002: 617–637; "Circular, Invisible, and Ambiguous Migrants: Components of Difference in Estimates of the Number of Unauthorized Mexican Migrants in the United States" (with Rodolfo Corona, Rodolfo Tuiràn, Karen A. Woodrow-Lafield and Jennifer Van Hook), *Demography* 38, 2001: 411–422; "Immigration and Labor Markets in the United States" (with S. Gonzalez Baker and R. Capps), in *Sourcebook on Labor Markets: Evolving Structures and Processes*, edited by Ivar Berg and Arne Kalleberg, New York: Plenum Press, 2001; "The Latino Middle Class: Myth, Reality, and Potential " (with S. Trejo, R. Capps, and M. Tyler), Claremont, Calif.: Tomás Rivera Policy Institute, 2001; "Introduction: Immigration and Its Relation To Race and Ethnicity in the United States" (with Stephanie Bell-Rose), in *Immigration and Opportunity: Race, Ethnicity and Employment in the United States*, edited by Frank D. Bean and Stephanie Bell-Rose, New York: Russell Sage Foundation, 1999; "Immigration, Spatial and Economic Change, and African American Employment" (with J. Van Hook and M. Fossett), in *Immigration and Opportunity: Race, Ethnicity and Employment in the United States*, edited by Frank D. Bean and Stephanie Bell-Rose, New York: Russell Sage Foundation, 1999; "Self-employment and the Earnings of Mexican Immigrants" (with D. Spener), *Social Forces* 77, 1999: 1021–1047; and "Immigration and the Social Contract" (with Robert G. Cushing, Charles Haynes, and Jennifer V. W. Van Hook), *Social Science Quarterly* 78, 1997: 249–268.

The editors of the American Sociological Association's Arnold Rose

Monograph Series in Sociology, especially Randall Stokes and Douglas Anderton, deserve a special note of thanks for an excellent job of managing the review process and for providing helpful suggestions regarding revisions of the manuscript. The comments of two anonymous reviewers were also of considerable benefit in our revisions of the manuscript, as were a couple of suggestions from Rubèn Rumbaut, our colleague at the University of California, Irvine, and co-director with the first author of the Center for Research on Immigration, Population, and Public Policy. Additionally, Carolyn Boyd and Gray Swicegood, our spouses, offered useful editorial comments on some of the chapters. Also, Suzanne Nichols, David Haproff, and Emily Chang of the Publications Department at the Russell Sage Foundation were enormously helpful during the production phase of the manuscript's preparation. And finally, we would like especially to thank Carolyn and Gray for being persons of such good cheer and for putting up with a not inconsiderable amount of crankiness and inconvenience during the long period of this book's gestation and writing.

Frank D. Bean
Gillian Stevens

= Chapter 1 =

Introduction: Immigration's Nuances and Complexities

T HE DESTRUCTION of the twin towers of New York's World Trade Center on September 11, 2001—carried out by persons who were neither citizens nor legal permanent residents—cast into bold relief the importance and contradictions of U.S. immigration policy. Those responsible for the suicide missions were able either to enter the country fraudulently or to remain here illegally after visas for legal entry had expired (Gorman 2001; Jenks 2001). A dramatic slowdown in international travel after the attacks took place, together with an apparent acceleration of a downturn in the U.S. economy that had begun well before the incidents occurred, illustrated that economic vitality in an increasingly interdependent global economy involves substantial flows of tourists, students, temporary workers, and permanent immigrants into the country (Maggs and Baumann 2001). The dilemmas for U.S. immigration policy became crystal clear (Meissner 2001). Should worries that further terrorist attacks might occur tilt admissions policies strongly in favor of restrictionism? Could the United States and other advanced postindustrial countries develop immigration policies that would provide security and facilitate ease of movement at the same time? Could both universalism and particularism be balanced in sensible and effective policies?

Since September 11, such immigration-related concerns have taken on unusual intensity and urgency. As important as these have been and as crucial as it is to deal with them, their frequent articulation also serves to remind us that preoccupations with immigration issues are anything but new. Debates about U.S. immigration policy have often commanded center stage among both the members of the general public and policy makers for the past quarter century. For example, during this period two national commissions, the Select Commission on Immigration and Refugee Policy (1981) and the U.S. Commission

1

on Immigration Reform (1997), released major reports recommending reforms in immigration law. Also, on three occasions substantial immigration reform legislation has been passed by Congress and signed into law. First, in 1986 Congress passed the Immigration Reform and Control Act (IRCA) in an effort to reduce unauthorized migration by legalizing migrants already living and working in the country and adopting employer sanctions in an attempt to make it harder for future migrants to find jobs (Bean, Vernez, and Keely 1989). Second, in 1990 Congress passed the National Immigration Act, which set a cap on annual legal immigration while providing increased numbers of visas for highly skilled workers (Bean and Fix 1992). Third, in 1996 Congress passed welfare reform and immigration legislation in part as an attempt to limit unauthorized migration by tightening access to public benefits for noncitizens (Espenshade, Baraka, and Huber 1997; Van Hook and Bean 1998b).

In 1965, with passage of the amendments to the Immigration and Nationality Act, the United States abolished national origin quotas as a basis for granting immigrant visas, and since the mid-1970s legislative initiatives have mostly involved efforts to limit immigration. By the end of August 2001, however, recommendations to increase immigration were being voiced frequently, demonstrating that U.S. immigration policy was on the verge of coming full circle from its previously largely restrictive emphases. For example, on September 5, just before the New York tragedy, President Vicente Fox of Mexico visited President Bush in Washington to publicize and lobby for recommendations on changing U.S. policy regarding Mexican migration (Sullivan and Jordan 2001). These included "regularizing" unauthorized Mexican migrants already in the United States and establishing a new "guest-worker" program for low-skilled laborers from Mexico, ideas motivated largely by the labor shortages stemming from the unusually strong economy of the late 1990s (Meissner 2001; Mexico–U.S. Migration Panel 2001). In short, in early September 2001 it seemed likely that a sharp turnaround in U.S. policy might take place away from the general thrust of a quarter century's emphasis. However, external events set the policy debates on a new course (Gorman 2002). Such dramatic twists and turns suggest the experience of the United States with the "new" immigration since 1965—the substantial increases in the numbers of persons coming from Asia and Latin America—and with the various issues underlying the policy reforms considered and adopted during the ensuing years warrants careful examination. This book undertakes such an examination. Its purpose is twofold: to conduct a review of social science research relevant to these issues and to introduce new research that focuses on the major issues that have driven the immigration-policy debates.

The results of our review and research have led us to conclude that on balance, the new immigration of the past four decades has had more positive than negative consequences for the United States. We also argue that it is often difficult to discern the positive aspects of immigration because several circumstances create the impression that unprecedented problems with the new immigration have emerged. One of these aspects is recent increases in unauthorized Mexican migration, a phenomenon that often causes consternation in part because it frequently is confused with legal kinds of immigration. Another aspect derives from changes in the nature of immigrant integration that both strengthen ethnic identities and increase the likelihood of their expression among many immigrants. This contributes to the impression that ethnic disharmonies rather than harmonies are on the rise, although we argue that the reverse is actually the reality. A third aspect is related to the fact that immigration's effects are not all positive, although the weight of the evidence indicates that the negative consequences are often exaggerated by observers and are more than offset by other positive consequences. More generally, and on the positive side of the ledger, one of the most significant developments is that immigration generates increased racial and ethnic diversity in many parts of the country, a change producing signs that the racial and ethnic boundaries that have long divided Americans are starting to break down. In the chapters that follow we present both a review of the empirical and theoretical research literature and our own new theories and research findings that provide the bases for these conclusions.

Why Are Immigration Issues Growing More Important?

Paying close attention to the results of policy-relevant social science research on immigration is important for several reasons. First, at the beginning of the twenty-first century, the United States finds itself occupying a new and historically unprecedented position—it is both the world's sole superpower and the most important locus of the new technologically driven information economy (Nye 2002). Immigration has been related to these developments in complex ways—sometimes operating as cause and sometimes as consequence of U.S. global military and economic power. Many envision immigration and globalization as essential to the future well-being of the country; others worry that these phenomena are threats to the vitality and security of the United States (Sassen 2000; Meissner 2001; Meissner and Martin 2001). Which of these views is more accurate and eventually comes to predominate will have important implications for the directions public policies are likely to take in the country over the next few decades. Formulating these policies requires taking stock of the social, demographic, and economic effects of immigration in the recent past. The United States is not likely to be able to mold the various dimensions of immigration into phenomena that reinforce rather than contradict its major policy goals for the future if it does not better understand the nature and consequences of immigration in the recent past.

Second, the new immigration and the policy proposals and reforms of the past thirty-five years have generated widespread ambivalence and, frequently, social tension among Americans (Rumbaut 1995). Indeed, as we will argue, immigration is a phenomenon that inherently generates ambivalence and contradictory responses. Policy reforms that reflect laissez-faire or single-factor approaches are not likely to be responsive to immigration realities or to stand much chance of gaining widespread public acceptance. Immigration is "messy," both as a phenomenon and in terms of the politics of public policy. As a result, it is not likely to be fruitfully addressed in the abstract or in its entirety, but rather will likely be reformed piecemeal and one aspect at a time. Under such circumstances, the results of social science research about the various immigration issues driving policy debates assume even greater relevance to the policy assessment and formulation process. In short, absent the viability of an overarching vision providing the rationale for modifying immigration policy, the results of social science research will loom particularly large in policy debates about reforms.

Third, immigration is increasing throughout the world. In the latter part of the twentieth century, the number of international migrants—by which we mean all kinds of international movers, not just those granted legal residency status—more than doubled (Martin and Widgren 2002). The United Nations Population Division estimates an increase from 75 million to 150 million international migrants between 1965 and 2000. The annual rate of increase was more than 2.5 percent per year over the last 15 years compared to an annual rate of increase in population growth of about 1.5 percent (International Organization for Migration 2001). And this growth is concentrated in a few countries, although it is spreading. Some countries, like the United States, have always been known as immigration countries (that is, as countries whose policies allow for substantial immigration). Others have not been known as immigration countries—Japan and Mexico, for example. Still others have not, at least until recently, either seen themselves or been known as immigration countries, even though they in fact have become countries of immigration. Germany is a good case in point. Almost all the developed countries in the world now receive migrants—either legal or illegal—from elsewhere, in one form or another. In this sense, most of the industrial countries of the world are now experiencing immigration, even if they have yet to view themselves as immigration countries.

Fourth, immigration is also increasing in significance because of economic globalization, the forces of which increasingly draw the countries of the world closer together (Friedman 1999; Gilpin 2000). Driven by technology and by the ascendance of the idea that freer international trade offers the prospect of more rapid economic growth, globalization has accelerated communications, capital flows, tourism, and trade among countries in many parts of the world. It has also exacerbated contradictions—antithetical themes and emphases that do not appear to fit well together, such as those encapsulated in the dichotomies "cosmopolitan-local," universalism-particularism," "McDonaldization-jihad" and "globalism-tribalism." Globalization also exposes contradictions between immigration and the public policies that are both causes and consequences of international migration. The major contradiction that many observers see emerging from this new international context is that many countries appear to support increased openness in flows of goods, capital, information, and technology, but not increasingly free flows of people (Massey, Durand, and Malone 2002). Globalization thus sets the context within which changes in migration and public policy must be interpreted.

Fifth, immigration is increasingly of great demographic importance to the United States. By the end of the twentieth century, immigration had become the major component of population change in the United States (McDonald and Kippen 2001), especially when the fact that almost 20 percent of all births in the United States now occur to foreign-born mothers (Ventura et al. 2000, table 13) is taken into account. Fertility rates peaked in the late fifties and early sixties and have since declined substantially. Soon after fertility peaked, immigration to the United States began to increase. As a result, immigration directly (through the arrival of new residents) and indirectly (through the childbearing of immigrants) now accounts for almost 60 percent of annual population growth in the country, making it the major component of population change (Bean, Swicegood, and Berg 2000). Simply from the perspective of sheer numbers, then, immigration has become an increasingly important phenomenon. This population growth has been accompanied by greater racial-ethnic and cultural diversity within the U.S. population, thus complicating in the minds of some observers the question of national identity, a subject to which we return.

Why Immigration Is So Complicated

Both immigration and its consequences, including the ways people respond to it, defy simple classification. A couple of concrete examples help to illustrate this point. Let's start with the business cycle. Over the five-year period 1996 to 2000, the United States generated about 14.3 million new jobs, or about 2.9 million new jobs every year (U.S. Bureau of Labor Statistics 2002). The unusual magnitude of this increase becomes clear if we examine it relative to population growth. Over the same five years, the United States population increased by a little less than 1 percent per year, or by about 12.3 million persons, or almost 2.5 million persons per year (U.S. Bureau of the Census 2001b). Note that this figure includes an estimate for new immigrants, both legal and unauthorized. Approximately how many new jobs would it have taken to accommodate this population growth? A useful rule of thumb is that about 150,000 new jobs are required every month in the United States to keep pace with the entrance of new workers into the labor market (Gosselin 2002a, 2002b). Applying this rule, the United States would have needed about 1.8 million new jobs per year during the latter half of the 1990s to accommodate new workers resulting from population growth, including immigration. In short, the country generated almost 1.1 million *more* jobs per year (2.9 million minus 1.8 million) than it would have needed to accommodate population growth at existing levels of employment during this time.

Where did the people come from who filled all these jobs? The answer is: from many places—from the ranks of the unemployed; from the previously retired; from increases in the numbers of persons holding more than one job; from persons who had stopped working or had become discouraged in looking for work because they thought they couldn't find jobs, including teenagers and racial and ethnic minorities. And also from unmeasured immigrants—that is, unauthorized migrants living in the country in greater numbers than expert observers thought were here. But the "excess" number of jobs was so large that hardly a voice was raised arguing that immigrants were taking the jobs of natives. In fact, most outcries were in exactly the opposite direction—claiming, as we note in chapter 9, that labor shortages, particularly of high-tech workers and low-skilled workers, more than justified new legislation mandating increases in the numbers of visas issued for highly skilled workers and new appeals for special guest-worker programs for low-skilled workers.

Now contrast this situation with the one that existed at the beginning of the 1990s. From the end of fiscal year 1989 to the end of fiscal year 1992, job growth in the United States was almost stagnant, increasing by only about 600,000 jobs for the entire period. The annual rate of population growth, however, was approximately the same over this period as it was in the latter half of the decade, meaning that the country added about 2.6 million persons per year to its population. Applying the rule of thumb noted above, roughly 1.8 million new jobs per year were needed to maintain existing levels of employment. But only about 200,000 jobs per year became available, a deficit of about 600,000 per year. Although such numbers are only ballpark figures, they provide useful indications of economic and population trends that dramatically illustrate the sharp changes in conditions that occurred in the country during the 1990s. These circumstances confronted both the immigrants arriving in the United States and the natives who reacted to their arrival. It is thus perhaps hardly surprising that both anti-immigration and anti-immigrant voices on the part of organizations calling for policy reforms were loud and strident in the first two or three years of the 1990s, but fell virtually silent during the latter half of the decade.

Now let's consider how such trends relate to actual responses on the part of the general public to immigration. One might expect the intensity of unfavorable views toward immigration to fluctuate with changes in the business cycle. To some extent, they have. In 1986, 49 percent of the respondents in a Gallup poll said they thought that in the United States "immigration should be decreased" (Gallup 2001). In 1994, shortly after the economic recession of the early 1990s, this figure rose to 65 percent. But by 2000 it had dropped to 38 percent. So attitudes about immigration do appear to be affected somewhat by the business cycle. But it is also interesting to note that, over the past thirty-five years, the period during which Gallup has been asking the same questions about immigration, there is also evidence of both continuity and ambiguity in Americans' minds about immigration issues. On the positive side, the percentage of respondents who say that "immigration should be kept at its present level or increased" has remained fairly high, varying from 46 percent in 1965 to 54 percent in 2000. Only in the period immediately after the stagnant job market of the early 1990s did the figure change much, dropping to 33 percent before going back up in the late 1990s. On the negative side, the data also show a substantial minority of respondents who said they thought immigration to the country should be "decreased," ranging from 33 percent in 1965 to 38 percent in 2000 (Gallup 2000). Over the past thirty-five years, then, a sizable group of Americans (about half) has been in favor of increasing or *not changing* immigration, whereas another group (about a third) has been in favor of decreasing immigration. As we note in the next chapter, immigration has nearly tripled over this period, from a total of 3.3 million entrants in the 1960s to about 10.0 million during the 1990s.

It is thus striking that the attitudes of Americans toward immigration are far from uniform. Immigration is undoubtedly not the most controversial public-policy issue the United States has faced in recent years. Certainly it is not the issue that has generated the most heated debate or intensity of feeling (in this regard, abortion rights and welfare come to mind, to note just two examples). But it clearly is a public-policy issue that is multifaceted and not easily categorized along a simple left–right or liberal–conservative political spectrum. And this complexity also makes it an issue that lends itself to contradictory groups of constituents supporting immigration legislation, which in turn generates contradictory legislative compromises. Such manifestations of contradiction underscore the need for an assessment of immigration and its effects.

Ambivalence and Major Immigration Issues

Why do many Americans apparently worry about immigration but not really want to decrease it from its present levels? A partial answer is that many Americans are simultaneously *both* nostalgic and troubled about immigration. On the nostalgic side of the ledger, positive sentiments toward immigration undoubtedly derive in part from the fact that many persons are the descendants of persons who themselves were immigrants in the not-too-distant past. Others are the descendants of more distant immigrants, some even of colonial settlers. Some observers, like the historian Oscar Handlin (1951), have even gone so far as to interpret this legacy as meaning that the history of the United States can largely be written as the history of immigration. But Americans also manifest confusion and ambivalence about immigration, emotions that are even built into the two major issues that lie at the root of concerns about immigration: the implications of immigration for sociocultural identity and the implications of immigration for the economy. By sociocultural identity we mean the ways people view and think of themselves in terms of language, social relationships, and racial or ethnic identification. By the economy we mean levels of aggregate economic growth and individual instances of economic well-being. In each of these domains occur processes that inherently generate ambivalent responses to immigration, and the two in combination can cause conflicting feelings about immigration within one person. And of course, responses to each issue are inevitably mixed across individuals. Some people will see identity changes in positive terms and others in negative terms; by the same token, some will gain economically from immigration, and others will lose. In addition, some who gain economically will see themselves as losing socioculturally, and vice versa.

Consider first the case of identity. Immigration inevitably involves social change because newcomers bring cultural differences with them. This leads to ambivalence because immigration contributes to anxiety about identity. There are a number of factors involved in such ambivalence, but one is simply that immigration by its very nature engenders mixed feelings. Immigration consists of persons moving from one part of the world to another, and destination societies cannot help but be changed by such movements, although perhaps in small ways. Included in the changes are new relationships between natives and newcomers, which means that at least some of the members of the host society come to see themselves in new ways. Immigration thus necessarily contributes in ways small and large to the emergence of new perceptions of social identity. Some persons will be fearful of such identity changes simply because they involve newness. Others will see these identity changes in positive terms because their relationships to the newcomers place them in newly defined social relationships that they think enhance their status and influence. Altogether, the identity changes accompanying immigration generate individual ambivalence and potential social tension between those whose status is enhanced and those whose status is not.

The second major way immigration affects the destination society is more instrumental, involving economic effects. The economic well-being of people already living in the society will either rise, fall, or stay the same on account of immigration—in other words, tangible costs and benefits are associated with immigration. Inevitably some people will gain and others will lose; furthermore, the economic benefits connected with immigration are unevenly distributed throughout the society. As we noted, there are many people who benefit economically from immigration during times of strong economic growth but are harmed by it when the overall economy is in decline. Thus, the economic implications of immigration can also generate individual ambivalence and social tension.

Most of the contemporary policy debates about immigration focus on economic issues (for example, Borjas 1999). This is partly because the sense of threat perceived to arise from immigration attaches to anxieties about sociocultural change that appear difficult to alleviate, so people take refuge in arguments emphasizing tangible economic costs. People often worry privately about matters of identity but talk publicly about economic impacts. But society cannot obtain the tangible economic benefits deriving from immigration without also experiencing its intangible sociocultural effects. Indeed, societies frequently seek what are at least perceived to be the economic benefits of immigration, only to be surprised to discover that immigration has other consequences. Note, for example, the oft-noted remark of a West German government official who, in response to a question about the nature of Germany's experience with guest workers, is reputed to have said, "Well, in the beginning we thought we were getting workers, but in the end we realized we were getting people."

Immigration, Complexity and Ambivalence, and Policy Approaches

What is the policy significance of this complexity and ambivalence? What approaches to immigration policy have been set forth in recent years? What are the features of current approaches that distinguish them from earlier endeavors? To answer these questions, we must first consider what the term "immigration" means and what the essential features of immigration are. First, it is important to remember that the term "immigrant" has a legal connotation: an immigrant is someone who has been granted a visa by a national government allowing that person to establish residence (and often to work) in the country. "International migrants" are a different category: all people who move from one country to another, some without having been granted such a visa. Thus, from a legal point of view, tourists, temporary students, and persons who illegally cross the border to live in the United States are not immigrants; they are international migrants. But what about people who have lived in the United States for two or three decades even though they entered illegally? Are such persons immigrants in a social science sense of the term even though in a legal sense they are not? In this book, the answer to that question is yes. That is, we consider settlement in the country as a criterion for use of the term "immigrant," in addition to the strictly legal criterion. Thus, we will define immigrants as legal immigrant entrants or persons who have established long-term residence in the United States, whether or not this has been done on a legal basis.

Our consideration of immigrants thus focuses on a behavioral basis for residence. We consider an immigrant to be someone who has settled in this country, either legally or illegally. We will have more to say about this later, particularly about what the term "illegal" means. But for the moment we want to emphasize that immigration is a phenomenon that by its definition comes about at least partly as a result of state policy (Zolberg 1999; Joppke 1999). Countries adopt rules about how many and what kinds of persons can enter for the purpose of establishing long-term residence. But even the numbers and kinds of persons who do this are affected by public policy because nations often implement border control practices that affect the ease or difficulty with which unauthorized border crossers can obtain entry (Andreas 2000; Bean et al. 1994). Thus, the implementation of border policies influences the numbers and kinds of persons who end up being considered illegal.

It is clear that public policy shapes various aspects of immigration processes, but other forces affect immigration as well. This may seem to be an obvious point, but it often is lost in debates about immigration. Some observers speak of immigration as if it is primarily affected by policy, as if the rules set up to permit some kinds of people to come to the United States can be largely separated from other sources of influence, such as family, personal, or political factors. Conversely, other observers speak as if the social and economic forces driving immigration operate to the exclusion of the influence of rules about what kinds of people can obtain visas or whether borders may be crossed. While it is always difficult to ascertain the relative influence of policy and other forces on immigration flows and patterns, it is crucial to recognize the fundamental importance of both kinds of effects.

In a very rough way, these two orientations constitute the beginning assumptions behind certain prominent recent efforts to justify modifying U.S. immigration policy. For example, proponents of one effort (see, for example, Borjas 1999) work on the assumption that policy can be molded largely to accomplish a single purpose. They argue that economic considerations should drive policy, that an effort should be made to develop a "rational" basis for immigration reforms, and that the basis for such rationality should be what is best for the country economically. The idea is that the current mishmash of policies should be replaced by policies encouraging the entry of immigrants with high skills because such people are most likely to generate economic gain for the country. This approach sees the results of social science research into specific immigration topics as somewhat irrelevant to current debates about immigration policy because such inquiries frequently fail to define a single highest-priority objective for policy.

Proponents of another type of recent effort tend to assume that economic and social forces overwhelm the influence of policy. These observers argue that current policy is largely ineffective because state policies often don't appear to affect migrant flows very much, or don't affect them in the manner intended, because policymakers often fail to understand the forces driving migration (see, for example, Massey, Durand, and Malone 2002). This perspective implies that social science research about the effects of policies is frequently beside the point because state policies are viewed as having either unintended effects or few effects because other factors trump policy factors. Ironically, analysts embracing such assumptions frequently still set forth policy recommendations, as exemplified in the set of thoughtful and far-sighted proposals recently offered by Douglas S. Massey, Jorge Durand, and Nolan Malone (2002) to address Mexican migration.

Neither of these assumptions about policy envisions that an assessment of what we know about the determinants and consequences of immigration—in particular of what we know about the consequences of particular immigration policies—is critical to the formulation of policy reforms. This is true in the former case because these analysts seek to superimpose a single overarching economic criterion on immigration policy and in the latter case because the policy makers despair of policy's having much impact anyway. The one view tends to see immigration policy as overly deterministic; the other sees immigration policy as underdeterministic. A preferable and more realistic alternative falls somewhere in between. Immigration and immigration policy in the United States, as well as their effects, are both complex and multifaceted, reflecting the often uneasy political compromises that have been reached among disparate and irreconcilable factions with contradictory agendas concerning immigration issues. They also reflect the ambivalence many Americans feel about immigration and indicate that immigration itself has multifaceted impacts, which reinforces personal and political ambivalence. Thus, neither purely rational nor relatively status quo approaches are likely to be satisfactory from the standpoint of generating viable immigration policies, the former because they ignore political complexity and the latter because they neglect compelling political needs to seek policy solutions. As Rumbaut has noted: "Politics and policy-making, like life itself, are . . . tangled, messy, uncertain, and contradictory. Condemned to try to control a future they cannot predict by reacting to a past that will not be repeated, policymakers are nonetheless faced with an imperative need to act that cannot be ignored as a practical or political matter" (1995, 311).

The Questions Addressed by This Book

In short, precisely because immigration engenders so much ambivalence, social tension, and contradictory responses, it is particularly important to understand its implications for American society. An effort to take stock of immigration needs to take place at two levels. One is at the concrete level of the issues that have driven the policy debates about immigration over the past three decades. Here we are basically concerned with three broad questions whose answers have had and will continue to have important implications for policy reform: First, how many and what kinds of persons migrate to the United States? Basically the broad policy issue here is the degree to which the numbers and types of persons coming are consistent with policies governing entry and with the social and economic policies and contexts within which arrivals occur. This requires understanding the reasons for migration, as well as the patterns of migration viewed in relation to changing contextual factors such as the strength of the economy. Chapter 2 examines these kinds of considerations. Because unauthorized migration from Mexico is such an important component of recent U.S. immigration and is viewed by many as the major glaring failure of U.S. immigration policy, we devote a separate chapter to this subject (chapter 3). Also, because welfare receipt is often viewed as another indication that U.S. immigration policies admit persons substantially different from those intended, we assess whether immigrants are more disposed to seek welfare than the native-born in chapter 4.

Second, what happens to immigrants after they arrive? For example, if they come to the United States with economic disadvantages, do these disadvantages disappear in time? This question is essentially the issue of immigrant incorporation, which we elaborate below. The policy issue is that if disadvantaged immigrants are being granted entry but cannot (or are not allowed to) join the economic mainstream, then doubts may be raised about the entry policies that permit such persons to come to the country. We examine this broad theme with respect to theoretical (chapter 5), economic (chapter 6) and sociocultural issues (chapters 7 and 8), focusing in the latter instance on linguistic incorporation and intermarriage.

Third, what effects do immigrants have on persons already living in the United States (including previously arriving immigrants)? The policy issue here is similar: If a given set of admissions criteria are bringing more or less the numbers and kinds of immigrants intended, if those immigrants are able to move into the economic mainstream within a reasonable period of time, but those entrants have negative effects on persons already here, then doubts may be raised about the entry policies allowing their admission. Here again we examine this theme with respect both to economic factors (chapter 9), where we focus on general economic and fiscal consequences of immigration, and sociocultural factors (chapter 10), where we focus on the implications of immigration for racial and ethnic composition.

A second level at which we inquire into the implications of immigration for the United States is more general. Thus, in addition to reviewing the research findings relevant to answering these questions, there is a need to ask, "What are the overarching implications of immigration for the United States?" This is a more abstract question: whether immigration in broad and general terms is contributing something positive or negative to the United States. Has the immigration of the past thirty years made us a richer or poorer society, a better or a worse society? And in what ways? What are the reasons for this? Among the many factors that affect the direction of debates about the significance of immigration, one that is particularly important is how immigration affects the color line in the United States. How does it influence the way Americans view themselves in racial and ethnic terms? How do the answers to such questions affect overall assessments of the significance of immigration for American society? These themes are taken up in chapters 10 and 11.

We do not attempt to deal here with all of the important topics relevant to immigration and immigration policy that might be examined. Naturalization, voting, and other forms of political behavior, along with transnational migration and ties, are examples of phenomena to which we devote little attention. The first three of these all fall within the purview of political incorporation, a subject of considerable importance but one whose relationship to sociocultural and economic incorporation remains ambiguous, particularly from the standpoint of what is cause and what is effect. Does political incorporation facilitate economic and socioeconomic incorporation, or is it the other way around? We do not think either the research literature or our own theoretical perspectives on this subject resolve these issues, which must be clarified before the policy significance of political incorporation can be assessed. Hence, we leave their examination for another time. Similarly, we do not spend much time on transnational migration, largely because the phenomenon has not been well defined and adequately distinguished from other kinds of migration. For example, how does it differ from circular migration, involving period spells of temporary migration? Moreover, a convincing case has yet to be made that the scale and significance of transnational migration for other phenomena are important enough to warrant extensive examination.

What makes immigration an especially fascinating subject in the U.S. context is that it is a phenomenon that reflects and elicits both the best and the worst features of the American experience. The national myth that the country is a nation of immigrants who have successfully pursued the American dream exemplifies the hope and optimism that many observers have noted is characteristic of American culture (Jaynes 2000; Bean et al. 1996). The nativist response that immigrants have often provoked reflects a strain in American culture and character that is more pessimistic, one that emphasizes the limits rather than the possibilities of American life. Both immigration and globalization increase cosmopolitanism and diversity in American life. Can the country's sense of national identity keep pace with these changes? Can it incorporate new elements to a sufficient degree to overcome worries about "newness" and "newcomers"? Will demographic and social and economic changes raise anxiety so much that old national identities become rigidified and lead to conflict? Answers to such important questions require objective social scientific assessment of what immigration has meant to the United States over the past half decade or so.

═ Chapter 2 ═

Migration Flows, Theories, and Contexts

A SSESSING the importance of immigration for the United States requires not only that we become knowledgeable about the shifting magnitude and nature of migration flows into the country occurring over the past few decades but also that we develop an understanding of the various theories about why such flows take place. It is also crucial that we consider the changes in the demographic and economic contexts that mark this period, shifts that may have altered the reception newcomers receive after they arrive. In doing so we must not lose sight of the diversity in the kinds of flows that have occurred. If we lump all flows together under the same category and speak of immigration in blanket terms, we risk glossing over important differences in outcomes related to the various kinds of flows that channel newcomers into the country, the various migration policy auspices through which such flows occur, and the various contexts into which such flows take place. Newcomers to the United States have become more visible in recent years, in part because their numbers have increased, but also in part because they have increasingly been coming from different countries than previously. As we will see, there is considerable heterogeneity among newcomers, many of whom are not immigrants. Thus, before we can speak knowledgeably about immigration's consequences, we need to delve more deeply into the various flows that contribute to migrant diversity, into the theories that help explain why international migration occurs, and into the fluctuations in recent demographic and economic conditions that have confronted migrants after they have arrived in the United States.

Kinds of U.S. Migration Flows

There have been four principal major migration flows to the United States in the post–World War II period: legal immigrants, refugees

16

and asylees, unauthorized migrants, and persons admitted for short periods of time on so-called nonimmigrant visas. One of the most important features of all these flows is that their volumes have generally been rising over this period. A second important feature of all the flows is that the share of persons from Hispanic and Asian countries has been increasing and has come to constitute a majority of each flow. Both of these changes have occurred at the same time that U.S. economic growth has slowed, wages have stagnated, and earnings inequality has increased, with the notable exception of strong economic growth during the latter half of the 1990s, which led to small countervailing trends in wages and earnings inequality at the end of the decade. As noted in the previous chapter, concerns about levels of immigration in the United States often reflect anxieties about potential changes in sociocultural identity and worries about economic conditions and job opportunities. Here we examine the recent changes in each of the major migration flows to the United States. Later in this chapter we focus on the changes in the demographic and economic contexts in which they have occurred. The results help to set the stage for determining the most important implications of U.S. immigration trends and policies for the country.

Overall Composition of Flows

A number of studies have examined changes in immigration trends and policies in the United States during the twentieth century (see, for example, Bean, Vernez, and Keely 1989; Borjas 1999; Reimers 1985; Reimers 1998; Suro 1998). All emphasize that the annual numbers of new entrants reached their highest totals during the first two decades of the century. The major pieces of legislation affecting immigrant flows are summarized in table 2.1. Owing to the passage of the National Origins Quota Act in 1924, the Great Depression during the 1930s, and an unfavorable immigration climate during World War II, immigration numbers dropped to 10 percent of these record-setting levels during the next twenty-five years. Specifically, the number of entrants decreased from over 700,000 per year during the first twenty years of the century to less than 70,000 per year from 1925 through 1945 (U.S. Immigration and Naturalization Service 1994). After this lull and continuing for nearly fifty years now, legal immigration has again moved steadily upward, and by the late 1980s and into the 1990s it reached levels approaching the all-time highs set in the early part of the twentieth century (figure 2.1). If the legalizations resulting from the Immigration Reform and Control Act of 1986 (IRCA) are

Table 2.1   Selected Major Legislation Administered by the Immigration and Naturalization Service, 1920s to 1990s

Title and Date	Major Provisions
Immigration Act of May 19, 1921 (first quota act)	Imposed national numerical limits according to the national origins of the white U.S. population in 1910.
Immigration Act of May 26, 1924 (National Origins Quota Act)	Recalibrated national origin limits using 1890 census figures.
Act of April 29, 1943	Provided for the importation of temporary agricultural laborers from South and Central America. Served as the legal basis for the Bracero Program, which lasted until 1964.
Displaced Persons Act of June 25, 1948	Admitted émigrés fleeing war-ravaged areas; operated outside of limits imposed by immigration selection system.
Immigration and Nationality Act of June 6, 1952 (McCarran-Walter Act)	Recodified national limits; also created separate preferences for skilled workers and relatives.
Refugee Relief Act of August 7, 1953	Admitted European refugees from Communist countries.
Immigration and Nationality Act Amendments of October 3, 1965	Eliminated national quotas; instituted a preference system for employment-based skills and family reunification.
Cuban Refugee Act of November 2, 1966	Admitted refugees from Cuba after the overthrow of the Cuban government.
Refugee Act of March 17, 1980	Provided set procedures for the attorney general to allow asylees to adjust to permanent-resident status.
Immigration Reform and Control Act of November 6, 1985	Banned employment of persons ineligible to work in the U.S.; provided amnesty to former illegal aliens under certain conditions.
Immigration Act of November 29, 1990	Instituted three preference categories: family-sponsored, employment-based, and "diversity" immigrants; expanded skilled immigration.

Source: Authors' compilation.

included in the totals, the levels in the early 1990s exceed all previous highs (U.S. Immigration and Naturalization Service 2002).

The results shown in figure 2.2 reveal the dramatically changing national origins of immigrants to the United States. Prior to 1960 the vast majority came from European countries or Canada (often over 90

**Figure 2.1   Average Annual Number of Immigrants by Decade and Percentage
Foreign-Born, 1910 to 2000**

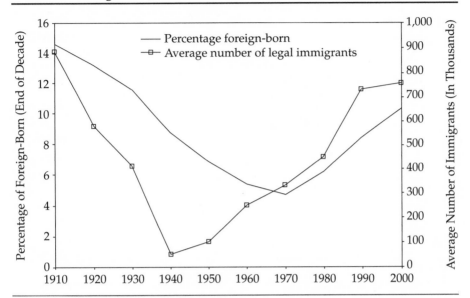

Sources: U.S. Bureau of the Census (various dates) and U.S. Immigration and Naturalization
Service (2002b).

percent when examined on a decade-by-decade basis). Even as late as
the 1950s, over two thirds (67.7 percent) of all arrivals were from these
countries. Things changed rapidly after the mid-1960s when family
reunification criteria rather than national origins quotas became the
main basis for granting entry visas (Bean, Vernez, and Keely 1989;
Reimers 1983). That the vast majority of immigrants now enter on the
basis of family criteria can be seen in table 2.2, which shows admissions for the year 2000 by class of admission. Almost three fourths
were   family-based   admissions   (235,280 + 51,000 + 347,870 =
634,150). By the 1980s the influence of the new criteria on national
origins of immigrants was clear. In that decade, only 12.5 percent of
legal immigrants came from Europe or Canada, whereas 84.4 percent
were from Asian or Latin American countries (U.S. Immigration and
Naturalization Service 1994).

These relatively recent changes in the national origin composition
of immigrants have begun to transform the United States from a
largely biracial society consisting of a sizable white majority and a

Table 2.2   Immigrants Admitted by Type and Class of Admission, 2000

Type and Class of Admission	Number
Total, all immigrants	849,807
Total, subject to worldwide numerical limits[a]	393,304
A. Family-sponsored preferences	235,280
1. Unmarried sons or daughters of U.S. citizens	27,707
2. Spouses or children of permanent residents	124,595
3. Married sons or daughters of U.S. citizens and their spouses and children	22,833
4. Siblings of U.S. citizens and their spouses and children	60,145
B. Employment-based preferences	107,024
C. Other (legalization dependents, diversity)	51,000
Total, not subject to worldwide numerical limits[b]	456,503
A. Immediate relatives of U.S. citizens	347,870
B. Refugee and asylee adjustments	65,941
C. Other	42,692

Source: U.S. Immigration and Naturalization Service (2002a).
[a]Worldwide numerical limits include family-sponsored preferences, legalized dependents, employment-based preferences, and diversity programs.
[b]Immediate relatives of U.S. citizens in previous editions of the *Statistical Yearbook* are included with admissions not subject to a numerical cap. Immediate relatives may immigrate without limit but the number affects the limit set for family-sponsored preference immigrants.

small black minority and a Native American minority of less than 1 percent into a multiracial, multi-ethnic society consisting of several racial and ethnic groups (Bean and Bell-Rose 1999; Passel and Edmonston 1994). This trend became discernible in the 1950s but began to accelerate in the 1960s (table 2.3). Since 1830 the U.S. census has contained a question about race or color; in 2000, for the first time this question allowed multiple responses, and the census also contained a separate question about Hispanic or Latino origin. In answer to the question on race, about 2.4 percent of all Americans chose two or more races, a percentage slated to grow as increases in intermarriage produce more Americans with a complex racial heritage. About 12.9 percent chose black or African American as a response, 4.2 percent chose Asian, 1.5 percent chose American Indian or Alaska Native, and 5.5 percent chose some other nonwhite race (U.S. Census Bureau 2002b). In answer to the separate question on Hispanic or Latino ancestry, more than one in eight Americans (13.4 percent) identified themselves as Hispanic or Latino. The apparent growth in the multiracial population and the clearly observed growth in the numbers of

**Figure 2.2   Average Annual Number of Immigrants Admitted to the
United States by National Origin, 1821 to 1998**

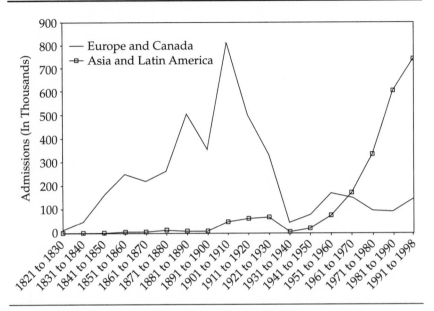

Source: U.S. Immigration and Naturalization Service (2002c).

Americans of Hispanic or Asian ancestries mean that the portion of
the population that is white and non-Hispanic is shrinking and that
blacks no longer constitute a majority of the minority population.

Refugees and Asylees

Like most other Western democracies, the United States did not place
the explicit and systematic admission of refugees under the purview
of immigration policy until after World War II, when it recognized the
victims of political persecution as "a distinct category of international
migrants to whom [it] owed special obligations" (Zolberg 1992, 55).
On June 24, 1948, the Soviet Union instituted the blockade of Berlin,
and on June 25, Congress signed into law the Displaced Persons Act,
permitting the entry into the United States of 205,000 of the hundreds
of thousands of displaced persons flooding into Western Europe and
the American-occupied zone of Germany. The drafters of the law
tried to connect the refugee resettlement provisions in the legislation
with U.S. immigration policy by stipulating that the number of refugees had to be charged against the immigration quotas of future

Table 2.3   U.S. Population by Race-Hispanic Origin, 1900 to 2000 (In Thousands)

Year	Total	Non-Hispanic White	Black	Hispanic	Asian	Native American
Population						
1900	76,195	66,225	8,834	656	243	237
1910	93,879	82,049	10,255	999	299	277
1920	110,747	96,969	11,512	1,632	389	244
1930	127,585	111,543	12,736	2,435	527	343
1940	136,928	119,425	13,767	2,814	577	345
1950	155,156	134,351	15,668	4,039	739	357
1960	182,055	154,969	19,071	6,346	1,146	524
1970	205,567	170,371	23,005	9,616	1,782	793
1980	226,625	180,392	26,482	14,604	3,726	1,420
1990	248,712	187,139	29,986	22,354	7,274	1,959
2000[a]	281,422	198,178	36,419	37,660	11,899	4,119
Percentage						
1900	100.0	86.9	11.6	0.9	0.3	0.3
1910	100.0	87.4	10.9	1.1	0.3	0.3
1920	100.0	87.6	10.4	1.5	0.4	0.2
1930	100.0	87.4	10.0	1.9	0.4	0.3
1940	100.0	87.2	10.1	2.1	0.4	0.3
1950	100.0	86.6	10.1	2.6	0.5	0.2
1960	100.0	85.1	10.5	3.5	0.6	0.3
1970	100.0	82.9	11.2	4.7	0.9	0.4
1980	100.0	79.6	11.7	6.4	1.6	0.6
1990	100.0	75.2	12.1	9.0	2.9	0.8
2000[a]	102.4	70.5	12.9	13.4	4.2	1.5

Sources: Adapted from Passel and Edmonston (1994, table 2.3) and U.S. Bureau of the Census (2000).
Note: Populations include the fifty states and the District of Columbia for 1900 to 2000.
[a]For the various racial-ethnic groups (but not the total), the numbers include persons identifying with the group alone or in combination, and thus their sum exceeds the total, and their cumulative percentage exceeds 100.0.

years. In the ensuing years, the issue of what to do about refugees continued to arise but was viewed as conflicting with other features of U.S. immigration policy, particularly the national origins quotas, which severely restricted admissions from some countries. As a result of this dilemma and because it was largely driven by foreign policy considerations, U.S. refugee policy essentially had to be crafted and implemented on an ad hoc basis.

Whatever the vagaries of postwar refugee policy, the effects of the numerous ad hoc admissions programs introduced another source of new entrants into the United States. Since the end of World War II, nearly 3 million refugees and asylees have been granted lawful permanent-resident status by the United States (U.S. Immigration and

Figure 2.3   Refugees and Asylees Granted Lawful Permanent-Resident Status by National Origin, 1946 to 1998

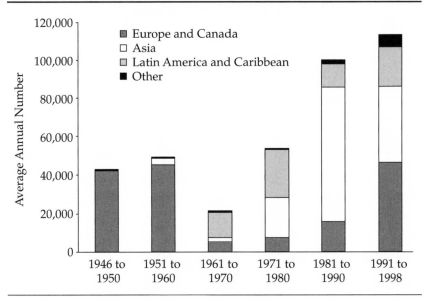

Source: U.S. Immigration and Naturalization Service (2002a).

Naturalization Service 2002a). During the 1940s and 1950s, the number of refugees and asylees averaged about 50,000 per year, a figure that declined to about 20,000 annually during the 1960s before moving to over 50,000 during the 1970s, to about 100,000 during the 1980s, and to well over 100,000 per year in the 1990s (figure 2.3). As with legal immigrants, the vast majority have come from Asia, Latin America, and the Caribbean (49.2 percent overall since 1945, and 82.2 percent during the 1980s), although both the relative and absolute numbers coming from the former Soviet Union have increased substantially since 1990. In sum, as figure 2.3 shows, the category of refugee and asylee admissions has constituted an increasing flow of persons into the country, predominantly Asian and Latino, over the past fifty years.

Illegal Immigrants

Persons who enter the United States illegally or enter legally and then stay illegally constitute another major flow into the country. The former are called "EWIs" by the U.S. Immigration and Naturalization Service because they "enter without inspection" (others simply call them undocumented or unauthorized migrants). Those who enter le-

Figure 2.4   Average Annual Number of Apprehensions by Decade, 1911 to 2000

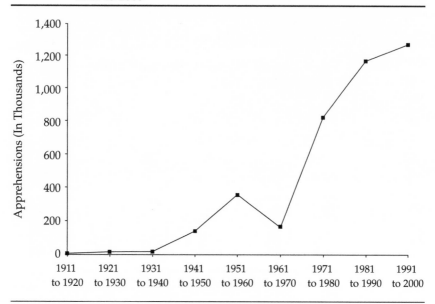

Source: U.S. Immigration and Naturalization Service (2002a).

gally but then stay illegally are called "visa-overstays" because they stay beyond the expiration date of their visas. Almost all of the unauthorized migrants enter at the U.S.–Mexico border, and the vast majority originate in Mexico, although in recent years substantial numbers from Central American countries have crossed that border (Bean, Passel, and Edmonston 1990). The visa-overstays do not come predominantly from any one country, although in recent years such persons have represented approximately half of the illegal population resident in the country at any one time (Warren 1990, 1992).

The Bracero Program, begun in 1942, was the result of an agreement between the American Embassy in Mexico City and the Mexican Ministry of Foreign Affairs, which was then implemented by the U.S. Congress in legislation passed April 29, 1943. The program provided a means whereby temporary contract laborers from Mexico could enter and work in the country legally (Calavita 1992). The program ended in 1964, and after this the flow of undocumented migrants from Mexico into the country began to increase. The flows of such persons into the country has become substantial as reflected in figure 2.4, which shows, by decade, the average annual number of apprehensions by the U.S. Border Patrol (mostly at the U.S.–Mexico border) of persons illegally resident in the United States (U.S. Immigration and Naturalization Service 2002a). There is little doubt that the increasing numbers of apprehensions indirectly reflect increases in the number of undocumented migrants entering the country (Espenshade 1995b), even though apprehension figures are for numbers of events—border crossings—not specific individuals, and thus cannot be interpreted as directly indicating the number of individuals who illegally reside in the country (Bean, Passel, and Edmonston 1990; Van Hook and Bean 1998a).

Migration involves a social process consisting of transitions over time from temporary (and illegal) status to permanent (and often legal) migration status (Massey et al. 1987). Partly as a consequence, the number of unauthorized migrants, together with the number of persons illegally residing in the country resulting from the process of visa-overstaying, started to grow in the 1960s and to increase substantially in the 1970s. The U.S. Bureau of the Census started including an annual net gain of 200,000 persons attributable to unauthorized immigration in its annual population estimates and projections in the 1980s and 1990s (Campbell 1994). Other sources estimated the size of this net component to be in the range 200,000 to 300,000 persons (Warren 1992). Because of the importance of Mexican migrants to the growth of this population, we examine Mexican unauthorized migration in more detail in the following chapter.

It is more difficult to gauge the racial and ethnic composition of unauthorized migrants than of authorized ones. The available evidence suggests that unauthorized migrants, like authorized migrants, are mainly Asian or Latin American in origin (Warren 1990, 1992; Warren and Passel 1987). This would suggest that the implications of unauthorized immigration for changing racial and ethnic composition are not greatly different from those of legal immigration, a conclusion corroborated by findings about the national origin composition of the persons who became legal immigrants under the provisions of the 1986 Immigration Reform and Control Act, of whom nearly 70 percent were of Mexican origin and over 90 percent were of Latin American or Asian origin (U.S. Department of Justice 1992).

Nonimmigrant Entrants

Nonimmigrants are persons admitted to the United States for a specified temporary period of time but not for permanent residence. Although the majority of nonimmigrants are tourists, large numbers of students and persons coming for various business and work-related

Figure 2.5   Annual Number of Nonimmigrants Admitted to the United States, Fiscal Years 1946 to 1999

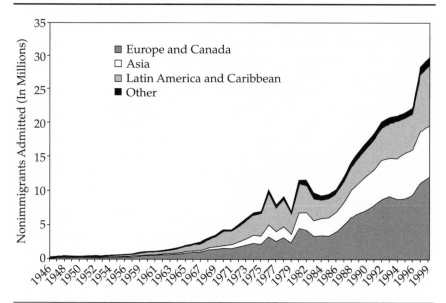

Source: U.S. Immigration and Naturalization Service (2002a).

reasons are also admitted. In fact, the numbers of people coming for business-related reasons have increased substantially in the past two or three years, an outcome facilitated by the Immigration Act of 1990 which included compromise provisions allowing easier nonimmigrant business entry in lieu of the even higher levels of employment-related immigration that some proponents wanted to include in the legislation (Bean and Fix 1992). During fiscal year 1999, 31.4 million nonimmigrant admissions to the United States were recorded. The largest number ever, it was an increase of more than 9 million over fiscal year 1995 (U.S. Immigration and Naturalization Service 2002a, 120).

Nonimmigrant admissions are an important source of flows into the country that hold significant implications for immigration issues that go beyond their sheer magnitude. The dramatic increases in nonimmigrant admissions in recent years reflect the mounting demand both for tourism and for business- and employment-related entry resulting from increased globalization of the economy. Nonimmigrant flows are the source of visa-overstays, who have been estimated to make up about half of all illegal residents in the United States (Warren 1992). The picture that emerges from numerous ethnographic studies of migration implies that the nonimmigrant entrants who become illegal migrants through visa-overstaying may do so through a social process that eventually results in many becoming legal immigrants. Hence, pressures on the legal immigration system are likely to increase as the volume of nonimmigrant admissions continues to climb steeply, even if the rate of visa-overstaying remains constant.

As the number of nonimmigrant entrants has steadily risen over the past decade, the national origins of these flows have become somewhat more diverse than is the case for other kinds of flows (figure 2.5). The percentage of nonimmigrant entrants from Asia, Latin America, and the Caribbean was about 56 percent in 1998, up from about 41 percent in 1965. The number and racial or ethnic identity of persons in the United States on nonimmigrant visas are also likely to affect public perceptions about immigration to this country. The average citizen seems rarely to distinguish among different kinds of immigrants, let alone among different kinds of nonimmigrants or between nonimmigrants and immigrants (Bean et al. 1987). Thus, the rapidly rising number of nonimmigrants, over half of whom are from Hispanic or Asian countries, undoubtedly contribute to the impression that Latino and Asian immigration to the United States is higher than it actually is.

Theories of Migration Causes

Clarifying what happens to immigrants after they arrive and the consequences they exert on others depends on understanding the reasons why people migrate. A variety of theoretical perspectives on the forces that drive international migration (see Massey 1998, 1999) embody different positions regarding the reasons for migration, the characteristics of migrants, and the nature of the receiving societies to which migrants move. Because the desire to work occupies such a central place in many migrants' decisions, we pay special attention to how various theoretical perspectives view the nature and operation of labor markets in advanced industrial societies. Below we briefly review these theoretical perspectives from the standpoint of how the forces and factors they emphasize shed light on the experiences and labor-market outcomes of immigrants in the United States.

Neoclassical Economic Theory

Neoclassical economists see migration as stemming from macrolevel imbalances between countries (or areas) in the supply of and demand for labor and the resultant wage differences these disequilibria generate (Harris and Todaro 1970). At the microlevel, these theorists assume that individuals make rational calculations concerning the benefits (usually assumed to be economic) of migrating relative to its costs (Todaro and Maruszko 1987). Migration thus represents an investment strategy for individuals to maximize their returns to labor power, and so migrants calculate their expected wages over their "time horizon," or the expected lengths of their stay at their destinations (Borjas 1990). Some migrants have short time horizons and therefore seek to maximize earnings within a framework of temporary, or circular, migration, whereas others have longer time horizons and are therefore more likely to settle permanently.

Costs of migrating may be incurred during the migration process or after settlement. For instance, Bean et al. (1994) assess the potential effectiveness of Operation Hold the Line, a U.S. Border Patrol operation in El Paso, Texas, in terms of the increasing costs borne by unauthorized migrants because of the program. Eschbach, Hagan, and Bailey (1999) assess the deterrent effect of U.S.–Mexico border enforcement in terms of the ultimate cost: risk of death while crossing. Migrants also consider expected costs of living after they settle at their destination. Living costs include rent, food, and clothing, and—especially in the United States—costs of housing and automobile transportation (Grasmuck and Pessar 1991; Hagan 1994; Hondagneu-Sotelo 1994). There may also be psychological costs of adjustment, or social benefits. For instance, women may find their social positions elevated, and men their social positions weakened in the United States, compared to their relative positions in their home countries (Hagan 1994; Hondagneu-Sotelo 1994). Expected wages and benefits must exceed expected costs of living after settlement to encourage migration, and social benefits must exceed psychic costs in order for migrants to stay in their new homes. Such factors may affect the gender composition of immigrant populations in receiving countries. For instance, if men incur psychic costs because their social status has declined, they may be more likely to return home; by the same token if women enjoy greater social benefits at their destination than in their home communities, they may seek to become permanent residents (Grasmuck and Pessar 1991).

A variant of microeconomic theory, human capital theory, stresses returns on investments in human capital. Workers invest in their education on the basis of expected returns over their time horizons (Becker 1964), in much the same way as migrants invest in moving to a new country and labor market. The concentration of larger, more prestigious educational institutions in developed countries may stimulate migration, and returns on education are often higher there than in developing countries. By moving to countries with better schools and more developed labor markets, migrants both enhance their investment in human capital and increase the likely return on that investment. Thus, human capital theory explains why countries like the United States attract so many well-educated migrants and cause a "brain drain" from other countries (Massey 1998).

New Economic Theories of Migration

Some theorists (for example, Stark 1991; Taylor et al. 1997) amend microeconomic theories by devoting emphasis to the intersection of labor-market factors and family or household variables in affecting migration decisions, and by incorporating the notion of minimizing risk along with maximizing earnings. This perspective also predicts that social rank, relative income, and potential for social mobility will influence migration. For example, Lowell Taylor et al. (1997) and Taylor (1994) emphasize that not only lower average wages but also greater social and economic inequality in Mexico stimulate migration to the United States. Similarly, Bryan Roberts and Augustin Escobar Latapi (1997) argue that urbanization generates emigration stemming from the urbanized environment's greater social inequality and atomization (that is, fragmentation of families) in Mexico's largest cities.

Among the factors generating such inequalities are "market failures," for example, in the availability of investment capital or land allocation, which often impede social and economic mobility in sending countries. Households in these countries respond by sending one or more members to foreign labor markets to generate income and capital that can be used to minimize short- and long-term risk (that is, household vulnerability to market failures) (Massey et al. 1998; Massey 1999). Members return income and capital to their home countries in the form of remittances, which are then either used for consumption or reinvested in household production, agriculture, or new small businesses (Lozano-Ascencio 1993; Taylor et al. 1997). In some communities in Mexico, the annual flow of remittances from the United States is greater than the annual income earned locally (Massey and Parrado 1994). Moreover, once reinvested, remittances may raise household income by more than the value of the remittances themselves, called "migration-induced multiplier effects" (Taylor 1992). Some Mexican households are "transnational" in the sense that they send members to the United States on a relatively permanent basis to earn supplemental income while other members remain in the home community where the remittances are invested (Roberts, Bean, and Lozano-Ascencio 1999).

Because they emphasize household organizational factors operating in response to external economic conditions, new household economic theories better allow for the possibility that migration may often be temporary, especially when not all family members migrate. This contrasts with neoclassical theory, which essentially implies that migration will be permanent, or at least last until macro-imbalances that give rise to individual decisions to move shift appreciably. Otherwise, neoclassical theory can explain return migration only by making recourse to differences in "preferences" (that is, differences in migration time horizons). But such preferences do not vary randomly. For example, using the theoretical concept of "social expected duration," Roberts (1995) explicates how labor-market conditions in both sending and receiving countries influence not only migrants' expected returns on their labor but also the length of their time horizons. Thus, in the case of labor migration from Mexico, neoclassical theory may provide an explanation for potential migrants' initial motivations to consider moving, but new economic theories, because of their more adequate explanation of circular migration, better enhance our understanding of the dynamics of labor flows from Mexico, especially those involving unauthorized migrants.

Labor-Market Segmentation Theory

In contrast to economic approaches, labor market segmentation theories emphasize how social stratification variables affect migration. Dual–labor market theory conceptualizes firms and their employees as stratified into primary and secondary sectors. The primary sector meets "basic demand" in the economy and consists of larger, better-established firms that provide more capital-intensive, better-paying jobs. The secondary sector meets fluctuating or seasonal demand and relies primarily on lower-paid, labor-intensive jobs (Averitt 1968; Massey et al. 1998; Piore 1979; Tolbert et al. 1980). Where human capital theorists argue that investments in education provide increasing returns for workers, segmentation theorists emphasize that barriers among segments and the nature of secondary-sector employment and demand prevent upward mobility and limit returns to human capital in the secondary sector. These conditions often dissuade native-born workers from taking secondary-sector jobs, especially when they are temporary or seasonal. Immigrants, however, are often willing to fill such jobs, especially if they expect to stay in the receiving country only a short time (Piore 1979). Thus, labor-market segmentation has implications both for the types of migrants who come to developed countries and for the structure of the labor market in which competition with native-born workers might occur.

Further segmentation may revolve around factors such as gender, ethnicity, and nativity. Waldinger (1996) and Bailey and Waldinger (1991) describe New York City's labor markets as typified by a hierarchy or "queue" of hiring preferences. They argue that "ascriptive" characteristics such as gender, skin color, ethnicity, and nativity influence employers' hiring practices. Once an immigrant proves he or she is productive at a job, the employer then stereotypes the immigrant group positively and continues to hire from that group in the future and place other groups lower in the queue.

Similarly, labor-market segmentation may derive from ethnic entrepreneurship: immigrants open businesses providing goods and services in the least desirable industries or in areas where ethnic-majority group members fear to go; these immigrant entrepreneurs have been called "middleman minorities" (Bonacich 1973; Bonacich and Modell 1980). Ethnic-owned businesses also serve co-ethnic communities, or—in the case of the strictest segmentation—serve ethnic enclaves that are geographically and economically distinct from the larger economy (Light and Karageorgis 1980; Portes 1987; Portes and Bach 1985; Portes and Jensen 1989; Portes and Stepick 1993; Wilson and Portes 1980). Such developments can generate both economic opportunity and segregation by nativity. Further differentiation also derives from the structure of men's and women's labor-market experiences. For example, immigrant men are often employed in construction (Stepick 1989) or migrant agriculture (Taylor, Martin, and Fix 1997), while many women work as domestics (Hagan 1994; Repak 1994; Repak 1995), child-care providers (Wrigley 1997), or sewing machine operators for the garment industry (Loucky et al. 1994; Morales and Ong 1991; Waldinger 1986). Labor-market segmentation shapes migration when immigrant entrepreneurs seek to attract immigrant labor for their businesses or when other employers continue to hire or decide not to hire certain immigrant groups on the basis of their ascriptive characteristics.

World Systems Theory

Analysts who apply the theory of world systems emphasize the influence on migration of the character of relationships among countries, and among regions and cities within countries. World systems theory is heavily influenced by the dependency critique of capitalism, according to which capital accumulation depends on reserves of labor and materials, thus promoting development in some countries and underdevelopment in others. Core (or more developed) countries build capital by exploiting the labor power and materials of less developed, or peripheral, countries (Furtado 1964; Wallerstein 1983). Core cities such as New York, Los Angeles, and London exercise control over the system through financial, labor, and commodity chains linking them to markets across the world. These links not only move labor-intensive production "offshore" to low-cost countries and regions of the world; they also concentrate capital in and attract migrants to core cities. Thus, New York, Los Angeles, and London have great numbers of immigrants from countries all over the world, but especially from those countries with the strongest financial and production links to these cities (Sassen 1988, 1991, 1994; Waldinger 1996).

The evolution of the global economy has not only stimulated international migration but also generated linkages between specific sending and receiving nations. The colonial and neocolonial history of capitalist expansion around the globe has resulted in ties between countries now in the semiperiphery—where industrialization is in its early stages—and core countries and their global cities in more developed nations. For example, Mexico and the Philippines, which are sites for large numbers of U.S. multinational manufacturing plants, also send the most migrants to the United States (Yang 1995). Migration to the United Kingdom has been dominated by citizens of former colonies in India and the Caribbean, and migration to France has occurred mainly from Algeria and Morocco (Castles and Miller 1998).

World systems theory is particularly useful in explaining why certain types of migrants fill certain types of jobs in global cities, for instance Asian garment entrepreneurs in Los Angeles. James Loucky et al. (1994) argue that growth in the garment industry in Los Angeles during the 1980s and 1990s was "inextricably linked" to large-scale immigration from Asia and Latin America. That growth occurred alongside the evolution of a commodity chain linking garment production in Asia and Latin America to retailers and their markets in the United States. Starting in the 1950s, a large share of U.S. garment production moved overseas, and this played a significant role in the Asian economic miracle. Then, the arrival of large numbers of immigrants in Los Angeles lowered labor costs, making domestic U.S. production competitive. In Los Angeles in the 1990s, the commodity chain included large numbers of small, Asian immigrant–owned garment shops employing mostly immigrant workers (Appelbaum and Gereffi 1994). Asian immigrants also created a new fashion market, and Asian entrepreneurs in California capitalized on their knowledge of this market and with their ties to producers in Asia to open new garment-related businesses (Cheng and Gereffi 1994). The garment industry is just one example of how a global chain of production has both influenced and been influenced by large-scale international migration.

Network Theory

Network theory seeks to explain at the microlevel how connections among actors influence migration decisions, often by linking individual immigrants with their family members and with jobs, both before and after arrival. Labor markets in sending and receiving countries create push and pull factors stimulating migration, but migration may continue after these push and pull factors have diminished. When large numbers of people have moved from one particular location to another, a process of "cumulative causation" is established whereby multiple ties to communities of origin facilitate ongoing and at times increasing migration (Massey et al. 1993; Massey 1994). The exchange of information and the formation of relationships of trust are the building blocks of migration networks. Migrants often do not know the general price of labor in their desired destination relative to that in their home country. Often, however, they do possess information about a particular job at a particular wage, and this information signals an opportunity in the destination labor market (Sassen 1995). Migrants also rely on informal trust relationships to minimize the risks associated with moving to a foreign land (Granovetter 1985, 1995; Granovetter and Swedberg 1992). These contacts with friends, families and employers provide an important means through which immigrants gain and accumulate social capital. By social capital we mean the repertoire of resources such as information, material assistance, and social support that flow through ties to kin, community, and institutions—churches, for example. These ties constitute an important element in the migration process (Massey 1990; Massey and Espinosa 1997). Social capital is enhanced as the number and intensity of social ties between a focal individual (the migrant) and other persons increases (Hagan 1998).

Empirical studies have documented the influence of network variables. In a survey of two sending communities in Michoacán, Mexico, Edward Taylor (1987) finds that having a close relative living in the United States strongly increased the likelihood of migration there, after controlling for age, sex, household income, prior migration, and the expected difference between earnings in Mexico and in the United

States. Using survey data for ten sending communities, Katharine Donato, Jorge Durand, and Douglas Massey (1992) find that social capital in the form of family connections raised Mexican immigrants' incomes, wages, and hours of work once in the United States. Thus, networks not only stimulate and channel migration, they also make it more lucrative. Studies documenting the presence and size of migration networks form an important basis for predicting future flows. Absent the imposition of significant checks on migration by state authorities, such networks can produce chain migration and thereby stimulate rapid increases in immigrant populations. Some authors argue this has been the case during the late twentieth century in the United States with respect to Asian and Latin American immigrant populations (for example, Reimers 1985).

Political Economy Theories

In addition to economic labor-market and network factors, the immigration policies of receiving countries also play an important role in affecting flows. According to James Hollifield's (1992) theory of "hegemonic stability," the world economic system rests on the political and military might of dominant states. Following the Second World War the victors established a global financial and trade system; they began with the international currency regime set up at Bretton Woods and followed this with the General Agreement on Tariffs and Trade (GATT), and the founding of the International Monetary Fund (IMF). The European Union (EU) and the North American Free Trade Agreement (NAFTA) represent the most recent formal attempts by great powers to establish structures and institutions to influence and regulate the global economy. Such attempts have been guided by neoliberal economic principles such as those relating to the ownership of private property and the legal rights of individuals and to protecting and enhancing the privileged position of capital.

Hegemonic states have employed the neoliberal economic order to regulate migration as well as global trade and finance, especially in times of labor shortages, when they have developed temporary direct labor importation programs. For example, by 1973—following decades of direct labor importation—between 10 and 12 percent of France and West Germany's labor forces consisted of temporary foreign workers, and Switzerland's labor force was 30 percent foreign-born (Salt 1981). Similarly, from 1946 to 1964 the United States imported 4.6 million temporary agricultural workers from Mexico under the Bracero Program (Calavita 1992). The United States continues to import temporary agricultural workers—about 17,000 such workers entered with these special work visas—called H-2A visas—in 1995. During recent legislative sessions, the U.S. House of Representatives has considered proposals to admit up to 250,000 agricultural workers under an expanded temporary migrant program (Martin 1997, 102–3). As these examples show, receiving countries often attempt to control immigration by encouraging temporary work patterns rather than permanent settlement.

The Demographic and Economic Contexts

As these discussions of immigration trends and theories indicate, the substantial rise in migration to the United States that has taken place since World War II has consisted of several different kinds of flows occurring for a variety of reasons. What kinds of contextual factors in the United States might have influenced the flows and the ways these were received? The increases in each of the flows may be seen as rooted to some extent in conditions that emerged out of the postwar economic expansion. From the end of World War II to the early 1970s, the United States experienced rising economic prosperity and increasing affluence. Levels of productivity were high and wages and personal incomes rose (Landau 1988; Levy 1987). Not by coincidence, the amendments to the Immigration and Nationality Act passed in 1965 eliminated the restrictive and discriminatory national origins criteria for the admission of immigrants that were embodied in the 1924 National Origins Quota Act and ratified in the Immigration and Nationality Act of 1952 (also known as the McCarran-Walter Act). Adopted in their place were more inclusionary family reunification criteria reflecting the domestic policy emphases of the era on improving civil rights and the foreign policy emphases on establishing better relations with newly independent Third World countries (Cafferty et al. 1983). Partly as a result of such policies in general and the family reunification provisions in particular, legal immigration began to rise substantially (Reimers 1983, 1985). At about the same time, because of the termination of the Bracero Program in 1964 and because of growing demand for inexpensive labor, unauthorized (mostly Mexican) immigration began to increase (Massey 1981). And, as we noted above, unlike the so-called "old" immigrants, who were mostly European in origin, the so-called "new" immigrants, both legal and unauthorized, came mostly from Third World Hispanic and Asian countries (Bean and Tienda 1987).

In the mid-1970s, growth in real wages began to level off, unemployment rose as the country experienced a recession (see figures 2.6 and 2.7), and calls for immigration reform began to emerge (Bean,

Figure 2.6   Hourly Earnings in Private Nonagricultural Industries, 1959 to 2000 (1982 Dollars)

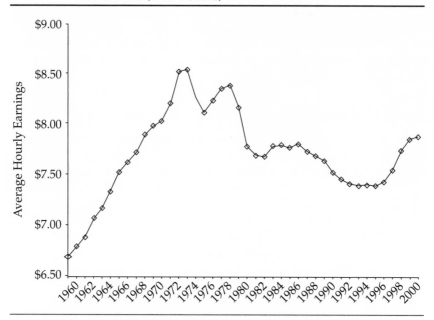

Source: U.S. Bureau of Labor Statistics, "Employment Estimates" (various dates).

Telles, and Lowell 1987). Frequently these consisted of restrictionist outcries against the new immigration, often stated in the form of un-proven claims about the pernicious nature of immigration and its harmful effects on the country. During the 1980s, a substantial body of social science research found little basis for the claims that immi-gration was generating strongly negative demographic, economic, or social effects. An important question is whether similar results obtain during periods of continuing high immigration and during periods of slow job and wage growth. These conditions characterized the first few years but not the second half of the 1990s. As of this writing, the strong economy of the latter half of the 1990s has collapsed into a significant recession during the period 2000 to early 2003. Thus, the issue of the country's capacity (or willingness) to absorb immigration remains a significant question.

Immigration has also frequently been viewed in terms of its impli-cations for population growth and, much less frequently, for eco-nomic growth (Borjas and Tienda 1987; Easterlin 1982; Morris 1985). With respect to population issues, many observers have noted that

Figure 2.7   Average Unemployment Rate and the Size of Civilian Labor Force, 1900s to 1990s

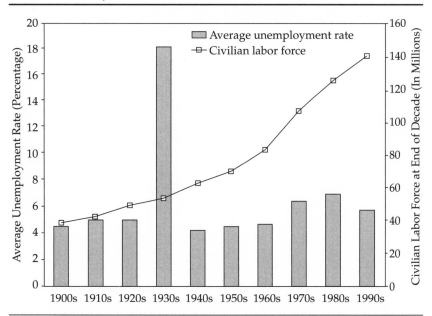

Sources: U.S. Bureau of the Census, *Statistical Abstract of the United States* (2001b and various dates); Council of Economic Advisers, *Economic Report of the President* (2002 and various dates).

the percentage of foreign-born persons in the population, even though rising during the 1970s and 1980s, has remained substantially below the percentage in the early part of the twentieth century (Borjas 1990; Passel 1987; Portes and Rumbaut 1990; Simon 1987) (see figure 2.1). Interestingly, however, immigration during the 1980s accounted directly for the same percentage of overall population growth as it did at the turn of the twentieth century (about 35 percent) (Easterlin 1982; Passel and Edmonston 1994). The apparent incongruity between the absolute and relative contributions of immigration to population growth is resolved by considering two factors. First, the fertility levels of the United States population were higher earlier in the century than they are now. Second, a larger proportion of immigrants returned to their countries of origin in the early part of the century than now appears to be the case. But whether measured in terms of absolute numbers, the percentage foreign-born in the population, or the contribution of net immigration to population growth, the volume of immigration during the 1980s and 1990s has not exceeded the immigration to the United States that occurred during the first twenty years of the twentieth century.

Efforts to assess immigration relative to the size of the economy have been much less frequent. Borjas and Tienda have examined immigration growth relative to the rate of growth in the civilian labor force. They note:

> Between 1951 and 1980, the U.S. labor force grew by 7.6 million, 12.3 million, and 22.5 million during each successive decade. On the basis of immigrant flows for each of these periods and assuming that all those admitted entered the labor force, recent immigrants could have accounted for at most 33 percent of this increase in employment during the 1950s, 27 percent during the 1960s, and 20 percent during the 1970s. (Borjas and Tienda 1987, 646)

The rate of aggregate unemployment during this period varied from around 4.0 percent in 1950 to around 6.5 percent in 1980 (see figure 2.7). Borjas and Tienda also point out that only about half of all immigrants admitted to the country entered the labor force upon arrival during this period. Thus, however measured, the rate of labor force growth during this period exceeded the rate of growth in immigration.

The economic circumstances of the 1950s, 1960s, and 1970s thus seemed more than sufficiently healthy to absorb the numbers of immigrants arriving at the time. During the 1980s, however, several trends changed. The rate of growth in immigration continued to increase while the rate of growth in the labor force began to decline. During the 1960s the growth rate in the U.S. labor force was 27 percent. Between 1970 and 1980 it dropped to 20 percent. By contrast, the growth rate in number of new immigrants jumped from 35 percent during the 1970s to 63 percent during the 1980s (see figure 2.1). Still, by the 1990s, the number of immigrants coming during the decade could have at most accounted for 54 percent of the growth in the labor force, assuming that every immigrant who came held a job, a highly implausible assumption (see table 2.4).

These changes in trends raise the interesting question of how the immigration experience of the late 1980s and 1990s compares both with other post–World War II years and with the early part of the twentieth century; that is, how the volume and growth of immigration compares to growth in the size of the economy. That this question so seldom seems to have been posed is surprising. To our knowledge, the examination by Borjas and Tienda (1987) of growth in immigra-

Table 2.4   Annual Percentage Change in Civilian Labor Force and the
Percentage That Immigrants Make Up of Labor-Force Change
by Decade, 1950 to 2000

Time Period	Annual Percentage Change in Civilian Labor Force	Number of Immigrants as a Percentage of Labor-Force Change
1951 to 1960	1.8	33.0
1961 to 1970	1.9	27.0
1971 to 1980	2.6	20.0
1981 to 1990	1.6	36.0
1991 to 2000	1.2	53.5[a]

Sources: U.S. Bureau of Labor Statistics, "Employment Estimates" (2001 and various years); U.S. Immigration and Naturalization Service (2002a).
[a]Excludes IRCA-adjusted immigrants.

tion relative to growth in the labor force represents one of few attempts to address the issue. Easterlin (1982) has broadly discussed the implications of immigration for growth in GNP, pointing out that at the simplest level of analysis, aggregate production clearly rises in some direct proportion to increases in immigration, but that the challenging problem is unraveling its effects on per capita output. To the extent that immigrants differ from the general population in characteristics that enhance production (higher proportions working, younger age structure of immigrant populations, perhaps greater motivation), the effects would be favorable. To the extent that their characteristics lower production (lower education, less knowledge of English), the effect would be negative. In either case, the effects are not likely to be large because immigrants are still a relatively small fraction of the population, and the characteristics of many immigrants are not enormously different from those of natives (Fix and Passel 1994).

The coincidence of trends in economic growth and immigration growth, though not indicative of a causal relationship between the phenomena, is nonetheless likely to be informative concerning the emergence of conditions likely to influence the reaction of natives to immigration. Figure 2.8 shows average annual rates of growth in per capita GNP for the decades of the twentieth century. During the first ten years of this century, when immigration reached the highest levels of any decade in the nation's history (and the population base was less than half the current base), the economy grew faster than either population or inflation. For example, from 1900 to 1910, after adjusting for inflation the economy expanded 2.8 percent faster than did population. In the 1950s, this differential was 1.6 percent, in the 1960s

Figure 2.8   Average Annual Change in Real GNP Per Capita by Decade, 1901 to 2000 (1996 Dollars)

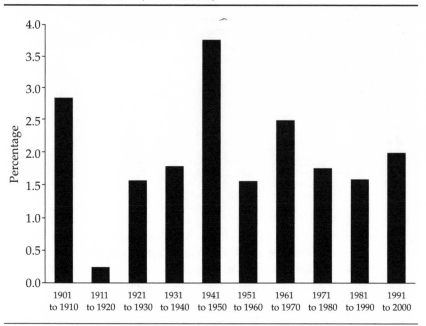

Source: U.S. Bureau of the Census, *Statistical Abstract of the United States* (2001b and various dates).

2.5 percent, in the 1970s 1.8 percent, and in the 1980s 1.6 percent. During the 1990s, the average was 2.2 percent, although from 1991 through 1993 it was only 0.4 percent. More substantial economic growth began in 1992. After an initial year or two of continuing employment and wage stagnation, the economy in the latter half of the 1990s expanded at rates that were stronger than at any other time in the twentieth century, and that also generated increases in real wages (figure 2.6). Increasingly, calls about labor shortages were heard rather than concerns about too much immigration. In 2000 the United States entered a recession, which continued into early 2003. The major question now is whether high rates of growth will resume in the next few years.

Summary and Conclusions

Over the past thirty-five years or so the United States has experienced a remarkable rise in the size and diversity of in-flows to the country.

These increases have occurred across all types of flows, from legal immigrants to refugees to unauthorized immigrants to nonimmigrants. All four types of flows have been characterized by the transition from migration originating mostly in European countries to migration coming mostly from Asian and Hispanic countries. This diversity in national origins now characterizes millions of nonimmigrants as well, so new immigration to the United States has substantially reinforced and increased the country's national-origin and racial-ethnic diversity. Recent patterns illustrate the applicability of the various theories explaining the origins and magnitude of the flows. That is, migrants of all types tend to come more often from countries with which the United States has had prior and continuing relationships (whether primarily political or economic). Within those countries, migration tends to involve more often persons who have family and friends in the United States and persons whose own earnings and whose family's investments stand to gain the most from the migration. The reception immigrants receive when they arrive is affected by the strength of the U.S. economy at the time of arrival. During most years over the past four decades, the economy has been reasonably strong. But during periods of recession and the times of stagnant or even shrinking employment connected with them, it has been more difficult to accommodate new arrivals. Although such periods have not usually been of long duration, they invariably heighten concerns about unauthorized labor migration and welfare receipt among immigrants, the subjects to which we turn in the next two chapters.

= Chapter 3 =

Mexico and Unauthorized Migration

U P TO this point we have considered the general phenomenon of international migration to the United States, noting the several kinds of flows that make up this migration, theories as to why such flows occur, and the economic and labor market contexts within which they have taken place. Often, analyses of immigration to the United States that are intended to shed light on immigration-related policy issues tend to treat immigration as a single phenomenon (see, for example, Borjas 1999). There are three major problems with such approaches. First, migrants from different origin countries are viewed as similar in terms of their reasons for migrating and the receptions they receive when they arrive in the United States. This may accord with desires to address immigration issues and potential policy reforms in universalistic terms, but the "one size fits all" approach fails to account for the fact that over the past thirty years immigrants to the United States from certain countries, especially Mexico, differ in important ways from immigrants from other countries (Suárez-Orozco 1998). The major feature that differentiates Mexicans from other immigrants is that so many of them are unauthorized low-skilled labor migrants. This carries significant implications, as we note below.

The second problem with viewing immigration as one homogeneous, generic phenomenon is that it tends to overlook the fact that the volume of Mexican migration to the United States over the past thirty years has vastly exceeded that coming from any other source country. This was especially true for the decade from 1991 to 2000, during which Mexico accounted for 24.7 percent of all legal entrants to the United States; in this period, the Philippines, in second place, accounted for only 5.6 percent.

A third and related problem is that those who take the generic view tend to ignore unauthorized migration, which is also mainly Mexican in origin. Many analysts estimate that Mexicans constitute an even greater presence among unauthorized migrants than among legal migrants (about 55 percent of all migrants versus about 7 percent for the next largest group, El Salvadorans) (U.S. Immigration and Naturalization Service 1999; Passel 1999). In sum, to speak of immigration without making a distinction between legal and unauthorized migration is to oversimplify substantially the reality of the U.S. immigration picture; and it is not possible to take unauthorized migration into account without paying special attention to the Mexican case.

These considerations lead us to devote an entire chapter to Mexico and Mexican migration. We do not intend in so doing to minimize the significance of immigration from other countries of origin. Rather, we simply bow to the reality that at this point in U.S. history Mexican migration is relatively large and is different in kind from other migration flows. Moreover, the U.S. and Mexican economies are so interdependent and the fates of the two countries so intertwined that Mexican immigration requires not only separate analysis but also perhaps exceptional treatment in immigration policy. We thus give it extra attention at this point, reviewing the history of Mexican emigration and its relationship to U.S. policy, its contribution to the evolution of the United States' Mexican-origin population, and the nature and size of the unauthorized Mexican migrant population in the United States.

Mexican Emigration and U.S. Policy

Mexican migration is important for U.S.–Mexico relations but the direction these relations will take in the future is uncertain (Weintraub 1997b). Whether the two countries continue to become more cooperative and to emphasize their increased integration or become more negative and promote further separation has the potential to affect myriad aspects of social and economic life in both countries. The rising importance of Mexico to the United States is reflected in the publication of a raft of books during the 1990s on Mexico and Mexican migration (see Bean et al. 1997; Oppenheimer 1995; Castañeda 1995; Fuentes 1996). It is also illustrated by the high priority the Democratic Clinton administration gave in 1993 to the passage of the North American Free Trade Agreement (NAFTA), an initiative begun in the first Bush administration, and by the loan-guarantee package put together by the Clinton administration to assist the Mexican government through the economic difficulties created by the peso devaluation of December 1994. As Andres Oppenheimer (1995, xi) noted: "No single country in the post–Cold War era affects the U.S. national interest in more ways than Mexico." While many observers may view this message as having been eclipsed by the recent attacks on the World Trade Center, recent growing turmoil in the Middle East, and the economic rise of China, there remains little doubt that Mexico is of considerable importance to the United States in numerous ways.

Perhaps the most important of these ways involves Mexican migration to the United States, which is occurring at the same time that the issue of immigration in general occupies a high place on the U.S. public policy agenda (see Brimelow 1995; Teitelbaum and Weiner 1995; Suro 1998; Borjas 1999; Portes and Rumbaut 2001; Clark 1998; Beck 1996). As noted in chapters 1 and 2, the importance of immigration issues in the United States over the past twenty years is reflected in the passage of a number of pieces of significant legislation. Given the importance of Mexico for the United States and the prominence of immigration (in both its legal and unauthorized dimensions) as a public policy concern, the intersection of these two issues is of special interest. In other words, both legal and unauthorized Mexican migration to the United States are of great importance to the United States.

Interestingly, however, until recently, when policy makers took up immigration issues, the question of Mexican migration in general has almost always been given only partial consideration, with Mexican *legal* immigration in particular either underemphasized or ignored altogether. This is illustrated in the foci of the two major reports mounted by the U.S. Commission on Immigration Reform, a bipartisan commission authorized by Section 141 of the Immigration Act of 1990. The mandate of the Commission was to review and evaluate the implementation and impact of U.S. immigration policy and to report its findings and recommendations to Congress. One report was conducted by the National Research Council and examined the demographic and economic effects of immigration in general on the United States (Smith and Edmonston 1997). The second study was carried out by the Mexico–United States Binational Migration Study Group (1997), which consisted of research teams that studied aspects of migration within each country and collaboratively analyzed the findings. This report focused predominantly (though not exclusively) on unauthorized migration from Mexico to the United States (Mexico–United States Binational Migration Study 1997). In a similar vein, the U.S. Congress has often focused specifically on illegal migration; for example, in 1996 it concentrated its legislative efforts on border control and on measures to slow unauthorized immigration. The de facto effect of this focus was to highlight only the unauthorized component of Mexican migration. Very little of the Congress's immigration reform package targeted legal immigration in general and Mexican legal immigration in particular. This is not atypical: in general little attention has been targeted on understanding and reforming both legal and unauthorized Mexican migration considered in tandem.

Historical Background

It is useful in considering the policy significance of unauthorized migration to understand the historical background of Mexican emigration to the United States. Until the Mexican Revolution (1910 to 1920), Mexico's agrarian hacienda system effectively tied rural inhabitants to the land (Katz 1988). Land holdings were heavily concentrated into large haciendas, and the vast majority of the rural population either possessed no land or had land holdings insufficient to maintain a family. This landless population put together a basic subsistence through sharecropping arrangements and seasonal labor on plantations, complemented by small-scale craft, service, and commercial activities. Survival depended on making use of the labor of almost all members of the household, from very young to very old. This pattern of rural subsistence discouraged not only the permanent migration of whole families, but also the migration of any household members, because all contributed to the family's subsistence. These patterns were already being disrupted before the Mexican Revolution, as railroads and the economic modernization introduced by Porfirio Díaz, the prerevolutionary president, expanded commercial agriculture and opened rural areas through more intensive trading networks. These changes and the greater population mobility they produced contributed to the Mexican Revolution. The fighting of the revolutionary years and the accompanying economic and social instability made previous strategies of rural survival even more difficult to sustain: local and regional economies offered few job opportunities, harvests were disrupted and destroyed, and commerce became more difficult. Instability in many parts of Mexico continued until the end of the 1920s, particularly in the west-central region of Mexico, where the Cristiada, the Catholic counterrevolutionary movement, pitted villages against each other and against central government. Under these conditions, long-distance migration to the United States became a more attractive option, especially for young and able-bodied males who would migrate seasonally but leave children, wives, and the elderly behind to eke out a meager existence in the village economy. For many others in these years, such as the middle classes, who were especially negatively affected by the revolution, migration to the United States became a permanent option (Knight 1986).

Given the instability of the years from 1910 to 1930 and an open land frontier with the northern neighbor, it is perhaps surprising that more people did not migrate from Mexico to the United States. From 1930 onward, Mexico's agrarian structure stabilized with the emergence of a strong central government and agrarian reforms that destroyed the old hacienda system in Mexico (Katz 1988). The new arrangements still permitted private farming, but imposed individual size limits on holdings. The ejido, or common, was created, partly out of property taken from haciendas, as a form of social property in which peasants and their families had individual farming rights, although they could not legally sell or lease these rights to others. Despite its limitations, agrarian reform was successful in restoring the social and economic viability of Mexico's agrarian structure. From the 1930s to the 1960s, the Mexican peasantry, mainly through the ejidal system and rain-fed agriculture, produced the food needed to feed an expanding urban population. Private commercial agriculture, which made extensive use of peasant migrant labor and some ejidos, provided a large part of the export revenues that helped finance Mexico's industrialization.

After the 1930s, the survival strategies of the Mexican peasantry were similar to those during the Porfiriato, but at a higher level of economic development (Katz 1988). Family labor was used to farm ejidal plots, care for animals, and undertake craftwork and, often, some trade. The developing road network intensified trade in agricultural products with the cities, creating commercial opportunities at the village level. Remittances from migrant laborers in the United States played an important part in Mexican village economies by generating the cash needed to make small investments in farming or housing. The scarcity of government credits to support ejidal farming made migrant earnings even more necessary. Migration to the United States was attractive because the wages were many times higher than could be obtained through migrant labor in Mexico. Such migration also tended to be greatest from areas where agriculture was highly market-oriented and thus the need for cash greater and contacts with the outside more intense. These were primarily in the west-central region of Mexico, the states of Guanjuato, Jalisco, and Michoacán, which already had long-established migrant links with California and the Southwest of the United States. Areas of mainly subsistence farming, particularly in geographically remote regions, such as Chiapas and Oaxaca, had few international migrants until the 1970s, though villagers worked seasonally in Mexican plantation agriculture.

The vitality of the Mexican agrarian structure from the 1930s to the 1960s helped ensure that international migration was primarily temporary (Gamio 1930; Taylor 1970). It was a strategy that enabled young heads of family or prospective heads of family to acquire some savings to set up their own households and to sustain their village-based families. Migrants returned because they had something to return to. In these years there was also a large-scale permanent outmigration of villagers, but this flow largely went to Mexico's expanding cities.

After 1930 rapid population increase in Mexico occurred as a result of sharp declines in mortality and, in the rural areas, consistently high levels of fertility. Despite their growth, the village economies could not absorb this population expansion, and there were more peasant farmers in Mexico in 1960 than there had been in 1910. From the 1930s onward, however, labor demand in the urban economies, particularly those of Mexico City, Guadalajara, and Monterrey, grew as Mexico undertook a substantial program of industrialization to replace imports with domestic products (called "import substitution"). The temporary character of Mexican cross-border migration, though based on conditions in Mexico, was undoubtedly also reinforced by U.S. actions and attitudes: From the 1920s onwards, U.S. immigration policy fostered the development of truly temporary migration from Mexico, through programs such as the Bracero Program and its predecessors. After the Bracero Program ended in 1964, U.S. immigration policy on unauthorized Mexican migration often operated by "looking the other way," even though occasional displays of control at the border appeased public concerns (Massey, Durand, and Malone 2002; Bean and Fix 1992).

The Contemporary Situation

By the 1970s, changes in the U.S. economy were altering the demand side of the migrant flow. The need for migrant labor in agriculture continued, even though mechanization reduced demand in some areas. The expansion of fruit and vegetable production in California and in new areas, such as the Northwest and Florida, increased demand for seasonal labor. But the principal change in the profile of migrant labor occurred when migrants started to take urban jobs. Although some earlier Mexican migrants had taken jobs in cities such as Los Angeles and Chicago, the massive migrant entry into such jobs dates from the 1970s, when the volume of Mexican migrants began to exceed substantially the numbers that could be absorbed in temporary agricultural work.

Partially responsible for the increase in the flow of Mexican migrants were conditions in Mexico, particularly the economic crises of the 1980s and the stagnation of the Mexican peasant economy (Escobar Latapi, Bean, and Weintraub 1999a, 1999b). But part of the reason was also the long-term shift in the pattern of demand in the United States labor market as employment in the U.S. economy became more service-based (Bean, Browning, and Frisbie 1984). This shift had a geographic and an occupational component, both of which created job opportunities for Mexican migrants (Escobar Latapi, Bean, and Weintraub 1999a). The U.S. economic expansion of the 1970s onward took place disproportionately in the states that had traditionally received Mexican migrants, the Sunbelt states of the Southwest and especially California. And some of the occupational shift in demand was toward skilled white-collar jobs and away from skilled and semi-skilled manual jobs.

There was, however, also an increase in demand for relatively unskilled jobs in service, retail, and construction activities to build the cities and the suburbs and to provide inexpensive consumer services for their inhabitants (Escobar Latapi, Bean, and Weintraub 1999a). These jobs required little English-language proficiency, and in times of high employment, there was not a ready supply of native-born Americans willing to work for low pay, often in poor working conditions. Though these jobs were insecure, they were not seasonal, like agricultural work, and thus offered migrants a basis for settling in the United States with their families. The crisis of the Mexican peasant economy meant that migrants were less likely than before to see themselves as returning to agriculture in Mexico while the crisis of the Mexican urban economy made migrating to a city in Mexico a less attractive alternative. Building upon networks that were usually still based on villages of origin but that included migrants who had already made the transition from agricultural to urban work, increasing numbers of Mexican migrants found their way to American urban areas and urban jobs in the 1970s, 1980s, and 1990s (Roberts, Bean, and Lozano-Ascencio 1999).

Mexican Migration and U.S. Responses

The high profile of Mexican migration for U.S. policy is relatively new. Until recently, Mexican migration, compared to that from other nations, was not particularly large and was relatively unrestricted, in practice if not always in the law, with exceptions such as the repatriation of large numbers of Mexican migrants in the 1930s and again in 1954. Compared to the massive immigrations from Europe in the last half of the nineteenth century and the first decades of the twentieth, until recently Mexican immigration made only a small contribution to U.S. population growth. Its pre–Second World War peak occurred in the 1920s, when the economic disruptions of the Mexican Revolution and the civil wars that followed led many Mexicans to migrate to the United States in search of jobs. In the 1920s, 459,000 Mexicans were registered as immigrating to the United States, equivalent to 3.2 percent of the total Mexican population in 1921. These numbers of Mexican immigrants were not surpassed until the 1970s, and they were not exceptionally high when compared to other immigrant flows to the United States. Several European countries—Italy, Germany, and the United Kingdom—contributed similar numbers of immigrants, and twice that number came from Canada in the 1920s. Even Ireland, long past the peak of its contribution to U.S. population growth, sent a higher percentage of its population as immigrants to the United States than did Mexico in these years. Some 5.2 percent of the Irish population immigrated to the United States in the 1920s, despite the attainment of Irish independence in 1921, which removed one major ostensible cause of Irish emigration.

Not only was Mexican migration not particularly heavy, but in addition, much of it, as noted above, was temporary in nature. Partly as a result, Mexican immigrants have had one of the lowest naturalization rates of any immigrant group (Jasso and Rosenzweig 1990, table 3.1). The census figures also suggest substantial emigration out of the United States by Mexican immigrants. Between 1901 and 1930, 728,000 Mexicans are recorded as immigrating to the United States, yet in 1930 the Mexican-born population in the United States was 641,000, and this figure would have included many unauthorized Mexicans. By 1950, the number of Mexicans in the United States had dropped to 452,000, reflecting not only mortality and the low level of immigration after 1930, but the forced repatriations of Mexicans in the 1930s. There are no satisfactory estimates of Mexican return migration to Mexico, but it is clear that the amount of return migration has been quite high in virtually all years, although it may have declined substantially during the 1990s as a consequence of beefed-up enforcement along the border (Bean et al. 1994; Reyes, Johnson, and Van Swearingen 2002; Massey, Durand, and Malone 2002; Mexico–United States Binational Migration Study 1998).

Until the 1960s, Mexican migrants to the United States were predominantly employed in temporary and seasonal types of work. The rapid expansion of Californian agriculture after World War II depended on a seasonal labor force. Work in fruit and vegetable production could not employ enough people year-round; consequently, it was attractive only to the newest entrants into the labor force, immigrant or not, who had no other sources of work. For most workers in California, seasonal work in agriculture was a step toward finding more permanent work either in the rural areas or in the cities, so turnover was high. The difficulties of recruiting a labor force from

California's resident population made Mexican migrant labor an attractive option for farmers. It was also attractive for the migrants themselves, who could earn much higher wages than in Mexico and could save enough to maintain their families in the villages and even enable some to invest in land or livestock. So long as the Mexican migrants wished to return, the arrangement suited both sides. Until the 1970s, most Mexican migrants did wish to return; but in the last three decades, Mexican immigration not only became greater in volume but also included a greater component of permanent immigration (Bean, Passel, and Edmonston 1990).

At this juncture Mexican migration became a critical issue for U.S. immigration policy, though this was not always made explicit. Other shifts in the flows of immigrants in the 1970s and 1980s played a part in changing immigration policy in the 1980s, particularly the increases in immigration from Asia. However, the major piece of legislation in the 1980s, the Immigration Reform and Control Act (IRCA) of 1986, and the policy debates around it were substantially affected by the peculiar challenge posed by Mexican immigration (Bean, Vernez, and Keely 1989). Whereas previous immigration policies toward Mexico had tended to operate according to the adage "If it ain't broke, don't fix it," IRCA represented a determined effort to find a solution to what were perceived to be immigration problems raised by Mexican migration (Massey, Durand, and Malone 2002). Confronted with the reality of millions of unauthorized Mexicans residing in the United States and the prospect of many more following them, IRCA, through legalization and employer sanctions, recognized de facto Mexican migrant settlement while it sought to limit employer demand for further migrant labor. As various observers have pointed out, the 1993 North American Free Trade Agreement (NAFTA) was, in policy terms, an arm of this strategy (Smith 1997; Weintraub 1997). By promoting economic development in Mexico, it was hoped that NAFTA would diminish the pressures on Mexicans to migrate to the United States in the medium and long term. Whether these hopes will be fulfilled cannot be reliably assessed in the period of time that NAFTA has been in effect, but early assessments do not indicate that NAFTA has been successful in curtailing migration flows (Massey, Durand, and Malone 2002; Weintraub 1997a).

The U.S. Mexican-Origin Population

Decades of both temporary and permanent migration have thus led to a substantial Mexican-origin population in the United States (Glick and Van Hook 1999). It has two principal components: individuals born in the United States who can trace their ancestry to Mexico and individuals born in Mexico who have subsequently moved to the United States. The latter group, Mexican-born individuals, can be broken down into three subgroups: naturalized citizens, legal immigrants, and unauthorized migrants from Mexico. The contribution of the Mexican-origin population to the total U.S. population has grown and continues to do so as a result of growth in each of these components. Here we present a brief discussion of the past and present size, growth, and distribution of the Mexican-origin population within the United States, focusing on changes in each component of the population. In the case of the unauthorized component, we present the most recent evidence of its size.

"Ethnicity denotes a social identity deriving from group membership based on common race, religion, language, national origin, or some combination of these factors" (Bean and Tienda 1987, 38). In part because ethnicity is a multidimensional concept, there have been changes in the way the U.S. Census Bureau has defined the Mexican-origin population over the past fifty years (see table 3.1). Prior to 1970, the Mexican-origin population could be identified through the use of various objective markers, including place of birth, parents' place of birth, mother tongue, and Spanish surname. While serving well to identify Mexican-origin persons who were either foreign-born or whose parents were born in Mexico, these markers failed to adequately identify third- or higher-generation Mexican-origin persons, especially those who no longer spoke Spanish at home or who no longer had a Spanish surname because of intermarriage. These limitations are especially problematic for identifying Mexican-origin persons whose families had a long history in the United States. In response to such issues, a new question was added to the 1970 census, allowing respondents of any generation to identify themselves as being of Mexican origin. This question was also included in the 1980, 1990, and 2000 censuses. Thus, measures of the size and distribution of the Mexican-origin population since 1970 depend on the ethnic self-identification of individuals, whereas measures in previous years relied on other kinds of ethnic classifications.

Irrespective of these changes in the measurement of the Mexican-origin population within the United States, measures of the size of the Mexican-origin population show steady growth over time, from 385,000 in 1910 to 20.6 million in 2000, as shown in table 3.2. This population nearly doubled in size in every decade except for the period from 1930 to 1960. Some of this growth can be attributed to natural increase. Mexican American fertility rates in recent decades have been approximately 35 to 40 percent higher than those of Anglos

Table 3.1 Identifiers Available in the United States Census or Current Population Survey for the Hispanic Population, 1950 to 2000

Year	Birthplace	Foreign Parentage	Mother Tongue	Home Language Other Than English	Spanish[a] Surname	Spanish Origin or Descent	Ancestry
2000	yes	no	no	yes	no	yes	no
Since 1994[c]	yes	yes	no	no	no	yes	no
1990	yes	no	no	yes	no	yes	yes
1980	yes	no	no	yes	yes	yes	yes
1970	yes	yes	yes	no	yes	yes	no
1960	yes	yes	yes[b]	no	yes	no	no
1950	yes	yes	no	no	yes	no	no

Sources: Bean and Tienda (1987) for 1950 to 1980 data; Bureau of the Census (1993); Current Population Surveys for 1994 and subsequent years; and U.S. Bureau of the Census (2001a).
[a]Available for only five southwestern states.
[b]Available for 25 percent of the foreign-born population.
[c]Current Population Survey (various dates).

Table 3.2   Total Mexican-Origin Population in the United States, 1910 to 2000

Year	Total Mexican-Origin Population (In Thousands)	Percentage of Total U.S. Population
2000	21,207	7.5
1990	13,393	5.4
1980	8,740	3.9
1970	4,532	2.2
1960	1,736[a]	1.0
1950	1,346	0.9
1940	1,077	0.8
1930	1,423	1.2
1920	740	0.7
1910	385	0.4

Sources: U.S. Immigration and Naturalization Service (1975); U.S. Bureau of the Census (1980, 1990); Current Population Survey (2002).
[a]Mexican-origin population calculated as a sum of the Mexican-born population and natives of Mexican parentage.

(Bean and Tienda 1987; Bean, Swicegood, and Berg 2000), whereas the two groups appear to experience more comparable mortality rates. Thus, even in the absence of migration the size of the Mexican-origin population would be increasing relative to the size of the Anglo population.

Mexican Immigration

Despite the relatively high rate of natural increase of the Mexican-origin population, the present-day size of the Mexican-origin population in the United States is mostly attributable to immigration from Mexico during the twentieth century. Edmonston and Passel (1994) estimate that this population would be only 14 percent of its current size had there been no immigration from Mexico over the last hundred years. Moreover, the number of immigrants from Mexico living in the United States has been increasing both in terms of absolute numbers and in comparison to other immigrant groups. Table 3.3 presents the size of the Mexican-born population in the United States since 1900. The flow of immigrants from Mexico has fluctuated throughout the twentieth century, but it is clear that the Mexican-born have become an increasingly large component of the total foreign-born population in the country. By 2000, 28.8 percent of foreign-born persons living in the United States were born in Mexico. Accompanying the growth in the Mexican-born population in this century have

Table 3.3   Total Mexican-Born Population in the United States,
1900 to 2000

Year	Mexican-Born Population (In Thousands)	Percentage of the Total Foreign-Born	Percentage of the Total Mexican-Origin Population
2000	8,771	28.8	40.8
1990	4,298	21.7	32.1
1980	2,199	15.6	25.2
1970	759	7.9	16.7
1960	576[a]	5.9	33.2
1950	454	4.4	33.7
1940	377	3.2	35.0
1930	617	4.3	43.4
1920	486	3.5	65.7
1910	222	1.6	57.7
1900	103	1.0	NA

Sources: U.S. Immigration and Naturalization Service (1975); U.S. Bureau of the Census (1980, 1990, 2000); Current Population Survey (2002).
[a]Mexican-origin population calculated as a sum of the Mexican-born population and natives of Mexican parentage.

been increases in the flow of migrants arriving from Mexico. The flow of immigrants has varied throughout the century, but despite these fluctuations, Mexican immigrants have become an increasingly large proportion of the total immigrant stream.

The number of Mexican immigrants arriving in the United States in each decade since 1900 is shown in table 3.4. It can be seen that the first large-scale increase in immigration from Mexico onto U.S. territory occurred between 1911 and 1920, when more than 200,000 immigrants arrived from Mexico; the volume doubled again in the twenties. After dropping back sharply during the 1930s and early 1940s, levels of immigration from Mexico began to increase with the introduction of the Bracero Program (bracero is Spanish for "hired laborer") in 1943. Starting in World War II, non-Mexican farm workers in California sought higher-paying jobs in the defense industry. The reduction in the available labor supply in agriculture prompted growers to place pressure on Congress to admit temporary workers from Mexico, and at the peak of the program, in 1956, 445,197 workers were recruited (Reimers 1992). These workers were expected to be temporary residents in the United States, but many stayed, and although growers fought to retain the supply of cheap Mexican labor, Congress refused to extend the program in 1964.

Table 3.4   **Legal Immigration from Mexico to the United States, 1900 to 2000**

Years	Number Arriving from Mexico in the Decade	Percentage of All Immigrants Arriving in the Decade
A. Published totals		
1991 to 2000	2,249,421	24.7
1981 to 1990	1,655,843	22.6
1971 to 1980	640,294	14.2
1961 to 1970	453,937	13.7
1951 to 1960	299,811	11.9
1941 to 1950	60,589	5.9
1931 to 1940	22,319	4.2
1921 to 1930	459,287	11.2
1911 to 1920	219,004	3.8
1901 to 1910	49,642	0.6
B. Numbers of Mexican arrivals, excluding IRCA legalizations[a]		
1991 to 2000	1,194,259	13.1
1981 to 1990	693,213	11.6

Sources: U.S. Immigration and Naturalization Service (2002a and various years).
[a]Numbers other than those legalizing their immigration status.

Despite the end of the Bracero Program in 1964, both unauthorized migration and legal immigration from Mexico continued to grow during the next three decades. The number of Mexican immigrants admitted legally to the United States recently increased dramatically, growing from almost 1.7 million (or 22.6 percent of the flow in the 1980s) to over 2.2 million (or 24.7 percent of the flow in the 1990s). The dramatic increase occurred because of the amnesty provisions of the 1986 Immigration Reform and Control Act (IRCA). Under IRCA, unauthorized migrants who had lived in the United States since 1982 or who had been working in the United States in agriculture for at least six months were offered the opportunity to legalize their migration status. Numbers of those entering the United States are therefore inflated because the counts include those legalizing their status under the IRCA provisions. Between 1989 and 1994, IRCA offered legal status to approximately 2 million unauthorized Mexican agricultural workers and other migrants who had been living illegally in the United States since 1982. Section B of table 3.4 shows the effect of the legalizations under IRCA on the size of the flow of immigrants from

Table 3.5   Number of Naturalizations Among Mexican-Born Persons in
the United States, 1950 to 1996

Year	Number of Naturalizations Among Mexicans	Number per Ten Thousand Mexican-Born Persons in the United States
1995	67,238	110.9
1990	17,564	40.9
1980	9,341	4.2
1970	6,195	0.8
1960	5,913	1.0

Source: U.S. Immigration and Naturalization Service (2002a and earlier years).

Mexico. When those who legalized their status under the amnesty provisions are removed from the official numbers of immigrants arriving in the decade, the size of the Mexican immigrant population entering between 1981 and 2000 is greatly reduced and is more comparable to the size of the flow during the 1950s, 1960s, and 1970s.

Another component of the Mexican-born population in the United States is immigrants who have become U.S. citizens. Table 3.5 presents the numbers of Mexicans who became naturalized citizens for selected years going back to 1960. Compared to other immigrant groups in the United States, Mexican immigrants have been slow to naturalize (Grebler 1966; Bean and Tienda 1987). There may be several factors influencing this comparatively low rate of naturalization, but English-language ability is frequently cited as the largest barrier to citizenship among Mexican immigrants (Reimers 1992). However, it is clear from table 3.5 that the proportion of Mexicans who are becoming citizens is increasing over time. Immigrants must reside in the United States for five years before becoming citizens of the United States. The number of immigrants becoming citizens increased substantially beginning in about 1994 as those who had legalized their status under IRCA became eligible for naturalization (U.S. Immigration and Naturalization Service 1998).

In addition to changes in its size and sources of growth, the Mexican-origin population has also experienced changes in its geographic distribution within the United States. Historically, Mexican-origin persons have been concentrated in five southwestern states: Arizona, California, Colorado, New Mexico, and Texas. The proximity of these states to Mexico made them a likely destination for immigrants. Mexican immigrants have also been more geographically concentrated than their U.S.-born Mexican-origin counterparts, although both groups are more likely to be found in the western or southern states than other Hispanic groups. Whereas Mexican immigration prior to World War II was largely to rural southwestern areas where jobs in agriculture, mining, and the railroads were found, more recent migrants have become increasingly urban although still concentrated in the Southwest (Bean and Tienda 1987).

Table 3.6 presents the geographic distribution of the Mexican-origin population from 1950 to 2000. By 1960 two states, California and Texas, contained the majority of the Mexican-origin population. However, the distribution of the Mexican-origin population within these states has changed significantly over time. For example, in 1960, Texas and California each contained around 41 percent of this population. By 2000, California still contained 41 percent of this population whereas Texas had less than 25 percent. That the fraction of the Mexican-origin population in California has remained so high suggests California remains a particularly attractive destination for migrants. In addition to a shift in the distribution of Mexican-origin individuals within the five southwestern states, there has also been a decrease in the proportion of this population found only in these five states. In 1970, 87 percent of the Mexican-origin population lived in the five southwestern states. By 2000, only about 76 percent of this population did. Other states such as Illinois, Michigan, and Washington have attracted increasingly large Mexican-origin populations as well (Bean and Tienda 1987). The decreasing geographic concentration of this group is likely to continue as the Mexican-origin population continues to grow in the twenty-first century.

While increasing numbers of Mexican migrants and their greater dispersal throughout the country are important features of the Mexican-origin population, perhaps the most distinctive and consequential characteristic of Mexican migrants is their very low level of human capital, as measured by education. Such low education levels result from the fact that educational attainment in Mexico is lower than in the United States and that the migration flow from Mexico consists largely of low-skilled labor (Bustamante 1998), as we noted above. Chapter 6 contains further information on education levels among Mexican foreign-born persons in the United States, together with data on the second, third, and later generations. But for the moment suffice it to note that the education levels of both male and female Mexican immigrants in the country in 1998 were about 38 percent below those of native white males and females. Although the education levels of Mexican-origin males and females have been rising in recent years, they have not been rising as fast as those of the native white population, meaning that the gap between Mexican immigrants and natives has been growing (Borjas 1999; Bean, Gonzalez

Table 3.6 Percentage of Mexican-Origin Population in the Five Southwestern States, 1950 to 2000

State	1950		1960		1970	
	Number (In Thousands)	Percentage of All Mexican Origin	Number (In Thousands)	Percentage of All Mexican Origin	Number (In Thousands)	Percentage of All Mexican Origin
Arizona	126	5.5	207	5.9	240	5.3
California	758	33.2	1,456	41.4	1,857	41.0
Colorado	119	5.2	152	4.3	104	2.3
New Mexico	249	10.9	276	7.9	119	2.6
Texas	1,027	45.0	1,423	40.5	1,619	35.7
Other states		–		–	593	13.1
Total	2,282	100.0	3,514	100.0	4,532	100.0
Percentage of Mexican-origin population in the five southwestern states					86.9	

State	1980		1990		2000	
	Number (In Thousands)	Percentage of All Mexican Origin	Number (In Thousands)	Percentage of All Mexican Origin	Number (In Thousands)	Percentage of All Mexican Origin
Arizona	396	4.5	619	4.6	1,296	6.3
California	3,637	41.6	6,071	45.3	8,456	41.0
Colorado	207	2.4	279	2.1	451	2.2
New Mexico	234	2.7	329	2.5	330	1.6
Texas	2,752	31.5	3,900	29.1	5,072	24.6
Other States	1,514	17.3	2,195	16.4	5,036	24.4
Total	8,740	100.0	13,393	100.0	20,641	100.0
Percentage of Mexican-origin population in the five southwestern states	82.7		83.6		75.7	

Sources: U.S. Bureau of the Census: (1970, "Persons of Spanish Origin," Subject Reports PC(2)-1-C; 1980, "Persons of Spanish Origin by State: 1980," Supplementary Report PC80-S1-7; "General Social and Economic Characteristics," United States Summary PC80-1-C1; 1990, "General Social and Economic Characteristics," United States Summary; 2000, "Demographic Profiles: 100-percent and Sample Data," available on-line at: www.census.gov.

Baker, and Capps 2001). This skills gap, when coupled with the labor-related nature of most Mexican migration, has important implications that will become evident in later chapters.

Unauthorized Mexican Migration

Over the past three decades, the component of the Mexican-born population that has attracted the most media attention is the unauthorized migrant population. This group has frequently galvanized public opinion and attracted the attention of U.S. policy makers (U.S. Commission on Immigration Reform 1994; Bean et al. 1997; Espenshade and Belanger 1998). Three of the special governmental initiatives undertaken to address immigration issues mentioned in earlier chapters are illustrative. First, in 1981 the Select Commission on Immigration and Refugee Policy (SCIRP), an initiative undertaken by President Carter, released its report, in which it noted that "one issue has emerged as most pressing—the problem of undocumented/illegal migration" (1981, 35). Second, in 1986 Congress passed the Immigration Reform and Control Act (IRCA) in an effort to reduce unauthorized migration. Third, in 1996 Congress passed welfare reform and immigration legislation partly to curtail unauthorized migration by limiting the public benefits available to noncitizen immigrants (Espenshade, Baraka, and Huber 1997; Van Hook and Bean 1998b).

An unauthorized migrant is a person who resides in the United States but whose status is not that of a U.S. citizen, permanent resident, or authorized visitor (Van Hook and Bean 1998a). Various labels have been applied to what we call here unauthorized migrants, including "undocumenteds," "illegals," "illegal aliens," and "illegal immigrants." Each of these terms has a somewhat different meaning and connotation (Keely 1977). We use the term "unauthorized migrant" because it best encompasses the population to which we are referring. We do not use the term "undocumented" because now many unauthorized migrants have documents. Nor do we use the term "illegal" (although in a technical sense these migrants are illegal) because the United States often does not systematically enforce laws making it illegal for employers to hire such persons.

Given the frequent preoccupation in the United States with unauthorized migration, and given that persons from Mexico by all accounts make up more than half of all unauthorized immigrants (Bean, Passel, and Edmonston 1990; U.S. Immigration and Naturalization Service 2000a), it is perhaps not surprising that many analysts and policy makers focus attention on how many unauthorized Mexican migrants there are in the United States while often ignoring research findings about other aspects of unauthorized migration. For example, a front-page story in *The New York Times* about the results of the Mexico–U.S. Binational Migration Study (Dillon 1997) emphasized the study's findings on the size of this population and didn't mention other results of the study. The unauthorized population is heterogeneous with respect to duration of stay. To avoid misunderstanding evidence about migration flows, it is particularly important to recall certain distinctions based on duration of stay, such as that between temporary and permanent migrants—in the terminology of sociologists, sojourners and settlers (Chavez 1988; Espenshade 1995a; U.S. Commission on Immigration Reform 1997; Bean, Vernez, and Keely 1989).

Much of the historical and current debate about unauthorized migration derives from differences in perceptions about whether sojourners or settlers dominate such flows. Insofar as the unauthorized migrant population is made up of sojourners, return migrants represent outflows that help to offset inflows. Outflow is a critical component because in the case of unauthorized Mexican migrants the majority of entrances has been offset by exits, at least until recently, as indicated by estimates of repeat entrances (Espenshade 1995b) and net flow (Passel and Woodrow 1987; Woodrow, Passel, and Warren 1987). During the 1970s, many observers mistook substantial numbers of border apprehensions as indicating large net inflows. By failing to account for outflow, such observers greatly exaggerated the rate of growth of the unauthorized migrant population. In effect, the error was to assume that there were more settlers than sojourners, whereas in fact just the opposite was the case.

Table 3.7 presents estimates of size of the unauthorized Mexican migrant population from 1980 to 2000. In 1980 this population was about 8 percent of the U.S. foreign-born population, 51 percent of the total Mexican-born population in the United States, and about 13 percent of the total Mexican-origin population in the United States. By 2000 the unauthorized Mexican population had increased to about 11 percent of the foreign-born population in the United States, but was only about 36 percent of the Mexican foreign-born population. While unauthorized migration from Mexico continues, legal immigrants constitute the largest component of the Mexican-born population in the United States despite all the publicity given to unauthorized migrants.

Questions about the size of the unauthorized population, particularly the unauthorized Mexican population, recently reemerged yet again in public discourse about immigration, this time over the results of the 2000 census. The unadjusted population count from that census, 281.4 million persons, substantially exceeded the number expected on the basis of the first round of demographic analyses re-

Table 3.7 Unauthorized Mexican Migrant Population as Percentage of Various Populations, 1980 to 2000

Year	Est. Number of Unauthorized Mexican Migrants (In Thousands)	Percentage of Total Foreign-Born Population	Percentage of Mexican Foreign-Born Population	Percentage of Mexican-Origin Population	Percentage of Total U.S. Population
2000	3,900	12.8	45.9	18.6	1.4
1996	2,700	11.0	40.4	15.0	1.0
1990	1,321[a]	6.7	30.7	9.9	0.5
1980	1,131[a]	8.0	51.4	12.9	0.5

Sources: 1980 estimates of enumerated unauthorized Mexican migrant population from Warren and Passel (1987); 1990 estimates from Warren (1994); 1996 estimates of the total unauthorized Mexican migrant population from Warren (1997); 2000 estimates from Bean et al. (2001).
[a]Estimate includes only the enumerated portion of the Mexican unauthorized population.

leased in early 2001: 274.6 million, a difference of 6.8 million persons. The figure derived from the demographic analyses was obtained by adding the most recent decade's births and immigrants to 1990 population counts and subtracting deaths and emigrants. Some observers immediately argued that the discrepancy of 6.8 million was almost entirely attributable to previously undetected unauthorized migration; if this had been true, the number of unauthorized migrants in the country in 2000 would have been twice as high as previously thought, in the range of 11 million to 12 million persons (see, for example, Cohn 2001; Zitner 2001).

What is the likelihood that such numbers are plausible? We can gain some insight into this question by examining the estimate for 2000 developed by Bean et al. (2001), who estimated about 3.90 million unauthorized Mexican migrants were in the country in March 2000. If Mexican unauthorized migrants constituted about 55.0 percent of *all* unauthorized migrants in 2000, as appeared to be the case in the mid-1990s, then the implied total of unauthorized migrants from all countries of origin in 2000 would have been about 7.06 million persons. This number is far below the figure of 11 million or higher that some observers speculated might be in the country in 2000. As Bean et al. note in the same study, even if the underenumeration rate of unauthorized migrants in the March 2000 CPS were twice as large as the value they used in their calculations, one would still come up with a figure of only 9.42 million. In short, though both Mexican and total unauthorized migration during the 1990s, especially during the latter half of the decade, certainly contributed more to the growth of the U.S. population than previously thought, without doubt they did not contribute enough to account for the gap between the census count and the number initially obtained from demographic analysis by the U.S. Bureau of the Census. Further research on the part of the U.S. Bureau of the Census (Robinson 2002) later documented that the size of the Mexican and total unauthorized populations were not as high as some of the more sensationalistic accounts were claiming.

An important question for the future concerns the degree to which economic growth and declining fertility in Mexico will lead to reduced migration to the United States over the next two or three decades. Birth rates in Mexico have fallen precipitously over the past couple of decades, from an average of about 6.1 children per woman in 1974 to about 2.4 children per woman in 1999 (CONAPO 1999). These drops have been so steep that each of the past six or seven Mexican birth cohorts has been smaller than the one immediately preceding it, reversing the pattern of steady increase that had obtained previously. Unless fertility goes back up, this means that the size of the Mexican labor force (by which we mean the number of persons each year looking for employment) could be expected to stop growing and perhaps start to shrink sometime between 2010 and 2015 (Mexico–United States Binational Migration Study 1997). Moreover, if economic growth in Mexico sustained reasonable but not unrealistic levels of 6 to 7 percent per year, the number of jobs in Mexico could easily within a decade equal the size of the workforce, a circumstance not present in the country for as long as anyone can remember. Given these trends, the question becomes: Would migration to the United States then start to subside? This can only be answered in a somewhat speculative manner because we cannot be confident that such developments will occur. In fact, though, even if they do, there are reasons to think Mexican migration might not slow down substantially, for reasons that have mainly do to with the kinds of forces that drive migration that were discussed in chapter 2. In the Mexican case, two probably stand out. The first is that so much migration has already occurred that it will continue to spawn more migration—the cumulative causation phenomenon noted by Massey, Durand, and Malone (2002). The second is that even if it becomes easier to find employment in Mexico, it is likely that there will continue to be economic reasons (such as higher wages) and family and household reasons to migrate. Thus, while certain kinds of pressures to migrate might ease under the scenario just outlined, other factors driving migration can be expected to continue.

Summary and Conclusions

Persons of Mexican ancestry have been part of the population of this country since its beginnings, and over the course of the twentieth century they have become an increasingly large component of the U.S. population. This growth is a result of both natural increase and immigration from Mexico, with legal migration contributing the most to the overall growth. The flow of migrants from Mexico to the United States has fluctuated with changes in the political and economic climates of both countries but has continued to increase substantially over time. The proportion of the Mexican-origin population in the United States made up of immigrants had been decreasing throughout the beginning of the century, but it has increased since 1960. Because the recent flow of legal and unauthorized labor migrants from Mexico has been so large, the proportion of the Mexican-origin population that is unauthorized will continue to be high and to influence public perceptions about immigration, because general immigration is often confused with this unauthorized migration.

The data and material presented in this chapter also highlight three main features of Mexican immigration to the United States that have substantial implications for our analyses in the rest of this book: the overwhelming size of the recent Mexican immigrant group; its predominantly labor-migrant nature; and the fact that so much of Mexican immigration consists of unauthorized migrants. The first feature makes Mexican immigration important; the second one structures the nature of Mexican immigration in ways that matter for almost all other outcomes one might examine; and the third means that many Mexican immigrants start their immigrant experiences far behind other immigrants and in a more shadowy existence (Chavez 1992). In addition, the last aspect almost guarantees that the public will often mistake legal Mexican immigrants for unauthorized immigrants. The importance of this factor—Mexicans as labor migrants—can hardly be overstated. Almost all Mexicans come here to work, usually thinking they will return to Mexico either soon or after a few years. Of course many end up staying here, but the fact they plan to return to Mexico, at least for a while, structures almost everything else they do. As we will see in the next chapter, this means that they are not as likely to receive welfare as natives, if one compares them with natives of similar socioeconomic standing. It also means that steady employment is often more important to them than trying to find jobs that pay more. Whatever the case, we will see time and time again in the following chapters that the labor-related nature of Mexican migration has a considerable influence on the topic being considered.

More broadly, the Mexican-origin population has and will continue to have an impact on the ethnic makeup of the United States. Not only will the proportion of the Mexican-origin population that is foreign-born continue to be large but also the Mexican-origin population in the United States will become an increasingly important component of the overall population. Latinos, of whom Mexicans are by far the largest group, recently became the largest minority ethnic group in the country. This growth has implications for the future social, economic, and political conditions of the United States. Its young age structure relative to non-Hispanic whites, for example, means that the Mexican-origin and Latino population will contribute more to the working-age population, will have a greater stake in the educational system, and may, as a result, become more politically active. In addition, since the Mexican-origin population in the United States seems especially likely to continue to be made up of a very high fraction of foreign-born individuals, both immigration policy in the United States and U.S. relations with Mexico will continue to retain their important places on the public-policy agenda of the United States.

= Chapter 4 =

Immigrant Welfare Receipt: Implications for Policy

T HE ISSUE of immigrant welfare receipt has played and continues to play a major role in national debates over the need to
reform immigration policy (Bean et al. 1997; Borjas 2002; Van
Hook, Glick, and Bean 1999). As noted in chapter 1, discussions about
immigration policy reform tend to revolve around three broad questions: How many and what kinds of immigrants come to the United
States? What happens to them after they arrive? And what effects do
they have on other residents of the country? Patterns of immigrant
welfare receipt are relevant to all three of these issues. Some observers think that higher immigrant than native welfare receipt indicates that immigrants violate the prohibitions of U.S. immigration
policy against admitting into the country people who will become
"public charges" (Borjas 1998b; Edwards 2001), thus suggesting a
need to modify existing immigration policies. Because poor immigrants are likely to take longer to move into the economic mainstream
(Duignan and Gann 1998), increasing rates of relative immigrant welfare receipt would also seem to reflect reduced prospects for successful immigrant incorporation. And finally, higher immigrant welfare
receipt could also affect natives because it might plausibly be indicative of increased competition with natives for scarce public resources.

Concern about immigrant welfare receipt during the 1980s and
1990s contributed to the passage in 1996 of the Personal Responsibility and Work Opportunity Reconciliation Act (PRWORA) (Weil and
Finegold 2002). This legislation, called the 1996 Welfare Reform Act
for short, involved the most significant changes in welfare policy that
have occurred over the past several decades in the United States. The
law made it much more difficult for noncitizens coming to the United
States after August 22, 1996, to gain access to welfare benefits and
placed explicit restrictions on noncitizen eligibility for receipt of Tem-

66

porary Assistance for Needy Families (TANF), food stamps, Medicaid, Supplemental Security Income (SSI) and other health and social
service programs (Capps 2001). The law also gave states the option of
extending some of these benefits to noncitizen immigrants, and many
have done so, although the number of programs restored has varied
substantially across states (Zimmermann and Tumlin 1999), thus leading to substantial state differences in the availability of programs providing benefits to noncitizen immigrants.

Despite its relevance to all three of the general questions driving
debates about U.S. immigration policy, immigrant welfare receipt is
arguably one of two major phenomena—the other being unauthorized immigration—most relevant to the first issue of whether unintended kinds of persons are being admitted. Many observers see
welfare-receiving immigrants and unauthorized immigrants as indications that immigrants falling outside the guidelines of existing policy are coming to the United States, which lends impetus to efforts to
reform immigration policy. In the previous chapter we addressed the
question of unauthorized migration, especially Mexican unauthorized
migration. In this chapter we focus on several issues that have dominated the debate on immigrant welfare receipt. One is the claim that
welfare usage—for immigrants and natives alike—is linked to welfare *dependency*. For example, some critics of U.S. immigration and
welfare policies argue that the immigrant cohorts that arrived during
the late twentieth century are unlikely to incorporate economically
and socially to the same extent as did the immigrant cohorts who
arrived during the early part of the century, and they link this to the
growth of the welfare state (Brimelow 1995). Since earlier cohorts
could not rely on welfare, those who were less successful emigrated
back to their countries of origin and those who stayed worked harder.
In other words, in this view welfare availability is a factor that erodes
the work ethic for all groups and in the case of immigrants may slow
adaptation and economic incorporation.

Another issue is the fear that the availability of welfare benefits in
the United States—whose value may exceed the average wage rate in
some developing countries—may act as a "magnet" for immigrants
(Borjas and Hilton 1996). Even if immigrants did not entirely base
their decision to immigrate on the calculation of welfare benefits potentially available to them in the United States, a welfare "cushion"
might reduce the risks of immigration, thus encouraging some to migrate who otherwise would not have. This could indirectly affect the
social and economic characteristics of those who ultimately make the
decision to come to the United States, even within the framework of
existing admissions policies. Still another issue is the kinds of factors

that have driven declines in immigrant welfare receipt compared to native receipt since the Welfare Reform Act was passed and what these factors imply about the need to reform immigration, welfare, or other kinds of policies. In this chapter we review the evidence to date concerning the levels and determinants of welfare usage among immigrants and natives. Our aim is to shed light on the degree to which immigrants receive welfare compared to natives, develop "dependencies" on welfare that may jeopardize motivations to work, are attracted to the United States because welfare acts as a magnet, or show declining welfare receipt for reasons that imply a need to reform immigration policy as opposed to other kinds of policy.

Before going further, it may be useful to introduce an issue that affects the interpretation of evidence about welfare receipt: Is the most appropriate unit of analysis for research on welfare receipt the individual or the household? And how does using households as opposed to individuals as units of analysis affect measures of nativity differences in receipt? At one level, this is an issue of methodology: How much difference does using one unit instead of the other make, and why? At another level it is an issue of policy: What is the most appropriate unit to use for analysis, given the policy issues being addressed, including those connected with policies governing the administration of welfare programs? Research has been undertaken to investigate the methodological question, and it will be examined in depth. We introduce the matter here in order to alert the reader to its relevance for the research results we review.

The policy issues derive in part from the fact that research based on the household as the unit of analysis yield larger nativity differences in welfare receipt than those based on the individual. This occurs in part because a substantial number of children born in the United States who are citizens live in households whose heads are unauthorized or otherwise welfare-ineligible persons (usually the parents of the citizen children). This enables these households to receive welfare. When such cases are analyzed at the individual level these birthright citizens are of course classified as natives. But some observers argue that such children would not be here if their immigrant parents were not here, and that their welfare receipt should thus be attributed to immigrants. This is an argument for relying on household-based analyses. A counterargument is that it is not the fault of the children that their parents are foreign-born; in any case, citizenship for those born here has long constituted the policy of the United States and their status as citizens is cast into question under the assumptions of household-based analyses. If important reasons exist to provide vulnerable children with welfare safety nets, then an argument could be made that these reasons should apply equally to all citizen children, regardless of whether they are born to natives or to immigrants. Unless one intends to embark on a critique of U.S. citizenship policy, this argument implies that one should classify welfare receipt by birthright citizens in the native category and suggests using individuals as the unit of analysis.

Levels of Immigrant Welfare Usage

In order to address the larger issue of whether immigrant welfare usage constitutes a problem and reflects a failure of admissions policies, it is important to accurately describe the extent to which immigrants receive welfare. The simple question of whether immigrants receive public assistance at higher rates than natives—and if so, to what degree—has played a prominent role in recent debates about the need to reform U.S. immigration and welfare policies (Bean, Van Hook, and Glick 1997; Smith and Edmonston 1997; U.S. Commission on Immigration Reform 1994; Borjas 1994). According to the 1980 census, approximately 8 percent of immigrant households—defined as households in which the household head or spouse of the household head is an immigrant—reported having received public-assistance income in 1979 (see table 4.1). During the same year, nearly the same percentage of native households—7.7 percent—reported having received public assistance. By 1989, the receipt level of immigrant households increased to 8.7 percent while the level among native households declined to 7.5 percent, thus producing a gap of 1.2 percentage points between native and immigrant households. By 1999 the gap had widened even further, to 1.7 percentage points.

On the surface these results appear simple and straightforward. But in order for research findings to have relevance and meaning for immigration policy issues, it is necessary to disaggregate immigrants along certain critical dimensions and to control for the influence of other variables. For example, it makes little sense to conclude that the

Table 4.1   Percentage of Immigrant and Native Households Receiving Cash Public Assistance, 1979, 1989, and 1999

	1979	1989	1999
Immigrant households	8.0	8.7	7.3
Native households	7.7	7.5	5.6
Difference (percentage points)	0.3	1.2	1.7

Sources: 1980 and 1990 1 percent PUMS; March 2000 Current Population Survey.

laws governing the kinds and numbers of legally admitted immigrants should be reformed simply on the basis of evidence that foreign-born households receive welfare at a higher rate than natives.
Such gross differences in receipt may have consequences (that is, they
may mean that more money per capita is spent on welfare receipt in
the case of immigrants than natives). But this says nothing about the
propensity of immigrants to rely on welfare as a source of support
compared to natives because such differences are too severely influenced by compositional factors. That is, they do not reflect the influence of differences between immigrants and natives in various other
characteristics that are themselves related to the likelihood of receiving welfare. For example, if poor families are more likely to receive
welfare than non-poor ones (which they are), and if a higher proportion of families are poor among immigrants than among natives, then
much of the higher gross receipt rate among immigrants may simply
reflect the two groups' different levels of poverty. If this is the case,
then gross differences have greater implications for welfare policy
than they do for immigration policy.

More relevant to the debate about the need to change immigration
policy would be data on rates of receipt adjusted for poverty and
other factors. If poor immigrants were more likely to receive welfare
than poor natives, then a stronger case could be made that something
might be awry in regard to immigration policy. In fact, as we shall
see, research results show just the opposite. Poor immigrants are actually mostly *less* likely to receive welfare than poor natives, a result
that implies they do not manifest a greater propensity to rely on welfare. Also, welfare levels vary considerably depending on how welfare is measured and who is counted as an immigrant. Different researchers have come to different conclusions about immigrant welfare
usage because they have examined different immigrant groups and
welfare programs and used different levels of analysis to measure
welfare usage. Below we examine these factors in order to develop a
more in-depth understanding and assessment of immigrant welfare
receipt.

Mode of Entry and Immigrant Status

Over the past couple of decades, the United States has received primarily three kinds of immigrants: refugees; persons who initially
came as primarily temporary labor migrants and originally entered
the country without documents (Hirschman 1978; Massey et al. 1987;
Portes and Bach 1985); and all other kinds of legal immigrants (Fix
and Zimmermann 1994); Fix and Passel 1994). The numbers and char-

acteristics of refugees, unauthorized migrants, and legal immigrants are affected by different types of U.S. policy. For example, the number of legal immigrants is determined by current immigration laws as they are enacted by the U.S. Department of State, while the number of unauthorized migrants is partially a result of the types and effectiveness of strategies such as border enforcement policies used by the Immigration and Naturalization Service for detaining and deporting such migrants. Different types of immigrants may be characterized as having different reasons for coming, different modes of entry, and different incorporation experiences after they arrive, all of which operate to affect, directly and indirectly, rates of receipt of public-assistance and naturalization.

Even prior to the welfare reform legislation of 1996, U.S. immigration policy established different eligibility rules for receiving public assistance for persons entering as refugees and persons entering as permanent resident aliens. Refugees were (and still are) immediately eligible whereas regular immigrants are not (Gordon 1987; Vialet 1993). In many respects, newly arrived refugees are encouraged to use welfare as a form of settlement assistance. Unauthorized migrants have been and still are ineligible for most kinds of welfare, although their U.S.-born children are eligible. Even if they subsequently become legal immigrants, their initial status indirectly may affect the probability of their seeking public assistance. On the other hand, the high levels of poverty among unauthorized migrants may lead to increased levels of public assistance receipt because their U.S.-born children are more likely to qualify for benefits. Even among legal immigrants, mode-of-entry distinctions can be critical because socioeconomic characteristics and eligibility for public assistance benefits vary significantly for specific legal statuses. Legal permanent residents, those who hold green cards, which permit them to work legally, face strict new eligibility restrictions under welfare reform, and nonimmigrants remain ineligible for most government benefits (Passel and Clark 1998).

While most data sources do not collect information about immigration status at entry, country of origin can be used to classify immigrants into roughly three groups that approximate immigrant status categories. The first is refugees, whom we identify as those coming from the eleven nations almost all of whose immigrants to the United States during the 1980s were refugees. These countries are the former Soviet Union, Cuba, Vietnam, Laos, Romania, Iran, Ethiopia, Cambodia, Poland, Afghanistan, and Nicaragua. In the 1990s, countries from the Balkans are added to this list. This classification strategy is viable because refugees have tended to come from only a relatively small number of countries (Fix and Passel 1994). In addition, countries that send refugees usually do not send large numbers of other legal immigrants. The eleven "refugee-sending" countries sent almost 90 percent of all refugee arrivals to the United States during the 1980s, and over 91 percent of the persons they sent came as refugees (U.S. Immigration and Naturalization Service 1994, 2002a).

The second group is labor migrants. Those coming from Mexico, El Salvador, and Guatemala are a group most likely to have arrived in the U.S. primarily for purposes of seeking employment—often temporary employment. Immigrants coming from these three countries constitute a disproportionate share of unauthorized immigrants to the United States (Fix and Zimmermann 1994; Fix and Passel 1994), and legal immigrants from these countries often initially came to the United States first as unauthorized labor migrants (Hirschman 1979; Massey et al. 1987; Portes and Bach 1985).

The third group is defined as all other foreign-born persons. Despite the heavy volume of recent immigration from Asian and Spanish-speaking countries, Current Population Survey (CPS) data for 2000 show that this "other" group still comprises about one half of all foreign-born households in the country; it is dominated by Europeans, Canadians, and some immigrants from non-refugee-sending Asian countries such as the Philippines, India, China, Korea, and Japan. The Current Population Survey is carried out monthly by the Department of Labor in order to measure unemployment and other labor force behaviors.

When welfare receipt is broken down into these three country-of-origin groupings, it becomes clear that welfare usage among the foreign-born is concentrated among refugees and labor migrants (see table 4.2). In 1979 and 1989, about 30 percent of Asian refugee households reported receiving some type of public-assistance income, and in 1999 this figure was about 19 percent. Welfare receipt is also high for the group originating from Mexico, El Salvador, and Guatemala and non-Asian refugees, ranging from 9.5 to 11.8 percent during the past two decades. Together, the refugee and labor migrant groups make up over 30 percent of all immigrant households and are not representative of the broader class of people who are admitted under U.S. immigration law. When refugees and most labor migrants are separated out, gross welfare receipt levels among the remaining immigrants are actually lower than those of native households. Moreover, and even more compellingly, the degree to which gross welfare receipt in each of these three major immigrant groups exceeded that of natives *dropped* between 1989 and 1999 (except, of course, in the

Table 4.2   Percentage of Immigrant and Native Households Receiving Cash Public Assistance, 1979, 1989, and 1999

	1979	1989	1999
Native households	7.7	7.5	5.6
Immigrant households	8.0	8.7	7.3
Mexico, Guatemala, El Salvador	12.0	11.7	8.8
Asian refugee	28.7	32.7	18.7
Non-Asian refugee	10.1	11.8	9.5
Other Immigrant	6.7	6.5	5.5
Difference from natives			
All immigrant households	0.3	1.2	1.7
Mexico, Guatemala, El Salvador	4.3	4.2	3.2
Asian refugee	21.0	25.2	13.1
Non-Asian refugee	2.4	4.3	3.9
Other Immigrant	−1.0	−1.0	−0.1

Sources: 1980 and 1990 1 percent PUMS; March 2000 Current Population Survey.

case of the "Other" category, whose level of welfare receipt was lower than that of natives to begin with).

Thus, the increase in the nativity gap in public-assistance receipt during the 1990s was entirely due to changes in country of origin composition, not to increases in country group–specific rates. That is, it resulted from higher proportions of refugees and labor migrants, not from relatively higher welfare receipt among immigrants. This suggests that the practice especially of admitting and providing settlement assistance to refugees and their families may contribute sub-

Table 4.3   Percentage of Immigrant and Native Households Receiving Cash Public Assistance, by Poverty Status, 1999

	Poverty[a]	Non-Poverty
Native households	18.8	2.0
Immigrant households	16.3	3.3
Mexico, Guatemala, El Salvador	13.5	4.5
Asian refugee	25.2	1.8
Non-Asian refugee	35.6	12.2
Other immigrant	15.2	2.7

Source: March 2000 Current Population Survey.
[a]Poverty is defined as receiving 150 percent or less of the official poverty income for the main family unit in the household.

stantially to statistically higher average welfare rates among the foreign-born in general. Disproportionate welfare receipt by immigrants—even if there were a consensus that it provides grounds for reforming immigration policy—would not be appreciably alleviated by changing general admissions criteria for legal immigrants, as some observers have advocated, as long as patterns of refugee and labor migrant admissions are not changed.

Also for considerable interest, as noted earlier, are comparisons of welfare receipt rates between relatively poor immigrants and natives, not comparisons involving all immigrants and natives. In 1999, looking only at immigrants and natives making less than 150 percent of poverty-level income, we find that welfare receipt among immigrant households is 2.5 percentage points *less* than it is among comparable natives (16.3 percent among immigrants receiving welfare compared to 18.8 percent among natives, as shown in table 4.3). And among the predominantly labor migrant group (Mexicans, Guatemalans, and El Salvadorans) falling below this income threshold, welfare receipt is fully 5.3 percentage points *less* than comparable natives (13.5 percent receiving versus 18.8 percent). In short, welfare receipt among poor Mexican and Central American immigrants, a group often stereotypically thought to exhibit a proneness to welfare dependency, falls considerably below the receipt level of poor natives. While the receipt of non-poor immigrants slightly exceeds that of natives, primarily because the receipt level of non-poor Asian refugee households (many of whom contain elderly parents, a situation we discuss later) is quite high in relative terms, these patterns make it clear overall that poor labor immigrants and non-refugee immigrants are actually quite a bit less likely to receive welfare than poor natives.

Age

Another useful way to distinguish welfare recipients is by age. In the United States, long-term economic support for the elderly through programs such as Social Security and Supplemental Security Income (SSI) has garnered widespread public support. Few expect needy elderly to work, and few are concerned that governmental support may erode the willingness of the elderly to seek employment. On the other hand, government aid for working-age adults, including single mothers of young children, has increasingly been viewed as problematic because it may create work disincentives (Murray 1994). Welfare usage among immigrants is concentrated among the elderly (Hu 1998; Fix and Passel 1994). Our own work shows that as recently as 1999, im-

Table 4.4   **Percentage of Immigrant and Native Households Receiving Cash Public Assistance, by Age Composition of Household, 1999**

	No Elderly in Household	Elderly Person in Household
Native households	5.7	5.6
Immigrant households	5.4	14.9
Mexico, Guatemala, El Salvador	7.5	23.1
Asian refugee	5.1	17.9
Non-Asian refugee	12.5	40.6
Other immigrant	4.0	10.9

Source: March 2000 Current Population Survey.

migrant households containing no elderly members exhibit public-assistance receipt levels lower than "nonelderly" native households (see table 4.4). Immigrant households containing at least one elderly person, on the other hand, exhibit welfare receipt rates that are much higher than any other age and nativity group.

One explanation for this age-based receipt pattern is that immigrants who arrive later in life do not have the time to build up the work history to qualify for Social Security or other retirement benefits. Fewer elderly immigrants qualify for Social Security income than elderly natives. In 1990, 78.3 percent of elderly immigrants versus 86.2 percent of elderly natives received Social Security income (Hu 1998). Moreover, elderly immigrants who arrived in the country earlier in life appear very similar to elderly natives with respect to both Social Security and welfare receipt. According to our own analysis of the 1990 census data, only 34.6 percent of elderly who arrived after the age of fifty-five received Social Security income, but among those who came prior to age fifty-five, nearly the same percentage, about 84.4 percent, received Social Security payments as did elderly natives. Data on welfare benefits parallels these findings. Michael Fix and Jeffrey Passel (1994) find that recently arrived elderly nonrefugee immigrants receive welfare at very high levels—about 25 percent. However, elderly immigrants who have been in the country at least twenty years are not much more likely to receive welfare (8.7 percent) than elderly natives (6.9 percent). These findings suggest that welfare receipt among immigrants may be linked to certain immigrants' being ineligible for Social Security, not with low labor-force effort among those of working age. This undermines the idea that welfare availability in the United States erodes the work effort of immigrants.

Type of Welfare

Just as there are differences in the receipt of public assistance by mode of entry and age, there are also differences by the kinds of welfare received. Of the three programs that provide cash assistance, Aid to Families with Dependent Children (AFDC, which in 1996 was replaced by Temporary Aid for Needy Families [TANF]) specialized in providing income to poor families with children; Supplemental Security Income provides income assistance to poor elderly, blind, and disabled persons; and "General Assistance," the smallest of the three cash-assistance programs, consists of a handful of state-run programs that provide cash payments to poor persons who do not qualify for AFDC, TANF, or SSI. It is important to examine immigrants' welfare usage by program because participation in the different programs may indicate different kinds and levels of need or dependency and different levels of public cost. Early studies of immigrant welfare usage did not distinguish by type of welfare primarily because the data were not available. Until 1994, when data relating to nativity and other immigration measures became available in the monthly Current Population Surveys on labor force behavior, most studies of differences between native and immigrant welfare receipt relied on census data because the census was the only source of data large enough to generate reliable estimates for particular national-origin immigrant groups (Van Hook, Bean, and Glick 1995). In the form in which census data are made available to users, however, they do not distinguish among AFDC, SSI, and General Assistance, the main cash-assistance welfare programs; all three of these types of welfare have often been lumped together in a single measure.

Now, however, there is a method that disentangles these programs by matching the characteristics of the recipient with the eligibility criteria of one of the three programs, and provides evidence from census data about type of program receipt (Van Hook, Bean, and Glick 1996). Generally speaking, recipients who do not have children in their immediate family unit and are disabled or are age sixty-five or older are classified as SSI recipients. Recipients with nondisabled children in their family unit who are neither disabled nor age sixty-five or older are classified as AFDC or TANF recipients. The recipients with neither AFDC nor SSI characteristics are classified as recipients of assistance from "other" programs (that is, "General Assistance"). As shown in table 4.5, until recently immigrant households were either less likely (in 1979) or no more likely (in 1989) than native households to receive AFDC income. By 1999, immigrant households were slightly more likely to receive TANF or AFDC (by about one percentage point), and

Table 4.5   AFDC and SSI Receipt Among Immigrant and Native Households, 1979, 1989, and 1999 (Percentage)

	AFDC or TANF Receipt			SSI Receipt		
	1979	1989	1999	1979	1989	1999
Native households	3.4	3.2	2.1	3.9	4.0	3.9
Immigrant households	2.7	3.5	3.2	5.1	5.1	5.3
Mexico, Guatemala, El Salvador	6.1	6.7	5.2	5.9	5.0	4.1
Asian refugee	22.1	22.8	4.3	5.9	13.6	16.7
Non-Asian refugee	1.7	2.3	2.0	8.0	9.3	7.7
Other immigrant	2.0	2.0	1.9	4.4	4.2	3.9
Difference from natives						
All immigrant households	−0.7	0.3	1.1	1.2	1.1	1.4
Mexico, Guatemala, El Salvador	2.7	3.5	3.1	2.0	1.0	0.2
Asian refugee	18.7	19.6	2.2	2.0	9.6	12.8
Non-Asian refugee	−1.7	−0.9	−0.1	4.1	5.3	3.8
Other immigrant	−1.4	−1.2	−0.2	0.5	0.2	0.0

Sources: 1980 and 1990 1 percent PUMS; March 2000 Current Population Survey.

levels of AFDC or TANF receipt are very low for both groups—less than 4 percent of immigrant and native households reported receiving AFDC income. In addition, excluding refugee and labor migrant households, we note that other legal migrants exhibited lower levels of AFDC or TANF receipt than did native households.

SSI receipt tends to be a bit higher among both immigrant and native households and the immigrant-native gap has remained steady at about one percentage point over the past two decades. Again, however, excluding refugee and labor migrant households, we see no significant difference emerge between immigrant and native households. Among the different country-of-origin groups, only Asians in the "refugee" category had very high AFDC and SSI receipt levels. For AFDC, receipt was high only in 1979 and 1989. One fifth of Asian refugee households reported receiving AFDC during these years. However, by 1999 only 4.3 percent reported TANF or AFDC income. At the same time, SSI receipt was relatively low in 1979 but increased starting in 1989, reaching 16.7 percent by 1999. These changes are likely due to demographic shifts that occurred among Asian refugees. Many of these refugees arrived with young families during the late 1970s and early 1980s, during which time they qualified for AFDC. As their children grew up they no longer qualified for TANF or

AFDC; at the same time, they aged into categories that made more of them eligible for SSI.

Noncash Assistance

So far we have examined only the receipt of cash assistance, but a wide array of noncash assistance programs also provide a variety of services to the poor. Food stamps are vouchers to cover the costs of groceries for poor persons and families. Housing assistance provides public housing and sometimes also vouchers to defray the costs of rent. Free and reduced-cost meals are provided to poor children at school. Finally, Medicaid provides medical insurance and may cover the costs of emergency medical care for poor persons without other health insurance. Most families and persons who qualify for cash assistance are automatically eligible to receive other types of assistance, such as food stamps, Medicaid, and free or reduced-cost school meals, but not all recipients of noncash assistance qualify for or receive cash assistance. Because of this, noncash programs tend to have larger caseloads than cash programs.

It is important to investigate immigrant participation in noncash as well as cash welfare programs because the costs of providing welfare to immigrants depends on their level of participation in both types of programs (Borjas and Hilton 1996). In fiscal year 1999, only about 18 percent of total expenditures for public assistance programs (nearly $300 billion) went to TANF and SSI; the remaining 82 percent went to noncash programs such as Medicaid ($177 billion), food stamps ($21.2 billion), and housing assistance ($25 billion). In terms of expenditures per recipient, about $3,000 was spent per year for each TANF recipient and $4,900 per SSI recipient. Medicaid is more expensive, costing about $5,847 per recipient per year. In addition, about $1,096 was spent for each household receiving food stamps, and $4,846 per household receiving some type of housing assistance.

George Borjas and Lynette Hilton (1996) used the Survey of Income and Program Participation, a Census Bureau survey designed to measure participation in various government programs, to evaluate immigrants' usage of the cash programs as well as five noncash programs: Food Stamps, Special Supplemental Nutrition Program for Women, Infants, and Children (WIC), energy assistance, housing assistance, and school breakfast and lunch. They found that even though immigrant households are only slightly more likely than native households to use cash assistance (9.1 percent versus 7.4 percent), they are much more likely to participate in at least one of the various means-tested cash or noncash programs taken together (26.1 percent versus 16.3

percent) (Borjas and Hilton 1996). Our own analysis of the March 2000 Current Population Survey shows similarly large differences between immigrant and native households. As of 1999, 17 percent of native households versus 27 percent of immigrant households reported receiving some type of cash or noncash public assistance (housing assistance, energy assistance, food stamps, Medicaid, and school meals) (see table 4.6).

The inclusion of school meals but not other types of programs as a type of welfare program disproportionately increases the immigrant-native differential in welfare receipt. Borjas and Hilton (1996) reported that the immigrant-native difference in the percentage who use cash assistance or Medicaid amounts to about 6 percentage points. Except in the case of the school lunch program, this six-percentage-point difference does not change much when other types of assistance are added to the analysis. For example, the differential still amounts to about six percentage points when considering receipt of *any* of the following: cash assistance, Medicaid, food stamps, WIC, energy assistance, or housing assistance. When the receipt of school lunches is considered along with the other types of assistance, the differential increases to roughly ten percentage points. In our own analyses of the 2000 CPS data, the nativity gap in welfare receipt is cut in half (from 10 to 5 percentage points) when school meals are excluded as a type of welfare. The influence of school meals is particularly dramatic for immigrant groups with many young children. For example, among Mexican, Guatemalans, and Salvadoran households, about 47 percent receive some type of cash or noncash assistance but only 30 percent receive assistance apart from school meals. The 17 percent difference represents the contribution of school lunches. Among nonrefugee, nonlabor migrant households, when school meals are excluded receipt levels for cash and noncash assistance programs are actually lower than among native households (14.7 versus 15.3 percent). Taking all immigrant households together, disproportionate participation in free or reduced-cost school meal programs accounts for about half of the nativity differential in receipt of cash and noncash welfare.

This fact substantially weakens the argument that very high levels of welfare usage by immigrants constitute a social problem. First, unlike some other noncash programs, free or reduced-cost school meals cost taxpayers very little: only $6.2 billion, or about $231 per recipient per year (U.S. House of Representatives 2000). Second, a strong case can be made for providing food assistance on humanitarian grounds and investing in human capital. The 1996 Welfare Reform Act specifies that all legal immigrants remain eligible for programs, services, or assistance specified by the attorney general as "necessary for the

Table 4.6 Receipt of Cash and Noncash Public Assistance Among Immigrant and Native Households, 1999 (Percentage)

			Country-of-Origin Grouping			
	Native	Immigrant	Mexico, Guatemala, El Salvador	Asian Refugee	Non-Asian Refugee	Other
Cash Assistance						
TANF	2.1	3.2	5.2	4.3	2.0	1.9
SSI	3.9	5.3	4.1	16.7	7.7	3.9
Vouchers						
Food stamps	5.4	6.2	9.6	11.5	8.7	3.9
Public housing	2.8	3.1	2.3	3.4	2.6	2.1
Rent vouchers	1.3	2.1	1.8	6.9	3.4	1.4
Energy assistance	2.2	1.3	0.8	2.1	1.5	1.0
Free or reduced school meals	5.7	14.7	32.1	14.7	7.9	7.7
Insurance						
Medicaid	12.0	18.0	26.4	25.8	17.9	12.6
Combinations of welfare						
Any cash assistance	5.6	8.0	8.8	18.7	9.5	5.5
Any vouchers	11.6	19.5	36.9	25.1	17.9	11.7
Vouchers, excluding school meals	8.6	9.2	13.1	14.6	12.7	6.6
Cash, vouchers, or insurance	17.3	27.2	46.9	36.1	24.9	18.1
Cash, vouchers, or insurance, excluding school meals	15.3	19.9	29.9	29.2	20.6	14.7

Source: March 2000 Current Population Survey.

protection of life or safety." Under this provision, programs like WIC and school lunches are exempt from the restrictions imposed by welfare reform, and energy and housing assistance may also be exempt. Third, the provision of food assistance directly to children is less likely to inhibit parents' motivations to work because no cash is provided directly to parents. Finally, the inclusion of school meals as a type of welfare for the purpose of comparing immigrant and native welfare usage is misleading because most of the recipients—children—are U.S.-born citizens, even those living in immigrant households. As of 1990, fully 80 percent of children living in immigrant households were born in the United States (Van Hook, Glick, and Bean 1999). Most of these children will remain in the United States as they grow up and enter the labor force. In short, for very little money, school lunch programs alleviate hunger and malnutrition among children while providing no cash to parents. Providing school meals to the children of immigrants is thus a low-cost investment in the second generation.

Net Versus Gross Differences

Researchers have also examined immigrant versus native welfare receipt while statistically controlling for the influence of such other factors as family structure, income, educational attainment, and age. As noted above, if immigrants were found to be more likely to use welfare than similar natives, particularly among those of working age, this would provide evidence of greater immigrant than native welfare dependency, which would imply that disincentives to work might have more effects with immigrants than with natives. Early studies conducted during the 1980s generally concluded that immigrants were no more or usually less likely than natives to receive welfare once differences in other variables had been taken into account (Blau and Schwartz 1984; Jensen 1991; Tienda and Jensen 1986). Borjas and Hilton (1996) similarly found that in the mid-1980s immigrants were no more likely than natives to receive cash assistance and were less likely to receive assistance when household composition, gender, education, and age were controlled. However, immigrant welfare usage increased during the 1980s, both absolutely and relative to natives (Borjas 1994, 1995). Studies examining these increases found that they are explainable in part by shifts in the national origins of immigrants (Borjas and Trejo 1991; Trejo 1992). Borjas and Hilton (1996) found that by the early 1990s, even after controlling for other factors, immigrants were more likely to use welfare than similar natives, whether welfare is defined as consisting of cash assistance, or various combinations of cash, noncash assistance, and vouchers. Such results appear to lend substance to the idea that U.S. immigration policy allows entry into the country of persons increasingly more likely to rely on welfare than previously was the case (Brimelow 1995, 146–51).

On the other hand, more in-depth work on this topic suggests that the trend of increasing welfare usage by immigrants is explained by increases in SSI receipt. Frank D. Bean, Jennifer Van Hook, and Jennifer Glick (1997) showed that in 1979, immigrants were no more likely than similar natives to use SSI, but this changed. In 1989, immigrants were more likely than statistically similar natives to receive SSI. Two groups—Mexicans and especially Asian refugees—accounted for much of the increase, with each group exhibiting higher levels of SSI receipt than natives even after researchers controlled for other variables. For AFDC receipt alone, however, we found similar results to those for the 1980s, when AFDC and SSI were not distinguished. In both 1979 and 1989, immigrants were less likely than similar natives to receive AFDC. In 1989, the AFDC receipt rate among immigrants would be expected to fall 1.1 percentage points below that of natives if immigrants had native characteristics. Another more recent study of AFDC recipients in California in 1992 shows that immigrants of various racial and ethnic origins do not receive AFDC payments for longer periods of time than similar non-Hispanic white natives (Ono and Becerra 2000). Also, even though Borjas and Hilton (1996) found significant differences between immigrants and natives in the two groups' receipt of certain combinations of public assistance programs, they found no significant differences in the receipt of AFDC or food stamps, nor did they find significant changes in the level of receipt of these kinds of welfare in different immigrant entry cohorts. Such results suggest that working-age immigrants—those who would qualify for AFDC or food stamps—are actually more *averse* to receiving welfare than natives. Moreover, this relationship has held constant over time.

Welfare Magnets

Another concern about immigrant welfare usage is that U.S. welfare benefits provide an incentive, and make it less risky, for potential immigrants to move to the United States. For example, some observers have noted that in China, manuals have been published for prospective immigrants that provide information about how to obtain U.S. welfare benefits (Rector 1996), including data on differences between benefits available in different states. These types of activities, while legal, have been interpreted by some as encouraging migration contrary to the spirit underlying U.S. immigration policy, which stresses self-reliance and hard work. If immigrants come to the United States expressly to obtain welfare, this would potentially undermine arguments for providing settlement assistance and poverty relief to poor immigrants, and strengthen the viewpoint that no immigrants should be allowed to receive welfare.

The consensus among researchers about the effect of state variations in welfare benefits on *internal migration within* the United States at one time was that there were no appreciable welfare magnet effects operating. This conclusion came from a variety of studies conducted during the late 1960s and early 1970s that found inconsistent and weak effects of state welfare benefit levels on interstate migration patterns (Moffitt 1992). However, later studies, which relied on improved econometric methods and better data, showed consistent, small, positive effects of state welfare benefit levels on the probability of internal in-migration (Moffitt 1992). Magnet effects were also found to have both international and interstate dimensions, influencing both the chances that an immigrant would come to the U.S. and immigrants' decisions as to where they would settle once they have made the decision to move. Each has different implications for assessing the degree to which welfare usage by immigrants is a problem. If welfare availability in the United States increases the chances that immigrants will make the decision to move to this country, it may be concluded that the availability of welfare has the effect of attracting some to come to the U.S. when they otherwise would not. If, on the other hand, state-level benefits affect where immigrants settle once they have made the decision to enter the United States, this has little bearing on the type of immigrant initially drawn to the country, only on immigrants' geographic distribution once they arrive.

Recent research by Borjas (1999) suggests that immigrants are more heavily clustered in states with high welfare benefits and are perhaps more drawn to these states by the benefits than are natives. This is particularly true for the recently arrived and households with children that are headed by a female. Although this result has important implications for the fiscal distribution of costs of immigration across states, it does not mean that immigrants are necessarily moving to the country expressly for the purpose of receiving benefits. As Borjas (1999) argues, immigration is selective of those who have already made the initial investment to come to the United States. The additional costs of choosing one location over another (say, a state with high benefits) are comparatively small. By contrast, U.S. natives include both movers and nonmovers. The state-level "magnet" effects are much weaker among natives because many have not already made the investment to move, and the costs of moving to another state typically outweigh any potential gains in welfare.

It is reasonable to think that prospective immigrants who have not yet made the investments necessary to immigrate are similar in this respect to U.S. natives. The gains from welfare to be made from immigration are probably too low to justify the high costs of moving internationally. It is more likely that immigrants make the decision to immigrate on the basis of a variety of factors, including the prospect of higher earnings, family reunification, and personal and political freedom. Perhaps the best group on which to test these ideas is elderly immigrants. We have already shown that working-age immigrants do not disproportionately use welfare, nor has their rate of welfare usage increased over time. As we have already pointed out, such patterns may occur because working-age immigrants are most likely come to the United States in order to work. But what about those who come later in life and are no longer working? Is the United States perceived internationally as a "retirement home"?

Welfare receipt among elderly immigrants compared to welfare receipt among elderly natives increased during the 1980s both absolutely and relatively, primarily because of increases in SSI receipt (Bean, Van Hook, and Glick 1997). Over the past ten to fifteen years, researchers have observed a substantial growth in the total SSI caseload owing in considerable measure to increases in the numbers of immigrants receiving benefits (Rector 1996; Specht 1995; U.S. General Accounting Office 1995). The Social Security Administration (SSA) reports that the number of noncitizens who receive SSI has increased substantially since 1982 (Ponce 1996). These data indicate that the total number of noncitizen recipients increased more than sixfold between 1982 and 1995, from 128 thousand to 785 thousand, and among the elderly, the caseload is reported to have increased from 98,000 to 536,000. Furthermore, the growth among noncitizens appears to have been faster than that observed for the entire SSI recipient population. Social Security Administration records show a fourfold increase in the proportion of the caseload attributable to noncitizens since the early 1980s, from about 3.3 percent to 12.2 percent. This pattern appears most dramatically among elderly recipients, among whom the percentage of noncitizens increased from 5 percent in 1982 to 26 percent in 1995. The increase among noncitizen caseloads in Social Security Administration records is exaggerated because the Social Security Administration did not update records for recipients who naturalized until 1996. Nonetheless, even when adjustments are made for this, the increase in the S.S. Administration's caseload among noncitizens remains substantial.

In light of these increases, it is important to examine the components of change in the SSI caseload that has been observed among elderly noncitizens. In particular, it is important to distinguish new arrivals and earlier arrivals on the one hand and increased rates of usage from increased numbers eligible for usage on the other. If *newly arrived* immigrants have increased their *rates* of SSI usage more so than is the case among earlier-arriving immigrants (particularly when rates of usage among those *eligible* for SSI are compared), it would imply that the former group, who are not likely ever to have worked in the United States, has been taking greater advantage of the availability of SSI, as the magnet hypothesis would imply. However, if this is not the case—if, rather, earlier-arriving immigrants who have been here long enough to have worked in the United States showed higher rates of receipt—this would imply that immigrant "aging in place" accounts for increased usage more than new immigration. In other words, if the increase in the noncitizen SSI caseload is *not* primarily the result of increases in rates of SSI receipt among elderly noncitizens, but rather is the result of substantial increases among persons living in the country for quite some time who have aged into categories that allow them to qualify for SSI (age sixty-five and over), much of the rise in the caseload would turn out to be the result of aging processes, not increases in rates among new immigrants, as would be expected by the magnet hypothesis.

To test these hypotheses, we draw on a variety of survey and administrative data sources, including Social Security Administration records, Immigration and Naturalization Service admissions and naturalization data, the 1 percent 1980 and 1990 U.S. Bureau of the Census Public Use Microdata Samples (PUMS) files, and the March 1997 Current Population Survey. The results of the analyses show that the noncitizen SSI caseload did not start to grow until the 1990s, and the major contributor to the growth has been the significant increase in the rate of receipt among those who have lived in the United States for more than ten years (a smaller increase occurred among recent arrivals). This factor accounts for about half of the total growth in the caseload and cannot be explained by increases in poverty among noncitizens. About one third of the increase can be accounted for by growth in the number of newly arrived elderly or near-elderly immigrants. The growth of this group may result from welfare acting as a magnet on elderly immigrants, but it is also important to note that the number of immigrants who enter the country as elderly or near elderly could have been increasing because of the family reunification provisions of immigration policy. One of these provisions, as noted in chapter 2, is that there are no numerical restrictions on the number of parents of U.S. citizens who may immigrate. As increasing numbers of postwar immigrants have naturalized, greater numbers have become eligible to bring their parents to the United States, which in turn has led to growth in the numbers of elderly and near-elderly immigrants. But *rates* of receipt among these persons have *not* been increasing.

In sum, the idea that the availability of SSI for elderly immigrants has acted as a magnet for poor elderly immigrants, thus accounting for the growth in the elderly immigrant SSI caseloads during the 1980s and 1990s, does not receive convincing support from the findings. Half of the increase in the SSI caseload resulted from increases in receipt levels among *earlier* arrivals; among recent arrivals, much of the increase can be attributed to growth in the elderly noncitizen population, not increases in receipt rates. If welfare were acting as a magnet for immigrants, receipt levels of recent arrivals—particularly among the eligible—would have increased along with increases in the size of newly arrived immigrant cohorts, but we do not find this to be the case. "Aging in place" and family reunification predominantly account for the growth in the caseload.

Unit of Analysis

As noted above, another factor that can affect conclusions about immigrant welfare receipt is that different studies have used different units of analysis or different units for the presentation of their results. A researcher might choose to focus on individuals or on a larger unit, aggregates of individuals such as families or households. Most studies that compare immigrant and native welfare use have relied upon aggregate-level units. In these studies, if one or more individuals within the unit receive public assistance income, then the entire unit is classified as a welfare-receiving unit.

But not all persons grouped together in aggregate-level units are identical with respect to welfare receipt and other important social indicators such as nativity status. For instance, no matter how many recipients a household contains, it is still counted as one household. Conversely, an immigrant household is counted as receiving welfare even if no immigrant household members received welfare—that is, U.S.-born household members receive it. This heterogeneity within households is no small issue. Although 95 percent of immigrants live in "immigrant" households and 95 percent of natives live in "native" households, it is estimated that one quarter of adults and 80 percent of children living in "immigrant" households are U.S.-born citizens (U.S. Bureau of the Census 1992b). Welfare receipt among immigrant households may be as much an indicator of receipt by U.S.-born citizens living in immigrant households as it is of receipt by immigrants.

The extent to which unit nativity composition is problematic for analyzing immigrant welfare receipt largely depends on how the U.S.-born children living in immigrant households are treated and, more precisely, on the unit on which the measurement of nativity is based. If such children are thought of as natives, then unit heterogeneity will appear much greater than if they are thought of as immigrants because their parents are immigrants. Adopting the household (or other aggregate units) as the unit of analysis and defining its nativity on the basis of the householder's nativity (as in Borjas 1994), or the nativity of the householder or the householder's spouse (as in Bean, Van Hook, and Glick 1997), assumes that native-born children are immigrants. Because nativity-related eligibility criteria for AFDC and other public assistance for children are based on children's place of birth, not the nativity of parents, and because immigrant parents are not eligible for AFDC benefits in their first five years of residence in the United States, some immigrant households can be classified as households receiving welfare even if they do so only because of the presence of a native-born child.

To examine the extent to which comparisons of immigrant and native welfare receipt are affected by the unit of analysis, Jennifer Van Hook, Jennifer Glick, and Frank D. Bean (1999) examined data from the 1990 and 1991 panels of the Survey of Income and Program Participation (SIPP). The survey's results showed that immigrants exceed natives in welfare use when larger units of aggregation are used. In both household-based comparisons (households, minimal household units [the smallest family unit within the household that could be its own household], and individuals) and family-based comparisons (family households, families, and family members), the immigrant level of welfare receipt is significantly higher than that for natives only in the cases of the most aggregated units (household or family households). It is not significantly higher in the cases of the smaller units. When all sources of welfare were separated into cash assistance received from AFDC and from SSI, the patterns observed for "any type of public assistance" are generally replicated, especially in the case of SSI (in other words, the use of larger-sized units made immigrant receipt appear higher relative to native receipt than when smaller-sized units were used). When nativity differentials were examined, the differences involving AFDC are not statistically significant for any of the units, whereas those involving SSI are, irrespective of the unit examined. When we produced new results for this chapter breaking receipt down by cash and noncash assistance, we still obtained this same pattern (that is, the nativity differences are much smaller when the individual is the unit of analysis) (see table 4.7).

All of the above results show that immigrant-native comparisons

Table 4.7   Immigrant-Native Difference in Cash and Noncash Public Assistance Receipt, for Households and Individuals, 1999

	Households	Individuals
Cash assistance		
TANF	1.1	−0.1
SSI	1.4	0.9
Vouchers		
Food stamps	0.8	0.3
Public housing	0.3	−0.1
Rent vouchers	0.8	−0.5
Energy assistance	−0.9	−1.3
Free or reduced school meals	9.0	−1.0
Insurance		
Medicaid	6.0	−0.6
Combinations of welfare		
Any cash assistance	2.4	0.7
Any vouchers	7.9	0.7
Vouchers, excluding school meals	0.6	0.7
Cash, vouchers, or insurance	9.9	0.8
Cash, vouchers, or insurance, excluding school meals	4.6	0.7

Source: March 2000 Current Population Survey.

of welfare receipt can depend on the unit chosen for the presentation of research results. When evaluated at the level of larger units, such as households or families, immigrants tend to exceed natives in the extent to which they receive welfare. When smaller units are used, however, there tend to be no differences between immigrants and natives in overall welfare receipt, particularly in the case of welfare programs that serve children. So which unit of presentation or analysis is preferable? The choice depends largely on the research question. If one is interested in studying the determinants of welfare usage, it is preferable to rely on units that approximate the unit that is used to determine eligibility, which for most types of welfare is the family or household. But if the research looks at the costs and effects of welfare usage, as does policy-oriented research, it may be better to examine individuals. But differences in use of various units of analysis notwithstanding, it is also clear that conclusions drawn in the previous sections of this chapter about the meaning of research results on immigrant welfare receipt, most of which are based on household-level analyses, are strong enough on their own terms to indicate that immigrant welfare receipt is not the problem that it is often made out to be.

Thus, our conclusions here do not depend entirely on considerations involving the unit of analysis, although they can be influenced by it.

Recent Declines in Caseloads: Lessons for Policy

In the latter half of the 1990s, the United States experienced the strongest economic growth of the twentieth century, and also a substantial decrease in welfare caseloads generally (Blank and Haskins 2001; Danziger 1999; Penner, Sawhill, and Taylor 2000). A number of studies have investigated the extent to which economic changes, along with welfare policy shifts, have contributed to these declines. For the most part, the studies have found that economic improvements during the 1990s probably mattered as much as policy changes for generating the reductions in caseload (Bell 2001; Moffitt 1992; Schoeni and Blank 2000). A few studies have also documented that welfare declines among immigrants exceeded those of natives during this period (Borjas 2002; Fix and Passel 2002; Lofstrom and Bean 2002). For example, Current Population Survey data indicate that receipt of welfare in any of four programs (AFDC or TANF, Food Stamps, Medicaid, or SSI) among native households fell from 15.5 percent to 13.7 percent, over the period 1994 to 2000. Among immigrant households, receipt in these programs fell from 23.6 percent to 20.9 percent. This figure shows a reduction in the difference between the two groups from 8.1 to 7.2 percentage points. The diminution of this gap in some of the individual programs was more striking. For example, immigrant households exceeded those of natives in AFDC receipt by 2.6 percentage points in 1994. The excess immigrant receipt dropped by more than 66 percent by 2000 (then TANF), to 0.8 percentage points.

What accounts for such differential declines? Some observers have argued that immigrants are differently affected by welfare reform than natives, in effect experiencing confusion and intimidation (or "chilling" effects) that cause them not to seek the benefits to which they are entitled (Borjas 2002; Fix and Passel 2002). Others have contended that immigrants are differentially influenced by changes in economic circumstances, arguing specifically that improvements in labor-market conditions account for much of the relative immigrant welfare decline (Lofstrom and Bean 2002). It is important to ascertain the nature of the factors driving such declines because they have significant implications for immigrant incorporation and social policy. If they occurred because changes in welfare policy make immigrants less likely than natives to seek or receive the welfare benefits for which they are eligible, the declines would imply bleaker incorporation prospects because this would mean that as a result of changes in welfare policy poor immigrants have lost one of the pillars of support undergirding their transition to the American economic mainstream. Research results showing the influence of such factors would thus imply a need to change welfare policy, particularly as it affects immigrants (Fix and Passel 2002). On the other hand, if the declines occurred because changes in economic conditions lead to increased employment and higher incomes, it would suggest the possibility of enhanced immigrant incorporation chances. But conversely, such trends would also suggest greater immigrant vulnerability to economic downturns, implying that immigrant incorporation prospects are likely to worsen disproportionately during hard economic times independent of changes in immigration or welfare policy. In this case, changes in immigrant welfare receipt as a function of labor-market changes should redirect our attention to the importance of employment-related as well as immigration and welfare policies for coping with immigrant poverty.

Using Current Population Survey data, Magnus Lofstrom and Frank D. Bean (2002) investigated the degree to which changing labor-market conditions contributed to the relatively greater declines in welfare receipt occurring among immigrants compared to natives from 1994 to 2000. In order to address this question, they constructed metropolitan and state-level indicators of nativity-specific unemployment and employment rates, measures that had not previously been available because of lack of data on country of birth in government surveys. (This information has been collected in the Current Population Survey since January 1, 1994.) Working on the premise that many immigrants constitute a disadvantaged source of labor, and thus one especially subject to the vagaries of the business cycle, they hypothesized that immigrant levels of unemployment and employment would be more adversely affected during times of economic retrenchment than those of natives, and subsequently recover more during times of strong economic growth. Such ideas provide a framework for predicting not only sharper welfare declines among immigrants but also steeper declines in states that suffer the most pronounced swings in the business cycle. They found that changes in labor-market conditions explain at least one third and probably more of the relatively greater decline among immigrants in welfare receipt over the period examined, a result that is robust to checks on the possibility that other properties of the areas in which immigrants and natives reside might account for the patterns.

What are the policy implications of these findings? Previous research has emphasized that the decline has seemed to be sharpest among noncitizens (Fix and Passel 1999, 2002), thus seeming to reflect a "chilling" effect associated with welfare reform. The occurrence of chilling effects seems to imply a need to reform welfare policies. Such reforms might consist of either more outreach to educate immigrants as to the law's actual provisions, more careful implementation in order to make sure the actual provisions instead of harsher practices are applied, or perhaps even repeal of the immigrant-specific provisions of the law itself. Lofstrom and Bean (2002), however, show that improved labor-market conditions on their own account for a significant portion of the reduction in the relative welfare gap since welfare reform. Their results do not rule out the possibility that increases in labor supply resulting from "chilling effects" might also account for as much as another one third. But their finding that the persistence of labor-market effects against all efforts to eliminate their influence lends viability to the idea that such factors made a difference *independent* of the effects of welfare policy reform or other unobserved factors.

One of these unobserved factors might be naturalization. Many of the immigrants most likely to receive welfare may have naturalized in the years immediately after welfare reform. If so, it could have resulted from confusion on the part of noncitizens, since immigrants who were already in the country before August 1996 did not have to naturalize to continue to receive benefits. In any case, the possibility of increased rates of naturalization provides still another explanation for declines in receipt among noncitizens. Such declines could have occurred because of the disproportionate movement of high-receipt households into the naturalized category, thus raising the average receipt level among naturalized immigrants (assuming receipt was higher among noncitizens to begin with, which in fact is the case). This possible change in naturalization behavior has been noted by Borjas (2002), who interprets it as indication that welfare is an incentive for immigrants to naturalize, noting, "Many immigrants will become citizens not because they want to fully participate in the U.S. political system, but because naturalization is a hurdle on the road to receiving welfare benefits." His policy recommendation is to make it more difficult to immigrate: "In the end, it is probably easier and cheaper to address the problem raised by the immigration of public charges not by 'ending welfare as we know it,' but by reforming immigration policy itself" (Borjas 2002, 8).

The policy implications of Lofstrom and Bean's (2002) research emphasize reforms other than those of either social welfare or immigrant admissions policies. Their study finds that changes in labor-market conditions account for a significant part of the declines in both immigrant welfare receipt and the nativity gap during the latter half of the 1990s. Given that improvements in labor-market conditions appear to have led to substantial declines in welfare participation, especially among immigrants, it is likely that deteriorating economic conditions would substantially increase future immigrant welfare receipt. In short, any increases in immigrant welfare in the years ahead are likely to result in significant part from decreased employment possibilities and increased unemployment. From a policy standpoint, these need to be addressed on their own terms. Thus, efforts to ameliorate the harsher effects that adverse labor-market conditions impose on immigrants compared to natives would appear to require considering employment policies that target immigrants, not just reforms of welfare and immigration policies.

Summary and Conclusions

The idea that immigrants receive welfare to a greater extent than natives has often been invoked as a major reason to reform immigration policy in the direction of greater restrictiveness, with such reforms usually aimed at tougher restrictions on entry of lesser-skilled immigrants. On close scrutiny, however, this idea does not hold up very well. Evidence that supports this notion tends to emerge only when researchers ignore distinctions among different kinds of immigrants and overlook different results for different kinds of welfare. Apparently supporting data also tend to emerge when researchers fail to take into account three phenomena relating to elderly immigrants and welfare: many recipients "age into" eligibility after already having been in the United States for long periods of time; growth in the elderly immigrant population stems from the family reunification provisions of U.S. immigration policy; and group-specific rates of elderly SSI receipt have not increased over time. By contrast, one of the most striking findings to emerge from analyses that control for the influence of other variables is that most immigrants, including Mexicans, whose historical and contemporary experiences as labor migrants shape their reasons for coming and their behaviors after arrival, are usually *less* likely than comparable natives to receive welfare, especially AFDC and TANF. None of these data provide much corroboration for the idea that welfare acts as a magnet to attract immigrants to the country or that immigrants manifest greater dependency on welfare after they arrive than natives.

It is the case, however, that recent years have witnessed some abuse of SSI by some elderly immigrant groups, and this may be the reason why the research record in the case of certain elderly SSI recipients indicates a level of welfare receipt that persists after all of the factors mentioned above are taken into account. Nonetheless, to argue that either immigration or overall welfare policy should have been reformed, or should still be further reformed, because of this one relatively small segment of the immigrant welfare-receiving population seems unwarranted. Whatever the case, the vast bulk of the evidence, when carefully analyzed and disaggregated as noted above, provides little indication of welfare abuse or dependency among the new immigrants. These findings, together with recent research showing that labor-market improvements explain greater relative immigrant declines in welfare receipt during the 1990s, suggest the need to refocus immigrant welfare-receipt research away from seeking evidence that would imply either a need to change immigration policy (and perhaps limit immigration) or to a need to reform welfare policy (and perhaps provide immigrants more government assistance). Rather, more research is needed on what can be done to expand and make more accessible the economic opportunities available to immigrants.

= Chapter 5 =

The New Immigrants and Theories of Incorporation

J UST HOW rapidly the new immigrants—by which we mean post-1965 immigrants—are becoming part of the American mainstream has constituted one of the major research issues fueling debates in recent years about the need to reform U.S. immigration policy. The general process marking this transition has most often been called assimilation. During the latter third of the twentieth century critics have often argued that this term has normative connotations that imply immigrants *should* become more like natives (see Brubaker 2001; Alba and Nee 1999; and Gans 1999b for discussions). This semantic controversy lies mostly outside the purview of this chapter, which examines theories about the convergence or lack of convergence between immigrant and native groups on various factors, including such variables as education and earnings. Most observers think that regardless of any prescriptive elements inherent in the notion of assimilation, immigrant group movement toward parity in education and earnings is practical and worthwhile (Hirschman 1983; Alba and Nee 1997). The normative liabilities of the term thus appear to apply less to phenomena like labor-market outcomes than to more socio-cultural phenomena.

As Richard Alba and Victor Nee (2003) have recently emphasized, early formulations of assimilation theory explicitly noted that newcomers affect their host societies even as these societies are affecting the newcomers. As we understand the term, then, assimilation means convergence of newcomer and host groups, with each affecting the other, not unidirectional movement of newcomers toward native groups. Because we are in agreement with a number of recent commentaries that have pointed out that neither the concept of assimilation nor concern with assimilation processes necessarily implies endorsement of normative goals as outcomes of the processes (Alba and

94

Nee 2003; Brubaker 2001; Morawska 1994), it is not in any "assimila-tionist" sense that we employ the concept of assimilation in our dis-cussions below. We also use the more general concept of incorpora-tion, by which we mean the broader processes by which new groups establish relationships with host societies. Assimilation is thus but one type of incorporation process.

A major reason incorporation matters in current debates about im-migration is that today's "hour-glass" economy appears to offer fewer chances for economic mobility than was the case in earlier decades (Bernhardt et al. 2001). If true, this shift would have both policy and theoretical significance. At the level of policy, many observers often interpret evidence indicating unsuccessful assimilation as implying that U.S. policies for admitting immigrants are operating to select per-sons into the country with unfavorable chances of joining the eco-nomic mainstream. In theoretical terms, such evidence would suggest that substantive changes either in the characteristics of immigrants or in the structural circumstances confronting new arrivals are now in-hibiting assimilation more than previously (see, for example, Massey 1995). The eventual successful blending of previous groups of immi-grants and natives, often noted in earlier studies and predicted by assimilation theory, might thus be occurring less frequently among more recent arrivals to the United States. In chapter 6 we present research results on the economic assimilation of the most important new immigrant groups.

First, however, we consider the multidimensional nature of assimi-lation and the ways its processes may be changing in the case of the new immigrants. We treat the concept here as having two major di-mensions, one economic and one sociocultural. As noted in chapter 1, sociocultural assimilation is the more complicated conceptually, in part simply because almost all observers would agree that economic assimilation is desirable whereas there is more ambivalence concern-ing sociocultural assimilation. But another reason is that sociocultural, unlike economic, assimilation, involves issues of racial and ethnic identity, particularly when immigrants arrive with national origins that differ from those of the ancestors of natives (Ignatiev 1995; Perl-mann and Waldinger 1999). If natives define these immigrants as ra-cialized minorities, the process can create or reinforce consequential discriminatory barriers (Castles and Miller 1998). Moreover, immi-grant and native racial-ethnic definitions may be at variance with one another. For example, immigrants who are black may choose to see themselves as members of an immigrant group rather than as a ra-cialized minority, whereas some natives may see such immigrants as members of disadvantaged minority groups (Waters 1999). How such identifications affect and are affected by economic assimilation thus becomes an important question.

Those with alternative theoretical perspectives on immigrant incorporation tend to view the connections between economic and sociocultural integration differently. For example, those taking assimilation approaches tend to see certain aspects of sociocultural assimilation (like language acquisition and acceptance of broad norms and values) as precursors of economic assimilation, whereas those with ethnic pluralist perspectives are less likely to posit a relationship between the two. In fact, however, recent theory and research imply not only that facets of sociocultural assimilation are becoming less likely to constitute prerequisites for economic assimilation but also that economic assimilation may even sometimes influence sociocultural assimilation, thus emphasizing the dynamic interplay between the two (Alba and Nee 2003; Gans 1999a, 1999b). This is particularly well illustrated in the complicated case of racial or ethnic identity. Recent research on reactive ethnicity—or the hardening of ethnicity that often results from having experienced ethnic discrimination—shows how economic assimilation can influence sociocultural assimilation, as in the case where mobility-blocked immigrants develop "oppositional" identities as a result of their lack of economic success (Portes and Rumbaut 2001). In the next three chapters, we introduce research results about economic and certain dimensions of sociocultural assimilation separately because, as we argue below, increasingly, some aspects of sociocultural assimilation may be consequences rather than causes of economic assimilation.

Theoretical Models and the Issue of Changing Incorporation

Addressing whether the pace of incorporation may be slowing thus involves considering the possibility that the nature of incorporation itself might be changing. To ascertain this, we must first understand theories of immigrant and ethnic group integration and the various kinds of factors they postulate as influencing economic and sociocultural mobility.

The Assimilation Model

The paradigm that has constituted the most prominent perspective on the issue of how rapidly immigrant groups attain upward mobility is *assimilation* theory, represented in the early work of Robert Park (1926),

William Thomas and Florian Znaniecki (1927), Oscar Handlin (1951), Irving Child (1943), Milton Gordon (1964), and in more contemporary writings of Herbert Gans (1979, 1988) and Richard Alba and Victor Nee (1997, 2003). This perspective envisions the process as one in which immigrants gradually begin to absorb and influence the cultural values and norms of the majority society, a process sometimes called cultural assimilation. In one of the most well developed early treatments of the subject, Gordon (1964) postulates several assimilation stages. After cultural assimilation (including linguistic) will come structural (educational, occupational and labor market, including wages, earnings, and employment), marital, and identificational assimilation. Within the structural category, some scholars draw a useful distinction between primary and secondary structural assimilation. The former refers to close, personal interactions between dominant and subordinate group members. The latter refers to "equal-status relationships between subordinate- and dominant-group members in the public sphere," for example, interactions structured by occupation, education, political position, and neighborhood of residence, and thus by implication labor-market factors (McLemore, Romo, and Gonzalez Baker 2001, 23).

The different stages of assimilation may occur at different rates among different groups. Gordon tended to view broad cultural assimilation not only as a precursor for other kinds of assimilation but also as irreversible. While the overall process may proceed through the stage of secondary structural assimilation without going further, once primary structural assimilation is attained, the process is likely to proceed to completion. In general, this viewpoint sees immigrant or ethnic and majority groups becoming more similar over time in their norms, values, behaviors, and characteristics. As noted above, while considerable debate has arisen over whether this similarity involves the subordinate group's becoming more like the dominant group (an "Anglo conformity" model) or the two groups' becoming more like each other (a "melting pot" model), in either case the model predicts a convergence of behavior and characteristics over time. This perspective would also entail the expectation that the members of later generations and those immigrants residing the longest in the United States would show the greatest decline in differences in behavior compared to the majority group. In this view, differences remaining by the third generation or later would reflect partial assimilation. In the case of labor-market factors, partial secondary structural assimilation could result in differences between the two groups in educational attainment and thus could account for later generational discrepancies in wages and unemployment.

The Ethnic Disadvantage Model

Other observers view the assimilation model as insufficient to explain fully the integration experiences of immigrant groups, as we shall discuss. Another major (and more recent) stream of thought notes the frequent persistence of incomplete assimilation among immigrant groups. This perspective, which we term the *ethnic-disadvantage* point of view, is reflected in the writings of Andrew Greeley (1971), Gerald Suttles (1968), Nathan Glazer and Daniel Moynihan (1963), Alejandro Portes and Robert Bach (1985), Alejandro Portes and Min Zhou (1993), and Alejandro Portes and Rubén Rumbaut (2001). To be sure, some of these writers emphasize ethnic pluralism as much or more than they do ethnic disadvantage. For example, some note the positive reasons for continued ethnic affiliations and activities, as Glazer and Moynihan did in *Beyond the Melting Pot*, which quite famously formulated a political-interest rationale for ethnic attachment. Such formulations provide a logic for the persistence of ethnic distinctiveness without assuming any accompanying ethnic group subordination. But in general, the major theme that runs through this literature is that increasing knowledge of the language of the new country and familiarity with its culture and customs often do not lead to increasing structural assimilation. Lingering discrimination and structural and institutional barriers to equal access to employment opportunities constitute obstacles to complete assimilation. Because socioeconomic opportunities for the first generation are evaluated relative to those in the country of origin, it is not until the second and third generations that the realization emerges that the goal of full assimilation may be more difficult and take longer than originally presumed. Such realities and the evaluation of them have social and cultural consequences, including the reemergence of ethnic consciousness. As Portes and Bach (1985, 25) note: "The rejection experienced by immigrants and their descendants in their attempts to become fully assimilated constitutes a central element in the reconstitution of ethnic culture."

As with the assimilation approach, this perspective would expect the immigrant generation to exhibit different characteristics than natives, even after taking into account other differences between immigrants and natives. By the second generation, however, language patterns and reference groups are in the process of shifting. For example, among first-generation Mexican-origin women, most (84 percent) have been found to use only Spanish at home (Portes and Rumbaut 1990), whereas by the third generation, the shift to English is nearly complete, with 84 percent using only English at home and 12 percent using both English and Spanish (Portes and Rumbaut 1990; Lopez

1982). Such patterns support the notion that the immigrant generation retains the country of origin as a primary reference group, whereas the third generation makes the transition to the country of destination as the reference group (Bean et al. 1994).

Part of the cultural and psychological conflict experienced by the second generation derives from the fact that it is socialized by the first generation, the group that evaluates its socioeconomic experience in the United States most positively. The result is strong efforts by the first generation to inculcate achievement aspirations in the second generation. Reinforcing the second generation's motivation to achieve is its desire to overcome the marginality involved in being caught between the old and the new (Child 1943). The second generation also begins to become more cognizant of the barriers that block access to complete assimilation, as it shifts its reference group to the United States instead of the old country (Hansen 1952; Bean et al. 1994). The second generation's experience of discrimination, together with a growing awareness of its relative socioeconomic standing compared to natives, undermines the second generation's motivation to transmit achievement aspirations to its children. Consistent with these ideas, Lisa Neidert and Reynolds Farley (1985) report a drop in average socioeconomic index score for third compared to second-generation groups, and Bean et al. (1994) and Reynolds Farley and Richard Alba (2002) find that levels of educational attainment and other labor-market outcomes in the third generation fall slightly below those of the second generation. Such findings suggest that real and perceived barriers to socioeconomic attainment can operate even in the third generation to discourage socioeconomic achievement, to reinforce the distinctiveness of the ethnic group, and reaffirm and revitalize ethnic patterns and customs.

The Segmented Assimilation Model

Thus, incorporation appears to elude some members of immigrant groups, even as late as the third generation. Some analysts have concluded that uneven patterns of success do not significantly undermine the validity of the theory of assimilation, but rather suggest that the process may follow a "bumpy" rather than "straight-line" course (Gans 1992a, 1992b). Others have noted that just as some members of immigrant groups become cut off from economic mobility, others find multiple pathways to incorporation depending on their national origin, socioeconomic status, contexts of reception in the United States, and family resources, both social and financial (Rumbaut 1999). As a result, the incorporation experiences of recent immigrants are more diverse than the scenarios provided by the assimilation and the ethnic-disadvantage models. Seeking to distill general tendencies from a multiplicity of trajectories, Portes, Rumbaut and Zhou (Portes and Zhou 1993; Portes and Rumbaut 2001; Zhou 1999) have amalgamated elements of both the straight-line assimilation and the ethnic-disadvantage approaches into a perspective they call *segmented assimilation.* They theorize that structural barriers limiting access to employment and other opportunities, obstacles that often are particularly severe in the case of the most disadvantaged members of immigrant groups, can lead to stagnant or even downward mobility, even as fellow immigrants follow divergent paths toward classic straight-line assimilation. Heavily disadvantaged immigrants may even reject assimilation altogether and embrace attitudes, orientations, and behaviors considered "oppositional" in nature.

The idea of segmented assimilation thus brings together elements of the classic, "straight-line," view of assimilation and the ethnic-disadvantage perspective. This combination represents a major advance in that it refocuses analytical attention on identifying the contextual and structural factors that separate successful assimilation from unsuccessful, or even "negative" assimilation. Portes and Rumbaut (2001) argue that it is particularly important to identify such factors in the case of the children of immigrants, or the second generation, because the operation at that level of significant structural impediments to mobility serves to thwart the onset of assimilation at perhaps its most critical juncture—the very beginning of the process among the children of immigrants (Rumbaut 1999). In essence, Portes and Rumbaut suggest that while many immigrants will find different pathways to mainstream status, others will find such pathways blocked and come to view themselves as members of disadvantaged and racialized minority groups as a result. Massey (1995) echoes these themes at another level in his arguments that new immigration and its meaning for opportunity and ethnicity are grounded in fundamentally different structural circumstances than was the case for previous generations of immigrants. The flows of new immigrants, especially those from Mexico, have occurred more continuously across longer periods of time than earlier migrations. In addition, economic transformations have resulted in increasingly segmented labor markets with fewer opportunities for economic and social mobility, especially for those with less education and lower skills. Moreover, the geographic concentration of the new immigration has created and sustained distinctive language and cultural communities on an unprecedented scale. In his view, these factors are slowing if not halting the traditional processes of assimilation that characterized European-origin populations and introducing a segmented opportunity structure that results in less movement away from ethnicity.

The Black-White Model and Mexican Immigrants

As insightful and useful as theories of incorporation have proved in the past, they are not fully adequate for explaining the progress of immigrants in joining the mainstream. The segmented assimilation model provides perhaps the most adequate depiction, because it offers a basis for understanding the dynamics of both success and failure, but its formulation, perhaps unintentionally, tends to emphasize factors that make for difficulties rather than ease of incorporation. The perspective has also focused predominantly on the circumstances of second-generation immigrant children, and within this frame often on adolescents, whose incorporation experiences are necessarily incomplete. Moreover, the age and developmental stage of adolescents make them prone to the adoption of some of the rebellious and oppositional tendencies predicted by the hypothesis. Thus, it is possible that some of the evidence advanced in support of the perspective's predictions about negative outcomes are attributable in part to life course factors rather than barriers to incorporation. In its emphasis on the second generation, research on segmented assimilation risks accentuating the negative outcomes of incorporation processes.

But there is also another reason that existing theories of assimilation may not apply satisfactorily to the experiences of the new immigrants. The theories have been constructed partially on an old black-white model of racial-ethnic relations that is ill suited for application to new arrivals whose skin color is not only often indistinguishable from that of whites, but whose historical experiences differ considerably from those of both blacks and European immigrants. Existing theories of incorporation offer essentially an optimistic (the assimilation theory) or a pessimistic (ethnic-disadvantage view) picture of the process, or a mixture of the two (segmented assimilation perspective). Which of these views has predominated has depended substantially, if not always explicitly, on whether or not a given immigrant group was treated as a "racialized," disadvantaged minority group. Ethnic-disadvantage perspectives have tended to regard immigrant groups as nonwhite minorities subject to discrimination. Assimilation perspectives have tended to view them less in racial or ethnic and more in nativity terms. Thus, the issue of immigration is inextricably confounded with the issue of race and ethnicity in the United States. To be sure, these features of the two perspectives are a matter of degree rather than absolute differences. Nonetheless, the question of changes in the pace of assimilation cannot be separated from the question of the extent to which the new immigrant groups tend to become disadvantaged and racialized minority groups in the United States.

The Mexican case exemplifies the difficulty of applying a strictly assimilation or ethnic-disadvantage perspective to new immigrants. Observers of the rise in the importance of the Mexican-origin population in the United States have often been uncertain how to characterize the experience of Mexican-origin persons in the United States and thus the degree of incorporation in the Mexican-origin population. Even though Mexican immigrants are diverse in terms of their migration status and modes of entry into the United States, the inclination has often existed (among both Mexican-origin persons themselves as well as others) to perceive the group's members in ways that often reflect the prior experiences of either European immigrants or African Americans. An assimilation perspective involves viewing Mexican-origin persons primarily as an immigrant group whose members have for the most part only recently come to the United States and whose incorporation may relatively quickly mirror that of earlier groups (Chavez 1989). In this view, one need only wait for natural incorporation processes to run their course, usually over three or four generations (McCarthy and Valdez 1985; Rodriguez 1999). An alternative perspective tends to envision Mexican-origin persons more as members of a disadvantaged minority group whose progress toward full economic parity with other U.S. groups is retarded by discrimination. In this view, substantial progress is not likely to occur simply with the passage of time but will require new policies both to help eradicate discrimination and to compensate for its past effects (Chapa 1990; Valdivieso and Dains 1986).

Analysts influenced by these two ways of looking at the Mexican-origin experience tend to organize economic statistics differently in seeking to shed light on the group's economic incorporation. Because the ethnic-disadvantage viewpoint is that all members of the group are subject to discrimination, its adherents tend to marshal data on income and jobs and other indicators for the entire national-origin group, irrespective of nativity status. By contrast, observers who treat Mexican-origin persons as members of an immigrant group tend to distinguish the foreign-born from the native-born on the grounds that the experience of Mexican-origin persons varies so much by nativity that data on this group must be disaggregated. For example, rather than arguing that discrimination shapes immigrants' experiences in the labor market, these observers hold that such outcomes as immigrant wages and employment are influenced more by English-language proficiency, human capital variables, and U.S. work experience. From this perspective, the examination of labor-market outcomes or other variables that include data on foreign-born and native-born persons lumped together is likely to yield misleading assessments of the economic achievements of many members of immigrant groups, especially Mexican-origin persons (see, for example, Bean, Berg, and Van Hook 1996; Trejo 1996, 1997).

Each of these points of view finds some evidence in support of its ideas. On the one hand, research suggests that persons of Mexican origin often face job discrimination, though not so much as African Americans (Bean and Tienda 1987; Perlmann and Waldinger 1999). Nonetheless, it is also evident that data aggregated by nativity present an incomplete picture of the accomplishments of those of Mexican origin. The gap in education and earnings between immigrant and native-born members of the same group clearly has more to do with origin-country differences in economic development than with discrimination. Bias resulting from the aggregation of statistics is likely to be especially severe in times of high immigration, as in the 1990s, when immigration, particularly from Mexico, rose because of the legalization programs associated with the 1986 Immigration Reform and Control Act (IRCA) and because of an economic crisis in Mexico (Bean et al. 1997; Massey, Durand, and Malone 2002).

Perspectives such as that of segmented assimilation argue that members of the new immigrant groups risk the kinds of outcomes that disadvantaged blacks have often experienced and that some national-origin groups are more vulnerable than others. At a minimum, sorting out the degree of economic progress among immigrant groups requires that research disaggregate racial and ethnic groups by nativity or (preferably) generational status. While this may seem like a banal observation, it bears repeating, as Rebeca Raijman and Marta Tienda (1999) have also emphasized, because even today it continues to be overlooked. Beyond this, understanding what is happening in the cases of the new immigrant groups requires recognition that even as incorporation may be occurring in regard to economic factors, it may at the same time be moving in opposite directions in regard to some sociocultural factors. Thus, the predictions of neither straight-line assimilation nor the ethnic-disadvantage perspectives, both of which are contained in the segmented assimilation framework, may fully characterize the experiences of many new immigrant groups. The new ethnic groups may not only have distinctive historical backgrounds, they also experience different modes of reception in the

United States (Portes and Rumbaut 1990; Portes and Zhou 1993; Bean et al. 1997). These factors may cause them to experience economic and sociocultural incorporation differently.

Existing Theory and Its Discontents

An examination of the origins of the two major theoretical perspectives on incorporation may illuminate how incorporation perspectives may need modification for new immigrant groups. A key difference between the assimilation and ethnic-disadvantage perspectives is how they view the connection between structural and cultural incorporation. That relationship has implications for the persistence and reformation of racial and ethnic identities, which in turn may affect the likelihood of new "racialized" minorities developing. In the classic "straight-line" model of assimilation (Gordon 1964) and its many variants (Crispino 1980; Alba 1990; Gans 1992b), newcomers are expected both to affect and to be affected by the fabric of American life so that immigrant minorities become ever more indistinguishable from natives, at least after several generations. Emerging out of the predominantly European-origin migration that took place at the beginning of the twentieth century, the formulation of this model was influenced by literary and artistic metaphors emerging from the experience (and strategy) of incorporation adopted by Jewish immigrants to establish a foothold and gain economic mobility in the United States. Canonizing this view was Milton Gordon (1964), who postulated that at least some aspects of acculturation were necessary (if not always sufficient) precursors to structural incorporation.

The dissatisfaction that developed with the model had partly to do with its incomplete depictions of the experiences of European migrants, but also partly with the inability of its integrationist counterpart to explain in another realm the experience of African Americans in America (Glazer and Moynihan 1963). Although African American customs, practices, ideals, and values by the early 1960s had come to mirror those of the larger population to a considerable degree, still missing was satisfactory African American structural incorporation. The prevailing optimistic view at the time was that the removal of legal barriers would in fairly short order lead to substantial structural incorporation of African Americans (Glazer 1997). In reality, however, though the elimination of such barriers to blacks resulted in some improvements in black economic situations, gains fell far short of parity with whites, with consequences that could readily be discerned by the mid-1980s (Wilson 1987; Glazer 1997; Bean and Bell-Rose 1999).

At about the same time, it was becoming increasingly clear that many white European groups continued to manifest aspects of ethnic distinctiveness despite their substantial structural incorporation (Alba 1990; Gans 1979; Waters 1990). Both of these trends contributed to the development of an ethnic pluralist perspective of incorporation that was predicated on the idea that cultural incorporation was neither inevitable nor necessary for structural incorporation (Greeley 1974). Researchers have demonstrated, however, that much of the ethnic revival among European immigrant groups during this period was symbolic, giving rise to the concept of *symbolic ethnicity*, at least among white ethnics (Gans 1979; Alba 1990; Waters 1990). As Mary C. Waters (1999) has noted, however, nonwhites, especially blacks, do not have the luxury of adopting "symbolic ethnicities." It was in part the reaction of nonwhite ethnics to lingering discrimination and disadvantage that contributed to the kind of ethnic revitalization emphasized by the ethnic-pluralist and ethnic-disadvantage perspectives.

Interestingly, the experiences out of which the assimilation, ethnic-pluralist, and ethnic-disadvantage perspectives arose and their assumptions about racial and ethnic group boundaries serve substantially to preserve distinctive racial and ethnic group identities. The multiculturalism of the United States in the latter part of the twentieth century, which both the ethnic-pluralist and ethnic-disadvantage perspectives reflect, emphasizes the worthiness of multiple racial and ethnic groups and the importance of tolerating the cultural differences manifested by such groups. At the same time, however, by taking the definition and thus the existence of such groups for granted and by assuming that the members of such groups will continue to see themselves in such terms in the future, multiculturalism tends to support the idea that sharp and distinctive boundaries divide racial and ethnic groups. Basically consistent with the tenets of multiculturalism, the ethnic pluralism and the ethnic disadvantage perspectives implicitly embrace the same orientation. Generally their assumptions are compatible with multiculturalism's effort to cope with the problem of barriers among groups by issuing calls for the tolerance of difference and the celebration of diversity, even while preserving the boundaries among groups.

The ethnic-pluralist and the ethnic-disadvantage paradigms thus basically accept the idea that the new immigrant groups are most appropriately viewed as nonwhite, "racialized" minorities. This is the case even though both the facial features and range of skin pigmentation of the groups to which the models have been applied vary enormously. Even the construction of "symbolic ethnicity" may be viewed as occurring in part because of multiculturalism, without whose triumph there would have been little need to reinforce and reify ethnic distinctiveness (Glazer 1997). The ethnic-disadvantage perspective similarly assumes continuing racial distinctiveness, albeit with a main emphasis on the nonwhiteness of new immigrants, the most dark-skinned of whom are seen as especially likely to develop not only a strong minority consciousness but also one that assumes an adversarial posture toward the white majority. In this regard, its tenets parallel those of John Ogbu (1994), who notes that racial or ethnic groups that have been involuntary migrants to the United States are particularly likely to develop such oppositional orientations.

A New Model of Changing Contingency Between Economic and Sociocultural Incorporation

The racial or ethnic identifications of the new immigrants may not follow the trajectories implied by the old models, a possibility that has been foreshadowed in the formulation of the ideas of "symbolic ethnicity" and "ethnic options" (Alba 1985, 1990; Gans 1979; Waters 1990). The assimilation and both the ethnic-pluralist and ethnic-disadvantage models, together with the historical experiences that have helped give rise to them (those of European immigrants and American blacks), seem inadequate to describe the situations and experiences of new immigrants in the later part of the twentieth century. As noted in chapter 2, most immigration during the 1980s and 1990s has been from Latin American and Asian countries (Portes and Zhou 1993; Neckerman, Carter, and Lee 1999). By the 1980s, only 12 percent of legal immigrants originated in Europe or Canada, whereas nearly 85 percent reported origins in Asia, Latin America, or the Caribbean (Bean et al. 1997; U.S. Immigration and Naturalization Service 1998), converting the United States from a largely biracial society consisting of a sizable white majority and a small black minority into a multiracial, multiethnic society consisting of several racial and ethnic groups. Not only are the majority of the new immigrants neither black nor white, but the largest group, Mexicans, as well as many other Latinos, come mostly from mestizo backgrounds. Also, the vast majority of recent immigrants are Latino labor migrants who entered the United States in the West, a region of the country in which many areas have long shown more tolerance for racial and ethnic diversity than the norm in the rest of the United States (Lee and Wood 1991; Farley and Frey 1994).

The old models of cultural accommodation and bipolar racial divides thus appear less relevant to the historical and contemporary experiences of Latinos than to earlier European immigrants (Rodriguez 2001; Suárez-Orozco and Páez 2002). And such dichotomies are scarcely more relevant for Asians, who come from so many countries of origin and often are so socioeconomically diverse that no single set of experiences can be thought to have played a defining role in shaping their identities (Lopez and Espiritu 1990). If cultural accommodation facilitated structural incorporation in the past, this has not seemed apparent or necessary for today's newcomers (Gibson 1988), resulting in a further decoupling of whatever traditional linkages had been thought to exist between acculturation and economic mobility (Alba 1990; Neckerman, Carter and Lee 1999). Rather, many of today's new Asian and Latino immigrants seem to have adopted a path of "selective assimilation" (Portes and Zhou 1993; Zhou and Bankston 1998) or "accommodation without assimilation" (Gibson 1988). Under these conditions, racial and ethnic identities are likely to become less constrained than previously presumed and more flexible and dynamic than emphasized by either the straight-line or ethnic-pluralist models. As a result, multiracial identifications may be more likely among Asian and Latino immigrants than among either black Afro-origin immigrants or native-born blacks, as a consequence of both higher rates of intermarriage and greater tendencies to see themselves in multiracial terms.

If Latinos' and Asians' internal identifications are less constrained, this may be because the native-born population is now less likely to constrain them. According to the ethnic-disadvantage model, the native-born, largely white population assigns an identity to the groups that tend to have the lowest status and the darkest skin, regardless of the groups' self-identification (Waters 1999). By contrast, in an assimilation model, the self-defined and externally defined identifications gradually merge and melt away. But the very size and socioeconomic diversity of the Latino and Asian immigrant streams may make them more difficult for the native-born to categorize easily. The immigrant groups of the early twentieth century may have had much less between- and within-group variation and thus may have been easier to stereotype. The diversity among contemporary immigrants may render racial and ethnic boundaries more negotiable than in previous generations. This diversity does not mean that stereotypes have not developed, because they have (for example, Asians are seen as the "model minority"). But they are also less likely to be pervasive.

Processes of self-identification may interact with socioeconomic status in complex ways, providing further indication that the relationship between sociocultural and economic aspects of incorporation may be changing from the sequential form implied in the assimilation model toward forms involving multiple contingencies and dynamic interplays. Racial and ethnic identification occurs at several levels: reactive, symbolic, and selective. Among those with the least status, reactive identification is most likely to arise from repeated discrimination and contribute to the subsequent hardening of oppositional attitudes. This interaction of socioeconomic status and identification suggests that ethnic identification is most intense among those of lowest status. Selective assimilation tends to develop among those with better prospects. Their status would make them more opportunistic than oppositional with respect to economic incorporation, and they would belong to ethnic networks and institutions with enough resources to offer greater support than available to poorer ethnicities in the ethnic enclave. In their case, high resource ethnic social ties would trump weaker interethnic ties, with the result that such people would be more likely to choose an ethnic identity. However, the choice might not entirely be theirs, since they might continue to face discrimination based on their ethnic or racial background. Symbolic ethnicity emerges among those who already are largely incorporated both culturally and economically. Such persons tend not to rely on co-ethnic networks and "ethnicity" for instrumental support but instead for expressive, individualistic needs (Alba 1990; Gans 1988). For them, ethnic identification is optional (Waters 1990).

Some research has found that the relationship between status and identification appears curvilinear (Neckerman, Carter, and Lee 1999). Ethnic identification seems to be highest among those of either lowest or highest status. Whereas reactive ethnicity may arise mainly among those of the lowest socioeconomic status, symbolic ethnicity seems most likely to occur among those of *highest* status. This stratum would have the most interest in its sociocultural heritage and the greatest freedom to assume an ethnic identity without incurring discrimination. The working class, on the other hand, would stand to gain the most from assimilation and might therefore shed much of its ethnic identity.

Such a curvilinear pattern would mean that the process of identificational assimilation, one of the seven types described by Gordon (1964), may increasingly occur autonomously from other types of incorporation. Gordon observed that the various dimensions of assimilation often empirically follow a sequence. Even though he also noted that this was not a necessity, the apparently growing separation of self-identification from other forms of incorporation is particularly striking. Identification is thus the one dimension of assimilation that is becoming both more subjective and autonomous; the other dimensions of assimilation named by Gordon involve behaviors or the atti-

Figure 5.1   Cross-Classification of Skin Color and Socioeconomic Status

	Socioeconomic Status		
	Higher	Middle	Lower
Skin lighter	Symbolic ethnicity	Straight-line assimilation	Straight-line assimilation
Skin darker	Selective assimilation	Bumpy-line assimilation	Reactive ethnicity

Source: Authors' configuration.

tudes of those outside the group. Thus, immigrants may be maintaining ethnic identifications despite considerable economic incorporation and despite social networks and perhaps even marriages that cross racial or ethnic boundaries, providing another example of attitude not always predicting behavior. Of course, such decouplings proceed most rapidly in the absence of strong discrimination or value conflict. Otherwise, external barriers would forestall incorporation. Among the low-status immigrants who face such external barriers and who develop reactive ethnicity, attitudes may remain tightly linked to behaviors. The independence of attitudes and behavior appears more likely to occur among the well-educated.

In general, skin color and socioeconomic status are likely to distinguish whether relatively "straight-line" assimilation, more "bumpy-line" assimilation, symbolic ethnicity, reactive ethnicity, or selective acculturation are most likely to emerge among new immigrant groups. As Waters (1999) observes, the concept of symbolic ethnicity applies best to the descendants of earlier-arriving white European immigrants, especially those of higher socioeconomic status. Among non-whites, the reaffirmation of "ethnicity" probably arises most in reaction to real and perceived discrimination, which immigrants of low socioeconomic status are most likely to encounter. Thus, if we cross-classify skin color and socioeconomic status, as in figure 5.1, we obtain the following six-fold indication of where straight-line assimilation, bumpy-line assimilation, symbolic ethnicity, reactive ethnicity, and selective assimilation might be most likely to emerge.

To the extent that such decoupling of self-identification from other forms of identification is occurring among the new immigrants, their ethnic identification may constitute an especially misleading indicator of their overall level of incorporation. Immigrants' actual behaviors, such as language usage and intermarriage rates, should be better indicators of sociocultural assimilation than subjective identification.

Although this point may seem obvious—language use and intermarriage have a long history as indicators of sociocultural assimilation—the advantage of behavioral indicators over ethnic identification deserves emphasis. Because the 2000 census has for the first time allowed individuals to identify themselves by more than one race, research in the next few years will inevitably focus on multiracial identities. Particularly if such research confirms the curvilinear pattern of ethnic identity among immigrants, observers who view such findings only through the lens of the old black-white model may mistakenly conclude that immigrants are not assimilating very rapidly, even if the overall behaviors of immigrants suggest otherwise. Fortunately, the census also contains data on language, educational level, occupation, and marriage that will provide a multitude of behavioral indicators of incorporation and thus a basis for a more complete assessment.

One question among the third and later generations of Asians and Latinos is the extent to which ethnic identity will remain reactive or selective, become symbolic, or, in the assimilationist model, disappear altogether. Racial and ethnic identity tends to be adaptable and thus may shift quite naturally during the process of incorporation. But the cross-sectional design of most studies of the second generation precludes study of the long-term evolution of identity and can unwittingly give the impression that ethnic identity is fixed. Because some of the largest changes happen in the third generation or later (Perlmann and Waldinger 1999), selective assimilation may well evolve into symbolic ethnicity.

A still larger question is whether immigrants are retaining their overall sociocultural and economic differences from the native-born population. On an identificational level, the answer appears to be yes. Members of immigrant groups of high and low status appear increasingly to be identifying themselves by racial or ethnic origins. But behavioral indicators of sociocultural assimilation such as intermarriage and language acquisition do not reflect any similar trends, suggesting a decline in ethnic separatism. Moreover, economically, such ethnic self-identification may be reflecting immigrants' achievements, in the case of symbolic ethnicity, or enabling immigrants to maximize achievement, in the case of selective assimilation. For immigrants who already enter with high socioeconomic status, retention of ethnic identity appears to have few costs and potentially many benefits. In fact, the rise of multiculturalism has mainstreamed the acceptability of diversity, so that retention of a *symbolic* level of racial or ethnic identification or even construction of a new pan-ethnic identity—

such as that of Latino as combination of multiple national origin groups—may paradoxically be part of the gradual process of incorporation. Because of these factors, maintenance of a racial or ethnic identification increasingly seems not to preclude other types of assimilation, and often even to be strengthened by both low and high economic assimilation.

The Mexican Case

The implications of what we have been saying about possibly new patterns of ethnic identity are particularly important in the case of the Mexican-origin group in the United States. This group is large and distinctive for its low levels of education, as we noted in chapter 3. It is also both a "new" immigrant group (in the sense that large numbers of Mexican immigrants have arrived since the elimination of national origin quotas in 1965) and an "old" immigrant group (in the sense that substantial numbers of Mexicans have been immigrating to the United States for quite a long time). Of course, a few of the members of the Mexican-origin population are the descendants of persons who were living in the territory that is now the United States when it was still part of Mexico, which causes some observers to claim that Mexican-origin persons are more like colonized minorities than immigrants. Whatever one's point of view on this matter, it nonetheless remains the case that the vast majority, indeed almost all, persons of Mexican origin in the country came as a result of voluntary migration (Bean and Tienda 1987; Edmonston and Passel 1999). As a consequence of this longstanding migration, the third and later generations in the Mexican-origin population are more numerous than similar generations for almost all of the other new immigrant groups. This means that some of the identificational dynamics by generation discussed above will have had a chance to manifest themselves. But it also means that a large fraction of the group is first or second generation and just beginning processes of assimilation.

But perhaps the most important dynamic for assessing the incorporation experience and success of the Mexican-origin group is the unauthorized status of so many of its first-generation entrants, both now and in previous decades. This separates the Mexican-origin group from all others, with the possible exception of Salvadorans and Guatemalans, whose numbers are substantially smaller and who did not migrate much to the United Sates until recently. Compared to other immigrant groups, then, and especially to other new immigrant groups, many Mexicans begin their immigrant experience with a unique handicap: their unauthorized status. They thus start the process of economic and sociocultural incorporation from a particularly disadvantaged position. If we liken immigration to entering a house through the "front" door (or "heaven's door," to use the title of a recent book on immigration) and seeking to climb to the upper floors where the long-term natives live, then it is important to realize that vast numbers of Mexicans came not through the front door but rather through a back entrance that channeled them straight to the basement. So if the usual expectation is that it might take a certain amount of time for immigrants to climb the floors of the house (about three generations, according to traditional assimilation models), then Mexicans are confronted with having to climb at least an extra flight of stairs. So it is logical we should think of their experience as requiring more time to reach some semblance of completion, perhaps four or five generations rather than three if the latter is viewed as an average. Certainly there is no doubt that many Mexican immigrants have longer journeys ahead of them than other immigrant groups because of their unauthorized status and their lower levels of education.

Now consider what this may mean in terms of how natives perceive the success of incorporation among Mexican immigrants. On the one hand, the identification dynamics discussed above may lead more and more Mexicans to retain some measure of identification as "Mexicans," even in cases where successful economic incorporation has occurred, for the reasons noted above. We have already discussed above that many native-born Americans may misinterpret the manifestations and expressions of such Mexican identities as indicating the lack of successful economic incorporation among Mexican-origin persons in general, especially if the native-born perceive Mexican-origin persons as members of a disadvantaged "racialized" minority group. Add to this all of the new immigrants, both legal and unauthorized, who have come to the United States in recent years and thus have not had time to progress very far economically, and the picture of a poor and not very successfully incorporating population gets reinforced.

Yet another factor in perceptions of Mexican-origin immigrants is that the sheer increase in the relative and absolute size of this group during the 1990s created ever-larger ethnic enclaves, thus substantially adding to the visibility of the population. In short, the changing dynamics of ethnic identification, the increasing proportion of the population with incomplete incorporation, and the rising conspicuousness of the group all conspire to suggest a bleaker incorporation picture than may actually be the case among Mexican-origin persons in this country. We return in the next chapter to further discussion of these issues.

Summary and Conclusions

Our examination of theories of incorporation and their applicability to the new immigrants indicates that ideas about incorporation must be revised if they are to fit the reception experiences of many of the new groups. The earlier theories of assimilation tended to assume that certain aspects of sociocultural assimilation preceded or occurred simultaneously with economic assimilation, and perhaps in certain circumstances even to act as a prerequisite for it. In the cases of the new immigrants, the question of racial and ethnic identification, which we view as one of the key facets of sociocultural assimilation along with language patterns and intermarriage, often seems to be shaped by immigrants' experiences with economic assimilation rather than the other way around. Some new immigrants develop their strongest sense of ethnic identity after they achieve a measure of economic success, the pattern and expression of this renewed ethnic consciousness often being reminiscent of the "symbolic" ethnicities that developed among European white ethnics during the 1960s and 1970s. Others maintain a strong sense of ethnic consciousness as a strategy for maximizing economic incorporation (Zhou and Bankston 1998; Waters 1999). Whatever the case, we suggest that the increased separation of sociocultural and economic assimilation has the effect of often confusing the American public about the nature and pace of overall assimilation. The continued manifestation of certain kinds of ethnic distinctiveness may reinforce the idea that integration may be proceeding slowly. Therefore an assessment of the degree of success of assimilation not only must focus on multiple facets of sociocultural assimilation like language acquisition and intermarriage but also must be sensitive to the fact that economic assimilation may increasingly occur independent of certain forms of identificational assimilation. We now turn our attention to the assessment of the degree of assimilation in terms of these multiple facets.

=== Chapter 6 ===

Immigrant Economic Incorporation

THE EXTENT to which the new immigrant groups are experiencing successful economic incorporation is one of the central issues driving current debates about the need to reform U.S. immigration policy. Political controversy about whether existing admissions policies should be changed is likely to intensify to the degree that immigrants are not experiencing positive economic incorporation, or are undergoing slower or more difficult incorporation processes than immigrants in the past. In recent years, the question of successful incorporation has also been raised in the case of the second generation. Attention has focused on the offspring of immigrants because it is the second generation that experiences lifetime exposure to the opportunities and constraints of American society (see Zhou and Bankston 1998; Portes and Rumbaut 2001). Relative lack of success among the second generation is likely to be interpreted by many as an even stronger indictment of immigration policies than any difficulties experienced by the first generation.

In this chapter, we address the matter of economic incorporation by examining labor-market outcomes among immigrants and their descendants, focusing primarily on wages and earnings. We concentrate on four main topics. First, in order to ascertain whether major categories of immigrants have experienced the same trends in earnings as non-Hispanic whites, we examine the levels and changes in earnings among major racial and ethnic and immigrant groups over the past twenty years, paying special attention to differences between the native- and foreign-born. Second, in order to ascertain what happens to immigrants themselves after they arrive, we review the results of recent research on the extent to which any nativity gaps in wages and earnings diminish the longer immigrants reside in the country. Third, we examine whether the degree of self-employment

114

and an important contextual factor, the relative size of the ethnic market or economy, enhance earnings prospects among Mexican immigrants who are not self-employed. Fourth, in order to ascertain the degree to which convergence in economic well-being between immigrants and natives occurs across generations, we present research findings on the education and labor-market outcomes of first-, second-, and third- or later-generation Mexican-origin persons, the largest recent U.S. immigrant group, compared to natives.

Earnings Trends

The work of social scientists seeking to describe, analyze, and explain immigrant economic well-being has often reflected the fact that until recently, literature on incorporation of immigrants into the labor market, particularly in urban contexts, has been dominated by studies of urban African Americans in the United States (Waldinger 2001). A resulting assumption has often been made that the research strategies and theoretical explanations applying to the African American case can be transferred to the immigrant case. One of the consequences of this is to treat immigrants and immigrant groups (by which we mean, in the case of the new immigrants, not only the immigrants themselves but also their descendants) as members of racial or ethnic minority groups that are disadvantaged because of persisting discrimination in the United States against people of color. While abundant evidence exists to document the enduring effects of racial discrimination in the case of blacks in this country, it has not been clear that immigrant groups are discriminated against to the same degree as are African Americans (Bean and Bell-Rose 1999; Perlmann and Waldinger 1999; Waters 1999), which calls into question tendencies to view the experience of immigrant groups as identical to that of African Americans.

Recent research also indicates that immigrants are more concentrated in lower-paying jobs than the native-born members of their ethnic groups, largely because of their lesser skills (Waldinger 2001). This implies that certain approaches to studying the economic situation of immigrant groups are not likely to be able to provide a full picture of immigrant incorporation. For example, an approach that treats immigrant groups as racial or ethnic minorities and lumps the foreign- and native-born together will understate economic progress by virtue of including the former with the latter. Also, an approach that focuses only on the immigrants instead of also on the second and later generations will cover too short a time span to reveal the effects of more complete incorporation experiences. A preferable strategy is to take into account nativity differences, and one that is even better where possible is also to make comparisons across more than two generations. The present chapter is one of few research endeavors that adopt the latter strategy, although we also present and review results based on the other approaches.

Despite the limitations of the approach, observers often judge the labor-market prospects of new immigrants by gauging what appears to be happening to the labor-market outcomes of the racial or ethnic groups to which immigrant groups belong. This approach portrays immigrants more as members of a racial or ethnic minority than as newcomers just starting out in their societies of destination. The vast majority of new immigrants to the United States since 1965 are Asian and Hispanic in origin (we use the terms Hispanic and Latino interchangeably to refer to persons of Hispanic origin in the United States). Because over 90 percent of Asians and Latinos have either come to the United States during the twentieth century or are the descendants of persons who have come during that time (Edmonston and Passel 1994), it is useful to examine the earnings trajectories of these two major groups, although doing so risks attributing to discrimination earnings differences that are actually due to generational change. Examining earnings trends for racial and ethnic groups by nativity helps to clarify the meaning of statistics about the incorporation experiences of immigrants. For example, we would be inclined to interpret differently an earnings gap between immigrants and natives occurring at the end of a period of rising inequality that affected all sectors of the population equally than we would one occurring at the end of a period where inequality affected immigrants more than natives.

The 1990s were times of uneven income growth in the population of the United States, as persons at the top of the income distribution experienced much more favorable earnings growth than those at the bottom (Bernhardt et al. 2001; Welch 2001). Since some immigrant groups tend to be concentrated at the bottom of the socioeconomic ladder, an important question is the extent to which the racial or ethnic groups of which immigrants are members have experienced these same general trends. Here we examine changes in individual earnings for full-time workers using data from the 1980 and 1990 censuses, together with pooled data from the 1996, 1997, 1998, and 1999 Current Population Surveys. We examine data on annual earnings for full-time workers, focusing on earnings information for the year before the survey, with all figures converted to 1998 dollars.

By focusing on full-time workers, we limit our analyses in certain respects. For example, lower-skilled black men have experienced a considerably harder time finding employment than lower-skilled men in other groups, even though the earnings gap between those blacks who are successfully employed and whites has narrowed to some extent (Bean and Bell-Rose 1999). By contrast, lower-skilled immigrant men have had little difficulty securing low-wage employment but have generally not managed to move from such employment to higher-paying jobs (Waldinger 2001). Our comparisons of immigrants and blacks thus tend to overstate the extent of an earnings gap between these groups. And because immigrants tend to work somewhat fewer hours than the members of other groups, our results also slightly overstate differences on account of this factor. We nonetheless focus on annual earnings because it indicates the general level of economic resources accruing to individuals on a yearly basis, thus providing a good reflection of overall economic incorporation.

The earnings trends over the past twenty years for all of the major racial and ethnic groups reflect a pattern of uneven prosperity, a pattern that has characterized the country as a whole. Persons likely to be at the top of the income structure (those with college education) saw their earnings rise over the two decades, irrespective of whether they were white, black, Asian, or Latino or male or female (see table 6.1). By contrast, persons likely to be at the bottom of the income structure (those with less than a high school education) saw their real earnings drop, irrespective of racial-ethnic group or gender. However, for those in the middle (those with high school education), the trend depended on gender but not on racial or ethnic group. Men in all four racial or ethnic groups suffered declines in real earnings across both decades (except for blacks during the 1990s). By contrast, all women experienced increases during the 1980s. During the 1990s, however, whites and blacks continued their increases, but Latinos and Asians did not. Thus, even with data that encompass the boom years of the late 1990s, years that brought at least small wage and earnings gains to persons at the bottom parts of the earnings distribution (U.S. Department of Labor 2001), the overall earnings situations of non-college-educated Asians and Latinos did not improve, even when earnings were rising among comparably educated whites and blacks.

These results would thus seem to suggest that the relative labor-market situations of non-college-educated Latinos and Asians have worsened over the past two decades, especially for men, thus implying that the incorporation prospects of Latino and Asian immigrants, many of whom have high school education or less, may have deteriorated as well. Stated differently, the increased income inequality that has emerged in the United States over the past thirty years involving declines in real earnings among persons in the bottom parts of the

Table 6.1 Average Earnings by Race-Ethnicity, Educational Attainment, and Gender, 1979 to 1998

		Male					Female				
					Percentage Change					Percentage Change	
Group	Education	1979	1989	1998	(1979 to 1989)	(1989 to 1998)	1979	1989	1998	(1979 to 1989)	(1989 to 1998)
White non-Hispanics	College	59,776	63,349	68,599	6.0	8.3	26,127	32,783	37,134	25.5	13.3
	High school	41,433	38,090	37,999	-8.1	-0.2	18,475	20,367	21,854	10.2	7.3
	< High school	33,661	28,682	26,858	-14.8	-6.4	14,901	14,490	13,685	-2.8	-5.6
Blacks	College	41,613	44,040	47,635	5.8	8.2	30,183	34,430	34,826	14.1	1.2
	High school	29,786	27,645	28,995	-7.2	4.9	19,700	20,627	20,909	4.7	1.4
	< High school	24,338	20,946	20,434	-13.9	-2.4	14,262	14,319	13,337	0.4	-6.9
Latinos	College	48,361	49,557	55,386	2.5	11.8	26,229	31,981	35,126	21.9	9.8
	High school	33,517	30,204	29,736	-9.9	-1.5	18,219	19,584	19,488	7.5	-0.5
	< High school	25,096	20,481	19,706	-18.4	-3.8	12,956	12,732	11,584	-1.7	-9.0
Asians	College	54,196	55,532	58,475	2.5	5.3	29,844	35,185	37,291	17.9	6.0
	High school	34,513	32,171	31,258	-6.8	-2.8	20,234	22,434	22,304	10.9	-0.6
	< High school	26,820	21,261	23,705	-20.7	11.5	15,070	15,456	14,521	2.6	-6.0

Ratios to White

White non-Hispanics	College	1.00	1.00	1.00	1.00	1.00	1.00
	High school	1.00	1.00	1.00	1.00	1.00	1.00
	< High school	1.00	1.00	1.00	1.00	1.00	1.00
Blacks	College	0.70	0.70	0.69	1.16	1.05	0.94
	High school	0.72	0.73	0.76	1.07	1.01	0.96
	< High school	0.72	0.73	0.76	0.96	0.99	0.97
Latinos	College	0.81	0.78	0.81	1.00	0.98	0.95
	High school	0.81	0.79	0.78	0.99	0.96	0.89
	< High school	0.75	0.71	0.73	0.87	0.88	0.85
Asians	College	0.91	0.88	0.85	1.14	1.07	1.00
	High school	0.83	0.84	0.82	1.10	1.10	1.02
	< High school	0.80	0.74	0.88	1.01	1.07	1.06

Sources: U.S. Bureau of the Census (1982, 1992b); Current Population Survey (1996, 1997, 1998, 1999).

income distribution seems to have hit the new immigrant groups harder than whites or blacks. If the cause of such inequality is predominantly technologically based changes in the economy that advantage high-skilled but disadvantage low-skilled workers, then this would imply that continued streams of low-skilled immigrants into the country would face diminished incorporation prospects. Before embracing this conclusion, however, we need to take into consideration that increasing numbers of immigrants have been entering the United States over the past two decades. If such immigrants are disproportionately low-skilled, the increasing proportions of Latino and Asian immigrants may account for the greater earnings declines observed among Latinos and Asians compared to whites and blacks. In other words, rising numbers of immigrants, who tend to start out in worse-paying jobs, may explain the worsening economic situations of Latinos and Asians, although it is not obvious why this should be more the case for men than women.

In order to assess this possibility, it is necessary to examine earnings trends separately by nativity. When we do this (see table 6.2), we find that although native-born Latinos and Asians tend to have higher earnings than the foreign-born members of these groups—and this is more marked for Latinos than Asians—trends in earnings between the foreign-born and the native-born within these groups are not discernibly different, especially in the case of Asians. Among Latinos, college-educated males have gained ground during the period examined, both absolutely and relative to comparable whites. Both Asians and Latinos with high school education have seen their earnings positions erode slightly. And the less-educated men of both groups appear not to have suffered as sharp a decline as their white counterparts, resulting in the striking pattern in the bottom panel of the table whereby the income positions of less well educated foreign-born Asians and Latinos relative to their white counterparts have actually improved somewhat over the two decades of the eighties and nineties. For example, Latino immigrants with less than a high school education moved from earning 70 percent as much as low-skilled whites in 1979 to 73 percent as much by 1998. Lower-skilled female immigrants, however, saw their earnings positions deteriorate somewhat relative to those of their white counterparts. However, none of these differences in trend compare in magnitude to the finding of a substantial difference in earnings between the foreign- and native-born Latinos at all time periods. This difference is all the more important because the earnings levels for Asians, both men and women, are quite close to those of whites over these decades. But the same cannot be said of Latinos, of whom even the native-born earned only about

77 to 88 percent as much as whites at the end of the 1990s, depending on level of education.

These figures suggest that the most challenging problems in the extent and pace of incorporation appear to involve the experiences of Latinos. Although there are variations in the degree to which the earnings of different Asian groups match those of whites, the closeness of the results for Asians overall suggests that any likelihood of identifying substantial instances of incorporation problems among Asians is much less than it is among Latinos. Thus we focus our further analysis on Latinos, asking the question: How much of any apparent incorporation difficulties find their locus in the experience of the Mexican-origin population? We begin by separating the Mexican-origin group from the overall Latino group and disaggregate by nativity. The results, shown in table 6.3, indicate that most of the income deficiencies noted above are concentrated among foreign-born Mexican males and females. In 1998, Mexican-born persons earned 60 to 79 percent of their Anglo counterparts' earnings, levels substantially below those of other groups. Although native-born Mexican-origin persons display higher relative earnings, they still fall below Anglos of comparable education. Clearly some of the most challenging incorporation hurdles for U.S. immigrants are those facing Mexican-origin persons.

Earnings by Length of Time in the United States

These results provide a way to understand the effects of nativity on relative immigrant group earnings. Latino immigrants in general and Mexican immigrants in particular suffer substantially lower earnings than other groups. Given that the fraction of Mexican immigrants in the Mexican-origin population grew from 0.23 in 1990 to 0.35 in 2000 (U.S. Bureau of the Census 1992b; U.S. Current Population Survey 2001), wage or earnings comparisons between immigrant groups and natives that failed to take nativity or national origin into account would be seriously misleading. Certainly this would be true for data from the 1980s, as indicated by the National Research Council's estimate that all of the decline then in relative immigrant wages among men and most of the decline among women was due to increases in the numbers of immigrants coming from low-education countries, especially Mexico and Central America (Smith and Edmonston 1997). In part for this reason, considerable attention has been focused on the issue of the growing gap between immigrants and natives in skills, a trend that has sometimes been described using the misleading and

Table 6.2 Average Latino and Asian Earnings by Educational Attainment and Nativity and Gender, 1979 to 1998

Group	Education	Male					Female				
		1979	1989	1998	(1979 to 1989)	(1989 to 1998)	1979	1989	1998	(1979 to 1989)	(1989 to 1998)
Latinos											
Foreign-born	College	50,501	49,270	50,215	-2.4	1.9	25,432	29,106	32,571	14.4	11.9
	High school	31,395	28,352	27,519	-9.7	-2.9	18,391	18,815	16,957	2.3	-9.9
	< High school	23,619	19,860	19,484	-15.9	-1.9	13,274	12,385	11,465	-6.7	-7.4
Native-born	College	46,270	49,854	60,600	7.7	21.6	27,011	34,385	37,116	27.3	7.9
	High school	34,921	34,604	31,666	-0.9	-8.5	18,108	20,102	21,381	11.0	6.4
	< High school	27,333	22,287	20,707	-18.5	-7.1	12,529	13,541	11,961	8.1	-11.7
Asians											
Foreign-born	College	54,356	54,714	58,322	0.7	6.6	29,388	34,549	36,802	17.6	6.5
	High school	30,651	30,490	30,047	-0.5	-1.5	18,730	21,429	21,108	14.4	-1.5
	< High school	24,163	20,814	23,413	-13.9	12.5	14,080	15,178	14,498	7.8	-4.5
Native-born	College	53,619	59,250	59,181	10.5	-0.1	31,239	37,564	39,077	20.2	4.0
	High school	40,057	37,093	35,237	-7.4	-5.0	22,616	25,638	26,119	13.4	1.9
	< High school	34,494	25,896	26,540	-24.9	2.5	19,684	20,731	14,818	5.3	-28.5

Ratios to White

Latinos							
Foreign-born	College	0.84	0.78	0.73	0.97	0.89	0.88
	High school	0.76	0.74	0.72	1.00	0.92	0.78
	< High school	0.70	0.69	0.73	0.89	0.85	0.84
Native-born	College	0.77	0.79	0.88	1.03	1.05	1.00
	High school	0.84	0.91	0.83	0.98	0.99	0.98
	< High school	0.81	0.78	0.77	0.84	0.93	0.87
Asians							
Foreign-born	College	0.91	0.86	0.85	1.12	1.05	0.99
	High school	0.74	0.80	0.79	1.01	1.05	0.97
	< High school	0.72	0.73	0.87	0.94	1.05	1.06
Native-born	College	0.90	0.94	0.86	1.20	1.15	1.05
	High school	0.97	0.97	0.93	1.22	1.26	1.20
	< High school	1.02	0.90	0.99	1.32	1.43	1.08

Sources: U.S. Bureau of the Census (1982, 1992b); Current Population Survey (1996, 1997, 1998, 1999).

Table 6.3 Average Mexican-Origin Earnings by Educational Attainment, Nativity, and Gender, 1979 to 1998

Group	Education	Male					Female				
		1979	1989	1998	(1979 to 1989)	(1989 to 1998)	1979	1989	1998	(1979 to 1989)	(1989 to 1998)
Mexican	College	42,501	44,414	54,755	4.5	23.3	26,044	32,102	32,502	23.3	1.2
	High school	33,830	29,690	29,489	-12.2	-0.7	17,316	19,126	19,206	10.5	0.4
	< High school	24,995	19,740	19,366	-21.0	-1.9	12,456	12,096	11,152	-2.9	-7.8
Foreign-born	College	40,434	35,080	41,387	-13.2	18.0	21,083	25,071	23,917	18.9	-4.6
	High school	30,573	26,188	26,291	-14.3	0.4	17,202	17,291	15,226	0.5	-11.9
	< High school	22,886	18,746	19,044	-18.1	1.6	12,451	11,354	10,833	-8.8	-4.6
Native-born	College	43,126	48,004	61,149	11.3	27.4	27,080	33,717	34,581	24.5	2.6
	High school	34,770	31,015	31,298	-10.8	0.9	17,341	19,621	20,770	13.1	5.9
	< High school	27,178	22,096	20,605	-18.7	-6.7	12,461	13,285	11,930	6.6	-10.2

Ratios to White

Group	Education	Male			Female		
		1979	1989	1998	1979	1989	1998
Mexican	College	0.71	0.70	0.80	1.00	0.98	0.88
	High school	0.82	0.78	0.78	0.94	0.94	0.88
	< High school	0.74	0.69	0.72	0.84	0.83	0.81
Foreign-born	College	0.68	0.55	0.60	0.81	0.76	0.64
	High school	0.74	0.69	0.69	0.93	0.85	0.70
	< High school	0.68	0.65	0.71	0.84	0.78	0.79
Native-born	College	0.72	0.76	0.89	1.04	1.03	0.93
	High school	0.84	0.81	0.82	0.94	0.96	0.95
	< High school	0.81	0.77	0.77	0.84	0.92	0.87

Sources: U.S. Bureau of the Census (1982, 1992b); Current Population Survey (1996, 1997, 1998, 1999).

pejorative phrase "declining immigrant quality" (Borjas 1985). This education gap, substantially documented with data from the 1980s, appears to have increased during the 1990s, even though average immigrant education did *not* decline but in fact increased, rising from 10.2 years of schooling in 1990 to 10.9 years in 2000 (U.S. Current Population Survey 2001). The gap grew because average native non-Hispanic white education levels increased faster, rising from 11.9 years of schooling in 1990 to 13.2 years in 2000. Such changes indicate that nativity differences in skills undoubtedly continue to account for part of the earnings differential between immigrants and non-Hispanic white natives during the 1990s.

Perhaps because the phrase "declining immigrant quality" has captured the imagination of immigration alarmists, changes in relative immigrant skills have often received the lion's share of attention as an explanation of declines in relative immigrant wages and earnings (Ellis 2001). As important as such changes are for explaining nativity gaps in economic well-being, however, other factors are also important. The information on educational level and earnings shown in tables 6.1 to 6.3 demonstrate the importance of nativity and national-origin composition for nativity differences in earnings. However, they also show the importance of changes in wage structure in accounting for relative declines in immigrant earnings. The earnings figures in those tables depict changes *within* racial-ethnic and skill categories, thus controlling roughly for the effects of nativity, race or ethnicity, and education on earnings differences and trends across the period. The figures thus more nearly reflect the influence of shifts in earnings structures per se.

But the earnings patterns of the immigrants may also reflect the influence of varying durations of time spent in the United States. Even if immigrants' earnings "caught up" with natives after they had worked in the country a certain length of time, nativity comparisons would still indicate differences in earnings to the degree that some immigrants were recent arrivals. Hence, the nativity differences shown above could still hide substantial incorporation. What are the results of research on the wage and earnings progress immigrants make the longer they are in the United States? Again, the findings are complex. Early analyses indicated that immigrants started out at lower wages when compared to natives but after twenty or so years caught up and then even surpassed native wage levels (Chiswick 1978, 1977). But because this research relied upon the examination of cross-sectional wage profiles by age, the results were subject to bias because the different age groups being compared varied in national-origin composition. Because the new immigrants were increasingly coming from countries with lower average levels of education, the younger immigrants had lower wages and earnings in part because of this factor rather than because they had not been in the country very long.

The best remedy for this problem would be longitudinal data, so that changes in the earnings of particular individuals could be examined over time. Since such data did not exist during the 1970s, alternative approaches were devised that involved following national-origin and age cohorts over time in order to remove the effects of varying national-origin composition by age. The results of these attempts to control for cross-sectional bias by examining synthetic age cohorts across different census periods tended to show that immigrants' earnings in fact fell considerably short of natives' even after they had been in the country for twenty to thirty years (Borjas 1987a, 1990). Still more recent research has argued that even comparisons involving synthetic age cohorts are subject to bias because they do not control for varying ages at arrival among immigrants. The examination of a given cohort at later periods tends to magnify immigrant-native wage differentials because the later period is more likely to include recent arrivals whose wages are lower. When this factor is taken into account, investigators find that as immigrants' length of time in the country increases, the wage deficit with natives is reduced further, but not eliminated (Myers 1998).

The most recent contribution to this line of research uses longitudinal data obtained by matching Social Security earnings records to cross-sectional panels of the Survey of Income and Program Participation (SIPP) and the Current Population Survey (Lubotsky 2000). Analyses of these data reveal still an additional source of bias in estimates of changes in relative immigrant earnings with length of time spent in the United States. This bias results from selective return migration by persons with low earnings. That is, immigrants with the lowest earnings are the ones most likely to return the soonest to their countries of origin. Taking this into account results in an increase in the nativity earnings gap over time. More specifically, previous analyses of census data generated results that implied that immigrant earnings relative to natives' earnings grew by about 25 percent during their first twenty years in the country. But when allowance is made for the portion of this that is attributable to selective return migration, this figure is cut roughly in half. In short, research on the labor-market experience of immigrants over the past twenty-five years does not provide much convincing evidence that the first generation achieves earnings parity with comparable natives by the end of the immigrants' employment careers. Thus the possibility of more complete incorporation with respect to economic well-being is deferred to the second- or even later-generation members of the immigrant group. And as the evidence above indicated, much of this tendency in the data is attributable to the experience of Mexican immigrants.

Self-Employment

On balance, the results of research on the labor-market incorporation of immigrant groups suggest a decline, if not elimination, of nativity differentials in earnings both with increasing duration of individual time spent in the United States and with rising generational status. Such results reflect the operation of the labor market in terms of its capacity to provide opportunities and rewards for immigrants who find jobs in the areas in which they live. They thus provide an important insight into the labor-market experiences of immigrants. But they do not constitute a complete picture of incorporation processes, because they reveal little about the implications for immigrant incorporation of the business activities initiated by immigrants themselves.

Self-employment can both directly and indirectly positively affect the dynamics of immigrant incorporation (Portes and Zhou 1996; Sanders and Nee 1996). To investigate this issue it is necessary to examine the extent to which entrepreneurship fosters socioeconomic well-being among immigrants. Self-employment is important in two regards. First, self-employment may enhance the economic prospects of self-employed immigrants themselves. Sociologists have gathered a considerable volume of evidence on this issue (Portes and Bach 1985; Sanders and Nee 1987; Zhou and Logan 1989; Bailey and Waldinger 1991; Nee, Sanders, and Sernau 1994), but their inquiries have yielded mixed results. Some studies have found positive effects of self-employment on income (Wilson and Portes 1980; Light 1984; Waldinger 1986; Portes and Zhou 1996), whereas others have found that self-employment is not associated with any benefits aside from the fact that self-employed immigrants often have higher levels of human capital than other immigrants (Bates and Dunham 1992; Bates 1994). Whatever the case, researchers have found that taking immigrant self-employment into account (as all of the studies of immigrant earnings discussed above do *not*) narrows the earnings gap between immigrants and natives even further (Lofstrom and Bean 2002).

Second, the presence in immigrant groups of high-income entrepreneurs may raise the prospects for economic success among other co-ethnic immigrant workers. Because their enterprises are already thriving, successful entrepreneurs are in a better position both to invest more in the ethnic economy and to meet their businesses' rising demand for co-ethnic workers (Bailey and Waldinger 1991). In order to assess how self-employment affects the incomes of co-ethnic immigrant workers, not just those of entrepreneurs themselves, David Spener and Frank D. Bean (1999) examined the extent to which the concentration of Mexican immigrant self-employment in U.S. metropolitan areas influences the earnings of non-self-employed Mexican immigrants. Previous sociological studies had concentrated on highly entrepreneurial immigrant groups such as Koreans (Light and Bonacich 1988), Chinese (Waldinger 1986), and Cubans (Portes and Bach 1985), whose populations were not sufficiently large or geographically dispersed to permit statistical examination of the effects of the concentration of self-employment on economic well-being. The one immigrant group large enough to constitute an exception, Mexican immigrants, had not been the focus of much research attention because the prevalence of self-employment in the Mexican origin population had been so low (Waldinger, McEvoy, and Aldrich 1990). However, recent case studies of Mexican immigrant entrepreneurs, in the context of a growing Mexican-origin population, suggest that both the degree and diversity of types of self-employment in this population have recently increased (Hansen and Cárdenas 1988; Alvarez 1983; Chapa and Cárdenas 1991; Villar 1994; Guarnizo 1995; Spener 1995). As a result, it has become possible to examine the impact of intercity variation in the impact of self-employment on immigrant economic well-being.

Immigrant entrepreneurship is most likely to foster economic gains for the entire immigrant group when it is beneficial for the entrepreneurs themselves. As noted, the results of research on the extent to which entrepreneurship exerts positive or negative effects on immigrant economic well-being have often been equivocal. The reasons are likely to be both theoretical and empirical. The theoretical raison d'être for immigrant entrepreneurship has often been the necessity for self-employment rather than the opportunity offered by such employment. Many analysts note that a major factor leading immigrants to seek self-employment and establish entrepreneurial niches is economic disadvantage, which may be due to lack of resources such as language, skills, and contacts necessary to compete for better employment or to more general labor-market barriers caused by exclusiveness and discrimination in the receiving society (Light 1979; Light and Rosenstein 1995). This view leads to the expectation that immigrant entrepreneurs will earn less than other workers, all else being equal.

Other theoretical formulations see immigrant entrepreneurship in a more optimistic light, emphasizing instead how the social and economic resources entailed in such activities can lead to income advances (Light and Karageorgis 1994). Immigrant enclaves—spatial

zones with high concentrations of ethnic employers, co-ethnic workers, and co-ethnic consumers (Logan, Alba, and McNulty 1994)—provide economic opportunities for both entrepreneurs and their employees, because such enclaves reduce enterprise transaction costs
(assuming hiring, production, and market interactions among co-ethnics proceed more smoothly and involve fewer errors) for all partici-
pants and provide jobs not otherwise available (Portes and Jensen
1989). Similarly, sizable ethnic economies often provide immigrant
and ethnic entrepreneurs opportunities to expand their service or
product markets to nonethnic group members and firms. Larger,
more diverse communities potentially generate greater opportunities
for ethnic entrepreneurs, because they may include businesses that
have broken the barriers of ethnically self-contained enterprises (Waldinger, McEvoy, and Aldrich 1990). Moreover, larger immigrant businesses may be more prevalent in enclaves and broader ethnic economies, and these business may be more likely to enjoy greater access
to capital resources and to generate economic success, thus leading to
the hypothesis that entrepreneurs, at least on average, will earn more
than other workers, all else being equal.

Which of these views provides a more accurate portrayal of the
role of immigrant self-employment in fostering economic advances?
Both are likely to operate to varying degrees in different settings,
which helps to explain the apparently conflicting findings of previous
research about whether entrepreneurship leads to economic gain.
And there is another factor that also influences research findings,
namely the mediating effects of the size of the ethnic group on self-
employment outcomes. Drawing on the tenets of organizational ecology (Freeman and Hannan 1983; Hawley 1984), M. D. R. Evans (1989)
has hypothesized that "the larger the immigrant group, the more favorable the [economic opportunity] for ethnic entrepreneurs since
their potential market is larger" (951). Taking this idea further, Spener
and Bean (1999) theorized that the relative size of the ethnic group
may also affect the kind of entrepreneurship opportunities available.
Ethnic-group size affects entrepreneurial outcomes because the wider
benefits of opportunity-induced entrepreneurship are more likely to
be greater when ethnic groups are relatively larger because such entrepreneurship is likely to be more capitalized and thus resource-
based. This means that on the one hand, disadvantage-caused self-
employment is likely to be relatively more prevalent in areas with
relatively smaller ethnic groups. On the other hand, more substantial
resource-based self-employment should be relatively more prevalent
in areas with relatively larger ethnic groups, ethnic enclaves, and ethnic economies. To the extent that this is the case, small-market entre-

preneurship is more likely to be associated with below-average earnings and large-market entrepreneurship with above-average earnings.

Testing these ideas in the Mexican immigrant case, Spener and Bean (1999) find that the concentration of Mexican self-employment across all metropolitan areas, regardless of city size, is negatively related to Mexican immigrant economic well-being, undoubtedly because Mexican self-employment does not generate enough special employment opportunities in the ethnic community overall to offset the effects of disadvantage-based self-employment. They also find, however, that in relatively larger Mexican-origin markets, Mexican entrepreneurship creates special job opportunities for co-ethnic workers that are not available to non-Mexicans. Given these dynamics, and excluding other factors, higher concentrations of Mexican immigrant self-employment lead to lower immigrant unemployment rates, which in turn boost wages not only for Mexican immigrants but also for other workers. Mexican immigrant-worker earnings are thus higher in cities where immigrant self-employment rates are higher and where the relative size of the ethnic group is larger. Thus, increasing levels of self-employment act to increase the pace of economic incorporation among Mexican immigrants.

Generational Differences

Up to this point, this chapter has focused on investigating trends in earnings among immigrant groups and on surveying the findings of research about the extent to which immigrant earnings improve the longer the immigrants reside in the country. We have learned that the greatest incorporation challenge confronting U.S. immigration policy involves the Mexican-origin immigrant group. In saying this we do not intend to ignore the arduous incorporation experiences of other immigrant groups, especially Dominicans, West Indians, Puerto Ricans, Salvadorans, Filipinos, and others. However, the sizes of these groups pale in comparison to the Mexican-origin group, either individually or collectively. Moreover, the Mexican-origin population is now becoming widely dispersed throughout the country, whereas these other groups tend to be concentrated in specific locales, many in New York City. Thus, the *major*, though not only, incorporation challenge the United States faces involves that of Mexican immigrants and their descendants.

Much of the challenge facing Mexican immigrants results from their low education levels—the declines in real earnings for low-skilled workers in the United States over time—and the fact that the Mexican immigrant group is so large. We have also found that the

economic standing of native-born Mexican-origin persons is appreciably higher than that of those born in Mexico. Even beyond this, native-born Mexican-origin persons themselves are not homogeneous,
particularly in regard to the length of time their ancestral families
have lived in the United States. An important question thus concerns
whether Mexican-origin natives whose families have resided here
longer have achieved greater economic well-being in comparison to
those whose families have arrived more recently. If the answer to this
question is yes—if we find that such persons are reasonably close to
achieving economic parity with non-Hispanic whites—it would imply a more positive prognosis about the likelihood of successful economic incorporation of newer Mexican immigrants than the evidence
so far appears to indicate.

To assess the degree to which Mexican origin persons who have
been in the United States longer have become more fully integrated
into the economic mainstream, we focus on patterns of intergenerational progress, comparing data on labor-market outcomes among Latino immigrants, their U.S.-born children, and their later descendants.
To differentiate the three groups, we use information about respondents' and also their parents' place of birth from the Current Population Survey data pooled for the years 1996, 1997, 1998, and 1999. Because the intergenerational comparisons utilize data from a single
time period (1996 to 1999), they cannot link actual immigrant parents
who entered the country quite some time ago with their actual U.S.-
born children who entered the labor market a couple of decades later.
An alternative approach would be to use data from successive time
periods and compare immigrant adults in some initial period with
their grown-up descendants twenty or more years later. Each approach has advantages and disadvantages. One benefit of the approach here is that using data from a single time period holds constant the social and economic environment, whereas the alternative
approach can give misleading results because economic conditions
change over time. For example, the civil rights movement may have
generated economic gains for *all* generations of Mexican-origin persons in the 1970s and 1980s. If so, then the improvements in education and earnings observed between Mexican immigrants in the 1960s
and their U.S.-born children in the 1990s would overstate the amount
of progress that is solely due to being a second-generation Mexican-
origin person who grew up in the United States rather than a Mexican-born person who grew up in Mexico.

Mexican-origin persons are the dominant subgroup of Latinos in
the United States, being over 60 percent of the Latino population. We
define the first generation as persons born in Mexico, the second as

Table 6.4   Generational Distribution of Persons of Mexican Origin, Ages Fifteen and Above (Percentage), 1996 to 1998

Recent immigrant[a]	21.2
Earlier immigrant	27.9
Second generation	22.4
Third or later generation	28.6
Total	100.0%
Sample size	33,072

Sources: Current Population Survey (1996 to 1998).
[a]Recent immigrants are defined as those who arrived in the United States within approximately ten years of the survey date.

Mexican-origin persons with at least one Mexican-born parent, and the third or later generations as Mexican origin-persons with two native-born parents. In many of our analyses, we split the first generation into "recent immigrants," those who have been in the United States for ten years or less, and "earlier immigrants," those who have spent more than ten years here. The overwhelming majority of Mexican-origin persons have been in this country for two generations or less (table 6.4). In particular, about half of Mexican-origin persons are foreign-born and slightly more than another fifth have at least one immigrant parent. By contrast, only 13 percent of Anglos and 9 percent of blacks were first or second generation in 1999 (Bean et al. 2001).

We focus first on educational attainment, which is a key determinant of how workers fare in the U.S. labor market. For both men and women, Mexican-origin persons average about three years less schooling than whites and two years less schooling than blacks; Mexican origin-men average 9.9 years of schooling, Mexican-origin women, 10.0; and immigrants, even fewer (see table 6.5). The educational disadvantage of Mexican immigrants is statistically driven by a disproportionate number of individuals without any secondary schooling. Fully half of Mexican-born persons have completed eight or fewer years of education. Moreover, more than 10 percent of native-born Mexican-origin persons are in this same category, whereas less than 5 percent of whites and blacks are. But an enormous educational improvement takes place between the first and the second generation: the second generation has on average about three and a half years more schooling than immigrants. Thus, a majority of the overall Mexican-origin educational disadvantage is due to the presence of large numbers of Mexican immigrants with very low education levels. Although the U.S.-born children of Mexican immigrants close most of the education gap, average schooling levels of all U.S.-born Mexican origin persons still trail those of whites by about a year and a half, mostly because U.S.-born Mexican-origin persons are about a third as likely to earn a bachelor's degree as Anglos and about five to six times more likely not to complete high school. One positive sign is that the average schooling of Mexicans rises somewhat between the second and third generations; this improvement is attributable largely to a substantial reduction in the fraction of individuals completing fewer than nine years of education.

We gain a better sense of how schooling levels have changed over time for U.S.-born Hispanics, including Mexicans, by comparing different age cohorts. Among men, the youngest cohort of U.S.-born Mexicans has on average over two years more schooling than the oldest cohort (table 6.6). This pattern suggests that substantial educational gains were made by U.S.-born Mexican-origin men over the thirty years that separate these cohorts. Moreover, the fact that these gains are much larger than those observed for non-Hispanic whites indicates that over this period Mexican-origin persons managed to erase a substantial portion of their educational deficit relative to whites. The progress for Mexican-origin men has primarily taken the form of a large reduction in the high school dropout rate, with relatively little improvement in college completion. For the most part, similar patterns emerge for women. In fact, educational progress has been even stronger for Mexican origin women than it has been for men. The sizable schooling deficit of women relative to men observed in the oldest cohort steadily shrinks across cohorts until it becomes a slight female advantage in the youngest cohort, and Mexican-origin women show much more improvement between the oldest and youngest age cohorts in the rate of college completion.

How do labor-market outcomes for Mexican-origin persons and blacks compare with those for whites, when we do not distinguish by generation? To answer this question we analyze important labor-market outcomes such as hourly wages, employment rates, and annual hours of work. Our results are derived from regression analyses that standardize for differences in age and geographic location within the United States and include only individuals who worked during the calendar year preceding the survey. On average, Mexican-origin men's hourly wages are 39.5 percent lower than those of non-Hispanic white men—a gap wider than the 25.9 percent wage gap of black men (table 6.7). Wage patterns are similar for women, although the magnitudes of the minority-white wage gaps are smaller among women than men.

(Text continues on p. 138.)

Table 6.5 Educational Attainment by Generation Among Mexican-Origin Persons, Ages Twenty-Five to Sixty-Four

	Men						
	Mexicans					Third + Generation Whites	Third + Generation Blacks
	Recent Immigrant	Earlier Immigrant	Second Generation	Third + Generation			
Average years of education	8.5	8.3	11.9	12.1		13.5	12.4
Percentage							
Zero to eight years	48.3	49.6	11.4	8.1		2.5	4.6
Nine to eleven years	14.8	15.1	12.3	13.9		6.4	13.3
Twelve years	24.9	22.0	35.8	40.3		34.6	43.1
Some college	7.4	9.1	28.5	25.8		26.5	26.0
Bachelor's degree and above	4.7	4.2	12.0	11.9		30.0	12.9
Total	100.0%	100.0%	100.0%	100.0%		100.0%	100.0%

Women

	Mexicans				Third + Generation Whites	Third + Generation Blacks
	Recent Immigrant	Earlier Immigrant	Second Generation	Third + Generation		
Average years of education	8.3	8.3	11.6	11.9	13.4	12.7
Percentage						
Zero to eight years	49.8	50.5	14.9	9.4	1.8	3.0
Nine to eleven years	16.5	14.7	13.4	14.8	5.8	12.9
Twelve years	21.1	21.2	34.2	37.6	36.6	38.9
Some college	7.8	10.0	25.7	27.4	28.7	29.7
Bachelor's degree and above	4.8	3.7	11.8	10.7	27.1	15.6
Total	100.0%	100.0%	100.0%	100.0%	100.0%	100.0%

Sources: Current Population Survey (1996 to 1998).

Table 6.6 Educational Attainment by Generation and Age

| | Men | | | | | |
| | All Hispanics | | Mexicans | | Third + Generation Whites | Third + Generation Blacks |
	Second Generation	Third + Generation	Second Generation	Third + Generation		
Average years of education						
Ages 25 to 34	12.7	12.5	12.5	12.4	13.5	12.6
Ages 35 to 44	12.2	12.4	11.9	12.3	13.5	12.5
Ages 45 to 54	12.2	12.2	11.9	12.1	13.8	12.5
Ages 55 to 64	11.1	10.8	10.5	10.4	13.0	11.2
High school dropout (percentage)						
Ages 25 to 34	16.3	17.6	17.9	18.6	7.3	11.3
Ages 35 to 44	21.9	16.3	22.2	18.0	7.7	15.3
Ages 45 to 54	23.9	22.4	25.7	24.9	8.1	19.8
Ages 55 to 64	34.9	41.6	40.1	45.5	15.2	37.1
College graduate (percentage)						
Ages 25 to 34	17.9	13.0	13.4	11.4	30.0	11.8
Ages 35 to 44	12.9	11.6	10.7	9.6	28.4	13.0
Ages 45 to 54	15.4	17.5	12.6	16.8	34.1	15.7
Ages 55 to 64	14.1	12.6	9.9	11.4	26.6	10.9

Women

	All Hispanics		Mexicans		Third + Generation Whites	Third + Generation Blacks
	Second Generation	Third + Generation	Second Generation	Third + Generation		
Average years of education						
Ages 25 to 34	12.8	12.6	12.6	12.6	13.7	12.8
Ages 35 to 44	12.2	12.3	11.7	12.2	13.6	12.9
Ages 45 to 54	11.7	11.8	11.3	11.4	13.5	12.7
Ages 55 to 64	9.8	10.5	9.2	10.0	12.7	11.9
High school dropout (percentage)						
Ages 25 to 34	14.6	16.8	16.6	17.5	5.8	11.9
Ages 35 to 44	23.0	18.1	28.5	19.6	5.8	11.6
Ages 45 to 54	26.6	27.5	29.8	31.4	7.3	17.3
Ages 55 to 64	49.0	43.0	53.9	50.0	14.8	32.1
College graduate (percentage)						
Ages 25 to 34	17.5	14.1	14.5	13.4	31.7	14.7
Ages 35 to 44	15.2	11.3	12.5	9.9	28.1	16.4
Ages 45 to 54	14.2	11.7	11.9	9.3	27.2	17.4
Ages 55 to 64	7.5	8.1	3.9	6.8	17.5	12.8

Sources: Current Population Survey (1996 to 1998).

Table 6.7   Labor-Market Outcomes by Ethnicity, Ages Twenty-Five to Sixty-Four

	Differential Relative to Whites			
	Hourly Wage (Percentage Differential)	Employment Rate	Annual Hours of Work	Self-Employment Rate
Men				
Blacks	− 25.9	− 12.2	− 222	− 8.0
All Hispanics	− 36.4	− 3.9	− 169	− 7.3
Mexicans	− 39.5	− 2.5	− 188	− 8.5
Women				
Blacks	− 14.0	− 3.0	19	− 5.2
All Hispanics	− 28.5	− 14.3	− 54	− 4.8
Mexicans	− 32.7	− 16.4	− 93	− 5.8

Sources: Current Population Survey (1996 to 1998).
Note: These comparisons control for age and geographic location. The calculations of hourly wages, annual hours of work, and self-employment rates are for samples that include only individuals who worked during the calendar year preceding the survey.

The share of Mexican-origin men who worked during the calendar year preceding the survey is 2.5 percentage points below the 91 percent employment rate of Anglo men. By contrast, black men are 12.2 percentage points less likely to be employed than white men. Employed white men average 2,226 hours of work per year, and Mexican-origin men annually work about 188 fewer hours than this. The employment rate of non-Hispanic white women is 78 percent; the corresponding rate for black women is just 3 percentage points lower; but the rate for Mexican-origin women is 16.4 percentage points lower. Thus the latter are significantly less likely to be employed than white or black women. Employed white women average 1,789 hours of work annually. Black women work slightly more hours than this, whereas Mexican women work somewhat fewer hours. Finally, among non-Hispanic whites the self-employment rate is 15 percent for men and 9 percent for women. For both men and women, Mexican-origin self-employment rates are less than the black rates and less than half the corresponding white rate.

To obtain results broken down by generation, we present in the first column of table 6.8 hourly wage differentials between the generation group and third-generation whites, when persons from all education levels are included. The next four columns report outcome differentials for persons in selected education categories: nine to eleven years of schooling, exactly twelve years of schooling, some college but no bachelor's degree, and a bachelor's degree but no postgraduate or professional degrees. By comparing the differentials among all

Table 6.8   Hourly Wage Differentials by Ethnicity and Generation, Ages Twenty-Five to Sixty-Four

	All Workers	Nine to Eleven Years	Twelve Years	Some College	Bachelor's Degree
		Percentage Differential, Relative to Third- and Later-Generation Whites			
		Selected Education Groups			
Men					
Third + generation blacks	−25.5	−16.4	−19.3	−17.1	−18.9
Mexicans					
Recent immigrant	−51.6	−27.2	−39.4	−33.4	−49.8
Earlier immigrant	−44.7	−15.3	−22.3	−27.5	−35.5
Second generation	−24.5	−14.6	−12.7	−13.0	−10.5
Third + generation	−26.1	−16.6	−15.2	−13.2	−11.9
Women					
Third + generation blacks	−13.7	−8.6	−9.2	−6.3	−6.5
Mexicans					
Recent immigrant	−51.1	−23.0	−34.1	−30.9	−34.8
Earlier immigrant	−43.8	−18.0	−19.6	−25.2	−25.2
Second generation	−20.4	−2.7	−11.8	−9.6	3.0
Third + generation	−20.0	−11.3	−9.9	−8.5	0.8

Sources: Current Population Survey (1996 to 1998).
Note: These comparisons control for age and geographic location. The sample includes only individuals who worked during the calendar year preceding the survey.

persons with the differentials for specific education groups, we can assess the role that education plays in maintaining the observed outcome differences between Latinos and whites. For example, suppose that within each education category average wages were the same for Latinos and whites, even though Latinos earn substantially less than whites when we compare workers from all education categories combined. This would indicate that the overall Latino wage disadvantage is entirely due to Latinos' having less education than whites. Conversely, if the wage deficits within education categories were similar to the overall wage deficit, this would indicate that education differences between Latinos and whites contribute little to the overall wage deficit.

Mexican-origin workers display marked wage growth between the first and second generations. For both men and women, U.S.-born Mexicans' wages are about 25 percent higher than those of recent Mexican immigrants and about 20 percent higher than those of earlier immigrants. Note that wage differences between foreign-born and U.S.-born Mexicans are generally much smaller within particular education categories than for workers from all education categories combined. For example, among men, the overall wage growth of 20 percent observed between earlier immigrants and the second generation shrinks to just 10 percent when we restrict the comparison to those with exactly twelve years of schooling, indicating that much of the wage progress across generations for Mexican-origin persons is driven by the intergenerational improvements in schooling already discussed. Intergenerational progress appears to stall after the second generation, however, as no further wage growth is evident between the second and third generations.

Within education categories, wage gaps relative to whites for U.S.-born Mexican-origin men generally are smaller than the corresponding wage gaps for black men. In particular, among the education categories representing men with at least twelve years of schooling, wage gaps for second- and third-generation Mexican-origin men range from 10 to 15 percent, whereas the analogous wage gaps for blacks range from 17 to 19 percent. Moreover, controlling for education leads to a bigger reduction in the wage gap for U.S.-born Mexican-origin men than it does for black men. These results highlight the prominent role that educational improvements can play in raising the economic status of Mexican Americans. Among women, minority-white wage gaps within education categories are relatively small for both blacks and U.S.-born Mexican-origin persons. As we saw for men, controlling for education dramatically shrinks the wage disadvantage of second- and third-generation Mexican-origin women. Women who possess a college degree do particularly well, with U.S.-born Mexican origin women of this group achieving wage parity with Anglo women.

Summary and Conclusions

The results presented here document the improvement in wages and earnings among the new immigrants the longer they reside in the country. Asian Americans have achieved substantially the same earnings levels as comparable native-born whites, but Latinos lag behind, in substantial measure because lower earnings in the Mexican-origin population "drag down" statistics for Latinos in general. Moreover, the data sources that constitute the basis on which such comparisons are made contain significant proportions of unauthorized Mexicans, which is a major contributing factor to the low earnings levels of the Mexican-born. Were it not for the presence of persons in the data whose migration status consigns them to lesser-paying jobs, the statistics for Latinos in general and Mexican-born persons in particular would look more favorable. But even native-born Mexican-origin men of high education do not achieve full earnings parity with non-Hispanic white males, suggesting that economic incorporation among Mexican-origin persons, while substantial, is nonetheless still incomplete. Taking self-employment into account, however, improves slightly the overall assessment because Mexican immigrant self-employment leads not only to higher earnings among the self-employed but also among the non-self-employed, at least in locales with substantial concentrations of Mexican-origin persons. By the third or later generations, the earnings picture suggests even further progress, particularly among college-educated women, whose earnings levels slightly exceed those of comparable non-Hispanic whites, even though college-educated males of Mexican origin still lag behind somewhat.

The fact that immigrants themselves (as opposed to the native-born later-generation members of immigrant groups) make earnings progress the longer they are here but do not achieve parity with natives implies that structural mechanisms may be at work limiting their mobility. Included among these are structures of labor-market segmentation and mechanisms of immigrant labor recruitment (Sassen 1995). Immigrants are drawn to areas containing other immigrants because their previous contacts with such persons, often through family relationships, become crucial factors in labor recruitment into low-wage work. The attraction of low-wage work is the availability of the jobs themselves, not comparisons of the wages of those jobs with wages paid in other jobs, at least in the country of destination. Such recruitment is replicated many times over, leading to cumulative causation in the tendency of immigrants of a certain national origin to become predominant in certain industries in certain locales, thus creating a tendency toward ethnic closure in those industries, and reinforcing segmentation in the labor market. Over time, some immigrants find pathways to partial upward earnings mobility, as research documenting the upward life course trajectory of immigrant earnings indicates. And the research evidence suggests this process is abetted by immigrant entrepreneurship in areas containing the greatest concentration of co-ethnics. But the fact that this trajectory is not steep enough to eventually lead to full earnings parity with comparable natives provides a telling clue that labor-market segmentation involving the partition of employment possibilities into better and worse jobs—with the latter being viewed by employers as the appropriate preserve for immigrants—continues to operate as a structural barrier that dampens first generation earnings, especially among Mexican-origin persons, many of whom are unauthorized. This further reinforces the idea introduced earlier in chapter 5 that a four- or five-generation model of immigrant incorporation provides an appropriate standard against which to gauge the "success" of immigrant group incorporation in the case of Mexicans. Applying such a model, we find in this chapter that Mexican immigrants have moved far enough along the path of economic incorporation for us to think that they will experience some degree of participation in the economic mainstream, as other immigrant groups have.

= Chapter 7 =

Linguistic Incorporation Among Immigrants

THE SOCIAL and cultural integration of immigrants and their children into American society is a critical issue for the immigrants, national descent groups, and American society. Theories concerning the social and cultural integration of national-origin groups in American society have largely focused on the language characteristics of immigrants as measures of the incompleteness of integration into a society firmly dominated by the English language and by English speakers. Speaking a non-English language has been assumed to attest to an attachment to a culturally defined group, and English skills have been viewed as a prerequisite for socioeconomic mobility. As noted in chapter 5, theories of incorporation, including both assimilation and cultural pluralism, often acknowledge the general possibility that convergence between minority and majority groups may result from changes in the attributes of both populations. In the case of language, however, processes of adaptation in the United States have tended, at least up to now, to be mostly one-sided; the dynamics of incorporation have been presumed to occur primarily within the minority-language group.

Unlike other major immigrant-receiving countries such as Canada or Great Britain, the United States has never made the language characteristics of prospective immigrants an explicit part of legislation regulating the flow of migration into the country. (One exception is the 1986 Immigration Reform and Control Act, which provided an opportunity for undocumented aliens to gain legal status if they met certain conditions, such as demonstration of English literacy [Terdy and Spener 1990].) Instead, immigration policy has shaped the language characteristics of entering immigrants implicitly by affecting the numbers of immigrants from national populations typified by specific language repertoires, that is, by fluency in specific non-English

143

languages and possession of lower or higher skills in English. Changes in the national origins of immigrants over the course of the last century thus have been accompanied by changes in the language repertoires of new immigrants, of the resident foreign-born population, and of their children. The significant shifts in the sources of immigration flows over the last third of the twentieth century are therefore in the process of shifting the linguistic characteristics of the foreign-born population, their immediate descendants, and the nation as a whole.

The dynamics of linguistic adaptation are complex, especially in a context in which the linguistic characteristics of the newest entrants and of the larger society are changing. At the minimum, linguistic adaptation involves changes in the numbers of immigrants entering with certain language repertoires, processes of English acquisition largely occurring within the foreign-born generation, and processes of language shift toward English (or minority-language loss) occurring within and between generations. Moreover, the processes of English acquisition and minority-language shift are intertwined, although they need not occur simultaneously.

Because immigrants' language repertoires correspond to their national origin and race—though only roughly—processes of language adaptation are part and parcel of processes of cultural assimilation and discrimination. Processes of English acquisition are also strongly implicated in labor force–related attainments. Nevertheless, it is worthwhile to consider processes of language adaptation apart from processes of cultural assimilation and social mobility. Discontinuities in the ability to speak a given language or dialect have the strong potential to divide communities, while a shared facility in a given language has the strong potential to unite. The Asian national-origin groups are strongly divided by language, whereas the Central and South American national-origin groups are not. The implications of these language differences in the formation of racially defined groups in the United States are still unknown. Unlike other cultural attributes, the ability to discard, maintain, or acquire a language is not entirely under individuals' control (Stromswold 2001). Acquiring a new language or maintaining a language first learned in childhood also requires individuals to have high levels of motivation as well as access to opportunities and resources to learn or continue to use the language, some of which must be available in or provided by the surrounding community.

Finally, there is the issue of one-sidedness in the linguistic adaptation of immigrant groups in the United States. The image of America as a monolingual English-speaking nation has reigned for at least a century. Still, the country does not have a federal language policy favoring the English language (or any set of languages) over others, and there have been periods of time when non-English languages have been tolerated and even encouraged (Kloss 1977). The Bilingual Education Act, passed in 1968 and reauthorized in 1994, and the Amendments to the Voting Rights Act, passed in 1975 and reauthorized in 1992, both sought to preserve the rights of minority-language speakers. Thus, American society is accommodating minority-language populations to some extent, although the nature and extent of the accommodations are a major source of contention. Many argue, for example, that the accommodations are far from sufficient in the efforts to socially and politically integrate minority-language populations into American society while others maintain that accommodation may retard the integration of minority-language populations by removing incentives to learn English.

This chapter first discusses how various theories of incorporation have treated the linguistic attributes of immigrants and immigrant groups. It then turns to a discussion of changes in the national origins of immigrants over time and the language characteristics of newly entering immigrants, the resident foreign-born population and their children, and the entire American population. Next, it provides an overview of processes of English-language acquisition and minority-language shift among immigrants. The chapter concludes with a discussion of how the contexts in which these processes occur may be changing.

Language Characteristics in Theories of Incorporation

The ethos underlying the post–World War II reforms in immigration policy and law, which moved immigration policy away from exclusionary and race-specific terms toward cultural and national pluralism, had its roots in the early twentieth century. For example, in an article titled "Democracy Versus the Melting Pot," Horace Kallen argued in 1924 that nationality groups in America should not be robbed of their cultural identities and coercively Americanized. He famously described America as an "orchestra" in which "every type of instrument has its specific timbre and tonality . . . as every type has its appropriate theme and melody, and the harmony and dissonances and discords of them all make the symphony of civilization" (Kallen 1988 [1924]).

In spite of Kallen's vivid aural analogy, not even those holding the most positive attitudes toward immigrants during that time period—

the "Americanizers"—entertained the prospect that immigrants should be encouraged to maintain their own language or that the United States should be host to a chorus of languages. The leaders of the Americanization movement in the 1910s hoped to mold foreigners into good Americans by teaching them civics, English, and the values of American society (Dixon 1916). It was a movement of "structured experiences" (Knobel 1996) in which social institutions such as settlement houses, schools, and the YMCA offered numerous evening programs aimed at "Americanizing" foreigners. In practice, however, the main focus of these programs was the teaching of English, which was considered to be the "first step" in the assimilation of the immigrant (Drachsler 1920; Hartmann 1967, 24).

Meanwhile, in the first quarter of the twentieth century, the linkages between race, nationality, and language were hardening. For example, in 1910 the U.S. Bureau of the Census attached a "mother-tongue" question to the census schedule that was to be used as an "index of racial character and origin" (U.S. Bureau of the Census 1913). In 1910 and 1920, coding instructions for the information gathered in answer to the "mother-tongue" question assigned the mother tongue of immigrant parents to their native-born American offspring, thereby revealing the presumption that mother tongue was an inherited rather than learned characteristic. In 1933, tabulations of the mother tongues of the U.S. population excluded members of racially defined groups such as Mexicans or Japanese. The rationale was that the information would be redundant, since "most persons of each of the other races speak one characteristic language" (U.S. Bureau of the Census 1933).

The inferred correspondence between language and nationality or race became incorporated into the theories and frameworks about the integration and incorporation of immigrant groups. Major theorists of assimilation such as Gordon wrote in an era in which relatively few immigrants and few Americans of European descent were unable to speak English. In the 1950s and 1960s, the major issues confronting the nation concerned the final steps in the social and political integration of European-descent groups, who were by then largely fluent in English, as "white Americans." The significant numbers of immigrants and native-born Americans who were fluent in another language, notably Mexicans and Mexican Americans, were still being viewed through the lens of race, nationality, or citizenship. Language characteristics were not the salient identifying feature. Instead, differences in languages were overshadowed by differences of race or nationality.

Theoretical frameworks of assimilation have thus largely assumed the language characteristics of new immigrants and their immediate descendants either as secondary cultural attributes and thus involved in early processes of acculturation, as reflecting participation in social networks and thus measuring processes of structural assimilation, or as an aspect of human capital and thus involved in economic and occupational mobility. Scholars have argued, for example, that mastery of a non-English language and extent of usage be used as indexes of "acculturation" (see, for example, Samora and Deane 1956). In this view, languages, particularly those learned as "mother tongues" in early childhood, carry the ethos of culture. Mother tongues provide the means to access a culture's literature, art, and history. (At its most romanticized, this perspective argues that a person's cultural and national affiliations are forever anchored to his or her mother tongue [Coulmas 1997].) Continued usage of the mother tongue therefore betrays a tight identification with the culture and sense of peoplehood embodied in the language. Conversely, shifting to use of English implies a loosening of the ties of membership and identification with the immigrant's national origins. In addition, because the English language is seen to be the standard-bearer of ideals of liberty and democracy, learning English conveys "an understanding of American industrial standards and an American point of view" (Kellor 1916).

Because languages are also means of communication among people, patterns of language use follow patterns of social interaction within and across culturally defined groups. Continued usage of a minority language, particularly in a setting dominated by another language, therefore conveys continued interaction with others sharing facility in the minority language and thus continued participation in the delimited community of people involved in the negotiation of that culture (Hammel 1990). Patterns of language use are thus integrally bound to social relationships within and across socially and culturally defined boundaries. Decreased use of a minority language is thus associated with a retreat from the community and its culture and perhaps movement toward another. Language shift toward English is thus associated with subprocesses of primary and secondary assimilation such as migration across state boundaries (Kritz and Nogle 1994), movement into suburbs (Alba, Logan, and Crowder 1997), and intermarriage (Stevens and Schoen 1988; Stevens and Swicegood 1987).

Language characteristics of immigrants are also implicated in theoretical frameworks that emphasize proficiency in English as a necessary resource in the pursuit of educational and labor force attainments. The relationship between skills in English and occupational attainments was anticipated and advertised early in the century. For example, in 1915 in the city of Syracuse, forty thousand handbills, printed in five languages (English, Polish, Italian, Yiddish, and German), read: "Can you speak well? Do you want to be an American citizen? It is hard to get a job in America without English. Go to night school and learn it!" (Dixon 1916, 23). Recent research of contemporary immigrants shows that their skills in English and levels of literacy in English are consistently strong predictors of occupational status and earnings (Chiswick 1991; Dávila and Mora 2001; Stolzenberg 1990). Moreover, this relationship may have strengthened during the 1980s (Mora 1998; Mora and Dávila 2000). Immigrants' skills in English are also strongly related to their levels of schooling (Warren 1994; White and Kaufman 1997), especially among those entering the United States during childhood or young adulthood. High levels of proficiency in English are thus viewed as a prerequisite for participating in the many social settings and institutions that most often presume an easy familiarity with the nation's dominant language.

The theoretical frameworks considering language characteristics of immigrants as an index of acculturation, participation in social networks, or a potential resource in occupational and related attainments have, however, been less successful in understanding how languages are implicated in the identity of the nation and what it means to be "American." It is incontrovertible, however, that the linguistic demography of the nation is being changed by immigration. We therefore turn to a discussion of changes in the language characteristics of immigrants over the last portion of the century and the ways these changes are altering the language characteristics of the nation as a whole.

Languages in the United States, 1980 to 2000

The U.S. Census Bureau has gathered information on the language characteristics of the American population for over a hundred years. Although the questions and subpopulations vary across census years, making it impossible to describe the changes in the language characteristics of the American population over the course of the entire century (see Stevens 1999 for details), the questions asked in the last three censuses were the same. Table 7.1 shows the languages (in major groupings) spoken by Americans aged five and over from 1980 to 2000. The table is based on data from the 1980, 1990, and 2000 U.S. censuses and, for the percentage of minority-language speakers in 2000 who are foreign-born, the supplementary survey to the 2000 census. All of the figures refer to people aged five years or more who reported speaking a non-English language at home in the census year.

Table 7.1   Numbers (In Thousands) and Percentages of Americans Speaking English Only or a Non-English Language at Home, 1980 to 2000

Language Spoken at Home	1980[a]	1990[a]	2000[a]
Total	210,248	230,446	262,375
	100.00%	100.00%	100.00%
English only	187,187	198,601	215,423
	89.03%	86.18%	82.11%
A non-English language (NEL)	23,060	31,845	46,951
	10.97%	13.82%	17.89%
Spanish	11,116	17,345	28,101
	5.29%	7.53%	10.71%
Other Indo-European language	7,941	8,790	10,018
	3.78%	3.81%	3.82%
Asian or Pacific Island language	2,231	4,472	6,960
	1.06%	1.94%	2.65%
Other language	1,772[b]	1,238	1,872
	0.84%	0.54%	.71%
Percentage NEL speakers who are foreign-born	42.19	48.45	55.3[c]

[a]1980 and 1990 figures are from the 1980 and 1990 U.S. censuses, as reported by Gibson and Lennon (1999). Unless otherwise noted, the figures for the year 2000 are from the 2000 U.S. census (U.S. Bureau of the Census 2002b).
[b]Includes some Indo-European languages.
[c]Percentage estimated from the Census 2000 Supplementary Survey (U.S. Bureau of the Census 2002a).

Because the question (and subsequent coding procedures) allowed only one language as a response, those who speak more than one non-English language at home are identified only by the first language they chose to report. Because the census schedules did not include questions asking about proficiency in the non-English language, it is unknown whether persons reporting that they spoke a non-English language are fully fluent in that language, a consideration that is probably more important for native-born than for foreign-born minority-language speakers. The figures also omit people who spoke a non-English language earlier in their lives but had shifted from usage of their non-English language to English by the time of the census, and people who speak a non-English language at the time of the census but did not use it at home.

Within a span of just twenty years, the absolute number of non-English language speakers more than doubled, from 23 million to 47 million with much of that increase being accounted for by increases in the numbers of people speaking Spanish or an Asian or Pacific Island language. The percentage of Americans speaking only English at home dropped from 89 percent to 82 percent and the percentages of Americans speaking Spanish or an Asian or Pacific Island language increased from 5.3 percent to 10.7 percent and from 1 percent to almost 4 percent, respectively.

In 1980, the majority (58 percent) of minority-language speakers were native-born. With the exceptions of the speakers of the indigenous North American languages and of Spanish speakers in the Southwest, the native-born portion of the non-English-language population in the United States consisted primarily of the U.S.-born children (and some grandchildren) of immigrants. This is because the high rates of language shift between generations over the course of the twentieth century quickly subtracted from the pool of speakers of languages other than English among later-generation Americans (Lieberson and Curry 1971; Stevens 1985). The inroads in the relative size of the native-born versus foreign-born minority-language population produced by high rates of intergenerational language shift were, however, counterbalanced by the virtual cessation of immigration of non-English speakers in the middle of the century. The return of high levels of immigration after the 1960s began to shift the nativity composition of the non-English-language-speaking population toward the foreign-born. By 1990, almost half (48 percent) of the minority-language speakers were foreign-born and the supplementary survey to the 2000 census suggests that in 2000, a small majority (55 percent) of non-English speakers were foreign-born. The shift would be even more pronounced but for the new second generation, which is native-born and also increasing in size. Many of the children of immigrants learn their parents' non-English language. As a result, although the relative percentage of native-born minority-language speakers dropped during the last portion of the twentieth century, the absolute number of native-born minority-language speakers grew between 1980 and 2000, from about 13 million in 1980 to over 20 million in 2000.

The nativity-specific numbers of non-English languages spoken by non-English-language American residents, largely immigrants and their children, is a lagged reflection of the timing and age distribution of major immigration streams over the last century. The increases in levels of immigration over the course of the last twenty years, and the consequent increases in the proportion of the total population that is foreign-born, are thus quickly changing the overall linguistic composition of the U.S. population as well as the nativity-specific composition of the minority-language population.

Non-English Languages
Spoken by Immigrants

The shifts in the national origins of immigrants entering the country over the last quarter of the twentieth century has dramatically changed the array of non-English languages spoken within the United States. Table 7.2 shows the distribution of non-English languages spoken by immigrants in the United States in 1980, 1990, and 2000 and the ratio of the number of speakers of each language in 2000 to the number in 1980. The changes between 1980 and 2000 in the absolute numbers of speakers of specific non-English languages clearly reflect the increases and decreases in levels of immigration from some countries during the 1980s and 1990s.

With the exception of Spanish, the numbers of Americans speaking a European language (or having a non-English mother tongue of European origin) were declining in the middle of the century; nevertheless, in 1960 the six biggest non-English mother-tongue populations were still European in origin (Fishman 1985b). Even by 1980 there were still well over half a million foreign-born speakers of German and Italian respectively. But the numbers of foreign-born persons speaking European-origin languages such as German, Italian, Greek, Hungarian, Dutch, or Yiddish, already in decline, dwindled as earlier-arriving immigrants died or left the U.S. and were not replaced by new immigrants who spoke those languages arriving during the 1980s and 1990s. Meanwhile, the number of foreign-born Spanish speakers increased 2.55 times between 1980 and 2000 while the number of speakers of Asian languages such as Chinese or Japanese and of Southeast Asian languages such as Thai, Mon-Khmer, Miao, or Vietnamese increased by between 2 and 11 times. By 2000, immigrants were most likely to speak Spanish, Chinese, Tagalog (one of the major languages spoken in the Philippines), Vietnamese, French, or Korean.

The changes in the national origins of the immigration streams entering the United States are responsible not only for changes in the overall array of languages spoken by immigrants but also for the different arrays of languages spoken by younger versus older Americans. Table 7.3, which is based on data from the supplementary survey to the 2000 census, shows the top ten minority languages spoken by children aged five to seventeen, adults aged eighteen to sixty-four, and by persons aged sixty-five and over.

The table shows that about two-thirds of children in the U.S. who spoke a minority language in 2000 spoke Spanish. The percentage is high, in large part, because of the growing predominance of immigra-

Table 7.2   Non-English Languages Spoken by Immigrants Aged Five and Over, 1980 to 2000

| Non-English Language Spoken at Home | Number of Speakers | | | |
	1980	1990	2000	Ratio, 2000/1980
All non-English languages	9,729,337	15,430,434	24,843,016	2.55
Spanish (includes creoles)	3,896,505	7,350,512	12,966,768	3.33
Chinese	494,855	1,088,296	1,249,429	2.52
Tagalog	402,968	746,443	973,421	2.42
Vietnamese	182,890	434,731	858,085	4.69
French (includes creoles)	376,060	534,192	736,095	1.96
Korean	237,516	530,860	683,409	2.88
Russian	127,605	186,514	643,043	5.04
German	627,998	529,678	471,472	.75
Arabic	164,953	251,409	420,776	2.55
Portuguese (includes creoles)	232,794	281,635	392,430	1.69
Italian	705,407	493,439	347,028	.49
Polish	260,341	286,896	339,612	1.30
Japanese	171,715	245,294	304,337	1.77
Hindi	115,774	287,067	251,681	2.17
Persian	94,395	178,354	210,243	2.23
Thai (Laotian)	73,542	173,226	197,502	2.69
Gujarati	32,065	87,539	182,680	5.70
Mon-Khmer (Cambodian)	15,089	113,910	170,923	11.33
Kru (Kwa)	22,454	58,172	153,610	6.84
Greek	215,700	181,965	144,130	.67
Armenian	69,995	115,017	134,976	1.93
Hebrew	49,044	74,985	109,646	2.24
Miao (Hmong)	14,638	62,699	92,979	6.35
Dutch	90,353	82,558	81,261	.90
Ukrainian	70,117	50,725	77,580	1.11
Romanian	24,058	53,493	75,450	3.14
Hungarian	105,298	87,024	55,449	0.53
Swedish, Danish, Norwegian	100,596	77,284	53,116	0.53
Serbo-Croatian	91,811	80,222	52,230	0.57
Yiddish	157,252	72,779	37,001	0.24
All other languages	505,549	633,516	2,376,654	4.70

Sources: Tabulations are based on data from the 1980 and 1990 U.S. censuses (Gibson and Lennon 1999) and from the Census 2000 Supplementary Survey (U.S. Bureau of the Census 2002a).

Table 7.3   The Percentages of Minority-Language Speakers Speaking the Ten Most Commonly Spoken Languages in 2000, by Age Grouping

	Children Ages Five to Seventeen	Adults Ages Eighteen to Sixty-Four	Adults Ages Sixty-Five and Over
Spanish	68.6%	55.8%	33.4%
French	3.4	5.2	4.5
Vietnamese	2.4	1.6	2.1
Chinese	2.3	4.3	6.6
German	1.8	4.6	7.8
Korean	1.7	2.2	a
Arabic	1.4	a	a
Russian	1.3	a	4.1
Tagalog	1.2	3.1	5.1
Miao (Hmong)	1.1	a	a
Italian	a	3.3	6.0
Polish	a	1.6	2.7
Japanese	a	1.4	2.1
Total[b]	85.2	83.1	74.4

Source: Census 2000 Supplementary Survey (U.S. Bureau of the Census 2002a).
[a]Not one of the ten most frequently spoken minority languages in this age group.
[b]The percentage of minority language speakers in this age group who speak one of the top ten languages.

tion from the Spanish-language countries in Central and Latin America in the last quarter of the twentieth century but the percentage of minority-language children speaking Spanish has also been pushed upward by the higher levels of fertility among the Spanish-speaking national origin groups in the United States (Bean, Swicegood, and Berg 2000), and the apparently higher rates of language retention between generations among the Spanish language population (Stevens 1985) especially in the American southwest.

Table 7.3 also shows that in contrast to the strong preponderance of Spanish speakers among minority-language children, only a little more than half of minority-language adults aged eighteen to sixty-four and a third of minority-language adults aged 65 or over spoke Spanish in 2000. Substantial percentages of adults spoke other minority languages, such as French, German, Chinese, or Italian. Linguistic diversity is clearly much greater among adult minority-language speakers than among children in the sense that significant percentages of adults speak different languages.

The higher levels of linguistic diversity among minority-language adults are a product of the confluence of several demographic and social processes. Some of the elderly European language speakers are the last survivors among the cohorts of non-English-language immigrants who entered the United States as children or young adults in the first third of the twentieth century. Other minority-language adults are the native-born descendants of the cohorts of European immigrants who entered in the first portion of the last century. Some of the older Asian-language speakers are the first few members of the large cohorts that began to enter the United States in the late 1960s as young adults and who are now entering the older age groupings while others entered the country as older adults during the 1970s or 1980s under the auspices of the family reunification provisions of immigration policy.

The diversity of languages spoken by immigrants has numerous implications for the incorporation of minority-language speakers and populations into American society. The preponderance of Spanish speakers among children, many of whom live in linguistically isolated households (defined as households that do not contain a person aged fourteen or over who speaks English "very well" or as his or her only language), points to the need for specialized services, particularly educational services, for Spanish speakers. At the same time, the wide variety of languages spoken by the non-Spanish minority-language children—the other 31 percent—highlights the difficulty of providing services to all young minority-language speakers, whether by means of traditional or transitional bilingual schooling programs or programs designed to enhance the chances of minority-language maintenance. The much higher levels of diversity among the elderly population suggests other problems. The wide array of languages spoken by significant percentages of the elderly coupled with their generally lower levels of English proficiency and the relatively high likelihood that elderly minority-language speakers live in linguistically isolated households (Mutchler and Brallier 1999; Stevens and Muehl 2001) point to a need for the provision of services and programs in a wide variety of languages in order to respond to the entire population of elderly minority-language speakers.

The discrepancies between the age groups—particularly the children and the elderly—in the array of minority languages spoken produce additional problems. Immigrant communities are often presumed to consist of demographically complete populations in the sense that their members span the entire age range. The discrepancies between the non-English languages represented among the younger and older minority-language speakers implies that many minority-language populations do not include all ages. Even if non-English-language children require or would benefit from specific educational, service-oriented, or ethnically based programs in their own minority language, it is possible that the pool of older adults with appropriate language skills from whom personnel can be found to manage or to participate in these programs is limited in size. The result is a shortage of appropriately qualified speakers who can work in educational and government institutions to provide bilingual services and programs (see, for example, August and Hakuta 1997). The difficulties associated with the ratio of the number of adult Spanish-language speakers to the number of young Spanish-language speakers is particularly acute because of the lower levels of education among the adult Spanish speakers (see chapter 6 for a description of the educational attainments of immigrant and native-born Americans by ethnic origins).

Changes in immigration policy, especially the implementation of the 1965 Immigration Act, have therefore changed the array and representation of minority languages represented among immigrants by changing the country of origins, and the corresponding non-English languages, spoken by immigrants and their children. Because immigration is highly selective of young adults, the shifts in the national origins of immigrant streams and the ancillary shifts in languages spoken by immigrants and their children have generated highly age-graded minority-language populations in the United States. Not only do different age groups require different arrays of services, but also the relative paucity of adult speakers of some minority languages has produced a relative shortage of personnel qualified to manage and participate in programs geared to particular age groups.

English-Language Skills at Time of Arrival

Recent censuses have gathered information on English proficiency for persons who reported speaking a non-English language at home. Of the approximately 31 million foreign-born persons over the age of five in 2000, about 80 percent reported speaking a non-English language at home and of these, less than half reported that they did not speak English "very well," the phrase often considered to denote fluency in English (U.S. Bureau of the Census 1993). The percentage of immigrants who do not speak English "very well" at the time they first enter the United States is, however, much higher. Many immigrants improve their English skills between their arrival and the time of the census, and some non-English-language immigrants who lack skills in English at time of entry and lack the motivation, opportuni-

Table 7.4   Level of Proficiency in English Reported by Recent Immigrants, by Official or Dominant Language of Their Country of Birth

| Speaks English | Total | Official or Dominant Language of Immigrant's Country of Birth | | | |
		English Dominant	English Official	Spanish Dominant	Other
Not well at all	19.5%	0.9%	1.6%	39.3%	11.6%
Not well	21.6	4.4	5.1	27.9	25.2
Well	19.8	5.7	20.1	13.0	28.8
Very well (or speaks only English)	39.0	89.0	73.1	19.9	34.4
Total	99.9	100.0	99.9	100.1	100.0

Source: Census 2000 Supplementary Survey (U.S. Bureau of the Census 2002a).

ties, or resources to learn English return to their country of origin before the census is fielded.

Because neither the census nor the Immigration and Naturalization Service collects information about the language skills of immigrants at time of arrival, we use an indirect approach to try to ascertain immigrants' skills at time of arrival. Focusing first on recently arrived immigrants, who have not had much opportunity to increase their levels of proficiency in English, we tie their reported skills in English to their countries of origin. Among recently arrived immigrants there is a strong correspondence between English skills and the language characteristics of their countries of origin. Immigrants born in countries in which English is a dominant language spoken by the general population—such as the United Kingdom, Australia and Canada—are almost all fully fluent in English. Many immigrants born in countries in which English is an official language, such as India and South Africa, are fluent in English. On the other hand, relatively fewer immigrants from countries in which Spanish is the dominant language—such as Mexico, Spain, and most Latin American countries—enter the country already fluent in English (see table 7.4).

The strong correspondence between country of origin and level of English proficiency at or near the time of arrival means that shifts in the country-of-origin distribution of immigrants can influence the overall prevalence of English fluency among newly arrived immigrants. Figure 7.1, which is based on data produced by the Immigration and Naturalization Service (U.S. Immigration and Naturalization Service 2001), shows the shifts over the twentieth century in the num-

Figure 7.1 Legally Admitted Immigrants by Decade and Language Characteristics of Country of Origin

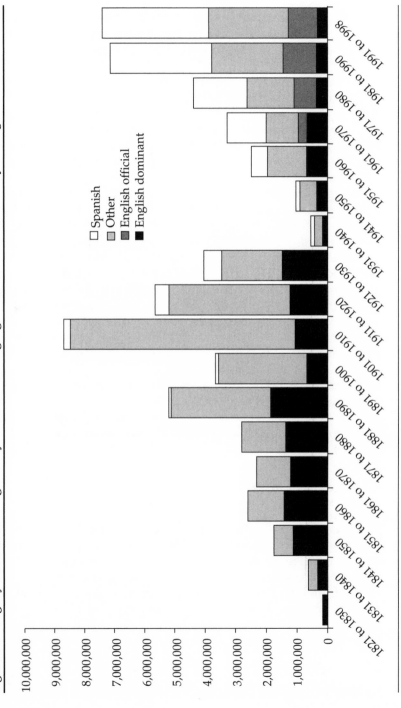

Source: U.S. Immigration and Naturalization Service (2001).

bers of legally admitted immigrants who have been classified by the language characteristics of their country of origin. The figure therefore omits the significant numbers of immigrants entering without documentation who tend to have low levels of proficiency in English (Chiswick 1991), and it does not refer to the language skills of individual immigrants. Still, the figure suggests that the English-language skills of newly legally admitted immigrants declined in the last third of the twentieth century. Geoffrey Carliner (2000), for example, estimates a decrease of .3 percent per year since 1970 in the probability that new entering cohorts of immigrants speak English "very well" or speak only English.

Immigration policy thus affects, inadvertently, the distribution of English skills among immigrants by affecting the overall distribution of countries of origin among newly arrived immigrants. The largely unanticipated shifts in the national origins of immigrants after the implementation of the 1965 Immigration Act have resulted in higher proportions of immigrants from countries in which English is neither a dominant nor an official language and has therefore resulted in higher proportions of immigrants entering the United States with lower levels of proficiency in English. In addition, recent results from the pilot study for the New Immigrant Survey, a panel study of new immigrants, show that the emphasis on family reunification is closely associated with lower levels of English proficiency among immigrants admitted under family preferences. About 58 percent of young adult immigrants admitted under the employment categories do not speak English "very well" but almost all persons (and their spouses) admitted under the sibling category do not speak English very well (Jasso et al. 2000b).

Changes in Language Attributes After Arrival

The language attributes of the first and second generations (immigrants and their native-born children, respectively) are the outcome of the language attributes of immigrants at the time they enter the United States and processes of change occurring after entry. Immigrants from non-English language countries can learn English as a second language or become more fluent in it. They may also increase the frequency with which they speak English vis-à-vis their minority language (a process known as intragenerational minority language shift). Immigrants may also choose to speak only English to their children. If their children learn and speak only English, then the minority language disappears between generations through intergenerational language shift, or "mother-tongue shift." These processes—the acquisition of English as a second language and minority language shift (both intragenerational and intergenerational)—have different causes and implications for the individuals involved, minority language communities, and the larger society.

Acquisition of English

After arriving in the United States, non-English-language immigrants face numerous pressures and incentives to learn English as a second or higher-order language or to increase their skills in English. Numerous researchers from a variety of disciplines including sociology, anthropology, economics, and linguistics have investigated the acquisition of English as a second or higher-order language among immigrants. There are several robust findings. The most important one, usually based on cross-sectional data, is that immigrants who have lived in the United States for longer periods of time have higher levels of proficiency in English than those who have lived in the United States for shorter periods of time (Carliner 2000; Espenshade and Fu 1997; Espinosa and Massey 1997; Jasso and Rosenzweig 1990; Stevens 1992).

Three possible explanations for the cross-sectional positive relationship between level of English proficiency and length of residence among immigrants are changes in levels of English skills across entry cohorts (as discussed above), selective emigration, and the acquisition of English skills while living in the United States. The changes in levels of English skills across entering cohorts at year of entry cannot, however, explain the increases in English proficiency that are routinely observed in cross-sectional comparisons of cohorts arrayed by year of entry. The possibility of selective emigration with respect to English skills suggests that immigrants who are less proficient in English at time of entry or who are less able or less motivated to improve their skills in English after arrival are more likely to return to their country of origin. But the available research suggests that the impact of selective emigration on the association between English skills and length of residence in the United States is minor (Lindstrom and Massey 1994; Stevens 1994) and cannot explain the strong positive relationship between skills in English and length of residence (which is synonymous with year of entry in cross-sectional data). Most of the cross-sectional association between immigrants' English skills and entry cohort must thus be attributable to immigrants' acquisition of English as a second or higher-order language while living in the United States.

A variety of theoretical approaches have been used in the study of second-language acquisition among immigrants. Linguists and psychologists often investigate the neurolinguistic, linguistic, and psycholinguistic subprocesses (which may be biologically based) underlying the acquisition of competency in phonology, syntax, lexicon, semantics, and communication. This research often focuses on the possibility that maturational constraints (or a sensitive period for second-language learning) govern the ability of non-English-language immigrants to become fluent English speakers (Long 1990). Linguists often point out, for example, that all else being equal, immigrants who have lived longer in the United States immigrated earlier in life. If maturational constraints govern the possibility of and extent of second-language acquisition, then the observed relationship between length of residence and English skills should be attributed to the operation of these constraints.

Social scientists, on the other hand, usually rely on human capital and exposure models in which second-language learning is presumed to be the outcome of opportunities and motivation. In human capital or exposure models, length of residence in the United States, a society firmly dominated by English, is often considered a simple and direct measure of immigrants' exposure to opportunities to learn the English language (as in Jasso and Rosenzweig 1990), although some social scientists, including sociolinguists, note that length of residence in the United States may reflect the general opportunities and pressures on immigrants to acculturate to various aspects of American society (Portes and Rumbaut 1990; Schumann 1986). Sociologists have begun to refine measures of the amount and degree of "exposure" to opportunities to learn English by considering societal contexts in which second-language learning and use may be differentially encouraged. For example, immigrants who live in a household with a native-born American who is likely to be fluent in English are more likely to have advanced English skills themselves because of the frequent opportunities to engage in conversations and discussions with a native English speaker.

Numerous studies have shown that educational attainment is particularly strongly associated with immigrants' proficiency in English, although scholars' interpretations of that relationship are often discipline-specific. Sociologists, for example, interpret the positive association between educational attainment and English proficiency as attributable to immigrants' length of participation in an English language–dominated environment, to the added cognitive skills relevant to second-language learning that are gained through more schooling, or to selection processes in which immigrants with better English skills achieve more schooling (see, for example, Espenshade and Fu 1997; Stevens 1994; Warren 1996). Economists, on the other hand, interpret the relationship between educational attainment and English-language proficiency as reflecting the higher relative costs of poor English skills among the better-educated (see, for example, Grenier 1984; Grin 1990).

Table 7.5 shows the results from an analysis of English-language proficiency among adult immigrants who were born in a non-English-language country. It includes some measures of exposure and opportunities for immigrants to learn English, as well as a measure of age at immigration, which is considered by linguists to be a reasonable proxy for the age at which second-language learning commences (Birdsong and Molis 2001; Johnson and Newport 1989). The data are from the supplementary survey to the 2000 U.S. census. As in the 2000 census, only persons who reported using a non-English language at home were asked whether they spoke English "very well," "well," "not well," or "not at all" in the supplementary survey and thereby were included in the analysis.

The first panel in table 7.5 shows that about 40 percent of immigrants born in a non-English-language country speak English "very well" and only about 10 percent do not speak English at all. On average, these immigrants entered the United States early in adulthood and have been in the country for several decades. The average level of education is high school graduation but the standard deviation is quite large. A large fraction of the immigrants appear to have attended school in the United States for at least a short time (although this variable was estimated by comparing the immigrants' time period of immigration, year of birth, and level of schooling and so is somewhat ambiguous). Most of the immigrants are married, a sizable fraction of the married immigrants have native-born spouses, and a majority report being employed in the labor force.

The coefficients in the last column of the table represent the logged odds that the respondent reports a higher level of proficiency in English rather than the immediately lower category, for example, "very well" rather than "well" or "well" rather than "not well," given a one-unit increase in the independent variable. The results support both social scientists' and linguists' expectations. The net effect of length of residence in the United States is strong and positive: the longer immigrants have lived in the United States, the more likely they are to report a higher level of proficiency in English. In addition, the net effect of age at immigration is negative. The older the immigrant at age of entry into the United States, the less likely he or she is to report a higher level of proficiency in English. The high levels of

Table 7.5   Means, Standard Deviations, and Coefficients for Variables in an Ordered Logistic Model Predicting Level of Proficiency in English Among Immigrants from Non-English-Language Countries

Variables	Proportion or Mean	Standard Deviation	Coefficients
Level of proficiency in English			
Very well	.41		
Well	.27		
Not well	.22		
Not at all	.10		
Length and timing of residence in U.S.			
Years in U.S.	22.38	15.50	.036*
Age at immigration	22.73	12.96	−.038*
Gender and family background			
Gender (female = 1)	.52	.50	−.076
Born in Spanish-language country? (yes = 1)	.38	.48	−.844*
Educational characteristics			
Years of education	12.30	4.47	.204*
Attended school in U.S.? (yes = 1)	.42	.49	.300*
Current family characteristics			
Married to native-born spouse? (yes = 1)	.15	.36	.878*
Married to foreign-born spouse? (yes = 1)	.43	.49	−.014
Not married (yes = 1)	.42	.49	a
Current major activity			
In labor force? (yes = 1)	.60	.49	.383*
Enrolled in school? (yes = 1)	.11	.31	.561*
Other activity? (yes = 1)	.29	.45	a
Model constants			
κ_1			3.022
κ_2			1.397
κ_3			−0.642
Model chi-square (with 10 df)			11,611

Source: Data from the Census 2000 Supplementary Survey (U.S. Bureau of the Census 2002a).
[a] Omitted category.
*Significant at .001 level.

English proficiency among the "1.5" generation—immigrants who entered the United States in childhood—may therefore be partly attributable to "maturational constraints" working in these immigrants' favor.

It is plausible, however, that the empirical relationship between age at immigration and lack of English proficiency is slightly overstated. The data describing "level of English proficiency" are based on respondents' self-assessments of how well they speak English. These self-assessments reflect their personal overall evaluations and expectations about how well they can communicate orally in English in social settings that are relevant to them. Of all the spheres of language competency, phonology appears to be the most sensitive to the age at which people begin to learn a second language (Bialystok and Hakuta 1994). Accents, even slight accents that do not deter communication, are readily decoded by linguistically naïve listeners. Because immigrants who immigrate later in life are likely to retain an accent even if they are communicatively competent in English, they may understate their level of proficiency in speaking English.

The coefficients for the social and demographic variables in the logistic model also show that immigrants' levels of proficiency are strongly predicted by their national origins, educational characteristics, marital characteristics, and labor force–related activities. More highly educated immigrants report higher levels of proficiency in English, particularly if they have completed at least some schooling in the United States. Immigrants with a native-born spouse are much more likely to report speaking at a higher level of proficiency than those with a foreign-born spouse or those who are currently not married. (This result is of particular interest given the high prevalence of cross-nativity marriages among immigrants of selected national origins—a topic we examine in the next chapter.)

The results presented in the logistic regression model also suggest that immigrants from Spanish-speaking countries are less likely to be highly proficient English speakers than immigrants from other non-English-language countries, even after controlling for a wide array of explanatory variables. This deficit could be attributable to several different factors. Results presented earlier in this chapter suggest that immigrants from Spanish-speaking countries report lower levels of proficiency in English than immigrants from other non-English-language countries shortly after they enter the country. Perhaps there are fewer opportunities to learn English or to begin learning English in Spanish-speaking countries than in other non-English-language countries and so immigrants from Spanish-language countries embark upon learning English in the United States with a smaller cache of

English skills than others. If this is the case, the continuing, seemingly inexorable spread around the globe of English as a world language will erase this differential in due time (Kachru 1992).

It is also possible that the lower levels of fluency in English among immigrants from Spanish-speaking countries reflect the higher proportions of unauthorized migrants from Spanish-speaking than from other non-English-language countries. Unauthorized migrants may lack the motivation to learn English because they anticipate only a short sojourn in the United States. They may also lack the necessary resources—including the appropriate documents—to participate in American social settings that encourage English-language learning. The growth in immigration from Spanish-speaking countries, the large native-born populations of Spanish speakers in the United States, and the geographic concentration of the Spanish speakers in California, the Southwest, and Florida also means that Spanish-speaking immigrants may be able to live in areas that lessen the need (and lower the number of opportunities) to learn English.

Minority-Language Shift

The "straight-line" theory of assimilation argues that the full incorporation of immigrants and immigrant groups requires that minority-language speakers learn English and then shift to the use of only English. The shift may occur within a generation, with minority-language speakers first learning and then increasing the extent to which they use English at the expense of continuing to use their minority language. While it is clear that non-English-language immigrants are likely to become more proficient in English, as demonstrated in the analysis in the previous section, it is less clear to what extent (or in which situations) immigrants shift to the use of English in lieu of their non-English language. It is also unclear what the implications of learning and using English are for immigrants' continued facility in their non-English languages. Unfortunately there are very few major sources of data that allow the investigation of shifts in patterns of language use, or measure language loss (sometimes referred to as first-language attrition) occurring within a generation. The U.S. censuses after 1970, for example, do not include measures of "mother tongue" or first learned language, and instead only assess whether a person speaks a minority language at home at the time of the census. It is therefore not possible to compare individuals' patterns of language use at the time of the census with patterns of language use at a younger age. For immigrants from a non-English-language country, it seems plausible that even those who speak only English at the time of the census or survey originally learned and spoke a non-English lan-

guage in childhood (although the assumption is not perfect). Moreover, even if the explicit comparison between patterns of language
use earlier and later in life were possible, there are still issues concerning the degree to which individuals retain full proficiency in their
non-English language.

The Survey of Income and Education (SIE), fielded in 1976 by the
U.S. Census Bureau, is one of the few major surveys that does include
a measure of "mother tongue." Analyses based on the SIE show that
the predictors of shifts in patterns of language use—from the presumably heavy reliance on a minority language in early childhood to
higher frequencies of English use later in adulthood—parallel those
predicting the acquisition of English as a second language (Stevens
1992). Foreign-born Americans with a non-English mother tongue are
less likely to shift to higher levels of English usage than their native-
born counterparts, and higher levels of education are associated with
higher levels of English usage among both foreign-born and native-
born generations. In addition, one of the most important predictors of
language shift is intermarriage. Couples in which the spouses do not
share the same mother tongue are very likely to speak only English
(Stevens 1985). The results are particularly telling when considering
language shift among the native-born generations, almost all of whom
learned English early in life. For native-born Americans, the impact of
variables such as "education" on pattern of English use can be read as
reflecting either the impact of the immediately surrounding context
and allied opportunities to use the minority language, rather than the
opportunities to learn English. In general, the research supports the
proposition that processes of intragenerational minority-language
shift are intertwined with processes of structural assimilation (Mirowsky and Ross 1984). Unfortunately these conclusions are very general because they are based on analyses of data sources such as the
Survey of Income and Education in which the measures of patterns of
language use are typically global in nature and do not pertain to any
specific social setting.

Intergenerational language shift (or "mother-tongue shift"), the
second form of language shift, occurs when children do not learn
their parent(s)' non-English mother tongue. There are two approaches
to assessing the extent of intergenerational mother-tongue shift. The
first is through a direct comparison of children's language repertoires
with those of their parents—an analytic approach that limits investigations to the subset of children living in the same household as their
parents at the time the data are collected. Studies using this approach
often show high rates of mother-tongue shift between the first and
later generations (Lopez 1978; Stevens 1985).

A second approach to the study of minority-language shift over generations examines communal shift, the gradual replacement of the non-English language with English over an extended period of time within an ethno-linguistic community. Over several generations, families and language communities progressively learn, and prefer to use, more and more English, and each succeeding generation learns (and uses) less and less of the minority language (Hakuta and D'Andrea 1992; Lopez 1982). Other allied research shows strong preferences for English vis-à-vis minority languages among first- and second-generation Vietnamese children in New Orleans (Zhou and Bankston 1998), and Spanish and Asian children in Florida and California (Portes and Rumbaut 2001; Portes and Schauffler 1994).

Often, research on minority-language shift focuses explicitly or implicitly on the "linguistic vitality" of the minority language, that is, its potential to survive over time. The acquisition of a minority language is often incomplete if children learn and use a minority language only in one domain, for example, only with family members in the home. The availability of institutional resources and incentives for maintaining and fostering the use of a minority language in a wide range of settings is therefore crucial in countering the downward drift over generations in levels of competency. Recent theories of cultural pluralism or segmented or selective assimilation acknowledge that stable bilingualism is a possible outcome that may be supported by educational and occupational incentives for individuals and communities (Yinger 1994; Portes and Rumbaut 2001. A wide-ranging survey in the United States concluded, however, that community resources for "intergenerational linguistic continuity . . . [are] not only generally weak but unconscious, unfocused, unspotlighted and undramatized" (Fishman 1985a). When considering the wider societal context, Chiswick (1991) concludes that the occupational and earnings rewards for fluency in a minority language are limited.

Because the U.S. census does not provide information on fluency in non-English languages, the large and increasing numbers of native-born Americans identified in recent censuses as "minority-language speakers" may overstate the apparent continuity of minority languages into the native-born generations because a significant fraction may not be fully fluent or literate in their non-English language. A recent survey of university students who reported speaking a non-English language at home provides clear evidence that many native-born Americans who spoke a non-English language in childhood do not acquire or maintain high levels of literacy into young adulthood. The native-born American students reported only slightly lower levels of proficiency in understanding and speaking their childhood home language than did the foreign-born students. But they reported markedly lower levels of proficiency in reading and writing their non-English language than the foreign-born students (Stevens and Gonzo 1998).

Nonetheless, educational institutions could support and encourage proficiency in non-English languages through the teaching of minority languages to English monolingual students, or by using minority languages as the means of teaching other subjects to any student. Joshua Fishman (1985a) argues that "ethnic-community mother-tongue schools" are, unfortunately, only meager language-maintenance auxiliary agencies; that they stabilize American ways of being ethnic rather than developing proficiency and literacy in minority languages and so fostering language maintenance. Viewed more broadly, competency in a second language is a major intellectual achievement and a source of cultural enrichment. Yet few children outside ethnolinguistic communities learn and become fully fluent speakers of a non-English language by virtue of being taught it (or being taught in it) in school. With the exception of the Spanish language, the mismatch between the foreign languages that are commonly taught in American schools—such as French, German, and Latin—and the languages that are spoken at home by many children of immigrants—such as Chinese, Korean, and Farsi—do not build upon the extant language repertoires of the minority-language children. Furthermore, most secondary schools do not orient their foreign-language instruction toward eventual adult use (Lambert 1994). Even universities, which often impose a foreign-language requirement for graduation upon their students, fail to build upon the extant language capabilities of many of their students (Stevens and Gonzo 1998).

On the other hand, many children of immigrant parents do have some facility in their parents' non-English language and the numbers are increasing. The demographic weight of the numbers involved could change patterns of language maintenance within and across generations. Research shows that persons with a non-English mother tongue use the language more often if there are larger numbers of persons sharing the language in the same demographic context (Stevens 1992). Lopez's (1982) research on the use of only English among Latino and Asian groups in Los Angeles shows that the presence of large numbers of immigrants may slow the pace of language shift toward English among native-born ethnic group members, perhaps because immigrant speakers, who are likely to be fully fluent in their non-English language, are less likely to speak English very well and so prefer using their non-English language with others in the community whenever possible. The continuous flow of immigrants, especially from Spanish-speaking countries, a globalizing economy, and the emergence of transnational communities (Portes 2001) may also be altering Americans' attitudes toward bilingualism and minority-language maintenance versus English monolingualism. The contexts in which minority-language speakers (and English monolingual Americans) live, go to school, and work are changing.

Summary and Conclusions

The language attributes of immigrants—their facility in non-English languages and their skills in English—are fundamental considerations in the social and cultural incorporation of immigrant groups. Many theories of assimilation and incorporation, however, view language characteristics only as indicators of processes of acculturation, identification, and assimilation. They also presume that the dynamics of integration and incorporation involving language characteristics are limited to the foreign-born minority-language population. This view is based on the experiences of European immigrants who entered the United States in the early twentieth century, among whom the probability of English acquisition was high (Labov 1998) and among whose descendents rates of mother-tongue shift across over the course of the twentieth century were strikingly high (Lieberson, Dalto, and Johnston 1975).

Whether or not the story will play out exactly the same way for the newest immigrants is unclear. On the one hand, there remain strong expectations that immigrants in the United States learn English. In 1994 the U.S. Commission on Immigration Reform stated this expectation as an obligation: "[I]mmigration to the United States should be understood as a privilege, not a right. Immigration carries with it obligations to embrace the common core of the American civic culture, to become able to communicate—to the extent possible—in English with other citizens and residents, and to adapt to fundamental constitutional principles and democratic institutions" (U.S. Commission on Immigration Reform 1994). The perception that immigrants and their children are, or should be, obligated to learn English is widespread. Over 90 percent of Mexican-origin persons in the United States agree that U.S. citizens and residents should learn English (de la Garza et al. 1992) and over two thirds of Asians and Hispanics believe that speaking English is "very important in making one an American" (Citrin, Reingold, and Green 1990). Although there are few longitudinal studies, studies based on cross-sectional data consistently demonstrate (as in this chapter) that immigrants' levels of English proficiency improve as they live out their lives in the United States. The children of immigrants, both the "1.5" generation and native-born children, are very likely to learn English early in their lives.

The language characteristics of contemporary immigrants are, however, different from those of earlier immigrants, and in many respects the context is different and is continuing to change. The lack of explicit attention paid in immigration policy to the language characteristics of prospective immigrants means that the array of language skills of newly admitted immigrants is largely an unanticipated by-product of their national origins. The languages spoken by contemporary immigrants differ from those spoken by earlier immigrants, and the perceived linkages between language, race, and national origins may be tighter. For example, George Sánchez (1997) argues that language differences have become involved in a new form of nativism that intertwines a new American racism with traditional hostility toward new immigrants. It seems possible that the differing receptions granted to immigrants of differing national and racial origins, and differences in personal and community resources, could result in immigrants' and their children's selecting different strategies with respect to language attributes. Mary C. Waters (1999) suggests, for example, that blacks of Caribbean descent appear to associate fluency in another language—or even just exhibiting a Caribbean accent while speaking English—as a means of dissociating themselves from the native-born American black population.

The demographic and social contexts differ as well. At the beginning of the twenty-first century, about 18 percent of the American population—more than one in six Americans—speaks a non-English language. The continuation of high levels of immigration from non-English-language countries may be increasing the perceived benefits of language maintenance and of bilingualism. The economic and social forces behind globalization increase the value of bilingualism and multilingualism for speakers of all languages. The call from the U.S. Department of Defense for interpreters with facility in the languages spoken in Afghanistan after the events of September 11, 2001, is a recent example of the acknowledged need for Americans with skills in even the less commonly spoken languages. The scenario of stronger language maintenance is particularly conceivable for the Spanish language in the United States. In three states—New Mexico, Texas, and California—over a quarter of the population speaks Spanish (U.S. Census Bureau 2002b). The continuing numerical dominance of immigrants from Spanish-speaking countries, the increasing economic ties between the United States and Mexico, and the long-standing native-born Spanish-speaking population in Florida, California, and the Southwest may be altering the understanding of the perceived value of Spanish in the United States. Polls in California suggest that about three quarters of Americans do not believe that it is a "bad thing" for immigrants to preserve their foreign languages (Field Institute, various dates).

Theories of the social integration of immigrants into American society have largely focused on the language characteristics of immigrants and their children as measures of the incompleteness of integration into a society still firmly dominated by the English language and by English speakers. The presumption that both processes of language adaptation—English-language acquisition and minority-language shift—are prerequisites for full incorporation follows from the importance of patterns of language use as indicators of acculturation, identification, and structural assimilation. Yet classic theories of assimilation rest on the assumption that learning and using English is the flip side of minority-language retention (that it's a zero-sum process) and that the dynamics of language change occur primarily within the minority group.

The assumption that learning and using English occur in tandem with minority-language shift may be too simplistic because it ignores the possibility of bilingualism, particularly within the native-born generations. It also ignores the impact of context. Almost all of the available evidence suggests that English acquisition proceeds quickly and, at an aggregate level, is complete within a generation or two. The increases in the aggregate numbers of minority-language speakers who are not proficient in English appear to be primarily a product of the influx of large numbers of immigrants who have not yet had access to the opportunities and resources to learn the country's dominant language. But the assumption that the trajectory of minority-language shift inevitably follows English-language acquisition is based on weaker evidence. Research, largely based on cross-sectional surveys, suggests that fluency in and usage of minority languages dissipate across generations. But it is often not clear when, over the progression of lifetimes and generations, the language shift occurred. For example, the intergenerational mother-tongue shift that resulted in the lower levels of Spanish usage among third-generation children at the turn of the twenty-first century may have occurred over a generation ago in the 1970s—a different context from today. A more nuanced understanding of processes of adaptation and integration should consider uncoupling the two processes and the impact of changes in the social and demographic contexts in which these processes occur.

Second, the view that the dynamics of language change occur only within the minority-language group has had at least one unfortunate corollary. If changes occur only in the minority-language group, then the responsibility for change rests on the shoulders of the minority group, and changes in the dominant society are not pertinent. Yet the linguistic characteristics of the American population as a whole are in a state of flux because of the historically vacillating impact of immigration and processes of English acquisition and minority-language shift within and between generations. Newly admitted non-English-language immigrants add demographic weight to extant minority-language communities (or establish new ones), change the linguistic characteristics of the native-born generations, and alter the balance of younger versus older speakers. The last several decades have seen an eruption of social and political controversies over the costs and benefits of providing services—particularly bilingual education—as well as the appropriate role of English vis-à-vis other languages in American society. These controversies clearly demonstrate that the increasing presence of minority-language immigrants in the United States is exciting strong and vociferous reactions. A more comprehensive understanding of the processes of adaptation and integration of immigrant groups thus requires considering how their language characteristics are affecting the larger American society.

= Chapter 8 =

The Incorporation
of Immigrants:
Patterns of Marriage

THE INCORPORATION of immigrant groups into the mainstream of American life is a central element in the debates about immigration policy. Whether—and how rapidly—racial and ethnic groups who immigrate to the United States are incorporated into the social and cultural fabric of American society is a particularly important aspect of immigration. High levels of racial and ethnic intermarriage provide strong evidence of sociocultural incorporation because the familial relations between members of different racially or ethnically defined groups bespeaks the lack of barriers to social interaction between group members and the fading or acceptance of cultural differences. High levels of racial and ethnic intermarriage have therefore been called the litmus test of the social and cultural incorporation of racially or ethnically defined groups (Alba 1995).

The incorporation of immigrant groups into American society can also be hastened by marriage between the immigrant and native-born generations. Marriages between the first and later generations result in the quick political integration of the foreign-born spouses and children and may also be associated with a quicker introduction of the foreign-born spouse to participation in social arenas dominated by native-born Americans. Although often neglected in research and discussions concerning intermarriage, levels of intermarriage across generational lines may in fact be an underappreciated aspect of (and shortcut to) the integration of immigrant groups into American society.

In this chapter, we describe patterns of intermarriage of immigrants with respect to national origins, race, citizenship, and nativity. We include discussions of some of the reasons why intermarriage is such an important barometer of incorporation, and how social and demographic contexts can modify patterns of intermarriage. To provide some background for the description and discussion of contemporary patterns of intermarriage, we first describe patterns of intermarriage with respect to national origins among immigrants and their descendants early in the twentieth century. We then discuss how elements of immigration policy have shaped patterns of marriage and intermarriage among immigrants during the latter part of the twentieth century.

Background

Early in the twentieth century, concerns were raised about the ability of the nation to integrate the "disparate racial elements" introduced through immigration from southern and eastern European nations. Contemporaneous and recent analyses of marriage patterns between the various European nationalities in the 1920s showed high "caste-like" levels of in-group marriage and low levels of intermarriage (Drachsler 1920; Pagnini and Morgan 1990). By 1960, however, a generation or so later, levels of intermarriage among Americans of European descent were much higher and educational attainment appeared to be trumping national ancestry as the more important dimension in marriage choices (Kalmijn 1993a). By 1980, only twenty years later, intermarriage had become the expectation among Americans of European descent: native-born Americans of European descent were more likely to be out-married (married to a member outside their ethnic group) than to marry a person of matching or overlapping European origin (Lieberson and Waters 1988). The social and cultural barriers between the European national groups, each of which was considered in the early twentieth century to be racially distinct—had become almost nonexistent in the American context. The high levels of intermarriage, which increased over time and generation during the twentieth century, both reflected and accelerated the processes through which Americans of European descent became American—or, more accurately, became white Americans.

The Immigration Act of 1924 had distinguished the desirability of Europeans according to nationality and ranked them invidiously. It also had banned the immigration of persons of nationalities racially ineligible for citizenship, such as Chinese, Japanese, and South Asians. Although Mexicans were not prevented from entering, the implementation of various provisions of immigration policy such as the literacy test, the ban on contract labor, and the formation of the

Border Patrol in 1925 helped drive the level of documented immigration from Mexico down during the 1920s (Ngai 1999).

But the rigid racial architecture underlying the Immigration Act of 1924 began to unravel in the 1940s. Small quotas were allotted to immigrants of previously barred races and national origins and special provisions were enacted for the spouses and fiancées of American soldiers. The Immigration Act amendments of 1965 mandated evenly distributed quotas of 20,000 each to states in the Eastern Hemisphere (comprising Europe, Africa, Asia, and Australia) and thus undid the national-origins quotas, which had come to be viewed as an illiberal deviation from American democratic tradition. The 1965 act also carried over provisions from earlier legislation for easing the migration of parents, spouses, and children of American native-born citizens, naturalized American citizens, and permanent residents by allowing some of them to enter the country as "immediate relatives," a newly defined category exempt from the world-wide cap.

The 1965 act thus provided a framework that encouraged the entry of immigrants with close familial ties to people in this country. When Congress enacted the law, it apparently had not considered fully how the continuation of the family provisions might change the national origins of immigrants entering the United States. Each immigrant entering under a country-specific quota could open a path for non-quota immigration. A Korean bride, brought in by her U.S.-born husband, could become a naturalized citizen within three years and bring her parents and siblings as non-quota immigrants, who could then in turn bring in their spouses and children.

Some scholars argue that the new immigration streams are more racially distinct than earlier immigration streams (see, for example, Alba and Nee 1999). In 1998, less than 15 percent of legally admitted immigrants were of European national origin, while 30 percent were of Asian, 23 percent were of Mexican, and 13 percent were of Central or South American origin (U.S. Immigration and Naturalization Service 2002b, table 2). Today, the largest immigration streams are of national origins that the 1924 National Origins Quota Act explicitly barred from the country or severely restricted because of these people's presumed inability to integrate into American society. The social and cultural integration of European immigrants entering the country in the first quarter of the century began in an era when immigrants from southern and eastern Europe were considered to be less desirable than those of northern and western Europe. However, high levels of intermarriage between Americans of various European nationalities in succeeding generations over the course of the mid-twentieth century were evidence of the diminution of social and cultural distinctions among Americans of European descent. Will the same happen to the different national origin groups that arrived in the latter third of the twentieth century?

Implications of Intermarriage

Intermarriage across racial or ethnic lines is considered a litmus test of assimilation because it affirms the dissolving of social and cultural barriers to the formation of formally acknowledged intimate relationships between members of socially or culturally distinct groups. Intermarriage also accelerates the dissolution or toleration of social and cultural distinctions in a variety of ways. The adults directly involved in mixed racial or ethnic marriages demonstrate and perhaps develop further sympathies with another socially defined racial or ethnic group. Moreover, their marriage affects the family relations of their relatives, whose social and kin networks now draw from at least two socially or culturally defined groups. Although racial intermarriage is increasing, it remains relatively rare in U.S. society. Still, about 20 percent of Americans have kinship networks that cross racial lines (Goldstein 1999). The effect of racially mixed marriages on the racial and ethnic composition of Americans' familial networks thus extends far into the general population.

Intermarriage also affects the social and cultural identities of the next generation, who now are of complex ancestry. In the case of intermarriage across racial or national-origin lines, putatively distinct physical markers of membership in one or the other group may be muted. Children are likely to learn some of the distinct mores and culture of both groups. In addition, culturally distinctive attributes may not be fully transmitted across generations. Children with only one parent who speaks a non-English language—a common occurrence in ethnically mixed marriages—are much less likely to learn that language than children with two non-English-language parents (Stevens 1985).

Intermarriage across racial and national-origin boundaries and the generation of offspring with complex lineages thus provide prima facie evidence of the blurring of racial and cultural distinctions in American society. By 1980, the increases in intermarriage over the course of the twentieth century had resulted in a large proportion of native-born Americans of European descent reporting two or more ethnic ancestries—in spite of the tendencies of parents to simplify their children's ancestries and in spite of the tendencies of young adults to focus on only one element of their ancestry after leaving their parents' home (Lieberson and Waters 1993). Contemporary levels and patterns of ethnic and racial intermarriage and the prediction of future levels and patterns of intermarriage are therefore important considerations in the projections of the racial and ethnic composition of the American population (Edmonston and Passel 1999; Waters 2000).

Race, ethnicity, and national origin constitute, however, only one dimension (or overlapping dimensions) of intermarriage. Another facet of intermarriage is marriage across generations—particularly the marriage of first-generation immigrants to native-born, or later-generation, Americans. Early in the twentieth century, marriage between the foreign and "native" stock (in other words, native-born Americans) was considered evidence of integration of foreign groups into the American population (Bossard 1939; Carpenter 1927). Julius Drachsler (1920) argued that a thorough-going assimilation of the foreign groups introduced through immigration would *require* frequent crossing of the generational divisions to fuse the foreign groups into the American population.

Cross-nativity marriages and their role in the social and cultural integration of immigrant groups disappeared from scholars' view in the middle of the twentieth century when levels of immigration sank. They may be, however, an important if underappreciated facet of the integration of immigrants and immigrant groups. For example, marriages between immigrants and native-born Americans are likely to be marked by the quicker social integration of the foreign-born spouse into social settings dominated by Americans than are marriages between two foreign-born spouses. A foreign-born person with a native-born spouse becomes eligible for naturalization more quickly than other immigrants. The offspring of marriages involving a native-born American parent are eligible for American citizenship whether the child is born in the United States or not. The children of cross-nativity marriages therefore are politically integrated with only minor efforts on their parents' part. Children with a native-born American parent are also very likely to learn English as a first (and only) language in childhood (Stevens 1985), and to identify themselves as American (Portes and Rumbaut 2001).

There are thus several reasons to investigate patterns of intermarriage and in-group marriage among immigrants. The levels of in-group marriage involving immigrants provide information on the extent of integration of new ethnic and racial groups in the United States and on the persistence of longstanding racial and ethnic designations in the American context. Patterns and levels of marriage within and between racial or national origin groups among the first generation also provides a baseline for the assessment of levels and patterns of in-group versus intergroup marriage in the native-born generations. Patterns and levels of marriage across generational lines—especially between the immigrant and the native-born generations—show the speed with which some immigrants and their children are being fully integrated into American society.

Correlates of Intermarriage

Levels and patterns of intermarriage are affected by more than the toleration or acceptance of socially or culturally defined groups in American society. Demographic and structural opportunities for people to meet potential partners with specific characteristics, preferences for partners with specific characteristics, and social institutions that encourage or discourage certain marriages are additional factors shaping patterns of intermarriage (Kalmijn 1998). Another factor is timing: immigrants may marry before entering the United States or some time after arrival. Patterns of intermarriage involving the immigrant generation are thus affected by demographic and structural factors operating in the immigrants' countries of origin as well as in the United States, by personal preferences for partners with specified attributes that were formed and perhaps modified in several different societies, and by the operation of social and familial institutions that may stretch around the world. Moreover, because it is possible that the act of marrying is linked to the act of immigrating, patterns of intermarriage are also affected by aspects of immigration policy and foreign relations.

It is particularly difficult to investigate the contribution of these factors on marriage patterns among persons who married before entry into the United States. The emphasis in this section is thus on how U.S. immigration policy may shape the marital characteristics of immigrants at time of entry and on patterns of intermarriage among immigrants currently residing in the United States.

Intermarriage and U.S. Immigration Policy

Various facets of immigration policy and foreign relations have affected the marital characteristics of foreign-born persons entering the United States. In general, the Immigration Act of 1990 implicitly favors married immigrants because of the emphasis on family reunification (Jasso and Rosenzweig 1986). First, principal immigrants can apply for visas for accompanying immediate family members, including their spouse. Second, after arrival, permanent resident aliens may sponsor spouses (and children) for entry under the family second preference, which is numerically limited. Third, native-born U.S. citizens, or permanent resident aliens who have become naturalized citizens, may sponsor their parents or spouses as "immediate relatives of U.S. citizens," a category that is not numerically limited.

Naturalized adult citizens may also sponsor married sons and daughters (family third preference), and adult brothers and sisters (family fourth preference). Christian Joppke (1999) further argues that many immigrants have used the family preference system in a stepwise fashion to sponsor their parents, who after naturalization can then easily sponsor their married sons and daughters. Immigrants entering the United States are therefore more likely to be married than native-born Americans of the same age (Greenwood and McDowell 1999; U.S. Census Bureau 2002a).

U.S. foreign relations have also affected the marriage characteristics of immigrants, especially female immigrants. The participation of men in major wars and conflicts outside the United States has often been accompanied by large numbers of marriages between American soldiers and civilians. The 1945 War Brides Act waived visa requirements for foreign nationals who married members of the American Armed Forces during World War II, and the 1946 Fiancées Act facilitated the admission to the United States of the fiancées of members of the American Armed Forces. Non-quota admission status was granted to the Chinese-national wives of American citizens in 1946, and in 1947, to wives of other nationalities then racially ineligible for admission (U.S. Immigration and Naturalization Service 2002a). These legislative reforms are noteworthy because they laid the basis for Asian family immigration, which had been a near impossibility under the exclusionary provisions of the 1924 National Origins Quota Act.

Over the last several decades the United States has retained large military bases in the Republic of Korea and Japan, as well as relatively large bases in Germany and some other NATO countries (U.S. Department of Defense 2001). The presence of U.S. military bases scattered across the world has resulted in large numbers of women migrating to the U.S. as wives of American servicemen (Jasso and Rosenzweig 1990). Many of the foreign-born spouses sponsored by American citizens are thus spouses of military personnel. Research based on the 1980 census suggested the presence in this country of over 40,000 "war brides" from Japan, China, the Philippines, India, Korea, and Vietnam (Saenz, Hwang, and Aguirre 1994).

In addition, some of the persons entering the United States as the spouses or fiancé(e)s of U.S. citizens are the result of relationships begun under the auspices of marriage agencies. Such agencies, many of which use the World Wide Web to advertise the attractions of prospective spouses living in countries such as the USSR, the Philippines, and Argentina, may be responsible for several thousand fiancées and newly married men and women entering the United States each year (Scholes 1999). Additional marriages between Americans living in the United States and persons living abroad are arranged or sponsored by families or national-origin communities in the United States because many foreign-born parents in these communities prefer for their native-born American sons and daughters to marry national compatriots and encourage them to do so (Foner 1997; Montero 1981).

Unfortunately, it is difficult to assess the detailed impact of policy on the patterns of intermarriage with respect to national origins, race, or nativity because of the general lack of data. Immigration and Naturalization Service data do not provide information on the national origins, race, or nativity of immigrants' spouses at time of arrival and the major cross-sectional surveys of immigrants currently living in the United States generally lack information on category of admission. It does seem plausible, however, that in many respects the emphasis on family reunification in U.S. immigration policy endorses the entry of immigrants who are married endogamously with respect to national origins, and the formation of marriages between foreign-born persons that are endogamous with respect to national origins. It also seems plausible that a large majority of marriages between foreign-born spouses and American citizens that are initiated by families and ethnic communities were encouraged for the specific purpose of ensuring marriages between persons of the same national and cultural background. On the other hand, it also seems likely that few of the marriages formed between foreign-born spouses (usually brides) and military personnel are endogamous, since so few military personnel are of the same national origin as the people of the country in which they are stationed. It also seems implausible that the majority of the relationships initiated under the auspices of marriage agencies are endogamous.

The Demographic Context of Marriages Occurring in the United States

Many immigrants marry or remarry after entering the United States. The probability of immigrants marrying a native-born American versus someone of their own national origin is thus subject to the demographic and structural features of the American marriage market. One of the most important demographic phenomena affecting levels of intermarriage is the sex ratio within the country-of-origin immigrant stream. The sex ratio at birth is 105 males to 100 females for almost all ethnic and racial groups. Mortality rates during infancy and childhood usually slightly favor females and so the sex ratio among young adults is usually about even.

For a variety of social, cultural, and economic reasons, however, migration streams, which are largely composed of young adults, often favor one or the other sex. For example, until the 1930s immigration to the United States was largely male; between the 1930s and 1978 and again during the 1990s, slightly more women than men were admitted to the country (U.S. Immigration and Naturalization Service 2002a). In addition, the migration streams from specific countries are very likely to be dominated by one sex (Donato 1990), sometimes extremely so. For example, the Chinese who were recruited to build the U.S. railroads in the mid-1800s were almost exclusively men and most of the Irish brought in as domestic servants during the late 1800s were women. Recent immigration from the Philippines has been predominantly female and immigration from Vietnam has been predominately male (Goodkind 1997). The more extreme the sex ratio among migrants, the more likely it becomes that the migrants marrying in the United States will contract marriages with persons of other national origins (Pagnini and Morgan 1990).

Other important demographic predictors of the relative frequency of intermarriage in a given context include the relative sizes of the national-origin or racially defined groups. If all else is equal, the larger a group, the more likely its members will be to marry endogamously. Kalmijn (1998) hypothesizes that immigrants born in countries that have historically sent larger numbers of immigrants to the United States are thus more likely to marry native-born Americans of the same national origin because of the larger number of potential partners. In addition, the more a national-origin group is concentrated in a particular geographic locale, the lower the rates of intermarriage. Thus the geographic concentration of ethnic or racial groups or nativity groups, whether measured at the state, city, or neighborhood levels, is associated with lower levels of intermarriage (Lieberson and Waters 1988; Stevens and Swicegood 1987; White and Sassler 2000). Social segregation—the uneven participation of members of immigrants and ethnic or national-origin groups in major social institutions such as schools and places of employment—further lowers the probability of intermarriage between immigrants of different ethnic or racial origins and between immigrants and native-born Americans (Bozon and Héran 1987; Kalmijn and Flap 2001; Mare 1991; Schoen and Kluegel 1988).

In addition to demographic or structural considerations, social preferences also play a role. In general, people appear to be attracted to prospective marriage partners who have characteristics that are similar to or match their own. In the United States, one of the most important dimensions of marriage markets is educational attainment (Lewis and Oppenheimer 2000; Mare 1991). Another is race (Kalmijn 1993b; Qian 1997). Length of residence in the United States is also a factor because in the American context this is strongly related to other processes of integration, such as the acquisition of English-language skills (Espenshade and Fu 1997; Stevens 1994), residential mobility and location (White and Sassler 2000), and thus the opportunity to meet and to attract potential marriage partners in an American setting.

The Marital Characteristics of Immigrants at Time of Admission

Because U.S. immigration policy favors married immigrants, a majority of immigrants—and an even larger proportion of adult immigrants—legally admitted to the country are married. Figure 8.1, based on data from the Immigration and Naturalization Service, shows the total number of immigrants admitted to the country, the number who were married, and the proportions of female and male immigrants who were married at the time of admission, for fiscal years 1975 to 1999. (Data on the marital status of immigrants admitted during 1980 and 1981 are not available.)

The percentages of immigrants who were married at the time they were admitted to the country increased between 1965 and the early 1970s and then vacillated around .50, ranging from a low of about .45 to a high of .55, until 1999. In every year, a higher percentage of female than of male immigrants were married at time of admission. The dip in the percentages of married immigrants admitted from 1989 to 1991 is probably accounted for by the slightly differing strategies used by immigrants admitted through the provisions of the Immigration Reform and Control Act (IRCA) of 1986. For example, Guillermina Jasso et al. (2000a) argue that for many of the couples residing illegally in the United States, just one spouse decided to pursue amnesty under IRCA as a means of safeguarding against the possible deportation of the entire family.

Unfortunately, detailed data on the marital and admission status of immigrants were not available until 1999. However, the Immigration and Naturalization Service does publish data showing the numbers of immigrants admitted to the country as spouses of U.S. citizens (who may be either native-born or naturalized) or as spouses of resident aliens (see figure 8.2). The numbers entering as spouses of resident aliens changed little during much of the 1980s but jumped in the

Figure 8.1   Numbers and Percentages of Immigrants Married at Time of Admission to the United States, by Year Admitted and Gender, 1965 to 1999

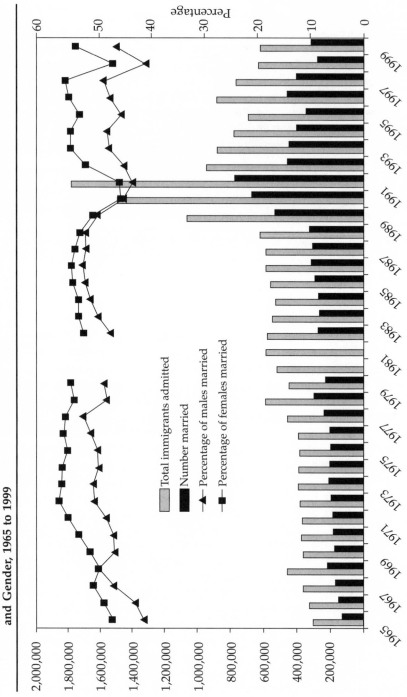

Source: U.S. Immigration and Naturalization Service (2001).
Note: Information on marital status not available for 1980 and 1981.

Figure 8.2   Numbers of Immigrants Legally Admitted to the U.S. as Spouses of U.S. Citizens or of Resident Aliens, 1965 to 1999

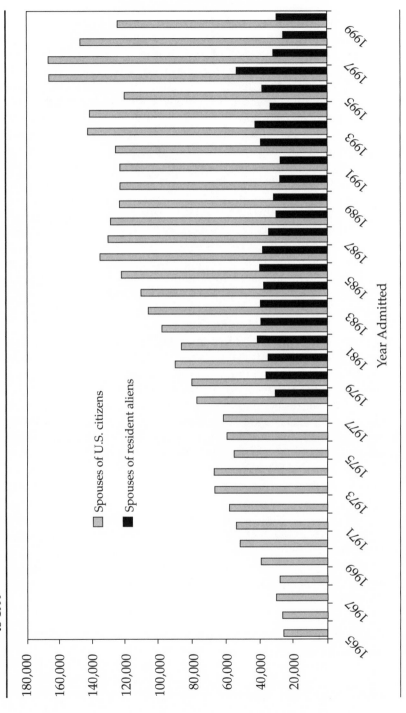

Source: U.S. Immigration and Naturalization Service (2001).
Note: Data on immigrants admitted as spouses of resident aliens not available before 1979.

mid-1990s. The probability of newly admitted immigrant spouses being sponsored by naturalized resident aliens may have increased in the 1990s as an outcome of policy enacted in the 1980s. Research based on interviews of immigrants from ten communities in Mexico further suggests that female migration in the mid-1990s reflected a process of family migration whereby wives migrated after their husbands obtained temporary amnesty under the provisions of IRCA (Donato 1993, 2001). Moreover, since these marriages were of longer than two years' duration, the newly admitted immigrant spouses were eligible for unconditional visas under the provisions of the 1986 Immigration Fraud Amendments Act.

The numbers of immigrants admitted as spouses of U.S. citizens increased steadily through the late 1970s until the mid-1980s, leveled off, and then peaked in 1996 and 1997. Research based on the New Immigrant Survey Pilot (Jasso et al. 2000b) suggests that about 40 percent of married immigrants aged eighteen and over who entered the U.S. or who adjusted their status to legal permanent resident in 1996 were sponsored by a native-born or foreign-born U.S. citizen. In many of these cases, the U.S. citizen appeared to be of Mexican origin and had been legalized under one of the provisions of the 1986 Immigration Reform and Control Act. IRCA-legalized aliens started becoming eligible to naturalize in fiscal year 1994, and consequently the mid-1990s immigrant entry cohorts included a large contingent of spouses of the IRCA-legalized and now naturalized migrants.

The Immigration and Naturalization Service data describing the marital characteristics of immigrants legally admitted to the country are, however, limited in several ways. They cover only immigrants who are legally admitted. With the exception of those who entered as the spouse of a U.S. citizen or of a permanent resident alien, no information is available describing the characteristics of the immigrant's spouse. We therefore turn to census data, which allow the description of the national origins, race, and nativity characteristics of married foreign-born persons and their spouses living in the United States in 1990. (Unfortunately, data from the 2000 census on the characteristics of married individuals are not yet available and other major surveys are too small to provide information about immigrants from specific countries of origin.)

Patterns of Intermarriage: National Origins, Race, and Nativity

There are numerous dimensions of intermarriage involving the immigrant generation. We focus first on national origin, which roughly corresponds to country of birth or country of origin. Basing our analysis on national origin glosses over important minority populations within each country, such as the Ainu in Japan, the Catalans in Spain, or the Québecois in Canada and so some facets of intermarriage across ethnic or racial lines are obscured, but this focus is dictated by the information available in the census. A further point is that within American society groups have formed along national lines after arriving in the United States, and in addition, the national origins of immigrants may reflect Americans' perceptions and understanding of the immigrants' ancestry and race. It is therefore unlikely that a focus on national origins is misleading with respect to patterns of intermarriage as a barometer of the relationships between culturally and socially defined groups

Unfortunately, recent U.S. census data do not include information on timing of marriage, marital status at time of entry into the country, or number of times the person has married. It is therefore impossible to determine which marriages occurred before the foreign-born persons migrated to the United States, which marriages are closely linked to the act of migration, and which occurred after arriving in the United States. For example, some immigrants may have been married well before migrating to the United States, entered as a married immigrant, divorced their spouse, and then remarried in the United States. The data from the census do, however, provide a cross-sectional overview of the outcome of these processes and thus provide a basis for discussion of the implications of patterns of intermarriage involving the foreign-born generation.

National Origin

Table 8.1 shows patterns of marriage by the national origins of married foreign-born men, and table 8.2 shows the same for married foreign-born women. The first line in table 8.1 shows, for example, that about 72 percent of married foreign-born men born in Portugal have wives who were born in Portugal, 9 percent have wives who were born in a foreign country other than Portugal, and about 19 percent have wives who were born in the United States. For each continent the countries of origin are ordered by the percentages of husbands with wives from the same foreign country. Among European countries, Portugal has the highest percentage of husbands with wives from the same country, and France has the lowest; only 15 percent of married male immigrants from France having wives from France.

Although the usual assumption is that most immigrants have spouses from the same country of origin—presumably because they

Table 8.1   Percentages of Married Foreign-Born Men with Wives Born in the Same Country of Origin, a Different Foreign Country, or the United States

Husband's Country of Origin	Wife's Place of Birth			
	Same Country as Husband	Different Foreign Country	United States	Total
Europe				
Portugal	72.1	8.7	19.2	100.0
USSR	61.9	15.0	23.2	100.0
Poland	55.3	16.9	27.8	100.0
Greece	53.3	9.8	36.9	100.0
Ireland	50.1	6.5	43.4	100.0
Italy	44.2	6.6	49.2	100.0
Hungary	42.6	19.8	37.6	100.0
Spain	31.6	24.3	44.1	100.0
Scandinavia	30.5	11.0	58.5	100.0
Czechoslovakia	28.9	22.2	48.9	100.0
United Kingdom	25.9	13.4	60.7	100.0
Switzerland	24.9	26.2	48.9	100.0
Germany	24.5	11.3	64.3	100.0
France	15.2	21.2	63.6	100.0
Asia				
Korea	93.0	3.3	3.7	100.0
Vietnam	91.8	5.2	3.0	100.0
Laos	91.5	6.2	2.3	100.0
Taiwan	88.1	8.4	3.5	100.0
India	82.6	9.9	7.5	100.0
Philippines	81.6	4.1	14.3	100.0
China	78.2	13.0	8.8	100.0
Pakistan	67.3	18.7	14.0	100.0
Iran	58.8	10.6	30.7	100.0
Japan	50.8	9.8	39.4	100.0
Iraq	47.6	31.1	21.3	100.0
North and South America				
Haiti	81.6	8.7	9.7	100.0
Cuba	74.5	9.1	16.5	100.0
Mexico	72.8	3.9	23.3	100.0
El Salvador	69.8	19.3	11.0	100.0
Dominican Republic	69.4	13.2	17.4	100.0
Guatemala	65.5	20.9	13.5	100.0
Colombia	65.5	15.7	18.8	100.0
Jamaica	64.5	10.1	25.5	100.0
Canada	25.4	7.3	67.4	100.0
Other country of origin	56.7	12.1	31.2	100.0
Total	61.4	9.5	29.1	100.0

Source: U.S. Bureau of the Census (1995).

Table 8.2   Percentages of Married Foreign-Born Women with Husbands Born in the Same Country of Origin, a Different Foreign Country, or the United States

Wife's Country of Origin	Husband's Place of Birth			
	Same Country as Wife	Different Foreign Country	United States	Total
Europe				
Portugal	79.0	4.4	16.7	100.0
USSR	70.9	12.6	16.5	100.0
Greece	68.5	9.1	22.5	100.0
Poland	61.3	13.7	25.1	100.0
Italy	57.5	4.2	38.3	100.0
Hungary	53.4	14.0	32.6	100.0
Ireland	40.9	9.7	49.5	100.0
Czechoslovakia	33.9	15.9	50.2	100.0
Spain	30.5	17.2	52.3	100.0
Scandinavia	30.1	6.9	63.1	100.0
Switzerland	28.8	21.9	49.3	100.0
United Kingdom	20.2	10.3	69.5	100.0
Germany	16.4	9.4	74.2	100.0
France	10.4	14.1	75.6	100.0
Asia				
Laos	94.8	3.7	1.6	100.0
India	89.1	6.1	4.9	100.0
Iran	86.0	6.5	7.5	100.0
China	82.1	7.0	10.9	100.0
Vietnam	79.7	7.4	13.0	100.0
Iraq	77.8	16.7	5.6	100.0
Pakistan	77.3	20.1	2.5	100.0
Taiwan	67.6	15.0	17.4	100.0
Korea	65.3	4.5	30.2	100.0
Philippines	63.5	5.1	31.5	100.0
Japan	28.7	5.8	65.5	100.0
North and South America				
Haiti	89.5	3.5	7.0	100.0
Cuba	78.6	7.6	13.8	100.0
Mexico	76.3	3.8	19.9	100.0
El Salvador	69.0	18.2	12.8	100.0
Dominican Republic	68.8	12.2	18.9	100.0
Jamaica	67.1	13.1	19.7	100.0
Guatemala	60.8	20.6	18.7	100.0
Colombia	54.7	21.4	23.9	100.0
Canada	21.7	6.7	71.6	100.0
Other	56.1	11.5	32.4	100.0
Total	58.6	8.3	33.0	100.0

Source: U.S. Bureau of the Census (1995).

entered the country together as young adults—the results presented in tables 8.1 and 8.2 show that this assumption is not fully warranted. Overall, only about 61 percent of foreign-born husbands and 59 percent of foreign-born wives living in the United States have spouses from the same country of origin, and some of these may have met and married their spouses after arriving in the United States. Moreover, there is a great deal of variation between continents, countries of origin within a continent, and the gender of the immigrant. Immigrants from Canada, a European country, or European region are in general less likely to have foreign-born spouses from the same country of origin than are immigrants from Asia or Central and South America.

Tables 8.1 and 8.2 also show that, in most cases, married foreign-born men from a specific country of origin are slightly less likely than their female compatriots to have a spouse from the same country of origin. For example, about 73 percent of Mexican husbands have Mexican wives while 76 percent of Mexican wives have Mexican husbands. That difference can be more extreme: only 48 percent of Iraqi husbands have Iraqi wives while over 78 percent of Iraqi wives have Iraqi husbands. In some cases the situation is reversed: over 90 percent of Korean husbands have Korean wives, whereas only 65 percent of Korean wives have Korean husbands. The same pattern holds for Japanese immigrants but at lower levels: Over 50 percent of Japanese husbands have Japanese wives but only 29 percent of Japanese wives have Japanese husbands.

Tables 8.1 and 8.2 also show that the origin-specific percentages of immigrants with spouses born in foreign-born countries that differ from their own are generally fairly low. These percentages are low for several reasons. The odds of the spouses from different foreign countries having met and married before migrating to the United States are low, and once in the United States, the odds of an immigrant's meeting and marrying an immigrant born in another foreign country are low because of linguistic and other cultural differences, the geographic segregation of different country-of-origin populations in the United States, and the relatively low numbers of foreign-born relative to native-born Americans in the United States.

Nativity

The percentages of immigrants with native-born American spouses also vary widely. Immigrants born in a European country or Canada are more likely than those born in Asia or in Central and South America to have native-born American spouses. There are a variety of reasons for this pattern. European and Canadian immigrants are more likely to have entered the United States already possessing skills in English (Stevens 1994). It is therefore easier for them to live in neighborhoods (Stevens and Garrett 1996), to go to schools, and to work in settings that are dominated by the English language and English speakers. The United States and Canada share an open border, and a very large percentage of Canadians live within one hundred miles of the United States. The ease of travel across the border allows numerous opportunities for Canadians to meet Americans and vice versa. Immigrants from Canada are therefore very likely to have been sponsored by a native-born American (Jasso and Rosenzweig 1989). In addition, because immigrants' countries of origin have shifted over time, immigrants from a European country are more likely to have lived in the United States for longer periods of time than immigrants from other countries and thus have had more time to meet and marry native-born Americans in this country, perhaps in a second or higher-order marriage.

It is also possible that race or national ancestry plays an important role. A large percentage of native-born Americans claim European descent. Racial cleavages between native-born Americans and immigrants of European or Canadian origins are therefore much less common than those between native-born Americans and immigrants born in Central or South America, Asia, or Africa. Moreover, because immigration streams in the nineteenth and twentieth centuries were dominated by Europeans, contemporary immigrants from Europe encounter many more opportunities to marry a native-born American of the same national origin than do contemporary immigrants from Asia or Central and South America.

The statistics presented in table 8.3 are from logistic models predicting the logged odds of a foreign-born man or woman having a native-born American spouse. The table shows in a slightly more formal fashion some of the relationships that are apparent in the previous tables showing percentage distributions. The more formal models have the advantage of allowing an evaluation of these relationships net of education—one of the most important social dimensions in marriage choices—as well as length of residence in the United States, race, and continent of origin. The coefficients in model 1 for each sex shows the relationships between education, time period of immigration, and the odds of an immigrant's being married to a native-born American. The impact of education is clear for both sexes: more highly educated immigrant men and women are more likely than less-educated immigrant men and women to be married to native-born Americans.

Table 8.3   Log Odds of a Married Immigrant Having a Native-Born Versus Foreign-Born Spouse, 1990

	Men			Women		
	Model 1	Model 2	Model 3	Model 1	Model 2	Model 3
Constant	−2.714*	−2.702*	−2.237*	−2.852*	−2.666*	−2.097*
Years of education	.073*	.090*	.085*	.122*	.110*	.111*
Year of immigration						
After 1986	ª	ª	ª	ª	ª	ª
1985 to 1986	.239*	.330*	.342*	.050	.140	.114
1982 to 1984	.425*	.537*	.568*	.171*	.257*	.247*
1980 to 1981	.105	.196	.219*	−.035	.045	.046
1975 to 1979	.494*	.604*	.581*	.391*	.463*	.446*
1970 to 1974	.755*	.814*	.813*	.787*	.852*	.839*
1965 to 1969	1.049*	.968*	.948*	1.106*	1.063*	1.041*
1960 to 1964	1.523*	1.312*	1.259*	1.636*	1.490*	1.047*
1950s	1.954*	1.636*	1.550*	2.022*	1.738*	1.719*
Before 1950	2.746*	2.424*	2.350*	2.490*	2.125*	2.114*
Continent of origin						
Europe or Canada	—	.412*	—	—	.518*	—
Asia	—	−1.188*	—	—	−.302*	—
Central or South America	—	.172*	—	—	−.473*	—
Other	—	ª	—	—	ª	—
Ethnic origin						
White	—	—	.031	—	—	−.132
Black	—	—	−.419	—	—	−1.032*
Asian or Pacific Islander	—	—	−1.997*	—	—	−.899*
Hispanic	—	—	−.591	—	—	−.897*
Other	—	—	ª	—	—	ª
Model Chi-square	7,725	9,593	10,700	9,077	10,252	10,234
df	10	13	14	10	13	14

Source: U.S. Bureau of the Census (1995).
ªOmitted category.
*Significant at .001 level.

The relationship between the time period when immigrants entered the United States and the odds of their being married to a native-born American, net of education, is strong and almost linear. The earlier a foreign-born person entered the country, the more likely he or she is to have a native-born spouse. The second model for each sex controls for continent of origin (Canada is placed in the same continental grouping as the European countries). The coefficients for year of immigration, net of time period of immigration, are slightly smaller but still significant. The third model for each sex replaces continent of origin with race or Hispanic origin as measured in the American context by the U.S. census. Again, the relationship between time of immigration and the odds of being married to a native-born American persists, although it is slightly weaker. The main conclusion is that the odds of an immigrant's being married to a native-born American increase the longer the person has been in the United States.

Race

The coefficients in table 8.3 for continent of origin and for race or Hispanic origin in the second and third models for each sex show sex-specific patterns. Men and women born in Europe or Canada are significantly more likely to have native-born American spouses than are men and women from an Asian or Pacific Island country or a Central or South American country—but the difference is much larger for men. When continent of origin is replaced by American race or Hispanic categories, the sex-specific pattern is even more striking. In addition to the differences between Asian men and women, there are differences between black foreign-born men and black foreign-born women in the odds of marriage to a native-born American. Black foreign-born women are much less likely to have a native-born American spouse than are black foreign-born men.

The race-specific results suggest that race, as defined in the American context, affects patterns of intermarriage within the foreign-born generation. The results presented in table 8.3 show the logged odds that immigrants with various characteristics, including race, marry a native-born American; they do not consider the race of the spouse. Table 8.4 shows the cross-classification of race or Hispanic origin for foreign-born men and foreign-born women and their spouses and, for purposes of contrast, for native-born men and native-born women as well. Although foreign-born white (non-Hispanic) men and foreign-born white (non-Hispanic) women are very likely to have white spouses, they are slightly less likely than native-born white men and women to have white spouses. In addition, black (non-Hispanic) immigrant men and women are less likely to have black spouses than are native-born black men and women. White immigrants and black immigrants are thus partly responsible for the increases in intermarriage across the white-black divide in American society (see also Kalmijn 1993b; Model and Fisher 2001). On the other hand, levels of racial endogamy are higher for foreign-born Asian men and women and for foreign-born Hispanic men and women than for their native-born counterparts.

The high levels of racial endogamy (or, conversely, low levels of racial intermarriage) in the United States are often considered evidence of persisting strong social and cultural barriers between the races, particularly between African Americans and others. The significant increases in racial intermarriage that have occurred over the last several decades (Stevens and Tyler 2002) suggest these barriers are diminishing. The results presented in table 8.4 suggest that the intermarriage patterns of immigrants are partially responsible for this statistical trend.

Nevertheless, a slight majority of immigrants have spouses of the same national origins as themselves (see tables 8.1 and 8.2) and thus are probably married endogamously with respect to race. Many, perhaps most, of these marriages occurred before the subjects immigrated to the United States and therefore say little about race relations in the United States. On the other hand, marriages between foreign-born and native-born Americans probably either occurred in the American context after the foreign spouse immigrated or were initiated by a native-born American. These marriages may therefore show particularly different patterns of racial endogamy and intermarriage.

Table 8.5 shows the cross-classification of racial or Hispanic origins for immigrant men and women with native-born American spouses. Recent research suggests that Asian immigrants in cross-nativity marriages are more likely to have white spouses than Asian immigrants with foreign-born spouses (Qian, Blair, and Ruf 2001). Table 8.5 shows that this pattern is not limited to Asian immigrants. Over 40 percent of Hispanic foreign-born wives in cross-nativity marriages have white spouses. Overall, higher percentages of immigrants in cross-nativity marriages have white spouses than immigrants in general. In general, the levels of racial endogamy are lower among cross-nativity marriages than among marriages involving two foreign-born spouses and marriages involving two native-born American spouses (see table 8.5). The relatively low levels of racial endogamy—particularly among black immigrants with native-born spouses—may reflect higher levels of acceptance of foreign-born than native-born blacks by native-born whites.

Table 8.4   Patterns of Racial Intermarriage for Wives and Husbands by Nativity, 1990 Census

Racial Origins	White	Black	Asian or Pacific Islander	Hispanic	Other	Total
Foreign-born wives						
White non-Hispanic	96.37	0.83	0.69	1.89	0.22	100.00%
Black non-Hispanic	3.86	93.69	0.20	2.10	0.15	100.00
Asian or Pacific Islander	19.16	1.31	77.99	1.33	0.21	100.00
Hispanic	11.16	0.85	0.79	87.02	0.18	100.00
Other	26.84	7.61	5.77	15.81	43.97	100.00
Foreign-born husbands						
White non-Hispanic	94.79	0.27	1.13	3.59	0.22	100.00
Black non-Hispanic	4.43	91.11	1.09	3.15	0.22	100.00
Asian or Pacific Islander	5.36	0.16	92.42	1.85	0.21	100.00
Hispanic	7.02	0.38	0.48	91.81	0.32	100.00
Other	26.75	6.61	2.19	10.87	53.58	100.00
Native-born wives						
White non-Hispanic	98.07	0.31	0.14	1.13	0.36	100.00
Black non-Hispanic	1.45	97.54	0.05	0.79	0.17	100.00
Asian or Pacific Islander	58.36	3.61	34.08	3.32	0.63	100.00
Hispanic	32.50	2.06	0.39	64.59	0.46	100.00
Other	53.96	2.58	0.49	3.96	39.00	100.00
Native-born husbands						
White non-Hispanic	96.55	0.11	0.72	2.24	0.39	100.00
Black	3.94	93.40	0.58	1.85	0.24	100.00
Asian or Pacific Islander	23.57	0.58	70.74	4.51	0.59	100.00
Hispanic	19.49	1.02	0.72	78.27	0.50	100.00
Other	51.51	1.87	1.14	4.59	40.90	100.00

Source: U.S. Bureau of the Census (1995).

Census data do not include information about parents' countries of birth and so cannot be used to distinguish patterns of intermarriage between the second generation and third (or later) generations, but the Current Population Surveys fielded in the latter part of the 1990s do. Table 8.6 is based on data from Current Population Surveys fielded in March from 1995 through 2001. The data are pooled to provide enough cases for analysis. The cell entries in the table are the sex-specific and race- or ancestry-specific percentages of marriages in which the respondent has a spouse of a different race or ancestry.

Table 8.6 shows the same pattern for foreign-born versus native-born white husbands and wives (although in more detail for the native-born generations) observed earlier in the census data. Foreign-

Table 8.5   Patterns of Racial Intermarriage for Foreign-Born Men and Women with Native-Born Spouses, 1990 Census

	Race of Native-Born Spouse					
	White	Black	Asian or Pacific Islander	Hispanic	Other	Total
Foreign-born wives						
White non-Hispanic	95.69	1.37	0.49	2.10	0.35	100.00%
Black non-Hispanic	13.85	81.33	0.00	4.11	0.71	100.00
Asian or Pacific Islander	79.25	5.22	11.34	3.36	0.84	100.00
Hispanic	42.47	2.77	0.43	53.72	0.61	100.00
Other	51.34	15.39	0.00	21.21	12.06	100.00
Foreign-born husbands						
White non-Hispanic	95.95	0.35	0.33	2.98	0.38	100.00
Black non-Hispanic	12.96	81.97	0.99	3.42	0.66	100.00
Asian or Pacific Islander	60.36	1.60	28.67	7.78	1.59	100.00
Hispanic	28.85	1.13	0.42	68.36	1.25	100.00
Other	54.80	17.55	0.00	10.06	17.59	100.00

Source: U.S. Bureau of the Census (1995).

born white husbands and foreign-born white wives are more likely than native-born white husbands and wives to have spouses of a different race or ancestry. Table 8.6 shows, in addition, that the difference in percentages of native-born white husbands and wives having spouses of different race or ancestry differs little between the second and the third generations.

For blacks, the patterns of intermarriage across generations appear to be sex-specific, although the small numbers of cases of second-generation black wives and black husbands make it difficult to reach any conclusions about a regular progression across the first, second, and third (and later) generations in levels of intermarriage. There are, of course, large numbers of third- and later-generation black Americans, and the number of foreign-born black immigrants in the United States has been growing steadily, albeit from a low base, since at least the 1970s. There has not, however, been enough time for black immigrants entering in the latter part of the twentieth century to have enough native-born children of marriageable age so that they would show up in statistical surveys in sizable numbers. This gap in the generations among black Americans is a reminder that second-generation Americans need not be the "children" of the current first generation (or the parents of the third generation), and that third generation Americans are not the children of the second generation. The small numbers of second-generation black husbands and wives thus

Table 8.6   Percentages of Married Men and Women, by Generation and Race or Ancestry, with Spouses of a Different Race or Ancestry

Generation	Race or Ancestry				
	White Non-Hispanic	Black Non-Hispanic	Asian or Pacific Islander	Hispanic	Other
Wives					
Foreign-born	4.25	5.33	17.59	10.49	—
Second generation	2.87	—	36.62	25.99	—
Third generation	2.62	3.08	40.46	31.17	60.8
Total	2.72	3.35	20.86	17.68	59.8
Number of cases	149,134	10,620	6,658	24,801	1,614
Husbands					
Foreign-born	5.97	6.22	6.22	7.68	—
Second generation	3.20	—	26.69	26.19	—
Third generation	3.11	7.18	29.47	30.94	59.74
Total	3.25	7.31	9.93	15.41	58.15
Number of cases	149,996	11,163	5,807	24,372	1,489

Source: Current Population Survey (1995 to 2001).
Note: — Percentage based on fewer than one hundred cases and therefore not presented.

provide a cautionary note in the reading of patterns over generations as unfolding over historical time when the data are limited to one time period.

The columns of percentages for wives and husbands of Asian or Pacific Island ancestry or of Hispanic ancestry all show the same pattern: an increase in the percentage of exogamous marriages between the first (foreign-born) generation and the second generation, and an additional, although much smaller, increase between the second and the third generations. The increasing levels of intermarriage across generations strongly suggests that the intermarriage patterns of Asians and of Hispanics will parallel those of European immigrants and their descendants over the course of the twentieth century.

Summary and Conclusions

The social and cultural integration of racial and ethnic groups introduced into the American context by immigration is a complex process. The extent and rapidity with which it occurs has numerous implications for relations between racial and ethnic groups; it may also change the understandings of race and ethnicity in the American context and perhaps the understanding of what it means to be "American." Levels of intermarriage across extant racial and ethnic boundaries are often considered a barometer of integration because levels (and patterns) of intermarriage reflect the strength of racially and ethnically based barriers to the formation of intimate social relationships and accelerate the loss of culturally important distinctions. In the European example, European national-origin groups, originally considered racially distinct in disparaging terms, intermarried in such rapidly increasing proportions over several generations that cultural and social distinctions were largely erased within a century. The native-born American population of European descent now lays claim to various European ancenstries so inconsistently as to imply that European-derived national origins are optional or largely symbolic (Farley 1991).

Whether the same process of integration, as marked and accelerated by intermarriage, will take place and at the same pace for the racial and ethnic groups introduced by immigration streams in the last portion of the twentieth century is unknown. The European case was marked by a virtual cessation of immigration during the middle third of the century, and some scholars have argued that the hiatus aided the assimilation, both structural and cultural, of the invidiously ranked European groups. The integration of the European groups may also have been aided by a lack of physical distinctiveness and by opportunities for economic and structural integration specific to the time period (Massey 1995).

Definitive answers are lacking as to what will happen over time and over generations, but it is still instructive to consider intermarriage patterns as reflecting and generating processes of incorporation. At the individual level, intermarriage with respect to national origin and race affects the incorporation of individual immigrants and their children into American society. Moreover, intermarriage across nativity and citizenship categories directly affects the political, and probably social, incorporation of immigrants and their children. The effects on individuals extend through their family networks and thus into the wider American population. And as the analyses presented in this chapter show, patterns of intermarriage across nativity overlay patterns of intermarriage across national origin and racial lines. The description of patterns of intermarriage involving the immigrant population also shows that the integration of national origin and racial groups through intermarriage starts in the first generation and continues into the native-born generations. The "succession of generations" may be a major engine of the incorporation of culturally distinct groups, but for some groups, the process is kick-started by the immigrant generation living through their lives in the American context.

Various aspects of immigration policy and foreign relations have some affect on the marital characteristics of immigrants at time of entry. The family reunification emphasis in U.S. immigration policy encourages the entry of immediate relatives—particularly spouses and fiancé(e)s—of successful applicants, of permanent residents, and of naturalized and native-born citizens. From the 1970s through the 1990s, about 50 percent of immigrants admitted to the country were married. Although the common image is one in which married immigrants admitted to the country are accompanied by their (also foreign-born) spouses, significant numbers of immigrants are admitted as spouses of U.S. citizens or permanent residents. In 1999, for example, of the 647,000 immigrants admitted, 330,000, or 51 percent, were married. Of the married immigrants, 115,000, or 35 percent, were principal immigrants and 57,000, or 17 percent, were derivative spouses. It is likely that many of these marriages were endogamous with respect to national origins and race. However, 128,000 (39 percent) of the married immigrants were spouses of U.S. citizens, and 29,000 (9 percent) were spouses of resident aliens (U.S. Immigration and Naturalization Service 2002b).

Overall, during the last quarter of the twentieth century about a quarter of immigrants legally admitted to the country each year were admitted as the spouse of an American citizen. In many cases the American citizen sponsor was a foreign-born naturalized citizen. And again, in many of these cases, it seems likely that the spouse sponsored by the naturalized citizen may be of the same national origin as his or her sponsor, and thus married endogamously with respect to national origin, race, and nativity. The implementation of various aspects of immigration policy—especially the provisions of the Immigration Reform and Control Act—in tandem with the complex and iterative nature of migratory behavior also appears to have encouraged the formation or re-formation of immigrant couples of the same national origin and research suggests this is particularly the case for Mexicans (Dávila and Mora 2001). Yet census data on the marital characteristics of immigrants residing in the United States also show that almost a third of married foreign-born persons living in the United States have native-born American spouses. A good percentage of the spouses sponsored by U.S. citizens must therefore have been sponsored by native-born American citizens.

Immigration and foreign relations policy may have played an unintended role in the formation of the large numbers of cross-nativity marriages by providing the opportunities for native-born Americans, especially male military personnel, to meet prospective partners abroad and to sponsor their entry into the country (Heaton and Jacobson 2000). The marketplace for foreign brides (and occasionally foreign grooms), possibly propelled by new technology, may also play a role in the arrival of foreign-born persons in the country. It seems plausible that many of these marriages cross boundaries of national-origin descent or race. (On the other hand, the apparently increasing probability that families or communities seek appropriate, that is, foreign-born, spouses from their country of origin as partners for American residents may result in some of these marriages being deliberately endogamous with respect to national origin or race.)

Most analyses of intermarriage have neglected the role of cross-nativity marriages. Yet marriage between the foreign-born and native-born generations allows the easier political integration of foreign-born spouses since the length of residence required for naturalization is shorter. The acquisition of U.S. citizenship for foreign-born children with an American citizen parent is almost guaranteed. Our analyses of census data also suggested that many immigrants contract marriages with native-born American citizens. In general, the longer an immigrant has lived in the United States (and thus the younger the age at immigration), the more likely he or she is to have a native-born American spouse. The relatively low levels of endogamy with respect to national origin (Stevens 2000) and the lower levels of racial endogamy in cross-nativity marriages than in other configurations suggest that the presumptive baseline of high levels of endogamy with respect to national origin in the foreign-born generation may be overstated.

The social and cultural integration of racial and national-origin descent groups introduced, and augmented, by immigration is a central consideration in debates about whom and how many to admit to the country. Theoretical frameworks and analyses considering the integration of social and culturally distinct groups have focused on processes of assimilation, including intermarriage, as they occur over time and generation. A common result is that the behaviors and experiences of the immigrant generation are used as a baseline against which progress of later generations is compared. To the extent that this comparison is warranted, the results presented here suggest that levels of intermarriage among Americans of Asian and of Hispanic descent increase through successive generations. Perhaps more important, the analyses presented here demonstrate that the processes of social and cultural incorporation, as indicated through intermarriage with respect to nativity, citizenship, and race, are well under way within the immigrant generation and that some of these processes have been facilitated, if inadvertently, by aspects of immigration policy.

= Chapter 9 =

The Economic and Fiscal Consequences of Immigration

I N PREVIOUS chapters we have focused on theory and research that help answer two of the three broad questions that, we suggested in chapter 1, drive most policy debates about immigration: What kinds of people immigrate to the United States? What happens to them after they arrive? In this and the next chapter we shift gears and focus on theory and research that can help answer the third broad question: What are the consequences of immigration for the United States and its residents? We focus in this chapter on the general aggregate economic and fiscal consequences of immigration, including an examination of labor-market implications. That recent immigrants are just as likely as natives to have graduated from college but at the same time are much more likely not to have completed high school implies that immigrants and natives play different labor-market roles (Waldinger and Lee 2001). It also suggests that significant interdependencies might exist in the United States between immigration and labor-market dynamics. If the foreign- and native-born populations were similar in their backgrounds and human capital characteristics, there would be little reason to think immigration might have substantial positive or negative impacts on the economy, including influences on native labor-market outcomes, beyond the scale effects of immigrants simply adding to population and economic growth (Smith and Edmonston 1997).

Immigrants constitute an increasingly important component of the labor-force in the United States. This is revealed by the percentage of the economically active population (those working or looking for work) made up by immigrants in 1999, 11.9 percent, which is greater than the percentage they represented of the general population in the same year, 9.9 percent (U.S. Current Population Survey 1999)—especially in high-immigration cities (see table 9.1). Migrants from certain

Table 9.1 Percentage Foreign-Born in Total and Economically Active Populations of High Immigrant and Low Immigrant Metropolitan Statistical Areas (MSAs), Thirty Largest MSAs, Persons Ages Sixteen and Over, 1998

	Total Foreign-Born Population	Percentage Foreign-Born in Total Population (A)	Percentage Foreign-Born in Economically Active Population[b] (B)
High immigrant MSAs[a]			
Los Angeles–Long Beach	3,483,099	35.8	45.3
New York	3,019,679	35.1	45.1
Chicago	1,097,255	14.3	17.0
Miami	1,025,997	48.9	59.7
Orange County, California	733,303	26.4	30.6
Total in the five high-immigrant cities	9,359,333	30.3	37.5
Difference between columns B and A		7.2	
Low immigrant MSAs[c]			
St. Louis	38,420	1.4	1.4
Pittsburgh	50,774	2.1	2.0
Kansas City	64,273	3.6	4.2
Cleveland	108,561	4.4	4.2
Baltimore	112,355	4.4	4.6
Total in the five low-immigrant cities	374,383	3.1	3.2
Difference between columns B and A		0.1	

Source: Authors' tabulations from 1998 March Current Population Survey.
[a] The five of the largest thirty metropolitan statistical areas (MSAs) with highest total foreign-born populations.
[b] The economically active population includes adults ages sixteen and older who were at work, working, laid off, or looking for work in March 1998. Adults in the armed forces and those not in the labor force are excluded.
[c] The five of the largest thirty MSAs with lowest total foreign-born populations.

countries, especially those likely to send labor migrants, are most heavily represented in U.S. immigration flows. A close look at immigration statistics reveals that employment-based immigration is a large but nevertheless a minority share of total legal immigration. In 1998 about 177,500 immigrants, or 11.7 percent of all legal immigration, were admitted under employment preferences, but 191,500 (29.0 percent) were admitted under family-sponsored preferences, along with another 283,000 (42.8 percent) as immediate relatives of U.S. citizens. An additional 54,500 (8.3 percent) were admitted as refugees or asylees for humanitarian reasons (U.S. Immigration and Naturalization Service 2000b, table 8). These shares did not vary greatly from year to year during the 1990s, because the quotas allocated to them were set into law by the immigration legislation of 1965, and were adjusted in the Immigration Act of 1990. Such figures illustrate that the provisions in U.S. immigration law favoring family reunification drive admissions more than employment factors. Family-based immigrants might be expected to show lower levels of education and thus lead to less favorable labor-market outcomes than employment-based immigrants. However, research by Elaine Sorensen, Frank D. Bean, and Leighton Ku (1992) reveals that family-based immigrants closely resemble employment-based immigrants in their labor-market behaviors and outcomes, thus implying that the emphasis on families in U.S. immigration law does not appear unduly to affect relative labor-market outcomes. (Of course we are talking here only about legal immigration.)

There may, however, be race- and gender-based differences in the labor-market implications of immigration. Concerning race, the case of African Americans is of particular interest because many blacks hold relatively low-skilled jobs, which could make them especially vulnerable to competition from unskilled immigrants. The gender discrepancy in the shares of the foreign-born and native-born populations that are economically active suggests that men and women may migrate for somewhat different reasons. Table 9.2 and figure 9.1 show that foreign-born men are more likely than native-born men to be economically active, whereas foreign-born women are less likely to be economically active than native-born women. The degree to which employment-based immigration might generate different labor-market characteristics and outcomes among men and women is a topic awaiting future research.

Economic and Fiscal Effects

Two of the major components of the third broad policy-relevant research question are the economic and fiscal effects of immigration on

Table 9.2 Proportions of Foreign-Born and Native-Born in Economically Active Population, by Age Group (1980, 1990, and 1996 to 1998)

Age Group	1980		1990		1996 to 1998	
	Native-Born	Foreign-Born	Native-Born	Foreign-Born	Native-Born	Foreign-Born
Men and women						
Sixteen and over	0.547	0.501	0.561	0.542	0.619	0.631
Sixteen to sixty-four	0.616	0.621	0.648	0.617	0.714	0.702
Twenty-five and over	0.585	0.519	0.603	0.574	0.669	0.670
Twenty-five to sixty-four	0.689	0.675	0.723	0.672	0.800	0.761
Men only						
Sixteen and over	0.664	0.629	0.642	0.654	0.684	0.762
Sixteen to sixty-four	0.728	0.750	0.717	0.718	0.769	0.827
Twenty-five and over	0.732	0.665	0.701	0.700	0.746	0.808
Twenty-five to sixty-four	0.832	0.831	0.808	0.788	0.865	0.893
Women only						
Sixteen and over	0.440	0.390	0.487	0.437	0.558	0.504
Sixteen to sixty-four	0.509	0.503	0.580	0.514	0.661	0.574
Twenty-five and over	0.455	0.397	0.515	0.459	0.600	0.537
Twenty-five to sixty-four	0.553	0.538	0.640	0.558	0.738	0.627

Sources: U.S. Census of Population and Housing (1982, 1992b); Current Population Survey, March sample (1996, 1997, 1998, 1999).

Figure 9.1   Proportion of Economically Active Population by Nativity and Gender, Ages Sixteen and Over in the United States, 1980, 1990, 1998

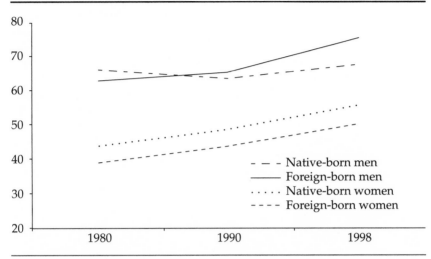

Sources: U.S. Census of Population and Housing (1982, 1992b); Current Population Survey, March sample (1996, 1997, 1998, 1999).

other groups and on the country as a whole. In a major effort to shed light on these issues, the U.S. Commission on Immigration Reform sponsored a major study in 1995 (U.S. Commission on Immigration Reform 1997). As part of its mandate the commission was required to submit a report to Congress on the impact of immigration on the country. The commission asked the National Research Council (NRC), the research branch of the National Academy of Sciences, to conduct an assessment of the demographic, economic (including labor-market), and fiscal effects of immigration on the country. The report was completed in 1997 (Smith and Edmonston 1997). Here we first consider economic and fiscal impacts as assessed by the NRC, and then we examine labor-market effects in greater detail. By economic impacts the NRC meant the sum total effects of immigration on aggregate gross domestic product operating through both supply and demand factors, including such mechanisms as reductions in the prices of goods resulting from increases in relatively cheap immigrant labor. By fiscal impacts the NRC meant the relationship between the taxes immigrants pay and the costs of their being here (Smith and Edmonston 1997).

In its assessment of immigration's economic effects on the country, the NRC concluded that overall and on balance, they are positive. That is, taking into account all of the various kinds of economic consequences connected with immigration, immigration works to generate a small net economic gain for the country (Smith and Edmonston 1997). However, the NRC research also indicated that such gains are not evenly distributed throughout the country and the population. Areas of the country with more highly skilled workers and the greatest concentrations of capital, as well as persons possessing these characteristics to greater degrees, receive a disproportionate share of the economic benefits of immigration. Persons with low levels of education and no capital are much less likely to benefit, or may even incur costs, as a result of immigration, although these costs are not sufficiently large to offset the gains to immigration accruing to the educationally and financially better endowed. But the overall economic effects are positive.

The NRC also investigated the fiscal effects of immigration—the extent to which the sum total of taxes paid as a result of the presence of immigrants in the country exceeds or falls below the sum total of the costs of services and benefits paid to immigrants. Whether the fiscal impacts of immigration have been positive or negative and the degree of this positive or negative impact has been one of the major controversies in the more general policy issue of the effects of immigration on U.S. natives. Research on this subject has been highly influential in the policy debate, particularly during economic slowdowns that have heightened anxieties about the economic costs of immigration. Such research has also been highly controversial, in large measure because different researchers have come to such widely varying conclusions about the magnitude and direction of fiscal impacts. For example, in early 1993, when the United States economy began growing again after the recession of 1990–1991 but not in sufficiently robust fashion to generate much in the way of increases in new jobs, one study estimated that the net cost of all legal and unauthorized immigrants in the United States was $42.5 billion annually (Huddle 1993). Another study, using the same data, came up with an estimated net gain from the presence of immigrants of as much as $30.0 billion annually (Passel 1994). The difference between these is $72.5 billion, a huge disparity by almost any standard, and an unusual example of how different researchers, even when using the same data, may not agree on what should be counted on the tax revenue or cost side of the ledger. This particular discrepancy reinforced the perception that the results of such research, at least up until the mid-1990s, often reflected more about the researchers' assumptions than about the actual net costs or benefits of immigrants.

It was partly in response to such discrepancies that the U.S. Commission on Immigration Reform asked the National Research Council to conduct the assessment of the demographic, economic, and fiscal effects of immigration on the country. Regarding fiscal impacts, the study pointed out that previous efforts to estimate the cost of immigration had almost all focused on developing "current account" estimates. That is, first they tried to add up tax revenues paid by immigrants (and sometimes taxes paid by natives in order to provide services for immigrants), then they added up the cost of the services and benefits that immigrants received. This was almost always done for a single year. Obviously, the results were completely dependent not only on revenue and expenditure data for that year but also on the characteristics of the immigrants in the country in that year. In short, these "current account" analyses were static, not dynamic, and failed to take into account the fact all of these factors are constantly changing. Not only revenue and expenditure patterns but also the characteristics of both the native and immigrant populations are constantly in flux, meaning that any estimate for only a single year provides an imperfect gauge of what the net cost or benefit of immigrants might be in the future. To take just one example, immigrants in the prime working ages pay substantially more in taxes and receive substantially less in benefits than older retired immigrants. Consequently, current account values will be significantly affected by the age composition of the immigrant population in the year for which estimates are calculated as well as by other changing characteristics of immigrants and natives over time, including the aging of these populations.

What, then, can be concluded about the fiscal impacts of immigration in the United States? First, in the short run (as indicated by the results of the NRC's estimates of the fiscal effects of those immigrants in the country in a particular year), the net fiscal impact of immigrants on native households appears to be negative, but relatively small—about $200 per household in 1996 dollars for all native households in the United States. This conclusion was arrived at by extrapolating to the entire country analysis carried out in New Jersey and California (Smith and Edmonston 1997, 282–89; Garvey and Espenshade 1998; Clune 1998), and it assumes that the cost burden is spread throughout the country. But when the NRC focused just on California, a state with a sizable immigrant population, the net cost per native household is much higher, about $1,200 per household.

Second, in the long run the net fiscal impact is estimated to be positive, rather than negative, primarily because so many of the recent arrivals are relatively young working age persons, often with children in the public school system (Smith and Edmonston 1997, 352–54; Lee and Miller 1998). This conclusion was based on the results of the dynamic analyses undertaken by the NRC to estimate the fiscal effects of immigrants in the country over the entire lifetimes of those immigrants. When aggregated into governmental jurisdictions, however, this positive impact was not distributed evenly among state, local, and federal levels of government. It was substantially positive at the federal level and substantially negative at the other two levels, but in the latter case not enough to prevent the overall effect on the entire country from being positive.

On balance, then, it is evident that it is difficult to reach definitive conclusions about the relative fiscal costs of immigration. In any case, the differences among the various estimates do not yield large enough positive or negative net balances to provide a clear basis for establishing policy directions. Having said this, however, there is one research result whose magnitude is so great that it continues to exert consequential effects on fiscal situations. This is that most of the taxes that immigrants pay (two-thirds to three-fourths) go to the federal government in the form of FICA (Federal Insurance Contributions Act), or payroll, taxes, and income taxes, whereas at least half of the "costs" of immigrants—education, health, and criminal justice expenses—are borne by state and local governments (Clune 1998; Smith and Edmonston 1997). Thus, a serious imbalance occurs in the jurisdictional distribution of the fiscal costs and benefits of immigration. This exerts a tremendous strain on state and local governments, one that is exacerbated during recessionary times and plays a substantial role in the emergence of anxieties about immigration during such times, in part because the costs are experienced more directly by state and local populations than are the revenues, which flow mostly to the federal government.

Labor-Market Effects

Another critical aspect of the larger question of immigration's impacts is the labor-market effects of immigration. This issue excites paramount interest because its consequences are felt much closer to people's daily lives than other, more abstract, effects, such as shifts in productivity. There has also been particularly keen interest in the labor-market effects of immigration for certain historically disadvantaged groups, especially African Americans. The questions of whether immigrants "drive down wages" and "take people's jobs," especially in relation to African Americans, have often captured public attention. Because of the importance of these issues, we address the matters here in some detail, devoting separate sections to the questions of immigration's labor-market effects on African Americans and women.

Interest in the labor-market effects of immigration is driven to a significant extent by the fact that many recent immigrants come with relatively low levels of education. Even though the distribution of educational attainment among immigrants shows the same relative concentration of high-education persons as among natives, it also reveals a higher proportion of low-education persons. For example, 20.4 percent of immigrants in 1995 reported sixteen or more years of schooling, 41.2 percent twelve to fifteen years, and 38.4 percent fewer than twelve years, whereas for natives the comparable figures were 20.4, 61.5, and 18.2 percent, respectively. Immigration's labor-market effects depend on, among other things, how immigrants are distributed geographically. The foreign-born population is not evenly dispersed throughout the country. California, New York, Florida, Texas, Illinois, and New Jersey (in that order) receive disproportionately large shares of newcomers: about 70 percent of all foreign-born persons in the United States lived in these six states in 1998 (U.S. Current Population Survey 1998). The labor-market consequences of immigration are likely to be felt most severely in these areas and less so in areas with few immigrants.

Interest in immigration's labor-market implications is also shaped by changes in economic conditions that have occurred in the United States over the past twenty-five years. Beginning in the early 1970s, growth in real wages began to slow down (Levy 1987, 1995), unemployment began to creep up (Farley 1996; Reischauer 1989), and calls for immigration reform began to emerge (Bean, Telles, and Lowell 1987). Most of the early research studies motivated by these conditions reported results suggesting that the labor-market effects of immigration on natives are small and contradictory in their direction (Altonji and Card 1991; Bean, Telles, and Lowell 1987; Borjas 1986, 1987a; DeFreitas 1988, 1991; LaLonde and Topel 1991; Stewart and Hyclak 1986; Taylor et al. 1988). Local case studies of the garment industry (Maram 1980), the restaurant industry (Vasquez 1981), and U.S. agriculture (Wise 1974) revealed lower wage levels and higher U.S.-worker unemployment levels associated with Mexican immigrant presence. One effort to specify the effects separately for Mexican unauthorized and legal immigrants found modest complementarity emerging between unauthorized men and their non-Hispanic white counterparts in the urban Southwest (Bean, Telles, and Lowell

1987)—in other words, higher wages among non-Hispanic workers was associated with greater numbers of unauthorized Mexican immigrants.

As real wages during the 1980s and early 1990s continued to stagnate and even to decline among less-skilled American workers (Kosters 1991; Levy 1995), and as income inequality further increased (Juhn, Murphy, and Pierce 1993; Karoly 1993; Levy 1997), interest in immigration's labor-market effects remained at a high level. As noted, analyses of the aggregate economic effects of immigration conducted during the 1990s tended to show that immigration works to benefit those who possess capital and higher skills but operates to impose an economic cost on those with lower skills (Borjas 1998a; Smith and Edmonston 1997). Moreover, some researchers found that immigration contributed to an increase in the earnings gap between low-skilled and high-skilled American workers (Borjas, Freeman, and Katz 1992, 1997), and others found that wage inequality has increased by larger amounts in those regions of the country experiencing the greatest immigration (Topel 1994). Such results, when viewed in combination with the results already noted, suggest that the effects of immigration may be more complex than many studies have indicated.

Theories of Labor-Market Impacts

The impact of immigration on native groups is viewed differently by economists and sociologists. Although economic theories provide a framework within which to analyze the consequences of immigration, such theories do not predict whether increasing immigration will have positive or negative impacts (Borjas 1984, 1989, 1990). For economists, ascertaining labor-market effects is thus an empirical matter that requires determining the extent to which immigrants are substitutes or complements in the process of production—whether they compete with native-born workers (substitute for natives) or enhance the productivity of natives (complement natives) (Borjas 1990). Various empirical approaches have been employed to estimate substitution and complementarity effects on labor-market outcomes (Borjas 1990; Bean, Telles, and Lowell 1987). Within the framework of these approaches, the labor-market outcomes of labor input groups (such as various native groups) are generally viewed as a function of the relative concentration and change in size of other labor input groups (such as immigrants). The finding that immigrants generate negative labor-market outcomes for other groups as they become more numerous indicates substitutability, whereas the finding of positive labor-market outcomes indicates complementarity.

Unlike economic theory, sociological theory provides more theoretical bases for predicting positive or negative immigration effects. As outlined classically in the work of human ecologists like Robert Park and Ernest Burgess (1921) and Amos Hawley (1945, 1950), and more recently and explicitly in the work of Fredrik Barth (1956, 1969), Peter Blau (1994), Amos Hawley (1970, 1986) and Susan Olzak (1992), the key theoretical proposition is that complementarity among social groups is enhanced when such groups occupy separate social structural locations and niches. Because scarce resources often lead to group competition—that is, because two or more racial or ethnic groups may "try to acquire the same valued resources, such as jobs, housing, or marriage partners" (Olzak 1992, 28)—social structural variables that foster complementarity and mitigate competition are of particular theoretical significance. Complementarity represents what Hawley (1986) terms "symbiosis" and competition, what he terms "commensalism." Other things being equal, especially groups' economic status, the tendency for the division of labor to evolve in the direction of specialization operates to enhance productivity. However, competition among socially differentiated groups for scarce resources may override this tendency to the extent that competing groups occupy the same social and spatial structures. Such competition will be minimized when groups show little overlap in social and spatial structural positions. Symbiosis or commensalism will also be more or less likely depending on the extent to which both scarce resources (jobs, in the present case) are rendered more or less plentiful and as the relative size of one of the groups pursuing such scarce resources becomes larger or smaller than the other.

In the case of immigrants, one way in which they might function as a complementary source of labor is illustrated by unauthorized migrants. Because of their willingness to fill low-paying, often temporary, jobs at the base of the social hierarchy (King, Lowell, and Bean 1986; Piore 1979), unauthorized migrants may fulfill an economic role that is both necessary and otherwise difficult to fulfill (Piore 1979; Massey, Durand and Malone 2002). Their ready availability and flexibility may enhance economic expansions and cushion the shocks of cyclical changes (DeFreitas 1988). Although the wages unauthorized workers receive have been found to be a function of their education, experience, and amount of job-specific training (Massey 1987), it is the economic niches they occupy and the employment conditions they are often willing to accept (as compared to those that legal immigrants or natives will accept), as well as the potential increases in demand and productivity that may accompany these, that lead to the possibility that such workers may complement native workers, at least under certain conditions.

Local Labor-Market Demand and
Structural Contingencies

Labor-market complementarity and competition may be affected not only by local labor demand but also by certain social and spatial structural features of the urban locales that are destinations for immigrants. The degree of complementarity or substitution occurring across local labor-market areas is variable rather than constant. The extent to which labor-market effects are positive or negative will accordingly be affected by social and spatial structural factors whose level and change increases (or decreases) the intensity of group efforts to acquire scarce resources and the tendency of groups to occupy non-overlapping social structures. The strength and vitality of urban labor markets as reflected by local area labor demand may thus affect the intensity of labor-market competition and complementarity between immigrants and natives. Specifically, the tightness of the local labor market may influence the direction and magnitude of immigration effects by lowering competition for scarce resources (jobs or higher wages).

Certain social and spatial structural features of local labor markets may affect complementarity and competition as well. During the 1970s and 1980s the United States shifted from a manufacturing-based to a more information- and services-based economy, and these changes affected some cities more than others (Sassen 1990). It is well documented that these shifts have been particularly hard on low-skilled workers, especially in the Northeast and Midwest (Holzer and Vroman 1991; Wilson 1987). Moreover, regions and cities vary considerably, not only in their pattern of restructuring (Kasarda 1985, 1989, 1995), but also in the extent to which they receive immigrants (Waldinger 1989). That cities like New York and Chicago experienced both net out-migration and the influx of large numbers of immigrants during the 1980s (Fix and Passel 1991) suggests that no single perspective on structure or change is likely to encapsulate fully the labor-market dynamics affecting the employment and earnings prospects of different racial and ethnic groups in urban areas.

Theories about spatial and skills mismatches, industrial and occupational restructuring, and job queuing point to factors affecting the likelihood that complementarity or competition will occur in the labor market. Originally formulated as an explanation of structural unemployment (Holzer and Vroman 1991), the spatial mismatch hypothesis has also been invoked to explain the emergence of underclass areas in inner cities (Kasarda 1989; Wilson 1987, 1996). The hypothesis links the development of urban poverty and the growth of such areas both to the decline of manufacturing jobs and to their movement to the suburbs (Wilson 1996). Less educated inner-city workers, because they lack the resources to relocate to the suburbs or to travel to jobs located there, suffer a "mismatch" between the location of employment and residential opportunities that impairs their economic well-being. All else being equal, the greater the infusion of low-skilled immigrants into cities, the greater any negative effects associated with mismatch. Conversely, any negative effects of low-skilled immigration on low-skilled natives can be expected to be most severe in areas of greater mismatch.

Although the spatial mismatch hypothesis points to some of the structural circumstances under which job competition and displacement between less-skilled immigrants and natives might be exacerbated, mismatch notions by themselves do not provide very satisfactory explanations of urban population and economic change because they provide little basis for understanding why large numbers of immigrants have moved into cities that have also experienced manufacturing declines. Urban economic restructuring perspectives, with their emphases on the globalization of the economy and the growth of the service sector (Sassen 1988, 1989, 1990), provide a better answer. Some cities that have experienced declines in manufacturing have also witnessed substantial increases in service jobs. Large postindustrial cities with substantial financial and business service sectors have generated large numbers of both new high-status, high-paying jobs and new low-status, low-paying jobs (Waldinger 1986, 1989, 1996). In short, an economic restructuring perspective, by focusing on the growth of services in their most advanced form, emphasizes increased demand for both high- and low-skilled labor. Because less-skilled immigrants have been willing to fill low-level, often unstable jobs, the economic restructuring hypothesis is better suited to explain both the decline in manufacturing employment *and* the increase in immigrant employment, at least as these have occurred together in certain kinds of cities.

More generally, the overall labor-market impact of low-skilled immigrants on natives in a given city depends on the change in the number of low-skilled manufacturing jobs, the degree of movement of low-skilled manufacturing jobs to the suburbs, the growth in high-level services, and the change in the supply of low-skilled jobs resulting from declines in the size of preferred groups standing higher in the job hierarchy (Gonzalez Baker and Newby 1999). These factors vary across local labor markets. In some, their relative balance will be such that immigrants and low-skilled workers can be absorbed more easily as replacement labor and as holders of new jobs in the service sector. In others their relative balance will be such that competition and displacement will be more likely to result. Frank D. Bean, Mark Fossett, and Jennifer Van Hook (1999) investigate the degree to which complementarity (or symbiosis) between immigrants and low-skilled groups will be enhanced the tighter the local labor market, the lesser the city's manufacturing decline, and the greater the city's growth in high-level services. Their research results indicate that immigrants enhance native labor-market outcomes under these conditions, thus providing another set of reasons about why overall labor-market effects of immigration have not consistently revealed the negative results generally expected.

Economic and Labor-Market Effects on African Americans

Given that immigrants continue to exhibit lower levels of schooling than natives, and that African Americans and most native minorities continue to have lower schooling levels than white natives (Farley 1996), research examining the economic and labor-market impacts of immigration on native minorities holds special resonance for immigration scholars and policy makers. We now devote particular attention to the case of African Americans in addressing the labor-market consequences of immigration because low-skilled African Americans are often viewed as the group most likely to find itself in competition with low-skilled immigrants.

But first, what role has immigration played in affecting the overall economic situation of African Americans? A recent research project examined this question (Hamermesh and Bean 1998). The study indicated that recent immigration to the United States appears to have exerted small but negative effects on the economic situation of African Americans. The research provides compelling documentation that the overall positive economic effects of immigration emphasized by the National Research Council study for the country as a whole do not extend to African Americans. This is perhaps not surprising, given that the NRC study also found that such benefits were concentrated among the highly skilled and the owners of capital (Smith and Edmonston 1997), two groups that include disproportionately fewer African Americans than whites.

What about labor-market effects on African Americans? It is sometimes argued that immigrants do not much affect the employment and wages of African Americans because blacks tend to live in the South (in 1998, about 55 percent of blacks resided in the eleven states the U.S. Census Bureau calls the South: Alabama, Florida, Georgia,

Kentucky, Louisiana, Mississippi, North Carolina, South Carolina, Tennessee, Texas, and Virginia), a region of the country containing relatively few immigrants, except for Texas and Florida. However, when one counts the blacks living in Texas and Florida (states containing lots of immigrants) together with those living in other states outside the South, the majority of African Americans (about 57 percent) live in parts of the country containing substantial numbers of immigrants (U.S. Current Population Survey 1998).

Further disaggregation reinforces this point. Investigating the implications of immigration for African Americans requires examining the structure and process of black employment. Given that blacks continue to be disproportionately concentrated in semiskilled and unskilled jobs (Farley 1996), the large numbers of new immigrants with low levels of education and work skills would seem particularly likely to influence African American labor-market outcomes. In the case of immigration's impact on unskilled workers, such impacts are thought to exert their influence through *local* labor-market dynamics, often represented in U.S. research studies by metropolitan areas (Sassen 1995). What does the evidence show about the extent to which blacks and immigrants reside in *separate* local labor markets? At first glance the answer seems to be that blacks and immigrants do indeed live in different places to a modest degree. Correlating the percentage black in 1990 with the percentage foreign-born across the 175 largest metropolitan areas in 1990 yields a figure of -0.12. However, this results entirely from the presence among these metropolitan areas of cities in the Deep South (Alabama, Georgia, Louisiana, North Carolina, and South Carolina), cities containing large black but very small foreign-born populations. With these Deep South cities removed, the correlation is 0.10, or just the opposite. In other words, in 1990 there existed some tendency for immigrants and blacks to concentrate in the same, not in different, places, except in the Deep South. These statistics on the tendencies for immigrants and blacks to live in the same places, whether examined by state or by city, do not support the idea that immigration will have few labor-market implications for African Americans because of the geographic distribution of immigrants.

Some research indicates reasons to expect variation in labor-market effects. From 1970 to 1980, unemployment rose from 4.5 to 7.1 percent in the overall population and from 6.9 to 13.2 percent among African Americans. Between 1980 and 1990, when unemployment decreased to 5.5 percent in the entire population, it merely fell to 11.3 percent among African Americans (U.S. Department of Labor 1971, 1981, 1991). And even by 2000, African American unemployment, 8.2 percent, still was higher than whites' unemployment, 3.4 percent (U.S. Department of Labor 2001). In accord with Richard Freeman's (1991) findings that unskilled black workers often do not benefit much from economic growth until relatively tight labor-market conditions develop, the labor-market effects of immigration on African Americans are likely to depend on the overall vitality and structure of the labor markets within which both immigrants and African Americans seek employment. It is thus not surprising that black economic opportunities in and migration to northern industrial cities increased during the 1920s and 1950s, when cheap immigrant labor was scarce (Kuznets 1977; Simon 1989).

But contemporary ethnographies document the tendency of employers to rely on immigrant social networks as their primary recruiting tool, to the exclusion of native-born workers, particularly African American workers (Waldinger 1997). At the same time, other evidence suggests that the presence of immigrants boosts African American wages and employment propensities, largely through an expanded public sector (which disproportionately employs African Americans) servicing a growing population (Muller and Espenshade 1985; Waldinger 1996). Also, many blacks worked in the manufacturing sector when the new immigration began. When manufacturing jobs held by African Americans decline and such workers must look elsewhere for employment, do low-skilled African Americans compete with low-skilled immigrants for expanding low-level service jobs, or is there sufficient growth in the demand for such employment to accommodate the needs of both groups? One view, which has been termed the job queuing hypothesis (following the work of Lieberson [1980]), postulates that ethnic groups are arranged in a hiring preference queue. All else being equal, employers do not move down the queue until all of the members of higher-ranked groups have been hired. Thus, when demographic or other change causes the size of the preferred white group at the top of the queue to shrink, a vacancy chain is set in motion that results in nonwhites moving up as replacements for whites. As the supply of white replacement labor diminishes, opportunities for immigrants and for blacks who have lost manufacturing jobs increase.

More successful and sizable ethnic economies provide relatively more employment opportunities for the members of that group, thus reducing the competitive effects of social structural overlap and increasing the possibility of complementarity. Samuel Cohn and Mark Fossett (1996) have found that, net of other factors, blacks experience better employment opportunities in areas where they are residentially concentrated, especially in larger cities. However, areas of black residential concentration are also likely to be areas of high segregation and such areas have historically evolved in ways that have also served to isolate and limit economic opportunities for African Americans in the larger society (Massey and Denton 1993). To a substantial degree, the residential segregation of African Americans represents a spatial structural mechanism of discrimination and is related to worse rather than better African American labor-market outcomes (Massey and Denton 1993). This tendency has been so strong that in most instances it undoubtedly overwhelms any positive tendency for blacks to benefit from residential concentration and from spatial structural separation.

In order to distinguish the negative and positive consequences of residential separation, Bean, Fossett and Van Hook (1999) coined the terms "residential segregation" for the (overwhelmingly larger) negative consequences of residential segregation and "residential autonomy" for possible positive consequences. All else being equal, these researchers noted that autonomy would be expected to negatively relate to niche overlap between immigrants and low-skilled groups, including African Americans, operating, all else being equal, to lessen the competitive labor-market impact of immigration. They found that greater complementarity occurs when immigrant and native residential autonomy is higher (because the concentration of native employment opportunities in native areas, *other things held constant*, will operate to minimize immigrant and native social structural overlap in such cases). They also found that more complimentarity is evident the greater the size of the immigrant group's co-ethnic economy (because it indicates less social structural overlap); the larger the minority group economy (because other things being equal, larger size indicates increased minority group employment opportunities and less structural overlap); and the smaller the size of the majority population (because a shrinking majority population will increase minority group employment opportunities).

Gender Variations in Labor-Market Consequences

Our discussion to this point makes few references to gender. In 1990, roughly 42 percent of immigrant workers in the United States were women and nearly 10 percent of the female labor force was foreign-born (Schoeni 1998). Despite this substantial presence of immigrant women in the United States, much of the research and literature on immigrant labor market outcomes has focused its analyses exclusively on men, as noted by Massey and Espinoza (1997). However, an emerging ethnographic and survey literature on gender and the migration decision suggests that migration decisions and profiles and labor market outcomes vary systematically by sex (Boyd 1989; Donato 1993; Hagan 1998; Hondagneu-Sotelo 1994; Repak 1994). Sociological analyses note that patriarchal value and behavioral systems in origin and destination countries differentially constrain potential labor migrants by sex and that gendered systems of labor-market returns can devalue work performed by women (Greico and Boyd 1998; Hagan 1998; Hondagneu-Sotelo 1994; Kanaiaipuni 1998; Kilbourne et al. 1994). In addition, gender perspectives on the migration decision suggest that women, while increasingly likely to participate in the labor force in destination countries, may attach more substantial weight to such family considerations as reunification with male partners who have migrated, responsibilities for child rearing, and normative systems regarding the appropriateness of female migration (Boyd 1989; Kanaiaipuni 1998).

Theoretical perspectives on the mechanisms by which labor migrants realize their migration objectives, as noted earlier, have focused heavily in recent years on the roles of social capital and social networks in facilitating migration. Social networks vary by sex in their structure, content, and effects (Boyd 1989). Although both men and women often realize their migration objectives through the recruitment and assistance of previous migrants, the specific role of same-sex network members in facilitating that process appears to be more salient for women. The resources provided by previous female migrants, particularly those with familial connections to potential female migrants in the origin community, can facilitate the migration process for subsequent cohorts even in opposition to the wishes of male migrant partners in destination countries and male family members in origin communities (Hagan 1998; Hondagneu-Sotelo 1994). Same-sex social network resources anchored in kin and origin-community ties reduce the perceived costs of the migration process with respect to personal safety for women. Furthermore, these networks are a critical component of labor-market incorporation in the destination community, an issue addressed in more depth below.

The substantial literature examining the labor-market characteristics of immigrants to the United States has largely however, restricted itself to men, prompting Schoeni (1998, 58), for example, to note that the "economist George Borjas's (1994) recent review of the performance of immigrants in the U.S. labor market referenced sixteen empirical studies, none of which examined women." Such research, predicated on men's human capital characteristics and migration patterns, notes that migrants from origin countries with high levels of socioeconomic inequality are less likely to be highly educated, for example, since the return to education is disproportionately high in the home country. Less educated migrants, then, can expect greater comparative returns by migrating to countries with less polarized socioeconomic structures. As U.S. policies have evolved to accommodate more migration from origin countries at intermediate stages of economic development—and thus with high socioeconomic inequality—an increasing share of immigrants with lower skill levels have entered the United States (Borjas 1994).

However, research suggests that such patterns are less likely to obtain for women, given gendered differences in the normative social systems that govern preferences and opportunities for work in origin countries. That is, legal and sociocultural constraints on women's labor force participation in the country of origin may become an incentive for women with certain skills to immigrate, particularly when female-typed occupational niches have developed in particular destination countries, even though men from the same source countries may not have similar incentives. One example of such gendered difference in the selectivity of migration is observed in migration from the Philippines to the United States. U.S. labor force participation rates for Filipina immigrants exceeds 85 percent, whereas the rate for males in the Philippines is just under 54 percent (Duleep and Sanders 1993; Schoeni 1998). This disparity corresponds to a disparity in years of completed schooling: Filipina adults ages twenty-five to forty-nine in the Philippines have 8.9 years of schooling, compared to U.S. Filipina immigrants' nearly fourteen years of completed schooling (Schoeni 1998).

Studies of immigration and its effects on U.S. workers have generally either omitted women from the analyses altogether or treated them as a residual "female" category, setting aside any possibility for comparisons across groups of working women. This omission is either attributed to the fact that groups of women workers are too similar, that their variation in hourly wages or annual earnings is much smaller than among men (Bean, Lowell, and Taylor 1988), or that they are too different, because immigrant versus native fertility differences lead to different labor force activity patterns, making comparisons difficult (Borjas 1990). Certain features of female labor-market experience suggest that gender variations in the labor-market consequences of immigration are likely. For example, women are concentrated in fewer occupational categories than men, owing to both supply-side and demand-side factors (England and Farkas 1986; Reskin and Padavic 1994).

If immigrant women enter a labor market featuring pervasive gender segregation, they compete directly with U.S.-born women in ways not comparable to the male labor force. Packed into fewer socially acceptable and structurally available job categories than men, women may experience gendered job crowding that exacerbates competitive pressures between immigrants and natives, even if such strong effects are not evident among men. This possibility is compounded by the fact that employers' adjustment mechanisms of capital substitution and offshore job flight are less feasible for many of the jobs in which women are disproportionately engaged, such as commercial and household domestic service, direct human services, and clerical and retail trade work. Such jobs are more dependent on human labor power and more anchored spatially than many of the manufacturing occupations that are filled predominantly by males. At the same time, certain other gender-specific labor-market features may offset this competition effect. For instance, much female-typed work in the United States involves clerical skills or direct contact with the public, thus demanding English-language skills immigrant women are particularly unlikely to possess. In 1980, over 40 percent of recent (less than five years in the United States) Mexican immigrant women spoke no English (Bean and Tienda 1987). By 1990, that figure exceeded 60 percent. Similarly, roughly half the working-age immigrant women in the United States from Indochina and Vietnam spoke little or no English in 1980 and 1990 (Schoeni 1998).

Network resource differences by gender also imply gender differences in labor-market incorporation. For example, a significant share of Latina immigrant employment involves domestic service work that frees native-born women to engage in market work outside the home, even as it relegates immigrants to an occupational niche from which it is difficult to escape. This is a pattern with substantial historic precedent for other immigrant women of color (Glenn 1992; Hagan 1994, 1998). These features of women's work experience imply possible gains in the wage and employment prospects for U.S. working women associated with the presence of immigrant women, if immigrant women boost U.S.-born women's wages by filling the lowest rungs on the female job queue—those not requiring English-language skills, such as domestic work (Reskin and Roos 1990)—or increase the labor supply for U.S.-born women in need of domestic and child-care services (Hagan 1998). These gains, furthermore, are not readily inferred from the patterns observed for men.

Given these features of U.S. labor markets, the influence of female immigration upon women's labor force experiences may differ from those of men. For example, the theory of a segmented labor market may suggest that immigrant women would enhance labor-market outcomes for U.S.-born women. But such segmentation may also be associated with limited prospects for immigrant job mobility out of the lowest-paying sectors of the economy in the case of women, thus implying greater job competition with unskilled U.S.-born women. This may be all the more true when one considers the degree to which higher-paying jobs in the female labor market require English skills immigrant women are so likely to lack. It is thus not surprising that research efforts examining labor-market dynamics among immigrant and U.S.-born women workers diverge in their conclusions. One project focusing on Mexican immigration to the metropolitan labor markets of the southwestern United States found that though immigrant women depress their own wage rates in the metropolitan labor markets where they are concentrated heavily, the net result of their presence on wages earned by U.S.-born women workers is positive (Gonzalez Baker 1999). Other projects more national in scope and focusing on particular racial or ethnic groups (for example, African Americans) at particular skill levels (for example, less than a high school education) found that the competitive effects of immigration observed among men are also observed for women (Butcher 1998). At present, substantial continued empirical work remains to be done on gender variations in the relationship between immigration and U.S.-born worker experiences.

High-Skilled Workers and the Economy

Our discussion up to this point has focused on the economic, fiscal, and labor-market consequences of immigration, with the emphasis on assessing the impacts on natives of immigrants in general or on lower-skilled immigrants in particular. But we need to bear in mind that, as noted previously, the educational distribution of the new immigrants is bimodal—that is, it is characterized by relatively sizable percentages of *both* highly and poorly educated immigrants. Thus, for example, the fraction of immigrants who have not completed high school exceeds that of natives, but the fraction who have completed college is about the same as that of natives. More specifically, immigrants are about half as likely to complete high school as natives (Martin and Midgley 1999), but they are *more* likely than natives to hold advanced degrees, especially in the case of immigrants who arrived during the 1990s (Hansen 1996). The question of the labor-market impact of high-skilled immigrants thus appears to be an increasingly important policy issue, particularly given the increase during the 1990s of workers with high levels of education. But in part because the growing number of migrants with upper-end skills has only recently become an issue, with pockets of controversy only recently emerging, the amount of research on the question of the impact of such workers has been minimal.

U.S. immigration policy has always included special provision for the entry of unusually high-skilled workers (Usdansky and Espenshade 2001). When it passed the Immigration Act of 1990, Congress devoted relatively more attention to skills as criteria for immigrant admission than at any time since 1952, when it passed the Immigration and Nationality Act (also known as the McCarran-Walter Act). That legislation included the largest set-aside up to that time for skilled immigrants, and for the first time skills were defined on the basis of education (Usdansky and Espenshade 2001, 34–37). The 1990 legislation substantially increased the number of employment-based slots (allowing them to almost triple to 140,000 by 1992), increased the number of employment-based preferences from two to five, and introduced a special category of high-skilled temporary worker through its adoption of the H-1B visa for nonimmigrants. The number of such visas was set at 65,000 annually. H-1B workers were to be paid the prevailing wage for their job and were permitted to stay three years (renewable for another three years), but no provisions were made for the family members of such workers. The impetus for these legislative changes was a growing concern during the late 1980s about looming shortages of high-skill and specialty workers, fears that were fueled by think-tank and government reports (for example, the Hudson Institute's "Workforce 2000" report and the 1990 "Report of the Council of Economic Advisors") that predicted that such labor shortages were indeed developing. Ironically, no sooner did the legislation pass than the country went into a recession, the effect of which was to reduce job growth to zero until nearly 1993 (U.S. Department of Labor 2002).

The major policy controversy over the past twenty years about the entrance of high-skilled workers has concerned the degree to which labor shortages of scientists and engineers and other high-tech workers have emerged (Cornelius, Espenshade, and Salehyan 2001). The economic boom in the United States during the latter half of the 1990s enormously strengthened the political leverage of high-tech businesses, whose representatives took the position that such shortages were real and substantial. The situation that developed in the case of the H-1B visa program during the late 1990s seemed to bear out their contentions. In 1997 for first time the 65,000 ceiling on H-1B visas set in 1990 proved insufficient to meet demand. Up until then the number of such visas had not been an issue, but now there were pressures to increase the ceiling. In 1998 Congress raised the number to 115,000 visas for 1999 and 2000, but in fiscal year 1999 the new supply of H-1B visas still ran out by June, with the result that in October of 2000 Congress rushed to extend the annual limit to 195,000 for a three-year period.

The timing was again ironic. At about the same time this last round of increases in H-1B visas was passed, the country went into another recession, which as of this writing was still afflicting the high-tech industry (Leonhardt 2002; Gosselin 2002a, 2002b). And as became clear to all observers by mid-2002, some of the economic growth of the late 1990s, although the exact amount remains uncertain, resulted from corporations artificially inflating their earnings reports, which implies that some of the "shortages" of high-tech workers during the late 1990s were also artificial. Such possibilities notwithstanding, controversies about the degree to which the native supply of high-tech workers fails to meet demand will probably not disappear anytime soon. While temporary visa holders, such as high-tech workers who obtain H-1B visas, are not immigrants in the legal sense of the term, their labor-market impacts may nonetheless be comparable to those of other high-skilled immigrants. They may be just as likely, or even more likely, to compete with high-skilled natives for jobs and wages. If they continue to come to the country during the early years of the new century in the expanded numbers provided for by the 2000 legislation, the question of their labor-market consequences is likely to be increasingly important, especially if job growth continues to stagnate. What will be even more needed then, but which does not currently exist to any satisfactory degree, are the kinds of careful systematic studies of the effects of high-skilled permanent and temporary workers that have been conducted on the labor-market effects of immigration in general and low-skilled immigration in particular (Gurcak et al. 2001).

Summary and Conclusions

The research results and theory presented and discussed in this chapter document the importance of immigrant workers in the labor force of the United States and outline the ways in which such workers affect and are affected by labor-market structures and processes. Immigration to the country has continued to increase over the past thirty years, much—but not all—of it concentrated among unskilled workers, even as economic restructuring has led to relatively fewer reasonably high-paying blue-collar jobs in the economy. In addition, immigrants constitute an increasingly larger share of the workforce than they do of the general adult population, especially in cities containing the largest fractions of immigrants. These factors imply that the mechanisms involved in attracting and channeling immigrants into certain local labor markets and certain parts of those markets involve the operation of additional and perhaps more complex forces than the conventional supply-and-demand factors emphasized by neoclassical economic theories. This is not to say that supply-and-demand factors are irrelevant to labor-market processes involving immigrants in the cities and areas in which they locate. It just means that such factors are inadequate to explain all aspects of such processes.

Other surveys besides this one have also concluded that immigrants generally have not generated much in the way of effects on the wages and employment of native workers (Friedberg and Hunt 1999). The relative absence of a relationship between rising numbers of immigrants and native workers' wages is often explained as being due to the fact that natives may move away from the areas into which immigrants locate, thus spreading the local labor-market effects of immigration over larger areas (Borjas 1999). Additional obscuring factors, as we have noted above, are that labor-market impacts vary by gender, race, and the structural arrangements in cities, thus reducing the likelihood of any single clear-cut pattern. However, it does appear to be the case that immigrants consistently exert negative effects on the wages and employment of *other immigrants* (Bean, Gonzalez Baker, and Capps 2001). The fact that these earlier-arriving immigrants do not all move away and do not avoid immigrant destination cities because of competition coming from newly arriving immigrants suggests that the factors governing the labor-market participation and consequences of immigrants are different from those of natives. A key research question for the future is the extent to which sufficient educational and employment opportunities will emerge to provide pathways for later generations of immigrant and other ethnic groups to move out of low-paying jobs in disadvantaged sectors of the labor market.

We have also examined the question of immigration's economic impact on African Americans. This cannot be fully assessed without looking at the history of black economic status in the United States over the past four decades or so. The overall record is mixed. Gains occurred in the late sixties and early seventies when civil rights laws and antidiscrimination policies in the form of affirmative action directives helped to lend a positive boost to the economic situation of blacks. Since then progress has stalled. Without question, much of this stagnation is due to the negative effects of economic restructuring on persons with only a high school education or less (Smith 2001), a group that includes disproportionate numbers of African Americans.

Some of it may also derive from the fact that immigration has on average worked against the economic interests of the black community, although the extent to which such an effect may have coincided with the influence of economic restructuring remains unknown. Whatever the case, researchers now conclude on the basis of the most recent evidence that one of the major forces for the improvements that have occurred in black economic status over the past forty years has been affirmative action (Bean and Bell-Rose 1999; Smith 2001).

On balance, however, the overall economic implications of immigration for African Americans appear less than benign. The fact that gains in black economic status ceased during the high immigration 1980s and 1990s after notable gains occurred following passage of antidiscrimination laws and the adoption of affirmative action policies in the 1960s and 1970s encourages the idea that immigration has done little to generate opportunities for economic advancement for native blacks. Moreover, this conclusion is buttressed by the compilation of research evidence indicating that immigration appears to worsen slightly the already precarious overall economic positions of African Americans, especially those with a high school education or less. Thus, the racial and ethnic diversification of the United States population over the past three decades brought about by immigration, a trend some analysts might have thought would bring advantages to nonwhite minorities, including blacks, seems at least at this point in time not to have improved the overall economic status of African Americans. Whether such diversification has led to other kinds of consequences that might be more salutary is the question we turn to in the next chapter.

=== Chapter 10 ===

Immigration and Race-Ethnicity in the United States

G IVEN THE United States' long and unfortunate experiences with racial exploitation and discrimination, an especially important topic involves the implications of immigration for race or ethnicity. This is true whether we are considering the consequences of the new immigration for the United States as a whole or for particular groups of native residents living in the country. As noted in chapter 2, the new immigration has increased considerably the racial and ethnic diversity of the U.S. population. And as noted in the previous chapter, research on the general economic implications of immigration for African Americans has revealed that somewhat lower levels of African American education and much lower levels of wealth and asset accumulation limit the economic gains blacks receive from immigration compared to majority whites (Hamermesh and Bean 1998). Moreover, low-skilled immigration sometimes seems to help and sometimes to harm the labor-market outcomes of African Americans, depending on structural and other contingencies in American cities. Thus, the economic effects of immigration for African Americans are ambiguous, or perhaps slightly negative, while at the same time generally positive for the country as a whole. What, then, can we say about immigration's sociocultural impacts, not only for African Americans, but also for the new immigrant groups themselves and for the country in general? Here we turn our attention to what is arguably the most important of these, what the new immigration means for racial and ethnic identity and for the "color line" in the United States.

Although some observers have argued that it is not yet clear whether the increasing racial and ethnic diversity resulting from recent immigration will ultimately prove to operate as a cohesive or a divisive force in American society (Suro 1998), it is reasonable to think that the transformation of the racial and ethnic composition of the U.S. population resulting from immigration may be affecting the dynamics of racial and ethnic relations in the United States and could be changing long-standing color lines in the process. The evidence we present here suggests that on balance this diversity is indeed beginning to modify the ways people view themselves in racial or ethnic terms and to break down the barriers that have often historically separated racial and ethnic groups in America. But this dynamic is occurring in a context of rising economic inequality. At a minimum, because immigration results in an uneven distribution of benefits throughout the general population and because it harms the labor-market outcomes of other (especially poor) immigrants, immigration serves to call attention to those groups in American society whose economic status is most precarious. Immigration thus also creates a growing need to adopt policies to enhance the socioeconomic opportunities of vulnerable groups and individuals least likely to receive the economic benefits associated with immigration, thus perhaps raising the price of the economic, humanitarian, and social benefits the country now enjoys as a result of its comparatively generous immigration policies. That those most in need of such policies are disproportionately concentrated among African Americans, Latinos, and certain Asian groups underscores the importance of addressing the policy domains of immigration and race or ethnicity jointly rather than separately.

To explore the implications of immigration for racial and ethnic groups in the United States, it is useful to clarify what we mean by the terms "race" and "ethnicity." Following the thinking of George M. Fredrickson (1988), we define race as a "consciousness of status and identity based on ancestry and color." Dropping the color criterion from this phraseology gives a useful definition of the term "ethnicity." Fredrickson's definition makes clear that race is a social construction and one that seems to fit the way the black population is viewed in the United States. In the cases of the new Latino and Asian immigrant groups, however, the term "race" does not by itself fit very well because it is not clear that color is (or is becoming) an attribute that society ascribes to immigrants from Latin America and Asia, at least on a consistent basis. For example, some Latinos view themselves and are seen by others as white, some as brown, and a few as black. We thus deliberately use the somewhat imprecise term "race or ethnicity" in the following discussion to refer to groups that are viewed or distinguish themselves on the basis of ethnic ancestry or color or both.

The Intersection of Immigration and Race or Ethnicity

In thinking about immigration and race or ethnicity, and in particular about how immigration affects the dynamics of racial and ethnic identity in the United States, which in turn may influence racial and ethnic relations, it is important to recall that immigration and race sometimes seem to represent features of the American experience that are very nearly polar opposites, at least as they have been characterized in the postwar period. Few phenomena have so captured the American imagination as immigration, and no concept has contradicted American ideals more than race (Cose 1992). The image of the successful immigrant enshrined in the Emma Lazarus poem at the base of the Statue of Liberty epitomizes not only the fulfillment of the American dream of equal opportunity and unlimited social mobility, but also the capacity of the American nation to offer the oppressed of the world the possibility of both freedom and prosperity. Indeed, the United States is often described as a "nation of immigrants," an idea Oscar Handlin elevated to near mythological status in noting that the history of America was synonymous with the history of immigration (Handlin 1951). Numerous books about immigration have incorporated into their titles some variation of the phrase "the golden door," words suggesting the possibility that newcomers and their descendants can achieve a better life in the United States than in the country they have left behind (see, for example, Borjas 1999; Reimers 1985; Waldinger 1996). This essentially optimistic and inclusionary view of immigration still resonates strongly in American culture, even as it is challenged by new concerns that competition for resources and environmental strains might place limits on the country's capacity to absorb new immigrants. As noted in chapter 1, the resulting tensions have created ambivalent attitudes about immigration in the 1980s and 1990s, leading to the development of sometimes seemingly contradictory positions toward immigration, such as adamant opposition to unauthorized migration but support for the continuation of current levels of legal immigration (Bean and Fix 1992).

The matter of race, and more specifically relations between whites and African Americans, is viewed very differently than is immigration. If immigration has often symbolized the hopeful and uplifting side of the American experience, the practice of slavery in many of the colonies and subsequent states for the first two and a half centuries of European settlement is a negative and exclusionary part of the historical picture (Tocqueville 1945 [1835]). If the incorporation of many strands of immigrants into the U.S. economic mainstream resents the success of the American experience, the lack of such incorporation in the case of the African American population a century and a half after the end of the Civil War represents for many observers the country's most conspicuous failure and an indication of the residual power of racial discrimination throughout American society (Fredrickson 1988; Rose 1997). Although social and economic progress among blacks has occurred, the questions of how much, when, how fast, and why are still the subjects of much debate and little consensus (Hacker 1995; Thernstrom and Thernstrom 1997). Even some of the most optimistic observers of the past three decades have not been able to conclude that blacks have reached economic parity with whites or that the prospects of social and cultural integration seem close at hand (see, for example, Glazer 1997).

Of course the themes of immigration and race are not totally separate, because blacks were some of the earliest immigrants, albeit involuntary immigrants, to North America. During the eighteenth century, African Americans were the single largest immigrant group arriving in the country (Berlin 1998). Despite this, their experience cannot be understood as one analogous to that of other immigrant groups. Most blacks came to the United States under chattel slavery that bound not only them but also their children to their owners for life (Morgan 1998). The modes of entry and the reception in America of immigrants from Africa were thus especially harsh and debilitating compared with the experience of immigrants from other countries and generally make it impossible to address the experience of blacks in this country as just another chapter in the story of immigration. At the same time it is an oversimplification to view the difficulties of recent immigrants as just another chapter in the history of racism in the United States.

Although it is misleading to treat the dynamics of immigration and race as essentially similar, neither is it satisfactory to treat race and immigration as completely separate phenomena. Perhaps because slavery has been such a blight on the national historical landscape, it has sometimes been easier to examine race in relatively compartmentalized terms. Thus, David Brion Davis notes that until recently, American historians have tended to study slavery largely in geographically limited ways, for example, as part of the history of the South (Davis 1998). In general, scholars' treatments of immigration have been conspicuous for the omission of any discussion of black perspectives or experience concerning immigration (note Glazer's [1997] observations on this point. Whatever the reasons for such com-

227

he tendency to think that immigration and race
ely separate issues continues even today. Thus, a
my of Science report argued that immigration
er the last thirty years held few implications
because most blacks live in different parts of
receiving most of the immigrants (Smith and
1). As we noted in chapter 9, however, when the states
Deep South are excluded, the actual geographic distribution of
immigrants and blacks does not support the idea that the two groups
live largely in different parts of the country and thus are unlikely to
have affected one another.

Part of the tendency to view immigration and race as separate issues in the postwar period may stem from a desire to forget that the
two have often been historically conflated, often in ways that do not
flatter the recollection. For example, the Chinese Exclusion Act of
1882 forbade the entry of Chinese largely for expressly racist reasons
(Reimers 1998). And much has been written recently about the considerable extent to which the immigrants of the nineteenth and early
twentieth centuries were treated as if they were "in-between" peoples—that is, midway between whites and blacks (Ignatiev 1995; Jacobson 1998). Indeed, a virulent racism has often seemed to provide a
handy device to be employed in the service of excluding immigrants
when it seemed desirable to do so (Higham 1963). Perhaps the optimism born of the U.S. victory in World War II and of the strong economy of the 1950s encouraged the idea that immigration and race issues could be approached as separate matters in the latter part of the
twentieth century.

If addressing immigration and race issues separately ever made
analytical sense, it certainly does not in the case of the post–World
War II period, during which the two issues have been intertwined in
often subtle ways. During those years, American conceptions about
immigration and race appear to have been mutually reinforcing,
sometimes optimistically and sometimes pessimistically, in a continuing reflection of the country's basic mythological orientation toward
both. This interplay also serves as a reminder that popular responses
to immigration and racial and ethnic relations, as well as reactions to
the public policies that have been contrived to address immigration
and racial and ethnic issues, can and do influence one another, sometimes for the better, sometimes for the worse. For example, the participation of blacks in the armed forces of the United States during
World War II set the stage for the civil rights movement of the 1960s
and for the eventual removal of legal barriers to the participation of
African Americans in the institutions of American society (Higham

1997; Morris 1984). To a considerable extent the same forces that sought to maximize equal opportunity for blacks through changes in the legal system contributed to the removal in 1965 of the discriminatory provisions of the National Origins Quota Act of 1924 and their replacement with family reunification criteria as the primary basis for the granting of entry visas to immigrants (Reimers 1985).

In similar fashion, the national mythology about the historic experiences of previous immigrants in overcoming hardship and discrimination and in fulfilling the American dream has often seemed to suggest that African Americans might also achieve integration and economic progress if only legal barriers to equal opportunity were eliminated (Glazer 1975). However, although progress has been made, the task of quickly achieving parity between the black and white populations has proved more difficult than the initially optimistic foresaw. Just as popular ideas about the historical experience of immigration raised hopes for black success as a result of the passage of civil rights legislation in Congress during the 1960s, so the slow progress actually made in bridging the divide between black and white has perhaps contributed to the emergence of a more pessimistic assessment about the benefits of immigration for America in the late twentieth and early twenty-first century. Moreover, if the optimistic outlook born of the country's experience with the successful incorporation of earlier immigrants has served to reinforce the hopeful idea that lingering discriminatory barriers to black achievement could be overcome by antidiscrimination policies, so too the de facto and de jure expansion of affirmative action policies to millions of recently arrived immigrants has contributed to the disillusionment of many Americans with such policies (Fuchs 1995, 1997; Suro 1998).

Effects of Immigration on Racial and Ethnic Composition

The implications of immigration for African Americans thus take on special resonance in the context of the question of how fully the black population has been incorporated into American society. The expectation that immigrants might influence the country in general and blacks in particular derives from changes in recent immigration. As noted in several previous chapters, the changing volume and national-origin composition of immigration has converted the United States from a largely biracial society consisting of a sizable white majority and a small black minority (and a very small Native American minority of less than 1 percent) into a multiracial, multi-ethnic society—one consisting of several racial and ethnic groups. This trend started in the 1950s and gained momentum in ensuing decades. By 2000, nearly a third of the U.S. population designated itself black, Latino, or Asian. The speed with which the Latino and Asian groups have grown has meant that the proportion of African Americans in the racial and ethnic minority population has been declining. In 1990, blacks were no longer a majority of this population, making only up 48 percent of racial and ethnic minorities. By 2001, their share had fallen to 40 percent (U.S. Current Population Survey 2001).

How much difference immigration has made to changing the racial and ethnic mix of the U.S. population and to its overall growth during the twentieth century can be ascertained by examining the contribution of immigration since 1900 to population growth for the major racial and ethnic groups, as distinct from the amount of growth that resulted from any excess of births over deaths among the pre-1900 entrants and native-born members of each of the groups. Barry Edmonston and Jeffrey Passel (1994) find that since 1900 immigration has accounted for about 30 percent of the growth of the total U.S. population. Even more significant, they find that immigration's contribution to the growth of the various major racial and ethnic subgroups has varied enormously, accounting for nearly all of the growth among Latinos and Asians (85.7 percent and 97.3 percent, respectively), but virtually none of the overall twentieth-century growth among blacks. Interestingly, however, since 1980 an increasing amount of black immigration from Africa and the Caribbean has begun to change this picture. According to Yanyi Djamba and Frank D. Bean (1998), black immigration accounted for almost a quarter of the population growth among blacks during the 1980s. Thus, immigration during the twentieth century has contributed to a decline in the relative size of the black population as a part of the overall racial and ethnic minority population in the United States, but recent increases in black immigration have begun to slow, if not reverse, this trend.

Although the numbers of new entrants coming to the United States has risen appreciably over the past thirty years (Bean et al. 1997), raising the percentage of the U.S. population that is foreign-born to over 11 percent by 2001 (U.S. Bureau of the Census 2001), the consequences of immigration for racial or ethnic diversity depend not only on the number of new entrants but also on how the foreign-born population is distributed geographically. As noted earlier, immigrants are not evenly dispersed throughout the country. California, New York, Florida, Texas, Illinois, and New Jersey (in that order) receive disproportionately large shares of newcomers; about 70 percent of all foreign-born persons in the United States lived in these states in 1998 (U.S. Current Population Survey 1998). As we will argue below, this appears to be breaking down some of the barriers that have traditionally divided groups in America.

Immigration and Racial-Ethnic Diversity

The increasing racial-ethnic diversity of the population of the United States resulting from immigration is thus contributing to the emergence of a more complex racial and ethnic system of stratification in the country than the one that existed in the recent past (since the end of World War II). The presence of so many immigrants adds another dimension of complexity to this system of stratification that may operate independent of race-ethnicity. That is, to the degree that immigrants, because of their limited English proficiency and other characteristics, are channeled into certain sectors of employment, labor-market segmentation along nativity lines in addition to labor-market segmentation along racial-ethnic lines may be increasing. Undoubtedly these two kinds of segmentation overlap to a considerable degree, but the substantially increased diversity introduced by immigration multiplies the possible dimensions along which segmentation can occur. It is not clear yet how to conceptualize these structural arrangements. Some of them appear to operate in ways that have positive implications for African American employment (for example, ethnic enclaves and patterns of residential autonomy), whereas others seem to operate in ways that have negative employment implications (for example, concentrations of ethnic- and immigrant-specific network hiring). An important challenge for future research is to conceptualize these new structural arrangements and to develop theories about their determinants and consequences that clarify the ways that new immigration affects not only native racial-ethnic minorities but also previous immigrants already in the country.

One possibility is that increased diversity is reducing the salience of some dimensions of racial-ethnic stratification but leaving others intact, or perhaps even enhanced. In that event, a major question involves the nature of the major racial-ethnic fault lines in American society that are persisting or being enhanced. The degree to which such fault lines delineate racial and ethnic divides along white-nonwhite lines or along black-nonblack lines is especially consequential. The posture the country adopts in regard to policies designed to enhance opportunity among the disadvantaged may be especially likely to influence the degree to which racial fault lines retain their salience. As noted above, further closures of the gap in socioeconomic attainment between African Americans and whites may be slowing or ceasing altogether, particularly with respect to education, and perhaps especially in regard to higher education. Some of this may be due to demographic changes triggered by immigration and some of it to the erosion of support for affirmative action. Recent research by Hoxby (1998) shows that immigration creates "crowding effects" in the use of preferences in granting admission and financial aid in private upper-tier institutions of higher education, thus perhaps diminishing opportunities for native-born African Americans to gain access to prestigious schools and the pathways to status and high income such schools often provide (Bowen and Bok 1998).

Theory building thus needs to focus on how the new and increased diversity deriving from immigration ultimately operates to affect racial-ethnic identity in the United States. David Reimers (1998) attributes much of the turn against immigration in the United States in the early 1990s (for example, Proposition 187 in California in 1994) to concerns that American identity is becoming fragmented and less Europe-oriented, even though this change of attitude coincided with an economic recession. In writing about the implications of Latino immigration for the United States, Roberto Suro (1998) notes: "Identity has once again become a problem for the United States, and as before, the crisis or reinvention will create a new identity that embraces the nation's new constituents. The presence of so many Latinos ensures that matters of race and language, of poverty and opportunity, of immigration policy and nationality will be central issues in the process" (321). One possible outcome of the process of identity redefinition is that racial-ethnic criteria are becoming less relevant as bases for identity formation, as well as workplace and occupational stratification and other forms of social organization in the United States. Increasing rates of racial-ethnic intermarriage in the United States over the past two decades provide an example of trends consistent with this possibility (Bean et al. 1997). And such phenomena as the emergence of an interracial political leadership group in Queens, New York, an area of extremely high racial and ethnic diversity during the 1980s and 1990s (Sanjek 1998), and the formation of collaborative organizations such as National Voices for an Inclusive 21st Century show that high levels of diversity may work to foster cooperation and solidarity rather than divisiveness and contention.

Racial and Ethnic Diversity and the Construction of Race and Ethnicity

How, then, does the increasing racial-ethnic diversity brought about by increasing immigration affect the ways people view themselves in racial-ethnic terms? Without question, immigration is transforming questions about race in the United States into questions about racial-ethnic relations. Because America is no longer merely a black and white society, questions are now being raised about the current placement and meaning of America's racial and ethnic color line(s) (Gans 1999a; Sanjek 1994; Skrentny 2001; Waters 1999). In fact, the use of the term "color" itself introduces ambiguities into racial-ethnic terminology. Sometimes the word is used to designate persons who are non-white, whereas at other times it is used more traditionally to refer only to blacks. Such multiplicities of usage, while assuredly not new, reflect transformations in the country that are currently broader and deeper than at any time since the first part of the twentieth century. Even in 1903, during a time of substantial immigration, it seems unlikely that the prominent African American social theorist W. E. B. Du Bois, who prophesied that the "problem of the twentieth-century is the problem of the color line" (1997 [1903], 45) could have anticipated that America's new immigrants in the late twentieth century would so drastically modify the racial and ethnic makeup of the United States, perhaps either changing or obscuring the very meaning of the term "color" in the process.

Social scientists have documented the processes by which racial categories have undergone reconstruction throughout our nation's history. For instance, previously "in-between" ethnic groups such as Irish, Italians, and Jews became "white," often by deliberately distinguishing themselves from blacks (Alba 1985, 1990; Brodkin 1998; Foner 2000; Gerstle 1999; Ignatiev 1995; Barrett and Roediger 1997). Even Asian ethnic groups such as the Chinese in Mississippi have changed their racial status from almost black to almost white by making concerted efforts to emulate the cultural practices of whites and distance themselves from blacks (Loewen 1988). The change in racial classification among ethnic groups from nonwhite to almost white or white illustrates that race is a cultural rather than biological category and that the "white race" has expanded over time to incorporate new immigrant groups (Alba 1985, 1990; Gerstle 1999; Omi and Winant 1994; Tuan 1998; Waters 1990, 1999). As Gerstle (1999, 289) explains, whiteness as a category "has survived by stretching its boundaries to include Americans—the Irish, eastern and southern Europeans—who had been deemed nonwhite. Contemporary evidence suggests that the boundaries are again being stretched as Latinos and Asians pursue whiteness much as the Irish, Italians, and Poles did before them."

Furthermore, because the construction of racial identities is a dialectical process—one that involves both internal and external opinions and processes—the way the native-born population categorizes immigrant ethnic groups is a crucial factor in how the group's racial and ethnic boundaries are determined (Loewen 1988; Nagel 1994; Portes and Macleod 1996; Portes and Rumbaut 2001). The U.S. native-born population traditionally followed the "one-drop" rule, which historically imposed a black racial identity on any person with even "one drop" of African American blood (Davis 1991; Nobles 2000; Wright 1994). By contrast, native-born Americans seem less concerned with defining the racial identity of Latinos and Asians. In addition, the very size and socioeconomic diversity of the Latino and Asian immigrant streams make it more difficult for the native-born to categorize them easily. Thus, the sheer racial, ethnic, and socioeconomic diversity among contemporary Latino and Asian immigrants may render racial and ethnic boundaries less definite and more negotiable than for blacks. Moreover, like earlier European immigrants, today's immigrants have not undergone the social history of slavery of African Americans, which gave rise to the black-white color line and cemented it. Hence, the bipolar racial divide may be less relevant to the historical and contemporary experiences of today's Latino and Asian immigrants (Lopez and Espiritu 1990; Rodriguez 2001). By contrast, the unique history and experience of black Americans in this country, especially with regard to slavery and de jure segregation, make the black-white racial divide qualitatively different from the Latino-white or Asian-white racial divides (Bailey 2001).

Although America's landscape has changed to one that is far more multiracial and multiethnic, theory and research in the fields of race and ethnicity have not always kept pace with the nation's vastly changing demographic scene, often pursuing the study of immigration and race as separate topics, as noted above. Thus, much theorizing about race and ethnicity continues to be couched in terms of the traditional black-white framework. For example, scholars sometimes treat at least some members of today's new immigrant groups as if they were racialized minorities who are subject to mobility barriers and levels of discrimination sufficiently strong to create the beginnings of a new rainbow underclass by the second generation (Castles and Miller 1998; Portes and Rumbaut 2001). Unlike African Americans, however, who were forcefully brought to this country as slaves, today's Latino and Asian newcomers are voluntary migrants, and consequently their experiences may be qualitatively distinct from those of African Americans. Hence, it may be inaccurate to treat them as racialized minorities who, like African Americans, encounter strong barriers to mobility and suffer discrimination. Instead, the newest immigrants may be more akin to the earlier European immigrants, who initially experienced discrimination but eventually became indistinguishable from and part of the larger white racial category. Which of these possibilities is more nearly correct has direct relevance for the way we think and interpret evidence about changes in racial and ethnic identities.

One important contingency in resolving this question concerns whether the members of immigrant groups see themselves and are treated by others primarily as racialized minorities. If they identify and are labeled as nonwhites, this undoubtedly tends to place them on the black side of the traditional black-white divide. If they identify and are labeled as immigrants, this tends to distinguish them from blacks and places them on the nonblack side of a black-nonblack divide. Which of these is more the case can affect how we interpret research results on intermarriage and multiracial identification. For example, if we assume that many immigrants are more like nonwhites than whites, then evidence of relatively high levels of intermarriage and multiracial identification among nonwhites (which here we take to include Latinos and Asians) might be taken to support the optimistic conclusion that the old black-white divide is breaking down. However, this interpretation may attribute to all nonwhites signs of incorporation that actually apply more to Latino and Asian subgroups than to blacks and lead to overly optimistic conclusions about the black experience.

Immigration and America's Color Lines

In the conclusion to her book *Black Identities*, Mary C. Waters (1999, 339) raises the following questions about immigration and America's color lines, "How will this wave of immigration affect American race relations? Where will the color line be drawn in the twenty-first century?" A number of social scientists have suggested that today's multiracial hierarchy could be replaced by a dual hierarchy consisting of "blacks and nonblacks" or "whites and nonwhites" (Gans 1999a, 1999b; Gitlin 1995; Sanjek 1994b; Waters 1999). Higher rates of intermarriage and multiracial identification for Latinos and Asians indicate that the racial hierarchy may be changing once again with race declining in significance for these groups, especially compared to blacks.

As emphasized in chapter 2, today's immigrants are notable because they are mainly non-European with the vast majority now hailing from the Latin American, Caribbean, and Asian countries. Immigrants and their children now account for 22 percent of the U.S. population, and according to projections by the National Research Council, the proportion of groups such as Latinos and Asians will continue to grow. If current trends continue, by the year 2050 the absolute sizes of America's Latino and Asian populations are expected to triple, constituting about 25 and 8 percent of the U.S. population, respectively (Smith and Edmonston 1997). The numbers of racial-ethnic intermarriages and of persons with multiracial backgrounds have risen along with the increased racial and ethnic diversity brought about by changes in immigration over the past three and a half decades. In the four decades since 1960, a time period that saw the rise of the new immigration, the intermarriage rate between whites and Asians and Latinos has increased tenfold (Jacoby 2001; Waters 1999). As we noted in chapter 8, almost one third of all married third-generation Asians and Latinos are married to a white. The increase in interracial marriage has also led to a growing multiracial population. Currently, one in forty persons identifies himself or herself as multiracial, and by the year 2050, this could rise to one in five (Farley 2001; Smith and Edmonston 1997).

What does current thinking and evidence about the new immigration, intermarriage, and multiraciality imply about America's racial and ethnic divides? At first glance, the new immigration might seem to indicate that race has become a less prominent social marker in the United States, pointing to the possible erosion of the traditional color line. However, this may be truer for some groups than others. While high levels of intermarriage, properly interpreted, and multiracial identification may indicate the loosening of racial and ethnic boundaries and a weakening of America's white-nonwhite color line, a crucial question is whether such tendencies are evenly distributed across all racial and ethnic groups. If the evidence points to substantial changes in group boundaries for only some groups, it would suggest that although America's basic color line might be changing, the process may be occurring more slowly for some groups than others.

An important strand of thinking about race provides further perspective on possible changes in the color line. In his seminal and influential work, *The Declining Significance of Race* (1980), William Julius Wilson argues that the direct effects of race on economic opportunities and outcomes have diminished significantly since the 1960s, contending that race per se and the racial characteristics of one's parents matter less in determining one's life chances than class. Thus, racial differences in earnings may persist, but they are now more likely to stem from racial differences in education rather than from direct racial discrimination (Sakamoto, Wu, and Tzeng 2000). Hence, according to Wilson, the color line between majority whites and nonwhite minorities in the United States has become much less sharply drawn (see also Sakamoto, Wu, and Tzeng 2000).

This reasoning and evidence can be applied to the likelihood of interracial marriage between whites and nonwhites and of multiracial identification. At least in those cases of marriages involving a white partner or one of the identities being white among multiracial individuals (which according to the results of the 2000 census made up 80.1 percent of the multiracial identities), Wilson's thesis implies that the likelihood of white-nonwhite interracial marriage and the likelihood of multiracial identification will be similar among all racial-ethnic groups. The greatest variance would be across class lines. If this is true, the factors that produce and reflect racial mixing, interracial marriage, and multiracial identification should be equally evident among all racial-ethnic groups, with perhaps somewhat lower levels of interracial marriage and multiracial reporting among blacks, for whom Arthur Sakamoto, Huei-Hsai Wu, and Jessie Tzeng (2000) find somewhat higher unexplained earnings disadvantages.

Wilson's ideas are highly influential, but they have not gone without criticism. One major line of criticism is based on the fact that progress in reducing the negative effects of pernicious, direct racial discrimination has not been matched by substantial progress in reducing the effects of indirect racial discrimination, especially residential segregation of blacks and its resultant consequences in limiting opportunities and labor-market outcomes for African Americans (Farley and Frey 1994; Massey and Denton 1993; Neckerman and Kirschenman 1991; Newman 1999; Patillo-McCoy 1999). Patterson (1998a, 1998b) makes a related argument: that black economic progress has been concentrated among those with high levels of education, and that blacks with lower levels of education continue to experience severe disadvantages.

Although research points to the continued disadvantage experienced by many blacks (Smelser, Wilson, and Mitchell 2001), America's newest nonwhite immigrant groups evince quite different patterns. As we noted in chapter 6, such disadvantage among Latinos (especially women) and Asians does not appear to persist much beyond the first generation, especially among the well-educated (Bean et al. 2001; Gibson 1988; Kao and Tienda 1995; Portes and Rumbaut 2001; Zhou and Bankston 1998). Hence, we may find evidence of the emergence of a new color line at the beginning of the twenty-first century, namely a black-nonblack line that will persist with greater strength than will the white-nonwhite or black-white color line. Furthermore, the black-nonblack line may operate more strongly in the case of blacks with lower levels of education than those with higher education. Therefore, less interracial marriage and multiracial identification may exist among blacks than among the other major racial-ethnic groups, with most of the deficit concentrated among blacks at lower levels of education and income.

Interracial Marriage in the United States

Social scientists conceive of intermarriage between whites and non-whites as a measure of decreasing social distance, declining racial prejudice, and changing racial boundaries (Davis 1941; Fu 2001; Gilbertson, Fitzpatrick, and Yang 1996; Gordon 1964; Kalmijn 1998; Lee and Fernandez 1998; Lieberson and Waters 1988; Merton 1941; Rosenfeld 2002; Tucker and Mitchell-Kernan 1990). Examining rates of interracial marriage between whites and nonwhites in order to explore the implications for America's color lines, we see in table 10.1 that intermarriage rates in the late 1990s for whites and blacks remain relatively low, at 5.8 and 10.2 percent of the total numbers of marriages involving at least one white or black person, respectively. By contrast, the intermarriage rate for Asians and Latinos is nearly three times the rate of blacks and more than five times the rate of whites. Among Asian and Latino marriages, 27.2 and 28.4 percent, respectively, involve a member of another racial or ethnic group, typically someone white.

The significantly higher rates of intermarriage among Asians and Latinos than among blacks indicate that racial and ethnic prejudice is less salient for these groups and that racial and ethnic boundaries are more fluid and flexible. The differential rates of intermarriage among nonwhite racial-ethnic groups suggest that race is not declining in significance for all groups at the same pace. The lower rates of intermarriage among blacks suggest that racial-ethnic boundaries are more prominent for blacks than for other nonwhite groups.

Although the white intermarriage rate accounts for only 5.8 percent of all white marriages, most interracial marriages involve a white partner because whites are by far the largest racial group. For example, of all black interracial marriages, 69.1 percent are with whites (table 10.1). For Asians and Latinos, the rate of intermarriage with whites is much higher, 86.8 and 90.0 percent, respectively. Hence, not only is the rate of intermarriage greater for Asians and Latinos than for blacks, but also the proportion of those married to whites is significantly higher among these new immigrant groups than among blacks. The corollary is that among the intermarried white population, we find that whites are least likely to marry blacks and most likely to marry Latinos, with Asians falling in between.

Of white intermarriages, more than half, or 55.2 percent, involve Latinos and slightly more than one fifth, or 20.7 percent, involve

Table 10.1 Rates of Exogamy Among Marriages Containing at Least One Member of the Racial or Ethnic Group

	White		Black		Asian		Latino		Other	
	Rate (Percentage)	Number	Rate (Percentage)	Number	Rate (Percentage)	Number	Rate (Percentage)	Number	Rate (Percentage)	Number
Total marriages	100.0	155,534	100.0	11,593	100.0	7,313	100.0	28,993	100.0	2,342
Same race	94.2	143,596	89.8	10,190	72.8	5,152	71.6	20,180	25.8	761
Intermarried	5.8	11,938	10.2	1,403	27.2	2,161	28.4	8,813	74.2	1,581
Racial or ethnic group										
White	—	—	69.1	848	86.8	1,788	90.0	7,949	88.4	1,353
Black	11.0	848	—	—	4.8	85	5.3	432	3.2	38
Asian	20.7	1,788	7.2	85	—	—	3.0	265	1.3	23
Hispanic	55.2	7,949	20.7	432	7.6	265	—	—	7.2	167
Other	13.1	1,353	3.0	38	0.8	23	1.7	167	—	—

Source: Current Population Survey (1995 to 2001).

Asians. By contrast, only 11.0 percent of white intermarriages involve a black partner. The disparities in the rates at which whites marry Latinos and Asians compared to blacks is even greater when we consider that blacks account for approximately 13 percent of the U.S. population and Latinos and Asians, only 6 and 4 percent, respectively. Hence, the social distance between whites and Latinos and Asians appears much less than it is between whites and blacks.

Multiracial Identification

The growth in intermarriage has resulted in the growth of the multiracial population in the United States. This population became especially highly visible in 2000, when for the first time in the nation's history the census allowed Americans to select "one or more races" to indicate their racial identification. This landmark change reflects the view that race is no longer conceived as a bounded category. Brought about by a small but highly influential multiracial movement, the change in the way the U.S. census measures racial identification provides a new reflection of changing racial boundaries (DaCosta 2000; Farley 2001; Hirschman, Alba, and Farley 2000; Waters 2000; Williams 2001). In 2000, 6.8 million persons, or 2.4 percent of the U.S. population (about one of every forty persons), identified themselves as multiracial (Greico and Cassidy 2001). These figures may not appear large, but a recent National Academy of Science study noted that the multiracial population could rise to 21 percent by the year 2050, by which time patterns of increasing intermarriage could mean that as many as 35 percent of Asians and 45 percent of Hispanics (meaning those claiming this race-ethnicity alone or in combination) could claim a multiracial background (Smith and Edmonston 1997). Of the multiracial or multiethnic population, 93 percent reported exactly two races, 6 percent reported three races, and only 1 percent reported four or more races.

While most individuals who reported a multiracial identification reported exactly two races, the two races selected is not evenly distributed across all racial groups. As table 10.2 illustrates, the groups with a high percentage of multiracial persons as a percentage of the total group include "Native Hawaiian or Other Pacific Islander," "American Indian and Alaska Native," "Other," and "Asian." Although "Latino" or "Hispanic," was not a racial category in the 2000 census, the Office of Management and Budget directive about the change in the race questions recommended continuing two questions regarding a person's racial or ethnic background: one about race and

Table 10.2   Multiracial Identification by Census Racial Categories

	Racial Identification[a] (Millions)	Multiracial Identification[b] (Millions)	Percentage Multiracial
White	216.5	5.1	2.3
Black	36.2	1.5	4.2
Asian	11.7	1.4	12.4
Other	18.4	3.0	16.4
American Indian and Alaska Native	3.9	1.4	36.4
Native Hawaiian or other Pacific Islander	0.7	0.3	44.8

Source: U.S. Bureau of the Census (2001a).
[a]Racial or ethnic group totals do not sum to the total U.S. population because multiracial persons are counted here in more than one group.
[b]Multiracial persons are counted for each race category mentioned.

a second about whether a person was of Spanish origin for self-identification of the Latino population in the United States.

What becomes immediately evident is that the groups with the lowest proportion of persons who claim a multiracial background are "whites" and "blacks." However, because whites account for 77 percent of the total U.S. population, most individuals who report a multiracial identity claim a white background (table 10.2). More specifically, although 5.1 million whites claim a multiracial background, this accounts for only 2.3 percent of the total white population. Like whites, the proportion of blacks who claim a multiracial background is also quite small, accounting for only 4.2 percent of the total black population. These figures stand in stark contrast to Latinos and Asians, 16.4 and 12.4 percent of whom claim a multiracial background, respectively. In sum, Latinos and Asians have much higher rates of multiracial reporting as a total percentage of their populations than whites and blacks.

Like intermarriage, multiracial identification reflects changing racial boundaries, and as with patterns in intermarriage, data on multiracial identification reveal that the boundaries are changing more rapidly for Latinos and Asians than for blacks. For example, from table 10.3 we see that the rate of black-white, Asian-white, and Latino-white multiracial reporting as a percent of the total black, Asian, and Latino populations are 1.9, 7.0, and 4.6 percent, respectively. In other words, Asians are 3.7 times more likely to report a multiracial identification that also involves a white identification than blacks, and Latinos are more than 2.4 times more likely to do so.

Table 10.3   Percentage of a Particular Racial-Ethnic Group Reporting a Multiracial Identity in Combination with Various Other Racial-Ethnic Groups

Group	Whites	Blacks	Asians	Native Americans	Others	Latinos
			Secondary Identity			
Whites[a]	—	0.3	0.4	0.5	1.1	0.9
Blacks[a]	1.9	—	0.3	0.6	1.1	0.8
Asians[a]	7.0	0.8	—	1.5	2.2	1.3
Native Americans[a]	25.5	4.6	4.1	—	2.4	4.5
Other[b]	11.9	2.2	1.3	0.5	—	9.7
Latinos	4.6	0.7	0.4	0.5	4.8	—

Source: U.S. Bureau of the Census (2001a).
[a]Are defined as non-Hispanic.
[b]Can be either Hispanic or non-Hispanic.

The rates of multiracial identification among the major racial groups indicate that patterns of multiracial reporting mirror patterns of intermarriage. Latinos and Asians are not only more likely to intermarry with whites than with blacks but also are more likely to report multiracial identifications than blacks. The higher rates of multiracial identification among Latinos and Asians, both as a proportion of the total Latino and Asian populations and vis-à-vis blacks, suggest that the racial boundaries may be more fluid or loosened for these groups. These national patterns of intermarriage and multiracial identification indicate that the racial divide may no longer fall between whites and nonwhites, as a traditional black-white model of race relations would presume. The patterns reveal that Latinos and Asians may be moving closer to whites faster than are blacks, indicating the possible emergence of a new color line, a black-nonblack divide, that may divide blacks from other racial-ethnic groups.

The Geography of the Multiracial Identities

While differences in multiracial reporting across racial groups are readily apparent, it is also noteworthy that rates of multiracial identification are not uniform across the country. For instance, 40 percent of all those who report a multiracial identification reside in the West, a region of the country that has often demonstrated more tolerance for social and racial or ethnic diversity than other parts of the country

Table 10.4   State Summaries: Most and Least Multiracial States

Rank	State	Number of Multiracial Persons	Multiracial Population (Percentage)	Percentage not Black or White[a]	Diversity
1	Hawaii	259,343	21.4	75.4	73.5
2	Alaska	34,146	5.4	29.0	51.3
3	California	1,607,646	4.7	46.9	66.0
4	Oklahoma	155,985	4.5	18.4	43.5
5	Nevada	76,428	3.8	28.2	52.9
6	New Mexico	66,327	3.6	53.6	61.4
7	Washington	213,519	3.6	17.9	36.7
8	New York	590,182	3.1	23.2	56.7
9	Oregon	104,745	3.1	14.9	29.5
10	Arizona	146,526	2.9	33.3	52.6
.	.	.	.	.	.
.	.	.	.	.	.
.	.	.	.	.	.
42	Tennessee	63,109	1.1	4.5	34.5
43	Iowa	31,778	1.1	5.3	14.1
44	Louisiana	48,265	1.1	5.2	50.4
45	New Hampshire	13,214	1.1	4.2	9.5
46	Kentucky	42,443	1.1	3.5	19.7
47	South Carolina	39,950	1.0	4.5	47.6
48	Alabama	44,179	1.0	3.8	43.8
49	Maine	12,647	1.0	3.0	6.9
50	West Virginia	15,788	0.9	2.3	10.4
51	Mississippi	20,021	0.7	3.1	50.0

Source: U.S. Bureau of the Census (2001a).
[a]Percentage *not* non-Hispanic white or non-Hispanic black.

(Baldassare 1981, 2000; Carter and Glick 1976; Godfrey 1988). As table 10.4 indicates, California leads the nation as the state with the highest number of multiracial persons and is the only state with a multiracial population exceeding 1 million. The multiracial population accounts for 4.7 percent of California's population, or one in every twenty-one Californians, compared to one in every forty Americas for the country as a whole.

Areas with high immigrant populations, and consequently high levels of racial and ethnic diversity, exhibit larger multiracial populations, and like the immigrant population, the multiracial population is clustered in certain states. In fact, 64 percent, or nearly two thirds, of those who report a multiracial identification reside in just ten states—California, New York, Texas, Florida, Hawaii, Illinois, New Jersey, Washington, Michigan, and Ohio—all of which have relatively high immigrant populations. In essence, states that have higher levels of diversity (as reflected in the percent of the population that is *not* non-

Hispanic white or non-Hispanic black), boast much larger multiracial populations than states that are less racially diverse. The patterns support the thesis that multiracial reporting is more likely in areas with greater levels of racial and ethnic diversity, largely brought about by the influx of the post-1965 wave of immigrants, particularly Latinos and Asians. We suggest that increased diversity through immigration increases the likelihood of multiracial identification because greater diversity leads to the loosening of racial boundaries, and consequently allows more flexibility in the identity options for multiracial persons.

On the opposite end of the diversity spectrum are states like West Virginia and Maine that have low racial minority populations and also exhibit very low levels of multiracial reporting. States like Mississippi, Alabama, South Carolina, and Louisiana, however, have relatively large black populations yet nevertheless exhibit low levels of multiracial reporting. In these southern states, the traditional dividing line between blacks and whites and the historically constraining "one-drop rule" appear to constrain multiracial identification, leading persons to identify monoracially as either white or black rather than adopting a multiracial identity (Davis 1991; Farley 2001).

The geography of multiracial reporting clearly indicates that the rate of multiracial reporting varies widely across the country, with the highest levels in states that exhibit the greatest racial and ethnic diversity brought about by the arrival of new immigrants to these areas. Hence, while national patterns in intermarriage and multiracial identification may indicate a loosening of racial boundaries, particularly in the case of Latinos and Asians, these shifts appear to be taking place more rapidly in certain parts of the country. Areas of the country that have lower levels of immigration and consequently less racial and ethnic diversity demonstrate the tenacity of the black-white divide. Hence, while some parts of the country like the West may exhibit the emergence of a new color line that falls between nonblacks and blacks, other areas such as the South show that the traditional black-white color line still endures.

Linking Diversity to Multiracial Identification

Simply noting that a few states with greater diversity appear to have higher multiracial reporting, however, does not provide a very strong basis for establishing a connection between growing diversity and the breakdown of racial and ethnic color lines. More needed are research results demonstrating more systematic bases for such linkages. Although it has been apparent for some time that the multiracial population is likely to continue to increase and that its existence and growth may have broader implications, the phenomenon has been relatively understudied in social science research. For example, only a handful of studies have examined the question of how interracial couples identify their multiracial children (Eschbach 1995; McKenney and Bennett 1994; Saenz et al. 1995; Xie and Goyette 1997), revealing that about 50 percent of American Indian–white and Asian-white intermarried couples report a white racial identity for their children. A somewhat larger but still not sizable number of studies have examined the ways multiracial individuals self-identify; these have often been based on small samples and have generated conflicting findings (Johnson 1997; Root 1992, 1996; Salgado de Snyder, Lopez, and Padilla 1982; Spickard 1989; Stephan and Stephan 1989). For example, Nelly Salgado de Snyder, Cynthia Lopez, and Amado Padilla (1982) found that 70 percent of multiracial children in California with one Mexican-origin parent identified as Mexican, a rate much higher than Cookie White Stephan and Walter Stephan (1989) found for multiracial Hispanic college students in New Mexico, where only 44 percent adopted a Hispanic identity.

As indicated above, old models of cultural accommodation and bipolar racial divides may be less relevant to the historical and contemporary experiences of Latinos (Rodriguez 2001) than for earlier immigrants. And such dichotomies are scarcely more relevant for Asians who come from so many countries of origin that no single context of reception or mode of incorporation can be thought to have played a defining role in shaping their identities (Lopez and Espiritu 1990). Moreover, as we argued in chapter 5, many of today's new Asian and Latino immigrants seem to have adopted paths of "selective assimilation" (Portes and Zhou 1993; Zhou and Bankston 1998) and "accommodation without assimilation" (Gibson 1988). Under these conditions, racial and ethnic identity appears to be less constrained than previously assumed and has become more flexible and dynamic than foreseen by either the straight-line assimilation or cultural pluralist models. Multiracial identifications are more likely among Asians and Latinos than among either black Afro-origin immigrants or native-born blacks, as a consequence of both higher rates of intermarriage and greater tendencies for Asians and Latinos to see themselves in multiracial or multiethnic terms. Places that have experienced more immigration may thus reveal larger relative sizes of racial and ethnic minority groups (at least in the case of Latinos and Asians) and increased diversity, with the latter in turn loosening racial and ethnic boundaries and increasing the likelihood of multiracial self-identification.

But a countervailing tendency is suggested by the literature on minority group size. An appreciable body of research indicates that larger relative minority group size increases perceptions of threat on the part of the majority group (Blalock 1967; Blumer 1958; Fossett and Kiecolt 1989; Schuman, Steeh, and Bobo 1985; Cohen 1999; Forbes 1997). Furthermore, under conditions of continuing immigration, a constant influx of new members of a given racial or ethnic group into areas already containing concentrations of group members will not only add to the group's relative size but may also reinforce the group's distinctive behavioral and cultural patterns (Massey 1995). In turn, this may increase and heighten the group's distinctive sense of ethnicity, foster ethnic insularity, and tighten racial and ethnic boundaries. Increased relative racial or ethnic and immigrant group size, though fostering diversity in a broad sense, may also lead to declines in intermarriage and thus make it less likely that the members of these groups will either come from multiracial backgrounds or come to perceive themselves in multiracial terms. In short, larger relative group size may foster multiracial identification through one pathway but diminish intermarriage and multiracial identification through others.

Previous research demonstrates that immigration and diversity affect identity choice. For instance, living among a large co-ethnic community or residing in an area that is greater than 20 percent Asian positively affects the degree to which interracially married Asians and whites identify their multiracial children as Asian (Saenz et al. 1995; Xie and Goyette 1997). Furthermore, Stephan and Stephan (1989) posit that the higher rates of multiracial identification of the Japanese in Hawaii (73 percent) compared to the Hispanics in New Mexico (44 percent) reflects the more multicultural environment in Hawaii. Eschbach (1995) too discovers vast regional differences ranging from 33 to 73 percent in the choice of an American Indian identity for American Indian–white multiracial individuals.

Although individual-level data from the 2000 census had not yet been released as of the writing of this chapter, state-level data on multiracial identification were available, and we examine these data here to provide an assessment of the effects of relative group size and diversity on multiracial reporting. For example, table 10.4 presents basic data for states on multiracial identification and racial and ethnic composition. We should note that we include in our measure of multiracial reporting Latinos who report in response to the U.S. census question on race that they possess both "white" and "other" racial backgrounds. Some scholars have suggested that such persons should not be included as multiracials because they are Latinos whose re-

Figure 10.1   State-Level Standardized Coefficients for Regressions of Diversity and Multiraciality on Relative Racial-Ethnic Group Sizes.

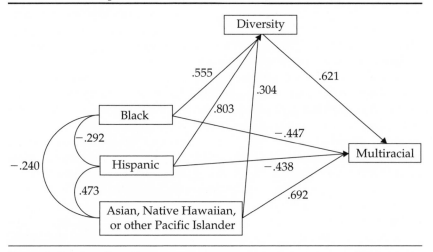

Source: Authors' configuration.
Notes: All standardized coefficients significant at p < .05.
Weighted by state population size.
N = 51.

sponses may reflect confusion about what the race question meant. Alternatively, we would suggest that among many Latinos, the categories "white" and "other" reflect "white" and "mestizo" backgrounds (Rodríguez 2000), suggesting, we would argue, that they indicate actual multiracial backgrounds. Whatever the case, we also reran the results we present below so as *not* to include these persons and found that this did not affect the pattern of our findings.

We present in figure 10.1 the estimates of a simple recursive model of the effects of relative group size on diversity and multiracial identification focusing on three major racial and ethnic groups: Latinos, African Americans, and Asians. The sizes of two of these, Latinos and Asians, have been substantially affected by immigration during the past decade. We use data from the 2000 census, and we construct from these data a simple measure of diversity, defined as one minus the Herfindahl Index of Concentration. This index indicates the degree to which the members of a population are concentrated in one of several subgroups. A high value on the Herfindahl Index means that one racial or ethnic group predominates in an area. A high score on the complement of the index means that no single group predominates. The values in the last column of table 10.4 show that Hawaii and California are the two highest-diversity states in 2000.

The findings make clear that states with relatively larger racial and ethnic groups (resulting in large part from immigration) have higher diversity scores and higher levels of multiracial identification. However, this positive effect of relative group size through diversity is partially offset by negative direct effects from relative group size in the cases of the Latino and (especially) black populations. But summing these direct and indirect effects reveals that relative group size exerts an overall positive effect on multiracial identification for Asians and Latinos, with much of this effect operating through increases in diversity. In other words, the positive effect of relative group size because of increased diversity is more than large enough to make up for the negative direct effect of relative group size. This pattern of findings thus provides further confirmation that the larger racial and ethnic groups resulting from higher immigration and generating greater racial and ethnic diversity appear also to lead to rising multiracial identification, lending additional weight to the idea that increasing diversity is operating to loosen traditional racial and ethnic group boundaries in the United States.

Summary and Conclusions

A significant proportion of the Latinos and Asians in the United States are either immigrants or the children of immigrants, and their understanding of race and ethnicity, racial boundaries, and the color line is shaped by a different set of circumstances in their case than in the case of African Americans. Moreover, as outlined in chapter 5, it appears that the processes of incorporation for Latinos and Asians increasingly do not require that they achieve full acculturation to achieve structural incorporation, meaning that Latino and Asian immigrants may have more leeway in retaining cultural and ethnic distinctiveness than even their earlier European counterparts. Most important, what sets the experiences of Latinos and Asians apart from those of African Americans is that the former are not rooted in a historical legacy of slavery and its resultant consequences of legal, systematic, and persistent discrimination and inequality from which the tenacious black-white divide was born. For these reasons, the racial and ethnic boundaries appear more fluid among the newest immigrants and whites than for native-born blacks. And gauging from patterns of intermarriage, whites also seem less concerned with constraining Latino and Asian identities and boundaries. America's traditional nonwhite color line thus appears to be shifting to accommodate new immigrant groups such as Latinos and Asians. Though the color line also appears to be loosening for blacks (for example, through increased intermarriage), this change seems to be occurring more slowly, demonstrating the tenacity of the black-white divide.

At this time, the unequal pace at which the color line is shifting for these three groups points to the emergence of a black-nonblack divide according to which Latinos and Asians are placed closer to whites than to blacks. This is most evident in areas with higher concentrations of immigrants and higher levels of racial and ethnic diversity, where higher levels of multiracial reporting indicate a breaking down of the barriers that have traditionally operated to separate whites and nonwhites in the United States. Immigration is playing a substantial role in this process, bringing a new group of persons to the country who are "in between" whites and blacks in terms of skin color and often other characteristics. The experiences of these newcomers, both historically (as in the emergence of a mestizo group among many Latinos [the mixing of early Spanish colonialists with indigenous populations]) and contemporaneously (as in the incorporation dynamics of many Asians), do not tend to reinforce the idea that the new immigrants constitute racialized minorities, either in their own or the receiving society's eyes. This serves to locate them in an intermediate position relative to whites and blacks. That the dissolution of racial and ethnic group boundaries has gone furthest in the areas with the largest relative numbers of Asians and Latinos (as indicated by levels of multiracial reporting) indicates that immigration is hastening the process of loosening boundaries between whites and nonwhites, even if these transitions appear to be occurring more slowly for African Americans than for the new immigrant groups.

=== Chapter 11 ===

Conclusions: Diversity and Change in America

HE EVIDENCE and arguments introduced in the previous chapters demonstrate that immigration has become a phenomenon of critical importance for American society. Recent annual levels of immigration are almost as high as, and in some years higher than, they have ever been. The national origins of immigrants have changed dramatically such that newcomers now swell the ranks of U.S. racial and ethnic minority groups. Unauthorized migration, predominantly Mexican in origin, continues largely unabated. These trends engender both optimism and pessimism. On the one hand, the economic boom of the United States in the latter half of the 1990s, which created annually more than a million more jobs than required to keep pace with non-immigration-related population growth, threw into bold relief the dependency of the American economy on immigrant labor, causing many to breathe a sigh of relief that substantial immigrant flows had forestalled even more severe labor shortages than those of that time. On the other hand, the attacks of September 11, 2001, and the implication that they were facilitated by easy entry to the country and lax immigration policies has heightened security concerns.

Americans continue to be ambivalent about immigration both because the phenomenon inherently tends to generate contradictory feelings, as noted in chapter 1, and because immigration tends to generate both positive and negative consequences. For example, when we consider the two major dimensions of immigrant incorporation and of immigration's consequences, the economic and the sociocultural, we saw in chapters 5 through 8 that successful economic and sociocultural incorporation can foster both higher education and earnings and more intermarriage and greater English proficiency at the same time that they lead to increased ethnic identity and conscious-

250

ness. This can create ambivalence in the minds of casual observers because on the surface, immigration appears to be generating contradictory outcomes (more prosperity on the one hand, but seemingly increasing ethnic fragmentation on the other). However, as we argued in chapter 5, we think many Americans are unnecessarily confused by this. Much of the ethnic distinctiveness that emerges among reasonably successful immigrants is more appropriately interpreted as consonant rather than dissonant with Americanization, for two reasons. First, immigrants often embrace distinctiveness as an explicit strategy for facilitating economic incorporation. And among immigrants who already possess middle-class status, such distinctiveness can be a mechanism of sustaining economic achievements (Zhou and Bankston 1998). Second, nothing is quite so American as nurturing and maintaining a distinctive subgroup, or "local" identity, within a larger national identity perspective. Rather than going against the American grain, such tendencies are actually part of the Americanization process (Alba 1990; Gans 1988; Glazer 1975; Fischer 1999). This is not to endorse a pollyannaish view of what is occurring among immigrants to the United States, because as we note below, external events can easily occur that may cause these processes to go awry. But it does provide an interpretation that accords with the increased levels of intermarriage and high levels of English language proficiency characteristic of immigrant groups in the United States.

In general, then, we conclude that on balance the overall consequences of immigration over the past thirty years or so have been more positive than negative for American society. To summarize more clearly why we reach this conclusion, it is helpful to review the three major policy-relevant questions with which we began this endeavor, together with the major issues within each of them.

1. Are the kinds and numbers of immigrants who have come to the United States in recent decades in line with the intentions of U.S. immigration laws and policies?

   • How many persons have been coming and what kinds of persons are coming? Are there major disequilibria in the annual flows? Have they fluctuated widely on a year-to-year basis in the numbers of persons coming, the kinds of persons coming, or their reasons for coming? Are the numbers and kinds of unauthorized immigrants too high, or subject to the kinds of fluctuations that are cause for concern? Do the levels and kinds of unauthorized migration run counter to U.S. policies in other areas?

- Is there indication that immigrants are more likely to be welfare recipients than natives? If so, are they also more likely to be welfare recipients than statistically comparable natives? Do tendencies to receive welfare vary depending on type of immigrant and type of welfare?

2. What kinds of incorporation experiences are the new immigrants having in the United States? Are some immigrants now not achieving full economic incorporation compared to the case of European immigrants arriving earlier in the twentieth century? Have patterns of sociocultural incorporation changed?

- How has thinking about incorporation changed over the past thirty years? Do changes in the countries where the new immigrants come from require changes in thinking about the nature and pace of immigrant assimilation? Have new theories emerged about the nature of the connections between structural (including economic) incorporation and sociocultural incorporation?

- What does the research record show about the relative and absolute degree of success of economic incorporation among the major new immigrant groups? Are there differences among immigrant groups in the nature and pace of economic incorporation? To what degree does more successful incorporation occur among later generational members of immigrant groups? Does successful economic incorporation require an extra generation or so for unauthorized Mexican immigrants?

- What does the research record show about the relative and absolute degree of success of sociocultural incorporation as indicated by patterns of language proficiency and use among immigrant groups in the United States? Are most members of immigrant groups proficient in English by the third generation? Is bilingualism prevalent? Is it an economic liability or asset?

- What does the research record show about the relative and absolute degree of success of sociocultural incorporation as indicated by patterns of intermarriage among members of immigrant groups? Do rates of intermarriage increase among the later generational members of national-descent groups? How are patterns of racial and ethnic intermarriage affected by patterns of marriage between immigrants and native-born Americans?

3. What are the consequences of immigration for the United States in general and for natives and earlier-arriving immigrants? If negative, are these consequences severe enough to warrant raising questions about immigrant admissions policies? If positive are they sufficient to conclude that immigration has generally been beneficial for the country?

    •   What are the major economic and fiscal (including labor-market) consequences of immigration? Have these generally been positive or negative over the course of the past thirty years? If some have been positive and some negative, what does the research record indicate about their relative balance?

    •   What have been the consequences of immigration for race and ethnicity in the United States? Has immigration changed patterns of the country's racial and ethnic composition? Has immigration increased racial and ethnic diversity? Have changes of these types led to changes in notions of race and ethnicity? Have these kinds of changes increased the likelihood of multiracial identification in the United States? If so, does this reflect a loosening of racial and ethnic boundaries and a modified color line in the United States?

We addressed each of these sets of issues in the chapters of this monograph, seeking to review the pertinent theoretical and research literature and to introduce new research findings where needed. The volume of immigration to the country has gradually increased over the past thirty years, to roughly 800,000 to 1.2 million new net immigrants per year, including both legal and unauthorized entrants. The largest portion of this flow has been immigrants from Mexico. Immigration has contributed about 35 to 40 percent of the country's almost 0.9 percent per year population increase during this period, with about one fourth to one third of immigration's contribution in most years involving persons from Mexico. In other words, Mexican immigration seems to have contributed directly to about 9 to 14 percent of U.S. population growth over many of the past thirty years. Because U.S. job growth during most of these same years was about two-and-a-half times the approximate level required to accommodate non-immigration-related population growth, immigration did not appear, very broadly speaking, to place undue pressure on the U.S. labor market, with the possible exception of generally short-lived recession periods.

There have, however, been two time periods that were exceptions to these generalizations. The first was from 1989 to 1992, when levels of legal immigration jumped upward as result of the floodtide of persons, the vast majority from Mexico, who became legal immigrants under the various legalization programs that were part of the 1986 Immigration and Reform and Control Act (IRCA). In these years the total annual number of new immigrants went from 800,000 or 900,000 during the early 1980s to about 1.5 to 1.6 million persons per year. Of course, a substantial minority of these persons were not in fact new entrants in the year that they were counted because they had already been living in the United States. It just happened that the year in which the statistics were issued for the "entries" of these persons was the year they officially became legal visa holders. Imprecision in the exact date when these persons arrived in the country does not, however, affect the main point here, which is that a much greater change in the number and status of persons than usual occurred at about this time. This was driven by IRCA and it led to more persons mostly from Mexico establishing legal residence in the country.

The second exceptional situation took place during the latter half of the 1990s, especially in the years 1998 to 2000, when an unusually large number of unauthorized immigrants entered the country, apparently as a result of the exceptionally strong job growth in the United States that started around 1994 and lasted until early 2001. A disproportionate number of these persons came from Mexico. New unauthorized annual immigration during these years has been estimated as high as 600,000 to 700,000 persons, figures which would place the total volume of immigration close to the levels occurring around 1990 that was brought about by the legacy of IRCA. In short, on two brief occasions over the past thirty years, spikes in U.S. immigration occurred that drove total immigration levels up by anywhere from a third to a half. These boosts involved either the arrival in the United States of more unauthorized migrants, mostly coming to work, or the legalization of unauthorized Mexican migrants if they were already here. In either case, it seems likely that an increase of this magnitude was large enough to be conspicuous. Moreover, given that each of these upturns was followed immediately by a recession, the increase in immigration that occurred probably resulted in something of a contrast effect. In other words, even though these bursts were short-lived, they stood out for two reasons: they involved more unauthorized Mexican migration, a kind of migration that has always been relatively unpopular simply because it occurs outside legal channels, and they were fairly sizable, something that was all the more noticeable because of an immediately succeeding recession.

Thus, it is likely that these periods exerted especially strong influence on public attitudes about immigration and helped to create considerable confusion about the nature and magnitude of the phenomenon in general. Much of the negative publicity about immigration has arisen in the wake of developments during these few years, helping to create an impression that most years are like these few. This reinforces ideas among many observers that immigration has been "out of control" and has caused negative economic and sociocultural effects on the country. And indeed, if all years over the past three decades had been like these years, the likelihood that immigration might have strained the social fabric and taxed the absorptive capacities of the American economy would undoubtedly have been far greater than it has in fact been. But these few years were the exception, not the rule. The general pattern over the past thirty years is that levels of immigration, both legal and unauthorized, have exhibited considerable stability and have not been unduly high, constituting about a third or slightly more of population growth. As such they provide little basis for concluding that immigration policy might be "broke" and need fixing. Having said this, however, we must also note that the few years that constitute departures from this pattern of moderation and stability serve to draw attention to one of the major features of the new U.S. immigration that should not be overlooked in thinking about the meaning of immigration for the United States, namely that much of it is from Mexico and much of it is unauthorized. Both of these have major implications for how we interpret research results about economic and sociocultural incorporation, as well as for relations between the United States and Mexico in a number of policy areas.

If unauthorized migration in general and unauthorized Mexican migration in particular has created confusion about the nature and magnitude of immigration patterns to the United States, our review of theory and research on economic and sociocultural incorporation has uncovered another major factor that also generates substantial confusion. The maintenance and in some instances reemergence of ethnic identity among immigrant groups fosters the idea that these developments and their various expressions are evidence that sociocultural incorporation may be occurring to a lesser degree than it did among earlier-arriving immigrants. Renewed ethnic consciousness appears to contradict the idea that successful incorporation has been taking place. But this is only the case if we presume that certain kinds of sociocultural incorporation occur before or necessarily accompany economic incorporation. As we noted in chapter 5, this is a notion born of narrow versions of assimilation theory, models influenced in part by the experience of European and some Jewish immigrants at the turn of the twentieth century. When we realize that this pattern does not fit the experiences of the new Asian and Hispanic immigrants very well, that in their cases a decoupling of ethnic consciousness and economic incorporation often seems to occur, we find that reasons for concern about the emergence and maintenance of ethnic identities tend to dissipate.

We presented two major pieces of evidence to argue that this decoupling has taken place. One is the finding that many new immigrant groups maintain their ethnic consciousness and immigrant group identity as a strategy for achieving successful economic incorporation, in part as a way to avoid being defined either by others or themselves as members of racialized minority groups. The second is that many later-generation members of immigrant groups often renew their embrace of their ethnic heritages after achieving considerable economic incorporation, a pattern reminiscent of the symbolic ethnicity that developed among later-generation European immigrants during the 1960s and 1970s. In both of these instances, the ethnic identity dimension of sociocultural incorporation no longer seems to accompany economic incorporation as readily as it once did, when ethnic identity tended to fade with rising economic incorporation.

Though the emergence of such ethnic consciousness may create confusion by appearing to contradict the idea that sociocultural incorporation has been taking place, substantial progress with respect to other dimensions of sociocultural incorporation, English language proficiency and intermarriage, has in fact been taking place, often at just as rapid a pace as it did for earlier-arriving European immigrants. Moreover, the increasing separation of the more subjective identity dimension of sociocultural incorporation from the more behavioral dimensions may serve to reinforce confusion among natives about the nature of the processes occurring among immigrants. When we focus our attention on what has been taking place "on the ground," so to speak, we find that levels of intermarriage and English-language proficiency are increasingly high. Thus, as measured by these concrete, behavioral measures, sociocultural incorporation among the new immigrants is proceeding to a substantial degree. In short, the high levels of English-language proficiency and intermarriage provide little basis for concluding that the experiences of the new immigrants with respect to sociocultural incorporation constitute cause for great concern about U.S. immigration policies.

Much the same conclusion emerges in the case of economic incorporation, with one important caveat. When we examine trends in earnings patterns by education among Asians and Latinos, together with changes in levels of earnings across generations, we find substantial evidence of successful economic incorporation among the new immigrants. Both earnings and education levels have increased over time, and earnings levels are noticeably higher among third- and later-generation members of these groups, especially in the case of Asians. Latinos lag behind somewhat, especially males. But when we examine earnings data separately by nativity, we find that much of the Latino gap is due to the lower earnings of the Mexican-origin group, and within this category, much of it to the immigrant instead of the native generation. In fact, among the third- or later-generation members of the Mexican-origin group, college-educated women earn as much as or more than educationally equivalent non-Hispanic white women, and college-educated men come close to their non-Hispanic white counterparts. The idea that the Mexican-origin population constitutes an exception to the pattern of continuing successful economic incorporation becomes reinforced, then, when data are examined that do not separate out the relatively low earnings of persons born in Mexico or Central America, especially those from Mexico who are by far the larger group. And on this matter it must also be said with some emphasis that the information used to assess economic incorporation within the Mexican-origin groups almost always comes from decennial census and Current Population Survey data. Both of these data sources contain substantial numbers of unauthorized Mexican migrants, persons whose especially low levels of earnings drag down the averages for the Mexican-origin group even more.

In short, with the notable exception primarily of unauthorized Mexican immigrants, the evidence for almost all groups points to a continuation of successful economic incorporation among the new immigrants. Little basis thus emerges on this account for concluding that legal immigrant admissions policies are in substantial need of repair. But it must be reiterated that this conclusion is often not the one that seems warranted by the data because the situations of unauthorized Mexican migrants so substantially cloud the picture. And the confusion has been exacerbated in recent years by the fact that such migration has been increasing. But this should not cause us to lose sight of the fact that even those Mexican-origin persons whose parents or grandparents or even more distant ancestors began their experience as unauthorized Mexican migrants are also experiencing substantial economic incorporation. This can be seen in the earnings growth occurring from the first to the second to the third or later generations. And we must remember that many Mexican-origin persons began their time in the United States as unauthorized migrants, or some of their ancestors did. This means that a substantial portion of the Mexican-origin population in the United States consists of unauthorized migrants or their descendants. Unauthorized persons, however, face more obstacles in the United States than authorized migrants, and these obstacles almost certainly hinder or deter their economic and sociocultural incorporation. Because children's educational and early occupational attainments are so strongly affected by their parents' attainments, the economic and sociocultural incorporation of the second (and perhaps third) generation of the Mexican-origin population in the United States will almost inevitably be less successful because of the disadvantaged start their parents, grandparents, or other ancestors had to endure in this country. When viewed through the prism of such a model, the experience of the Mexican-origin group with respect to economic incorporation appears much more sanguine.

Research on the labor-market consequences of immigration on other groups continues to generate either largely inconclusive results, findings showing inconsequential negative or positive effects, or findings showing that effects are contingent on other factors such that overall consequences become canceled out. The one exception to this generalization concerns labor-market consequences for earlier-arriving immigrants. In this case the research literature indicates that new arrivals tend to harm earlier arrivals, decreasing their job prospects and lowering their wages and earnings. Perhaps through this mechanism, immigration thus may account for a small amount of the increases in earnings inequality over the past thirty years (Reed 2001), as well as place an additional burden on the incorporation prospects of the low-skilled, especially in the case of unauthorized immigrants. But because all immigrants constitute still only about 11 percent of the population, the impact on the overall labor-market effects is slight. In short, overall the labor-market consequences of immigration have not been found large enough to provide a basis for concluding that immigrant admissions policies are problematic.

Some basis thus exists for feeling positive about the overall economic consequences of immigration. What can we say about the demographic consequences of immigration? We have already noted that the relatively small volumes of legal and unauthorized immigration in most years (enough roughly speaking to cause increases in population growth of about 0.35 percent, or about one third of one percent) are not disruptive and help the economy to cope with labor shortages and the society to forestall the aging of the population. The consequences for racial and ethnic population composition are more noticeable. We have examined the ways immigration has transformed the

United States from a largely biracial population to a multi-ethnic, multiracial society. The important question here, however, is not simply one of composition, but rather one of the implications of this diversity for the nature and strength of the country's color lines. W. E. B. Du Bois (1997 [1903]) said that in the United States, "[T]he problem of the color line will be the problem of the twentieth century." Will this also be true in the twenty-first century, and perhaps even more so because of immigration? Or will it instead be the case that the ethnic diversity born of the new immigration is loosening racial and ethnic group boundaries in the country? We have presented evidence in the last chapter about why we think the latter is the more accurate picture: because we find multiracial self-identification (a product of both intermarriage and the willingness to report multiple-race backgrounds, reflecting the dilution of racial and ethnic boundaries) most prevalent in places with the greatest racial and ethnic diversity. This diversity is greatest in areas with the most immigration.

In summary, many of the allegations about immigration's negative features and consequences do not hold up when examined carefully in light of the research evidence. Immigration is not creating welfare dependency among immigrants, nor does the evidence indicate that welfare is a magnet for immigrants. Moreover, there is little indication that incorporation is not occurring in the cases of some of the new immigrants, or that they are taking natives' jobs or driving down the wages of other groups, although they do appear to have a negative effect in this regard on earlier-arriving immigrants. On balance, then, the scorecard on immigration shows more positives than negatives. The major minuses are that immigration contains a large unauthorized component, mostly from Mexico, a phenomenon that is a negative not because the migration is Mexican in origin but because it is unauthorized; that low-skilled workers in the country do not receive much in the way of the benefits associated with immigration, and may even be slightly harmed (although the small negative outcomes that provide evidence for this conclusion may just as likely result from deeper secular trends in industrial restructuring and changing technology-based patterns in wage structures); and that immigration leads to serious strains between the federal government and state and local governments because of substantial inequities in taxes received on the federal level and the costs of social services provided at local levels.

By contrast, the list of pluses is long: immigration serves humanitarian purposes by allowing the United States to participate in taking in a portion of the world's refugees; it provides for reunification of families (a large portion of current immigration involves the entry of spouses and family members of citizens); it contributes a modest and relative stable portion of U.S. population growth without which the United States might face the prospects of an even more rapidly aging population and perhaps even population decline; it contributes an important and seemingly much-needed component to the country's low-skilled workforce, because immigrants are willing to do jobs that natives won't do or feel they are overqualified to do; it exerts an overall positive effect on the economy; and perhaps most important, it is leading to a broader and deeper racial and ethnic diversity in the population, which appears to be loosening racial and ethnic boundaries and modifying color lines such that they are not as sharply drawn as before, although this process seems to be proceeding less rapidly in the case of blacks than in the cases of the new immigrant groups.

Thus, the weight of the evidence indicates that present levels and patterns of U.S. immigration, if maintained in the future and if not overridden by other forces, will continue to generate what are, on balance, a favorable ratio of benefits to costs for American society. In saying this, we do not want to be misunderstood as arguing that a positive scenario is inevitable. Indeed, there are clouds to this silver lining, two of which in particular loom on the horizon. The first concerns unauthorized migration, and the second the now thirty-year trend toward increasing inequality in America in earnings and wealth. Unauthorized migration is a concern, first, because it is simply illegal. Its continuance thus does not fit within the United States identity as a country of laws, and it may be the major area of United States–Mexico public policy that so far has fallen outside the growing pattern of bilateral cooperation between the two countries (Bean et al. 1997). Furthermore, unauthorized migration confuses the public about the issue of immigration generally and thus carries the potential to upend what has basically been a fairly stable and generally favorable legal migration regime in the United States over the past thirty-five years. If policy makers ignore this uncomfortable situation simply because it seems hard to change, or alternatively because it is easy to overlook during years when economic and job growth are strong, they risk a virulent and potentially harmful backlash against legal immigrants and immigration during years when circumstances become more difficult. Such reactions tend to occur when the economy is in recession, or when external threats or attacks like those on the World Trade Center lead to heightened public anxieties about national and personal security. Policy reforms are needed that would help forestall such possibilities by curtailing unauthorized migration—especially migration from the largest source country, Mexico, but also from other countries. And in the Mexican case, these policies need to work through mechanisms that involve bilateral cooperation between the United States and Mexico and minimize the dangers of border enforcement. One option in this regard would be to increase legal Mexican migration in ways that maximally reduce illegal entries (Bean et al. 1997; Massey, Durand, and Malone 2002). In addition, as was attempted when the United States supported the North American Free Trade Agreement (Wintraub 1997), the United States needs to work more closely with Mexico to develop policies that increase that country's rates of economic growth. But it is very important that such policies be structured in ways that do not preclude technology transfers to Mexico (and other developing countries) and that are not undercut by other government actions, such as those that provide subsidies to U.S. industries, like agricultural corn producers, which force their Mexican counterparts to compete on uneven playing fields because the subsidies give advantages to U.S. growers (Rosenberg 2002). And it is especially important to implement such reforms over the next fifteen to twenty years, when further economic growth initiatives will be particularly important for Mexico because population pressures stemming from previously high Mexican birth rates will not yet have abated (Mexico–U.S. Binational Migration Study 1997).

Increasing inequality in earnings is also a problem, particularly because the growing gap in pay between rich and less well off working Americans results not only from the former gaining ground faster than the latter but from less well off working Americans actually losing ground in terms of real earnings over time (Bernhardt et al. 2001; Danziger and Gottschalk 1993). If this trend continues, and especially if the country does not return soon to the levels of economic growth attained in the latter half of the 1990s, growing inequality may engender a substantial social and political backlash in the country that could involve immigrants once again becoming scapegoats, as they so frequently have in the past, for frustrations resulting from injurious and unjust secular forces not of their own making. The combination of continuing high levels of unauthorized migration and inequality-induced social disruption could prove especially incendiary. A more optimistic view is that the relative generosity of the country's immigration policies for more than three decades now, which have substantially increased the country's national-origin diversity and strengthened its economy, if left to continue their influence and if allowed to work in combination with far-sighted economic policies that spread the benefits of economic growth to the entire population, promise to continue to foster universalistic values by further diminishing the salience of the kinds of color lines that have been such a burden to American society in the past.

═ References ═

Alba, Richard. 1985. *Italian Americans: Into the Twilight of Ethnicity*. Englewood Cliffs, N.J.: Prentice Hall.

———. 1990. *Ethnic Identity: The Transformation of White America*. New Haven, Conn.: University Press.

———. 1995. "Assimilation's Quiet Tide." *The Public Interest* 119(1): 3–18.

———. 1999. "Immigration and the American Realities of Assimilation and Multiculturalism." *Sociological Forum* 14(1): 3–25.

Alba, Richard D., John R. Logan, and Kyle Crowder. 1997. "White Ethnic Neighborhoods and Assimilation: The Greater New York Region, 1980–1990." *Social Forces* 75(3): 883–912.

Alba, Richard, and Victor Nee. 1997. "Rethinking Assimilation Theory for a New Era of Immigration." *International Migration Review* 31(4): 826–74.

———. 1999. "Rethinking Assimilation Theory for a New Era of Immigration." In *The Handbook of International Migration: The American Experience*, edited by Charles Hirschman, Josh DeWind, and Phillip Kasinitz. New York: Russell Sage Foundation.

———. 2003. *Remaking the American Mainstream: Assimilation and the New Immigration*. Cambridge, Mass.: Harvard University Press.

Altonji, Joseph G., and David Card. 1991. "The Effects of Immigration on the Labor Market Outcomes of Less-Skilled Natives." In *Immigration, Trade, and the Labor Market*, edited by J. M. Abowd and R. B. Freeman. Chicago: University of Chicago Press.

Alvarez, Robert. 1983. "Mexican Entrepreneurs and Markets in the City of Los Angeles: A Case of an Immigrant Enclave." *Urban Anthropology* 19(1–2): 99–124.

Andreas, Peter. 2000. *Border Games: Policing the U.S.-Mexico Divide*. Ithaca, N.Y.: Cornell University Press.

Appelbaum, Richard P., and Gary Gereffi. 1994. "Power and Profits in the Apparel Commodity Chain." In *Global Production: The Apparel Industry in the Pacific Rim*, edited by Edna Bonacich, Lucie Cheng, Norma Chinchilla, Nora Hamilton, and Paul Ong. Philadelphia: Temple University Press.

August, Diane, and Kenji Hakuta. 1997. *Improving Schooling for Language-Minority Children: A Research Agenda*. Washington, D.C.: National Academy Press.

264   References

Averitt, Robert T. 1968. *The Dual Economy: The Dynamics of American Industry Structure*. New York: W. W. Norton.

Bailey, Benjamin. 2001. "Dominican-American Ethnic-Racial Identities and United States Social Categories." *International Migration Review* 35(3): 677–708.

Bailey, Thomas, and Roger Waldinger. 1991. "Primary, Secondary, and Enclave Labor Markets: A Training Systems Approach." *American Sociological Review* 56(4): 432–45.

Baldassare, Mark. 1981. *The Growth Dilemma: Residents' Views and Local Population Change in the United States*. Berkeley: University of California Press.

———. 2000. *California in the New Millennium: The Changing Social and Political Landscape*. Berkeley: University of California Press.

Barrett, James R., and David Roediger. 1997. "Inbetween Peoples: Race, Nationality and the 'New Immigrant' Working Class." *Journal of American Ethnic History* 16(3): 3–44.

Barth, Fredrik. 1956. "Ecological Relationships of Ethnic Groups in Swat, North Pakistan." *American Anthropologist* 58(6): 1079–89.

———. 1969. *Ethnic Groups and Boundaries*. Boston: Little, Brown.

Bates, Timothy. 1994. "Social Resources Generated by Group Support Networks May Not Be Beneficial to Asian Immigrant–Owned Small Businesses." *Social Forces* 72(3): 671–90.

Bates, Timothy, and Constance R. Dunham. 1992. "Facilitating Upward Mobility through Small Business Ownership." In *Urban Labor Markets and Job Opportunity*, edited by George E. Peterson and Wayne Vroman. Washington, D.C.: Urban Institute Press.

Bean, Frank D., and Stephanie Bell-Rose, eds. 1999. *Immigration and Opportunity: Race, Ethnicity, and Employment in the United States*. New York: Russell Sage Foundation.

Bean, Frank D., Ruth R. Berg, and Jennifer Van Hook. 1996. "Socioeconomic and Cultural Incorporation and Marital Disruption Among Mexican Americans." *Social Forces* 75(2): 593–617.

Bean, Frank D., Harley L. Browning, and W. Parker Frisbie. 1984. "The Sociodemographic Characteristics of Mexican Immigrant Status Groups: Implications for Studying Undocumented Mexicans." *International Migration Review* 18(3): 672–91.

Bean, Frank D., Roland Chanove, Robert G. Cushing, Rodolfo de la Garza, Gary P. Freeman, Charles W. Hayes, and David Spener. 1994. *Illegal Mexican Migration and the United States–Mexico Border: The Effects of Operation Hold the Line on El Paso–Juarez*. Washington: U.S. Commission on Immigration Reform.

Bean, Frank D., Rodolfo Corona, Rodolfo Tuiran, Karen A. Woodrow-Lafield, and Jennifer Van Hook. 2001. "Circular, Invisible, and Ambiguous Migrants: Components of Difference in Estimates of the Number of Unauthorized Mexican Migrants in the United States." *Demography* 38(3): 411–22.

Bean, Frank D., Robert G. Cushing, Charles W. Haynes, and Jennifer V. W. Van Hook. 1997. "Immigration and the Social Contract." *Social Science Quarterly* 78(2): 249–68.

Bean, Frank D., Thomas J. Espenshade, Michael J. White, and Robert F. Dymoski. 1990. "Post-IRCA Changes in the Volume and Composition of Undocumented Migration to the United States: An Assessment Based on Apprehensions Data." In *Undocumented Migration to the United States: IRCA and the Experience of the 1980s*, edited by Frank D. Bean, Barry Edmonston, and Jeffrey S. Passel. Washington, D.C.: Urban Institute Press.

Bean, Frank D., and Michael Fix. 1992. "The Significance of Recent Immigration Policy Reforms in the United States." In *Nations of Immigrants: Australia and the United States in a Changing World*, edited by Gary P. Freeman and James Jupp. New York and Sydney: Oxford University Press.

Bean, Frank D., Mark Fossett, and Jennifer Van Hook. 1999. "Immigration, Spatial and Economic Change, and African American Employment." In *Immigration and Opportunity: Race, Ethnicity and Employment in the United States*, edited by Frank D. Bean and Stephanie Bell-Rose. New York: Russell Sage Foundation.

Bean, Frank, Susan Gonzalez Baker, and Randy Capps. 2001. "Immigration and Labor Markets in the United States." In *Sourcebook on Labor Markets: Evolving Structures and Processes*, edited by Ivar Berg and Arne Kalleberg. New York: Plenum Press.

Bean, Frank D., Lindsay B. Lowell, and Lowell J. Taylor. 1988. "Undocumented Mexican Immigrants and the Earnings of Other Groups in the United States." *Demography* 25(1): 35–52.

Bean, Frank D., Jeffrey S. Passel, and Barry Edmonston. 1990. *Undocumented Migration to the United States: IRCA and the Experience of the 1980s*. Washington, D.C.: Urban Institute Press.

Bean, Frank D., C. Gray Swicegood, and Ruth Berg. 2000. "Mexican-Origin Fertility: New Patterns and Interpretations." *Social Science Quarterly* 81(1): 404–20.

Bean, Frank D., Eduardo Telles, and Lindsay Lowell. 1987. "Undocumented Migration to the United States: Perceptions and Evidence." *Population and Development Review* 13(4): 671–90.

Bean, Frank D., and Marta Tienda. 1987. *The Hispanic Population of the United States*. New York: Russell Sage Foundation.

Bean, Frank D., Jennifer Van Hook, and Jennifer E. Glick. 1997. "Country-of-Origin, Type of Public Assistance, and Patterns of Welfare Recipiency among U.S. Immigrants and Natives." *Social Science Quarterly* 78(2): 432–51.

Bean, Frank D., Georges Vernez, and Charles B. Keely. 1989. *Opening and Closing the Doors: Evaluating Immigration Reform and Control*. Santa Monica, Calif.; Washington, D.C.; and Lanham, Md.: Rand and Urban Institute Press.

Beck, Roy Howard. 1996. *The Case Against Immigration: The Moral, Economic, Social and Environmental Reasons for Reducing U.S. Immigration Back to Traditional Levels*. New York: W. W. Norton.

Becker, Gary S. 1964. *Human Capital: A Theoretical and Empirical Analysis, with Special Reference to Education*. New York: Columbia University Press.

Bell, Stephen H. 2001. "Why Are Welfare Caseloads Falling?" Discussion paper. Washington, D.C.: The Urban Institute.

Berlin, Ira. 1998. *Many Thousands Gone: The First Two Centuries of Slavery in North America*. Cambridge, Mass.: Harvard University Press and Belknap Press.

Bernhardt, Annette D., Martina Morris, Mark S. Handcock, and Marc A. Scott. 2001. *Divergent Paths: Economic Mobility in the New American Labor Market*. New York: Russell Sage Foundation.

Bialystok, Ellen, and Kenji Hakuta. 1994. *In Other Words: The Science and Psychology of Second-Language Acquisition*. New York: Basic Books.

Birdsong, David, and Michelle Molis. 2001. "On the Evidence for Maturational Constraints in Second-Language Acquisition." *Journal of Memory and Language* 44(2): 235–49.

Blalock, Hubert M. 1967. *Toward a Theory of Minority-Group Relations*. New York: John Wiley & Sons.

Blank, Rebecca M., and Ron Haskins. 2001. *The New World of Welfare*. Washington, D.C.: Brookings Institution Press.

Blau, Peter M. 1994. *Structural Contexts of Opportunities*. Chicago: University of Chicago Press.

Blau, Peter M., and Joseph E. Schwartz. 1984. *Crosscutting Social Circles: Testing a Macrostructural Theory of Intergroup Relations*. Orlando, Fla.: Academic Press.

Blumer, Herbert. 1958. "Race Prejudice as a Sense of Group Position." *Pacific Sociological Review* 1(1): 3–7.

Bonacich, Edna. 1973. "A Theory of Middleman Minorities." *American Sociological Review* 38(3): 583–94.

Bonacich, Edna, and John Modell. 1980. *The Economic Basis of Ethnic Solidarity: Small Business in the Japanese American Community*. Berkeley: University of California.

Borjas, George J. 1984. "The Impact of Immigrants on the Earnings of the Native-born." In *Immigration Issues and Policies*, edited by V. M. Briggs and Marta Tienda. Salt Lake City: Olympus.

———. 1985. "Assimilation, Changes in Cohort Quality, and the Earnings of Immigrants." *Journal of Labor Economics* 3(October): 463–89.

———. 1986. "The Self-employment Experience of Immigrants." Working paper. Cambridge, Mass.: National Bureau of Economic Research.

———. 1987a. "Immigrants, Minorities, and Labor Market Competition." *Industrial and Labor Relations Review* 40(3): 382–92.

———. 1987b. *Self-selection and the Earnings of Immigrants*. Cambridge, Mass.: National Bureau of Economic Research.

———. 1989. "Economic Theory and International Migration." *International Migration Review* 23(3): 457–85.

———. 1990. *Friends or Strangers: The Impact of Immigrants on the U.S. Economy*. New York: Basic Books.

———. 1994. "The Economics of Immigration." *Journal of Economic Literature* 32(December): 1667–1717.

———. 1995. "The Economic Benefits from Immigration." *The Journal of Economic Perspective* 9(2): 3–22.

———. 1998a. "Do Blacks Gain or Lose from Immigration?" In *Help or Hindrance? The Economic Implications of Immigration for African Americans*, edited by Daniel Hamermesh and Frank D. Bean. New York: Russell Sage Foundation.

———. 1998b. "Immigration and Welfare: A Review of the Evidence." In *The Debate in the United States over Immigration*, edited by Peter Duignan and L. H. Gann. Palo Alto, Calif.: Hoover Institution Press.

———. 1999. *Heaven's Door: Immigration Policy and the American Economy*. Princeton, N.J.: Princeton University Press.

———. 2002. "The Impact of Welfare Reform on Immigrant Welfare Use." Report. Washington, D.C.: Center for Immigration Studies.

Borjas, George J., Richard B. Freeman, and Lawrence F. Katz. 1992. "On the Labor Market Effects of Immigration and Trade." In *Immigration and Trade*, edited by Richard Freeman and George Borjas. Chicago: University of Chicago Press.

———. 1997. "How Much Do Immigration and Trade Affect Labor Market Outcomes?" *Brookings Papers on Economic Activity* 1: 1–67.

Borjas, George J., and Lynette Hilton. 1996. "Immigration and the Welfare State: Immigrant Participation in Means-Tested Entitlement Programs." *Quarterly Journal of Economics* 111(2): 575–604.

Borjas, George, and Marta Tienda. 1987. "The Economic Consequences of Immigration." *Science* 235(February): 645–51.

Borjas, George J., and Stephen J. Trejo. 1991. "Immigrant Participation in the Welfare System." *Industrial and Labor Relations Review* 44(2): 195–211.

Bossard, James H. 1939. "Nationality and Nativity as Factors in Marriage." *American Sociological Review* 4(6): 792–98.

Bowen, William G., and Derek Curtis Bok. 1998. *The Shape of the River: Long-term Consequences of Considering Race in College and University Admissions*. Princeton, N.J.: Princeton University Press.

Boyd, Monica. 1989. "Family and Personal Networks in International Migration: Recent Developments and New Agendas." *International Migration Review* 23(3): 638–66.

Bozon, Michel, and Francois Héran. 1987. "Finding a Spouse. Part 1: Changes and Morphology of the Place of First Encounters." *Population* 42(6): 943–85.

Brimelow, Peter. 1995. *Alien Nation: Common Sense About America's Immigration Disaster*. New York: Random House.

Brodkin, Karen. 1998. *How Jews Became White Folks, and What That Says About Race in America*. New Brunswick, N.J.: Rutgers University Press.

Brubaker, Rogers. 2001. "The Return of Assimilation? Changing Perspectives on Immigration and Its Sequels in France, Germany, and the United States." *Ethnic and Racial Studies* 24(4): 531–48.

Bustamante, Jorge A. 1998. "Some Thoughts on Perceptions and Policies." In *Migration between Mexico and the United States*, edited by Mexico–United States Binational Migration Study. Mexico City and Washington, D.C.: Mexican Ministry of Foreign Affairs and U.S. Commission on Immigration Reform.

Butcher, Kristin F. 1998. "An Investigation of the Effect of Immigration on the Labor-Market Outcomes of African-Americans." In *Help or Hindrance?: The Economic Implications of Immigration for African Americans*, edited by Daniel Hamermesh and Frank D. Bean. New York: Russell Sage Foundation.

Cafferty, Phyllis, Barry R. Chiswick, Andrew Greeley, and Teresa A. Sullivan. 1983. *The Dilemma of American Immigration*. New Brunswick, N.J.: Transaction.

Calavita, Kitty. 1992. *Inside the State: The Bracero Program, Immigration, and the I.N.S.* New York: Routledge.

Camarota, Steven A. 2001. "Immigration from Mexico: Assessing the Impact on the United States." Report. Washington, D.C.: Center for Immigration Studies.

———. 2002. "The Open Door: How Militant Islamic Terrorists Entered and Remained in the United States, 1993–2001." Report. Washington, D.C.: Center for Immigration Studies.

Campbell, Paul R. 1994. *Population Projections for States, by Age, Sex, Race, and Hispanic Origin: 1993–2020*. P25-1111. Washington: U.S. Government Printing Office for U.S. Bureau of the Census.

Capps, Randy. 2001. "Hardship among Children of Immigrants: Findings from the 1999 National Survey of America's Families." Report. Washington, D.C.: Urban Institute Press.

Carliner, Geoffrey. 2000. "The Language Ability of U.S. Immigrants: Assimilation and Cohort Effects." *International Migration Review* 34(1): 158–82.

Carpenter, Niles. 1927. *Immigrants and Their Children. 1920*. Washington: U.S. Government Printing Office.

Carter, Hugh, and Paul C. Glick. 1976. *Marriage and Divorce: A Social and Economic Study*. Cambridge, Mass.: Harvard University Press.

Castañeda, Jorge G. 1995. *The Mexican Shock: Its Meaning for the United States*. New York: The New Press.

Castles, Stephen, and Mark J. Miller. 1998. *The Age of Migration: International Population Movements in the Modern World*. New York: Guilford.

Chapa, Jorge. 1990. "The Myth of Hispanic Progress." *Journal of Hispanic Policy* 4: 3–18.

Chapa, Jorge, and Gilbert Cárdenas. 1991. *The Economy of the Urban Ethnic Enclave*. Austin, Texas: Lyndon B. Johnson School of Public Affairs and Tomás Rivera Center.

Chavez, Leo R. 1988. "Settlers and Sojourners: The Case of Mexicans in the United States." *Human Organization* 47(2): 95–107.

———. 1992. *Shadowed Lives: Undocumented Immigrants in American Society*. Fort Worth, Tex.: Harcourt Brace Jovanovich College Publishers.

Chavez, Linda. 1989. "Tequila Sunrise: The Slow but Steady Progress of Hispanic Immigrants." *Policy Review* 48(spring): 64–67.

Cheng, Lucie, and Gary Gereffi. 1994. "U.S. Retailers and Asian Garment Production." In *Global Production: The Apparel Industry in the Pacific Rim*, edited by Edna Bonacich, Lucie Cheng, Norma Chinchilla, Nora Hamilton, and Paul Ong. Philadelphia: Temple University Press.

Child, Irving L. 1943. *Italian or American? The Second Generation in Conflict*. New Haven: Yale University Press.

Chiswick, Barry R. 1977. "Sons of Immigrants: Are They at an Earnings Disadvantage?" *American Economic Review* 67(February): 376–80.

———. 1978. "The Effect of Americanization on the Earnings of Foreign-born Men." *Journal of Political Economy* 86(5): 897–921.

———. 1991. "Speaking, Reading, and Earnings among Low-Skilled Immigrants." *Journal of Labor Economics* 9(2): 149–70.

Citrin, Jack, Beth Reingold, and Donald Green. 1990. "American Identity and the Politics of Ethnic Change." *Journal of Politics* 52(4): 1124–54.

Clark, William A. V. 1998. *The California Cauldron: Immigration and the Fortunes of Local Communities.* New York: Guilford Publications.

Clune, Michael S. 1998. "The Fiscal Impacts of Immigrants: A California Case Study." In *The Immigration Debate: Studies on the Economic, Demographic, and Fiscal Effects of Immigration,* edited by J. P. Smith and Barry Edmonston. Washington, D.C.: National Academy Press.

Cohen, Jean L. 1999. "Does Voluntary Association Make Democracy Work?" In *Diversity and Its Discontents,* edited by N. J. Smelser and J. C. Alexander. Princeton, N.J.: Princeton University Press.

Cohn, D. 2001. "Another Case of Undercount." *The Washington Post National Weekly Edition,* March 26–April 1, p. 31.

Cohn, Samuel, and Mark A. Fossett. 1996. "What Spatial Mismatch? The Spatial Proximity of Blacks to Employment in Boston and Houston." *Social Forces* 75(2): 557–73.

CONAPO. 1999. "La Situacion Demografica de Mexico." Mexico City: Consejo Nacional de Poblacion.

Cornelius, Wayne A., Thomas J. Espenshade, and Idean Salehyan. 2001. *The International Migration of the Highly Skilled: Demand, Supply, and Development Consequences in Sending and Receiving Countries.* La Jolla, Calif.: Center for Comparative Immigration Studies, University of California, San Diego.

Cose, Ellis. 1992. *A Nation of Strangers: Prejudice, Politics, and the Populating of America.* New York: William Morrow.

Coulmas, Florian. 1997. "Mother Tongue—for Better or Worse." In *Language and Its Ecology: Essays in Memory of Einar Haugen,* edited by Stig Eliasson and Ernst H. Jahr. New York: Mouton de Gruyter.

Council of Economic Advisers. 1990. "Report of the Council of Economic Advisers." Washington: U.S. Government Printing Office.

———. 2002 (and earlier years). *Economic Report of the President, 2001.* Available on-line at: *www.access.gpo.gov.eop.*

Crispino, James A. 1980. *The Assimilation of Ethnic Groups: The Italian Case.* Staten Island, N.Y.: Center for Migration Studies.

DaCosta, Kimberly. 2000. "Remaking the Color Line: Social Bases and Implications of the Multiracial Movement." Ph.D. diss., University of California, Berkeley.

Danziger, Sheldon H. 1999. *Economic Conditions and Welfare Reform.* Kalamazoo, Mich.: Upjohn Institute.

Danziger, Sheldon H., and Peter Gottschalk. 1993. *Uneven Tides: Rising Inequality in America.* New York: Russell Sage Foundation.

Dávila, Alberto, and Marie T. Mora. 2001. "Hispanic Ethnicity, English-Skill Investments, and Earnings." *Industrial Relations* 40(1): 383–88.

Davis, David B. 1998. "A Big Business." *New York Review of Books* 45: 50–53.

Davis, F. James. 1991. *Who Is Black? One Nation's Definition.* University Park: Pennsylvania State University Press.

Davis, Kingsley. 1941. "Intermarriage in Caste Societies." *American Anthropologist* 43(3): 376–95.

DeFreitas, Gregory. 1988. "Hispanic Immigration and Labor Market Segmentation." *Industrial Relations* 27(2): 195–214.

———. 1991. *Inequality at Work: Hispanics in the U.S. Labor Force.* New York: Oxford University Press.

de la Garza, Rodolfo, Louis DeSipio, F. Chris Garcia, John Garcia, and Angelo Falcon. 1992. *Latino Voices: Mexican, Puerto-Rican, and Cuban Perspectives on American Politics.* Boulder, Colo.: Westview Press.

Dillon, Sam. 1997. "U.S.-Mexico Study Sees Exaggeration of Migration Data." *New York Times*, August 31, 1997, p. 1.

Dixon, Royal. 1916. *Americanization.* New York: Macmillan.

Djamba, Yanyi K., and Frank D. Bean. 1998. "African Americans, African Immigrants, and Black Immigrants from Countries South of the United States: Toward an Afro-Labor Queue." Unpublished paper. Population Research Center, University of Texas, Austin.

Donato, Katharine M. 1990. "Recent Trends In U.S. Immigration: Why Some Countries Send Women and Others Send Men." Paper presented at the Annual Meeting of the Population Association of America, Toronto, Canada (March 12–14).

———. 1993. "Current Trends and Patterns of Female Migration: Evidence from Mexico." *International Migration Review* 27(4): 748–71.

———. 2001. "A Dynamic View of Mexican Migration to the United States." In *Immigrant Women*, edited by R. J. Simon. New Brunswick, N.J.: Transaction.

Donato, Katharine M., Jorge Durand, and Douglas S. Massey. 1992. "Changing Conditions in the U.S. Labor Market: Effects of the Immigration Reform and Control Act of 1986." *Population Research and Policy Review* 11(2): 93–115.

Drachsler, Julius. 1920. *Democracy and Assimilation: The Blending of Immigrant Heritages in America.* New York: Macmillan.

Du Bois, W. E. B. 1997 [1903]. *The Souls of Black Folk*, edited by D. W. Blight and R. Gooding-Williams. Boston: Bedford Books.

Duignan, Peter, and Lewis H. Gann. 1998. *The Debate in the United States over Immigration.* Palo Alto: Hoover Institution Press.

Duleep, Harriet, and Seth Sanders. 1993. "The Decision to Work by Married Immigrant Women: Evidence from Asian Women." *Industrial and Labor Relations Review* 46(4): 667–90.

Easterlin, Richard. 1982. "Economic and Social Characteristics of the Immigrants." In *Dimensions of Ethnicity*, edited by S. Thernstrom. Cambridge, Mass.: Belknap Press and Harvard University Press.

Edmonston, Barry, and Jeffrey S. Passel. 1994. *Immigration and Ethnicity: The Integration of America's Newest Arrivals.* Washington, D.C., and Lanham, Md.: Urban Institute Press.

———. 1999. "How Immigration and Intermarriage Affect the Racial and Ethnic Composition of the U.S. Population." In *Immigration and Opportunity: Race, Ethnicity, and Employment in the United States*, edited by Frank D. Bean and Stephanie Bell-Rose. New York: Russell Sage Foundation.

Edwards, James R., Jr. 2001. "Public Charge Doctrine: A Fundamental Principle of American Immigration Policy." Washington, D.C.: Center for Immigration Studies.

Ellis, Mark. 2001. "A Tale of Five Cities? Trends in Immigrant and Native-Born Wages." In *Strangers at the Gates: New Immigrants in Urban America*, edited by Roger Waldinger. Berkeley and Los Angeles: University of California Press.

England, Paula, and George Farkas. 1986. *Households, Employment, and Gender: A Social, Economic and Demographic View*. New York: Aldine de Gruyter.

Eschbach, Karl. 1995. "The Enduring and Vanishing American Indian: American Indian Population Growth and Intermarriage in 1990." *Ethnic and Racial Studies* 18(1): 89–108.

Eschbach, Karl, Jacqueline Hagan, and Stanley Bailey. 1999. "Death at the Border." *International Migration Review* 33(2): 430–54.

Escobar Latapi, Augustin, Frank D. Bean, and Sidney Weintraub. 1999a. "The Dynamics of Mexican Emigration." In *Emigration Dynamics in Developing Countries*, edited by Reginald Appleyard. Vol. 3. Aldershot, U.K., and Brookfield, Vt.: Ashgate.

———. 1999b. *La Dinamica de la Emigracion Mexicana*. Mexico City: CIESAS y Miguel Angel Porrua.

Espenshade, Thomas J. 1995a. "Unauthorized Immigration to the United States." *Annual Review of Sociology* 21: 195–216.

———. 1995b. "Using INS Border Apprehension Data to Measure the Flow of Undocumented Migrants Crossing the U.S.-Mexico Frontier." *International Migration Review* 29(2): 545–65.

Espenshade, Thomas J., Jessica L. Baraka, and Gregory A. Huber. 1997. "Implications of the 1996 Welfare and Immigration Reform Acts for U.S. Immigration." *Population and Development Review* 23(4): 769–801.

Espenshade, Thomas J., and Maryanne Belanger. 1998. "Immigration and Public Opinion." In *Crossings: Mexican Immigration in Interdisciplinary Perspectives*, edited by Marcelo M. Suarez-Orozco. Cambridge, Mass.: Harvard University Press.

Espenshade, Thomas J., and Haishan Fu. 1997. "An Analysis of English-Language Proficiency Among U.S. Immigrants." *American Sociological Review* 62(2): 288–305.

Espinosa, Kristin, and Douglas Massey. 1997. "Determinants of English Proficiency Among Mexican Immigrants to the U.S." *International Migration Review* 31(1): 28–50.

Evans, M. D. R. 1989. "Immigrant Entrepreneurship: Effects of Ethnic Market Size and Isolated Labor Pool." *American Sociological Review* 54(6): 950–62.

Farley, Reynolds. 1991. "The New Census Question about Ancestry: What Did It Tell Us?" *Demography* 28(3): 411–30.

———. 1996. *The New American Reality: Who We Are, How We Got Here, Where We Are Going*. New York: Russell Sage Foundation.

———. 2001. "Identifying with Multiple Races: A Social Movement That Succeeded but Failed?" Ann Arbor, Mich.: Population Studies Center, University of Michigan.

Farley, Reynolds, and Richard Alba. 2002. "The New Second Generation in the United States." *International Migration Review* 36(3): 669–701.

Farley, Reynolds, and William H. Frey. 1994. "Changes in the Segregation of Whites from Blacks During the 1980s: Small Steps Toward a More Integrated Society." *American Sociological Review* 59(1): 23–45.

Field Institute. Various dates. "Polls: Full Questions and Study Information." Available on-line at: *www.field.com/fieldpollonline*.

Fischer, Claude S. 1999. "Uncommon Values, Diversity, and Conflict in City Life." In *Diversity and Its Discontents*, edited by Neil J. Smelser and Jeffrey C. Alexander. Princeton, N.J.: Princeton University Press.

Fishman, Joshua A. 1985a. "Ethnicity in Action: The Community Resources of Ethnic Languages in the United States." In *The Rise and Fall of the Ethnic Revival: Perspectives on Language and Ethnicity*, edited by Joshua A. Fishman. New York: Mouton.

———. 1985b. "Mother-Tongue Claiming in the United States Since 1960: Trends and Correlates." In *The Rise and Fall of the Ethnic Revival: Perspectives on Language and Ethnicity*, edited by Joshua A. Fishman. New York: Mouton.

Fix, Michael, and Jeffrey S. Passel. 1991. "The Door Remains Open: Recent Immigration to the United States and a Preliminary Analysis of the Immigration Act of 1990." Report. Washington, D.C.: The Urban Institute.

———. 1994. "Setting the Record Straight: What are the Costs to the Public?" *Public Welfare* 52(2): 6–15.

———. 1999. "Trends in Noncitizens' and Citizens' Use of Public Benefits Following Welfare Reforms: 1994–97." Report. Washington, D.C.: The Urban Institute.

———. 2002. "The Scope and Impact of Welfare Reform's Immigrant Provisions." Report. Washington, D.C.: The Urban Institute.

Fix, Michael, and Wendy Zimmermann. 1994. "After Arrival: An Overview of Federal Immigrant Policy in the U.S." In *Immigration and Ethnicity: The Integration of American's Newest Arrivals*, edited by Barry Edmonston and Jeffrey S. Passel. Washington, D.C.: Urban Institute Press, for the Immigrant Policy Program and the Urban Institute.

Foner, Nancy. 1997. "The Immigrant Family: Cultural Legacies and Cultural Changes." *International Migration Review* 31(4): 961–74.

———. 2000. *From Ellis Island to JFK: New York's Two Great Waves of Immigration*. New Haven and New York: Yale University Press and Russell Sage Foundation.

Forbes, H. D. 1997. *Ethnic Conflict*. New Haven, Conn.: Yale University Press.

Fossett, Mark A., and K. Jill Kiecolt. 1989. "The Relative Size of Minority Populations and White Racial Attitudes." *Social Science Quarterly* 70(4): 820–35.

Fredrickson, George M. 1988. *The Arrogance of Race: Historical Perspectives on Slavery, Racism, and Social Inequality*. Middletown, Conn.: Wesleyan University Press.

Freeman, John, and Michael T. Hannan. 1983. "Niche Width and the Dynamics of Organizational Populations." *American Journal of Sociology* 88(6): 1116–45.

Freeman, Richard. 1991. "Employment and Earnings of Disadvantaged Young Men in a Labor Shortage Economy." In *The Urban Underclass*, edited by Christopher Jencks and Paul E. Peterson. Washington, D.C.: Brookings Institution Press.

Friedberg, Rachel M., and Jennifer Hunt. 1999. "Immigration and the Receiving Economy." In *The Handbook of International Migration: The American Expe-*

rience, edited by Charles Hirschman, Josh DeWind, and Philip Kasinitz. New York: Russell Sage Foundation.

Friedman, Thomas L. 1999. *The Lexus and the Olive Tree: Understanding Globalization.* New York: Basic Books.

Fu, Vincent Kang. 2001. "Racial Intermarriage Pairings." *Demography* 38(2): 147–60.

Fuchs, Lawrence H. 1995. "A Negative Impact of Affirmative Action: Including Immigrants in Such Programs Flies in the Face of Civil Rights." *The Washington Post,* February 25–26.

———. 1997. "The Changing Meaning of Civil Rights, 1954–1994." In *Civil Rights and Social Wrongs: Black-White Relations Since World War II,* edited by John Higham. University Park: Pennsylvania State University Press.

Fuentes, Carlos. 1996. *A New Time for Mexico.* New York: Farrar, Straus & Giroux.

Furtado, Celso. 1964. *Development and Underdevelopment.* Translated by R. W. de Aguiar and E. C. Drysdale. Berkeley: University of California Press.

Gallup Poll News Service. 2000. "Opinion Poll." Available on-line at: *www. gallup.com/poll/immigration.*

———. 2001. "Opinion Poll." Available on-line at: *www.gallup.com/poll/ immigration.*

Gamio, Manuel. 1930. *Mexican Immigration to the United States: A Study of Human Migration and Adjustment.* Chicago: University of Chicago Press.

Gans, Herbert J. 1979. "Symbolic Ethnicity: The Future of Ethnic Groups and Cultures in America." *Ethnic and Racial Studies* 2(1): 1–20.

———. 1988. *Middle American Individualism: The Future of Liberal Democracy.* New York: Free Press.

———. 1992a. "Comment: Ethnic Invention and Acculturation: A Bumpy Line Approach." *Journal of American Ethnic History* 11(1): 42–52.

———. 1992b. "Second-Generation Decline: Scenarios for the Economic and Ethnic Futures of the Post-1965 American Immigrants." *Ethnic and Racial Studies* 15(2): 173–92.

———. 1999a. "The Possibility of a New Racial Hierarchy in the Twenty-first Century United States." In *The Cultural Territories of Race,* edited by M. Lamont. Chicago and New York: University of Chicago Press and Russell Sage Foundation.

———. 1999b. "Toward a Reconciliation of 'Assimilation' and 'Pluralism': The Interplay of Acculturation and Ethnic Retention." In *The Handbook of International Migration,* edited by Charles Hirschman, Josh DeWind, and Philip Kasinitz. New York: Russell Sage Foundation.

Garvey, Deborah L., and Thomas J. Espenshade. 1998. "Fiscal Impacts of Immigrant and Native Households: A New Jersey Case Study." In *The Immigration Debate: Studies on the Economic, Demographic, and Fiscal Effects of Immigration,* edited by J. P. Smith and Barry Edmonston. Washington, D.C.: National Academy Press.

Gerstle, Gary. 1999. "Liberty, Coercion, and the Making of Americans." In *The Handbook of International Migration,* edited by Charles Hirschman, Josh DeWind, and Philip Kasinitz. New York: Russell Sage Foundation.

Gibson, Campbell J., and Emily Lennon. 1999. "Historical Census Statistics on the Foreign-Born Population of the United States: 1850–1990." Population Division Working Paper No. 29. Washington: U.S. Bureau of the Census.

Gibson, M. A. 1988. *Accommodation Without Assimilation: Sikh Immigrants in an American High School*. Ithaca, N.Y.: Cornell University Press.

Gilbertson, Greta A., Joseph P. Fitzpatrick, and Lijun Yang. 1996. "Hispanic Intermarriage in New York City: New Evidence from 1991." *International Migration Review* 30(2): 445–59.

Gilpin, Robert. 2000. *The Challenge of Global Capitalism: The World Economy in the 21st Century*. Princeton, N.J.: Princeton University Press.

Gitlin, Todd. 1995. *The Twilight of Common Dreams*. New York: Metropolitan.

Glazer, Nathan. 1975. *Affirmative Discrimination: Ethnic Inequality and Public Policy*. New York: Basic Books.

———. 1997. *We Are All Multiculturalists Now*. Cambridge, Mass.: Harvard University Press.

Glazer, Nathan, and Daniel P. Moynihan. 1963. *Beyond the Melting Pot: The Negroes, Puerto Ricans, Jews, Italians, and Irish of New York City*. Cambridge, Mass.: M.I.T. Press.

Glenn, Evelyn Nakano. 1992. "From Servitude to Service Work: Historical Continuities in the Racial Division of Paid Preproductive Labor." *Signs: Journal of Women in Culture and Society* 18(1): 1–43.

Glick, Jennifer E., and Jennifer Van Hook. 1998. "The Mexican-origin Population of the United States in the Twentieth Century." In *Migration Between Mexico and the United States: Binational Study*, Vol. 2. Research Reports and Background Materials. Mexico City and Washington, D.C.: Mexican Ministry of Foreign Affairs and U.S. Commission on Immigration Reform.

Glick, Jennifer E., Frank D. Bean, and Jennifer V. W. Van Hook. 1997. "Immigration and Changing Patterns of Extended Family Household Structure in the United States." *Journal of Marriage and the Family* 59(1): 177–91.

Godfrey, Brian J. 1988. *Neighborhoods in Transition: The Making of San Francisco's Ethnic and Nonconformist Communities*. Berkeley: University of California Press.

Goldstein, Joshua R. 1999. "Kinship Networks That Cross Racial Lines: The Exception or the Rule?" *Demography* 36(3): 399–407.

Gonzalez Baker, Susan. 1999. "Mexican-Origin Women in Southwestern Labor Markets." In *Latinas and African American Women at Work: Race, Gender, and Economic Inequality*, edited by Irene Browne. New York: Russell Sage Foundation.

Gonzalez Baker, Susan, and C. Alison Newby. 1999. "Changing Faces, Changing Jobs: Occupational Succession in the High Immigration U.S. Metropolis." Paper presented at the Annual Meeting of the Population Association of America, New York (March 25–27).

Goodkind, Daniel M. 1997. "The Vietnamese Double Marriage Squeeze." *International Migration Review* 31(1): 108–12.

Gordon, Linda W. 1987. "Southeast Asian Refugee Migration to the United States." In *Pacific Bridges: The New Immigration from Asia and the Pacific Islands*, edited by J. T. Fawcett and B. V. Carino. New York: Center for Migration Studies.

Gordon, Milton M. 1964. *Assimilation in American Life: The Role of Race, Religion, and National Origins*. New York: Oxford University Press.

Gorman, Siobhan. 2001. "A Nation Without Borders." *National Journal*, December 1, pp. 3648–56.

———. 2002. "Reframing the Debate." *National Journal*, March 2, 618–21.

Gosselin, Peter G. 2002a. "Economic Recovery Sluggish, Uneven, New Figures Show." *Los Angeles Times*, August 1, p. A1.

———. 2002b. "Economy Suffers Another Setback." *Los Angeles Times*, August 3, A1.

Granovetter, Mark. 1985. "Economic Action and Social Structure: The Problem of Embeddedness." *American Journal of Sociology* 91(3): 481–510.

———. 1995. "The Economic Sociology of Firms and Entrepreneurs." In *The Economic Sociology of Immigration*, edited by Alejandro Portes. New York: Russell Sage Foundation.

Granovetter, Mark S., and Richard Swedberg. 1992. *The Sociology of Economic Life*. Boulder, Colo.: Westview Press.

Grasmuck, Sherri, and Patricia R. Pessar. 1991. *Between Two Islands: Dominican International Migration*. Berkeley: University of California Press.

Grebler, Leo. 1966. "The Naturalization of Mexican Immigrants in the United States." *International Migration Review* 1(3): 17–32.

Greeley, Andrew. 1971. *Why Can't They Be Like Us? America's White Ethnic Groups*. New York: E. P. Dutton.

———. 1974. "Political Participation Among Ethnic Groups in the United States: A Preliminary Reconnaissance." *American Journal of Sociology* 80(1): 170–204.

Greenwood, Michael, and John McDowell. 1999. *Legal U.S. Immigration: Influences on Gender, Age, and Skill Composition*. Kalamazoo, Mich.: W. E. Upjohn Institute for Employment Research.

Greico, Elizabeth, and Monica Boyd. 1998. "Women and Migration: Incorporating Gender into International Migration Theory." Paper presented at the annual meetings of the Population Association of America, Chicago (April 18).

Greico, Elizabeth M., and Rachel C. Cassidy. 2001. "Overview of Race and Hispanic Origin." Report for U.S. Department of Commerce, Economics and Statistics Administration, U.S. Bureau of the Census. Washington: Government Printing Office.

Grenier, Gilles. 1984. "Shifts to English as Usual Language by Americans of Spanish Mother Tongue." *Social Science Quarterly* 65(2): 527–50.

Grin, François. 1990. "The Economic Approach to Minority Languages." *Journal of Multilingual and Multicultural Development* 11(1–2): 153–573.

Guarnizo, Luís. 1995. "La Economía Étnica Mexicana En Los Angeles: Acumulación Capitalista, Reestructuración De Clase Y Transnacionalización De La Migración." Paper presented at the V Reunión Nacional de Investigación Demográfica, Colegio de México, Mexico City, June 5.

Gurcak, Jessica C., Thomas J. Espenshade, Aaron Sparrow, and Martha Paskoff. 2001. "Immigration of Scientists and Engineers to the United States: Issues and Evidence." In *The International Migration of the Highly Skilled:*

Demand, Supply, and Development Consequences in Sending and Receiving Countries, edited by W. A. Cornelius, T. J. Espenshade, and I. Salehyan. La Jolla: Center for Comparative Immigration Studies, University of California, San Diego.

Hacker, Andrew. 1995. *Two Nations: Black and White, Separate, Hostile, and Unequal*. New York: Ballantine.

Hagan, Jacqueline Maria. 1994. *Deciding to Be Legal: A Maya Community in Houston*. Philadelphia: Temple University.

———. 1998. "Social Networks, Gender, and Immigrant Incorporation: Resources and Constraints." *American Sociological Review* 63(1): 55–68.

Hakuta, Kenji, and Daniel D'Andrea. 1992. "Some Properties of Bilingual Maintenance and Loss in Mexican Background High-School Students." *Applied Linguistics* 13(1): 72–99.

Hamermesh, Daniel, and Frank D. Bean. 1998. *Help or Hindrance? The Economic Implications of Immigration for African Americans*. New York: Russell Sage Foundation.

Hammel, Eugene A. 1990. "A Theory of Culture for Demography." *Population and Development Review* 16(3): 455–85.

Handlin, Oscar. 1951. *The Uprooted: The Epic Story of the Great Migrations That Made the American People*. Boston: Little, Brown.

Hansen, Kristin A. 1996. "Profile of the Foreign-born Population in 1995: What the CPS Nativity Data Tell Us." Paper presented at the Annual Meeting of the Population Association of America, New Orleans (May 6–8).

Hansen, M. L. 1952. "The Third Generation in America." *Commentary* 14(5): 492–500.

Hansen, Niles H., and Gilberto C. Cárdenas. 1988. "Immigrant and Native Ethnic Enterprises in Mexican American Neighborhoods: Differing Perceptions of Mexican Immigrant Workers." *International Migration Review* 22(2): 226–42.

Harris, John R., and Michael P. Todaro. 1970. "Migration, Unemployment and Development: A Two-Sector Analysis." *American Economic Review* 60(1): 126–42.

Hartmann, Edward George. 1967. *The Movement to Americanize the Immigrant*. New York: AMS Press.

Hawley, Amos H. 1945. *Dispersion Versus Segregation: Apropos of a Solution of Race Problems*. Ann Arbor: University of Michigan Press.

———. 1950. *Human Ecology*. New York: Ronald Press.

———. 1970. *The Metropolitan Community: Its People and Government*. Beverly Hills, Calif.: Sage.

———. 1984. "Human Ecological and Marxian Theories." *American Journal of Sociology* 89(4): 904–17.

———. 1986. *Human Ecology: A Theoretical Essay*. Chicago: University of Chicago Press.

Heaton, Tim B., and Cardell K. Jacobson. 2000. "Intergroup Marriage: An Examination of Opportunity Structures." *Sociological Inquiry* 70(1): 30–41.

Higham, John. 1963. *Strangers in the Land*. New Brunswick, N.J.: Rutgers University Press.

————. 1997. *Civil Rights and Social Wrongs: Black-White Relations Since World War II*. University Park: Pennsylvania State University Press.

Hirschman, Charles. 1978. "Prior U.S. Residence Among Mexican Immigrants." *Social Forces* 56(4): 1179–1202.

————. 1979. *Theories and Models of Ethnic Inequality*. Durham, N.C.: Center for International Studies, Duke University.

————. 1983. "America's Melting Pot Reconsidered." *Annual Review of Sociology* 9: 397–423.

Hirschman, Charles, Richard Alba, and Reynolds Farley. 2000. "The Meaning and Measurement of Race in the U.S. Census: Glimpses into the Future." *Demography* 37(3): 381–93.

Hollifield, James F. 1992. *Immigrants, Markets, and States: The Political Economy of Postwar Europe*. Cambridge, Mass.: Harvard University Press.

Holzer, Harry J., and Wayne Vroman. 1991. "Mismatches and the Urban Labor Market." In *Urban Labor Markets and Job Opportunity*, edited by George Peterson and Wayne Vroman. Washington, D.C.: Urban Institute Press.

Hondagneu-Sotelo, Pierrette. 1994. *Gendered Transitions: Mexican Experiences of Immigration*. Berkeley: University of California Press.

Hoxby, Caroline M. 1998. "All School Finance Equalizations Are Not Created Equal." Cambridge, Mass.: National Bureau of Economic Research,

Hu, Wy. 1998. "Elderly Immigrants on Welfare." *Journal of Human Resources* 33(3): 711–41.

Huddle, Donald. 1993. "The Costs of Immigration." Unpublished paper, Rice University, Houston, Texas.

Hudson Institute. 1991. "Workforce 2000." Indianapolis, Ind.: Hudson Institute.

Ignatiev, Noel. 1995. *How the Irish Became White*. New York: Routledge.

International Organization of Migration. 2001. *World Migration Report 2000*. Geneva: International Organization for Migration.

Jacobson, Matthew Freye. 1998. *Whiteness of a Different Color: European Immigrants and the Alchemy of Race*. Cambridge, Mass.: Harvard University Press.

Jacoby, Tamar 2001. "An End to Counting Race?" *Commentary* 111(6): 37–40.

Jasso, Guillermina, Douglas S. Massey, Mark R. Rosenzweig, and James P. Smith. 2000a. "Assortative Mating Among Married New Legal Immigrants to the United States: Evidence from the New Immigrant Survey Pilot." *International Migration Review* 34(2): 443–59.

————. 2000b. "The New Immigrant Survey Pilot (NIS-P): Overview and New Findings about U.S. Legal Immigrants at Admission." *Demography* 37(1): 127–38.

Jasso, Guillermina, and Mark Rosenzweig. 1986. "Family Reunification and the Immigration Multiplier: U.S. Immigration Law, Origin-Country Conditions, and the Reproduction of Immigrants." *Demography* 23(3): 294–311.

————. 1989. "Sponsors, Sponsorship Rates and the Immigration Multiplier." *International Migration Review* 23(4): 856–88.

————. 1990. *The New Chosen People: Immigrants to the United States*. New York: Russell Sage Foundation.

Jaynes, Gerald D. 2000. "Introduction: Immigration and the American

Dream." In *Immigration and Race: New Challenges for American Democracy*, edited by G. D. Jaynes. New Haven, Conn.: Yale University Press.

Jenks, Rosemary. 2001. "The USA Patriot Act of 2001." Washington, D.C.: Center for Immigration Studies.

Jensen, Leif. 1991. "Secondary Earner Strategies and Family Poverty: Immigrant-Native Differentials, 1960–1980." *International Migration Review* 25(1): 113–37.

Johnson, Jacqueline S., and Elissa L. Newport. 1989. "Critical Period Effects in Second Language Learning: The Influence of Maturational State on the Acquisition of English as a Second Language." *Cognitive Psychology* 21(1): 60–99.

Johnson, Kevin. 1997. "The New Nativism: Something Old, Something New, Something Borrowed, Something Blue." In *Immigrants Out! The New Nativism and the Anti-Immigrant Impulse in the United States, Critical America*, edited by J. F. Perea. New York: New York University Press.

Joppke, Christian. 1999. *Immigration and the Nation-State*. New York: Oxford University Press.

Juhn, Chinhui, Kevin M. Murphy, and Brooks Pierce. 1993. "Wage Inequality and the Rise in Returns to Skill." *Journal of Political Economy* 101(3): 410–42.

Kachru, Braj B. 1992. *The Other Tongue. English Across Cultures*. Urbana: University of Illinois.

Kallen, Horace. 1988 [1924]. "Democracy Versus the Melting Pot." *The Nation* 100: 190–94 and 217–20.

Kalmijn, Matthijs. 1993a. "Spouse Selection Among the Children of European Immigrants: A Study of Marriage Cohorts in the 1960 Census." *International Migration Review* 27(1): 51–78.

———. 1993b. "Trends in Black-White Intermarriage." *Social Forces* 72(1): 119–46.

———. 1998. "Intermarriage and Homogamy: Causes, Patterns, Trends." *Annual Review of Sociology* 23: 395–421.

Kalmijn, Matthijs, and Henk Flap. 2001. "Assortative Meeting and Mating: Unintended Consequences of Organized Settings for Partner Choices." *Social Forces* 79(4): 1289–1312.

Kanaiaipuni, Shawn M. 1998. "Invisible Hands: The Structural Implications of Women's Activities for the Mexican Migration Process." Paper presented at the Annual Meeting of the American Sociological Association, San Francisco (March 12–14).

Kao, Grace, and Marta Tienda. 1995. "Optimism and Achievement: The Educational Performance of Immigrant Youth." *Social Science Quarterly* 76(1): 1–19.

Karoly, Lynn A. 1993. "The Trend in Inequality Among Families, Individuals, and Workers in the United States: A Twenty-Five-Year Perspective." In *Uneven Tides: Rising Inequality in America*, edited by Sheldon Danziger and Peter Gottschalk. New York: Russell Sage Foundation.

Kasarda, John D. 1985. "Urban Change and Minority Opportunities." In *The New Urban Reality*, edited by P. E. Peterson. Washington, D.C.: Brookings Institution Press.

———. 1989. "Urban Industrial Transition and the Underclass." *The Annals of the American Academy of Political and Social Science* 501.

————. 1995. "Industrial Restructuring and the Changing Location of Jobs." In *State of the Union: America in the 1990s*, edited by Reynolds Farley. New York: Russell Sage Foundation.

Katz, Friedrich. 1988. *Riot, Rebellion, and Revolution: Rural Social Conflict in Mexico*. Princeton, N.J.: Princeton University Press.

Keely, C. B. 1977. "Counting the Uncountable: Estimates of Undocumented Aliens in the United States." *Population and Development Review* 3(4): 473–81.

Kellor, Frances A. 1916. "Americanization by Industry." *Immigrants in America Review* 2(1): 15–26.

Kilbourne, Barbara S., Paula England, George Farkas, Kurt Beron, and Dorothea Weir. 1994. "Returns to Skill, Compensating Differentials, and Gender Bias: Effects of Occupational Characteristics on Wages of White Women and Men." *American Journal of Sociology* 100(3): 689–719.

King, Allen G., Lindsay B. Lowell, and Frank D. Bean. 1986. "The Effects of Hispanic Immigrants on the Earnings of Native Hispanic Americans." *Social Science Quarterly* 67(4): 673–89.

Kloss, Heinz. 1977. *The American Bilingual Tradition*. Rowley, Mass.: Newbury House.

Knight, Alan. 1986. *The Mexican Revolution*. New York: Cambridge University Press.

Knobel, Dale T. 1996. *America for the Americans: the Nativist Movement in the United States*. New York: Twayne Publishers.

Kosters, Marvin H. 1991. *Workers and Their Wages: Changing Patterns in the United States*. Washington, D.C.: AEI Press.

Kritz, Mary, and June Nogle. 1994. "Nativity Concentration and Internal Migration among the Foreign-Born." *Demography* 31(3): 509.

Kuznets, Simon. 1977. "Two Centuries of Economic Growth: Reflections on U.S. Experience." *American Economic Review* 67(1): 1–14.

Labov, Teresa G. 1998. "English Acquisition by Immigrants to the United States at the Beginning of the Twentieth Century." *American Speech* 73(4): 368–98.

LaLonde, Robert J., and Robert H. Topel. 1991. "Immigrants in the American Labor Market: Quality, Assimilation, and Distributional Effects." *American Economic Review Papers and Proceedings* 2(81): 297–302.

Lambert, Richard D. 1994. "Some Issues in Language Policy for Higher Education." *Annals of the American Academy of Political and Social Science* 532: 123–37.

Landau, Ralph. 1988. "U.S. Economic Growth." *Scientific American* 258(6): 44–52.

Lee, Barrett A., and Peter B. Wood. 1991. "Is Neighborhood Racial Succession Place-Specific?" *Demography* 28(1): 21–40.

Lee, Ronald D., and Timothy W. Miller. 1998. "The Current Fiscal Impact of Immigration and Their Descendants: Beyond the Immigrant Household." In *The Immigration Debate: Studies on the Economic, Demographic, and Fiscal Effects of Immigration*, edited by J. P. Smith and Barry Edmonston. Washington, D.C.: National Academy Press.

Lee, Sharon, and Marilyn Fernandez. 1998. "Trends in Asian American Racial/Ethnic Intermarriage: A Comparison of 1980 and 1990 Census Data." *Sociological Perspectives* 41: 323–42.

Leonhardt, David. 2002. "New Report Shows U.S. Economy Slowed Significantly for Quarter." *The New York Times*, August 1, p. 1.

Levy, Frank. 1987. *Dollars and Dreams: The Changing American Income Distribution*. New York: Russell Sage Foundation.

———. 1995. "Incomes and Income Inequality." In *State of the Union: America in the 1990s*, edited by Reynolds Farley. New York: Russell Sage Foundation.

———. 1997. *The New Dollars and Dreams: American Incomes and Economic Change*. New York: Russell Sage Foundation.

Lewis, Susan K., and Valerie K. Oppenheimer. 2000. "Educational Assortative Mating Across Marriage Markets: Non-Hispanic Whites in the United States." *Demography* 37: 29–40.

Lieberson, Stanley. 1980. *A Piece of the Pie: Blacks and White Immigrants Since 1880*. Berkeley: University of California Press.

Lieberson, Stanley, and Timothy J. Curry. 1971. "Language Shift in the United States: Some Demographic Clues." *International Migration Review* 5(2): 125–37.

Lieberson, Stanley, Guy Dalto, and Mary Ellen Johnston. 1975. "The Course of Mother Tongue Diversity in Nations." *American Journal of Sociology* 81(1): 34–61.

Lieberson, Stanley, and Mary C. Waters. 1988. *From Many Strands: Ethnic and Racial Groups in Contemporary America*. New York: Russell Sage Foundation.

———. 1993. "The Ethnic Responses of Whites: What Causes Their Instability, Their Simplification, and Inconsistency?" *Social Forces* 72(2): 421–50.

Light, Ivan. 1979. "Disadvantaged Minorities in Self-Employment." *International Journal of Comparative Sociology* 20(1–2): 31–45.

———. 1984. "Immigrant and Ethnic Enterprise in North America." *Ethnic and Racial Studies* 7(2): 195–216.

Light, Ivan Hubert, and Edna Bonacich. 1988. *Immigrant Entrepreneurs: Koreans in Los Angeles, 1965–1982*. Berkeley: University of California Press.

Light, Ivan, and Stavros Karageorgis. 1980. "Chinatown: The Socioeconomic Potential of an Urban Enclave." *Ethnic and Racial Studies* 16(4): 742–43.

———. 1994. "The Ethnic Economy." In *The Handbook of Economic Sociology*, edited by Neil J. Smelser and Richard Swedberg. Princeton, N.J., and New York: Princeton University Press and Russell Sage Foundation.

Light, Ivan, and Carolyn Nancy Rosenstein. 1995. *Race, Ethnicity, and Entrepreneurship in Urban America*. New York: Aldine de Gruyter.

Lindstrom, David P., and Douglas S. Massey. 1994. "Selective Emigration, Cohort Quality, and Models of Immigrant Assimilation." *Social Science Research* 23(4): 315–49.

Loewen, James. 1988. *The Mississippi Chinese: Between Black and White*. Prospect Heights, Ill.: Waveland Press.

Lofstrom, Magnus. 2002. "Labor Market Assimilation and the Self-Employment Decision of Immigrant Entrepreneurs." *Journal of Population Economics* 15(1): 83–114.

Lofstrom, Magnus, and Frank Bean. 2002. "Assessing Immigrant Policy Options: Labor Market Conditions and Post-Reform Declines in Immigrant Welfare Receipt." *Demography* 39(4): 617–37.

Logan, John R., Richard D. Alba, and Thomas L. McNulty. 1994. "Ethnic Economies in Metropolitan Regions: Miami and Beyond." *Social Forces* 72(3): 691–724.

Long, Michael H. 1990. "Maturational Constraints on Language Development." *Studies in Second Language Acquisition* 12(3): 251–85.

Lopez, David E. 1978. "Chicano Language Loyalty in an Urban Setting." *Sociology and Social Research* 62(2): 267–78.

————. 1982. *The Maintenance of Spanish over Three Generations in the United States.* Los Alamitos, Calif.: National Center for Bilingual Research.

Lopez, David, and Yen Espiritu. 1990. "Panethnicity in the United States: A Theoretical Framework." *Ethnic and Racial Studies* 13(2): 198–224.

Loucky, James, Maria Soldatenko, Scott Gregory, and Edna Bonacich. 1994. "Immigrant Enterprise and Labor in the Los Angeles Garment Industry." In *Global Production: The Apparel Industry in the Pacific Rim*, edited by Edna Bonacich, Lucie Cheng, Norma Chinchilla, Nora Hamilton, and Paul Ong. Philadelphia: Temple University Press.

Lozano-Ascencio, Fernando. 1993. "Bringing It Back Home: Remittances to Mexico from Migrant Workers in the United States." Monograph Series, no. 37. San Diego: Center for U.S.-Mexican Studies, University of California, San Diego.

Lozano-Ascencio, Fernando, Bryan R. Roberts, and Frank D. Bean. 1999. "The Interconnections of Internal and International Migration: The Case of the United States and Mexico." In *Migration and Transnational Social Species*, edited by L. Preis. Aldershot, U.K., and Brookfield, Vt.: Ashgate.

Lubotsky, Darren. 2000. "Chutes or Ladders?: A Longitudinal Analysis of Immigrant Earnings." Unpublished paper. Princeton University, Princeton, N.J.

Maggs, John, and David Baumann. 2001. "The Stimulus Skirmish." *National Journal*, October 13, pp. 3162–73.

Maram, Sheldon L. 1980. "Hispanic Workers in the Garment and Restaurant Industries in Los Angeles County." In *Monograph No. 12 in U.S.-Mexican Studies.* San Diego: Center for U.S.-Mexican Studies, University of California, San Diego.

Mare, Robert D. 1991. "Five Decades of Educational Assortative Mating." *American Sociological Review* 56(1): 15–32.

Martin, Philip. 1997. "Do Mexican Agricultural Policies Stimulate Emigration." In *At the Crossroads: Mexico and U.S. Immigration Policy*, edited by Frank D. Bean, R. O. de la Garza, B. R. Roberts, and S. Weintraub. New York: Rowman & Littlefield.

Martin, Philip, and Susan Martin. 2001. "Immigration and Terrorism: Policy Reform Challenges." Paper presented at the Conference on Immigration, Brussels (October 14–15).

Martin, Philip, and Elizabeth Midgley. 1999. "Immigration to the United States." *Population Bulletin* 54(2). Washington, D.C.: Population Reference Bureau: 1–44.

Martin, Philip, and Jonas Widgren. 2002. "International Migration: Facing the Challenge." *Population Bulletin* 57(1). Washington, D.C.: Population Reference Bureau: 1–40.

Massey, Douglas S. 1981. "Dimensions of the New Immigration to the United States and the Prospects for Assimilation." *Annual Review of Sociology* 7: 57–85.

———. 1987. "Understanding Mexican Migration to the United States." *American Journal of Sociology* 92(6): 1372–1403.

———. 1990. "The Social and Economic Origins of Immigration." *Annals of the American Academy of Political and Social Science* 510: 60–72.

———. 1994. "Immigrants and the American City." *American Journal of Sociology* 99(5): 1346–48.

———. 1995. "The New Immigration and Ethnicity in the United States." *Population and Development Review* 21(3): 631–52.

———. 1999. "International Migration at the Dawn of the Twenty-first Century: The Role of the State." *Population and Development Review* 25(2): 303–22.

Massey, Douglas S., Rafael Alarion, Jorge Durand, and Humberto Gonzalez. 1987. *Return to Aztlan: The Social Process of International Migration from Western Mexico*. Berkeley: University of California Press.

Massey, Douglas, Joaquin Arango, Graeme Hugo, Ali Kouaouci, Adela Pellegrino, and J. Edward Taylor. 1993. "Theories of International Migration: A Review and Appraisal." *Population and Development Review* 19(3): 431–66.

———. 1998. *World in Motion: Understanding International Migration at the End of the Millennium*. Oxford and New York: Clarendon Press and Oxford University Press.

Massey, Douglas S., and Nancy A. Denton. 1993. *American Apartheid: Segregation and the Making of the Underclass*. Cambridge, Mass.: Harvard University Press.

Massey, Douglas S., Jorge Durand, and Nolan J. Malone. 2002. *Beyond Smoke and Mirrors: Mexican Immigration in an Era of Economic Integration*. New York: Russell Sage Foundation.

Massey, Douglas, and Kristin E. Espinosa. 1997. "What's Driving Mexico-U.S. Migration? A Theoretical, Empirical, and Policy Analysis." *American Journal of Sociology* 102(4): 939–99.

Massey, Douglas, and Emilio Parrado. 1994. "Migradollars: The Remittances and Savings of Mexican Migrants to the USA." *Population Research and Policy Review* 13(1): 3–30.

McCarthy, Kevin, and R. Burciaga Valdez. 1985. *Current and Future Effects of Mexican Immigration in California*. Santa Monica, Calif.: Rand Corporation.

McDonald, Peter, and Rebecca Kippen. 2001. "Labor Supply Prospects in 16 Developed Countries, 2000–2050." *Population and Development Review* 27(1): 1–32.

McKenney, Nampeo R., and Claudette E. Bennett. 1994. "Issues Regarding Data on Race and Ethnicity: The Census Bureau Experience." *Public Health Reports* 109(1): 16–25.

McLemore, S. Dale, Harriet D. Romo, and Susan Gonzalez Baker. 2001. *Racial and Ethnic Relations in America*. Boston: Allyn & Bacon.

Meissner, Doris. 2001. "After the Attacks: Protecting Borders and Liberties." Washington, D.C.: Carnegie Endowment for International Peace.

Meissner, Doris, and David Martin. 2001. "Terrorism and Immigration: Our

Borders, Security, and Liberties." Washington, D.C.: Carnegie Endowment for International Peace.

Merton, Robert K. 1941. "Intermarriage and the Social Structure: Fact and Theory." *Psychiatry* 4: 361–74.

Mexico–United States Binational Migration Study. 1997. *Migration Between Mexico and the United States.* Mexico City and Washington, D.C.: Mexican Ministry of Foreign Affairs and U.S. Commission on Immigration Reform.

Mexico–U.S. Migration Panel. 2001. "Mexico-U.S. Migration: A Shared Responsibility." Washington, D.C., and Mexico City: Carnegie Endowment for International Peace and the Insituto Tecnologico Autonomo de Mexico.

Mirowsky, John, and Catherine E. Ross. 1984. "Language Networks and Social Status Among Mexican Americans." *Social Science Quarterly* 65(2): 551–64.

Model, Suzanne, and Gene Fisher. 2001. "Black-White Unions: West Indians and African Americans Compared." *Demography* 38(2): 177–86.

Moffitt, Robert. 1992. "Incentive Effects of the U.S. Welfare System: A Review." *Journal of Economic Literature* 30(1): 615–26.

Montero, Darrel. 1981. "The Japanese Americans: Changing Patterns of Assimilation Over Three Generations." *American Sociological Review* 46(6): 829–39.

Mora, Marie T. 1998. "Did the English Deficiency Earnings Penalty Change for Hispanic Men between 1979 and 1989?" *Social Science Quarterly* 79(3): 581–94.

Mora, Marie T., and Alberto Dávila. 2000. "English Skills, Earnings, and the Occupational Sorting of Mexican Americans Working Along the U.S.-Mexico Border." *International Migration Review* 34(1): 133–57.

Morales, Rebecca, and Paul Ong. 1991. "Immigrant Women in Los Angeles." *Economic and Industrial Democracy* 12(1): 65–81.

Morawska, Ewa. 1994. "In Defense of the Assimilation Model." *Journal of American Ethnic History* 13(2): 76–87.

Morgan, Phillips. 1998. *Slave Counterpoint: Black Culture in the Eighteenth-Century Chesapeake and Lowcountry.* Chapel Hill: University of North Carolina Press.

Morris, Aldon D. 1984. *The Origins of the Civil Rights Movement.* New York: Free Press.

Morris, Milton. 1985. *Immigration: The Beleaguered Bureaucracy.* Washington, D.C.: Brookings Institution Press.

Muller, Thomas, and Thomas J. Espenshade. 1985. *The Fourth Wave: California's Newest Immigrants.* Washington, D.C.: Urban Institute Press.

Murray, Charles. 1994. *Losing Ground: American Social Policy, 1950–1980.* New York: Basic Books.

Mutchler, Jan E., and Sara Brallier. 1999. "English Language Proficiency Among Older Hispanics in the United States." *The Gerontologist* 39(3): 310–19.

Myers, Dowell. 1998. "Dimensions of Economic Adaptation by Mexican Origin Men." In *Crossings: Mexican Immigration in Interdisciplinary Perspectives,* edited by Marcelo M. Suarez-Orozco. Cambridge, Mass.: Harvard University Press.

Nagel, Joane. 1994. "Constructing Ethnicity: Creating and Recreating Ethnic Identity and Culture." *Social Problems* 41(1): 152–76.

Neckerman, Kathryn M., Prudence Carter, and Jennifer Lee. 1999. "Segmented Assimilation and Minority Cultures of Mobility." *Ethnic and Racial Studies* 22(6): 945–65.

Neckerman, Kathryn M., and Joleen Kirschenman. 1991. "Hiring Strategies, Racial Bias, and Inner-city Workers." *Social Problems* 38(4): 433–47.

Nee, Victor, Jimy M. Sanders, and Scott Sernau. 1994. "Job Transitions in an Immigrant Metropolis: Ethnic Boundaries and the Mixed Economy." *American Sociological Review* 59(6): 849–72.

Neidert, Lisa, and Reynolds Farley. 1985. "Assimilation in the United States: An Analysis of Ethnic and Generation Differences in Status and Achievement." *American Sociological Review* 50(6): 840–50.

Newman, Katherine S. 1999. *No Shame in My Game: The Working Poor in the Inner City.* New York: Alfred A. Knopf and Russell Sage Foundation.

Ngai, Mae M. 1999. "The Architecture of Race in American Immigration Law: A Reexamination of the Immigration Act of 1924." *Journal of American History* 86(1): 67–92.

Nobles, Melissa. 2000. *Shades of Citizenship: Race and the Census in Modern Politics.* Palo Alto, Calif.: Stanford University Press.

Nyden, Philip, Michael Maly, and J. Lukehart. 1997. "The Emergence of Stable Racially and Ethnically Diverse Urban Communities." *Housing Policy Debate* 8(2): 491–534.

Nye, Joseph S. 2002. *The Paradox of American Power: Why the World's Only Superpower Can't Go It Alone.* New York: Oxford University Press.

Ogbu, John U. 1994. "Racial Stratification and Education in the United States: Why Inequality Persists." *Teachers College Record* 96(2): 265–98.

Olzak, Susan. 1992. *The Dynamics of Ethnic Competition and Conflict.* Palo Alto, Calif.: Stanford University Press.

Omi, Michael, and Howard Winant. 1994. *Racial Formation in the United States: From the 1960s to the 1980s.* New York: Routledge.

Ono, Hiromi, and Rosina M. Becerra. 2000. "Race, Ethnicity and Nativity, Family Structure, Socioeconomic Status and Welfare Dependency." *International Migration Review* 34(3): 739–65.

Oppenheimer, Andres. 1995. *Bordering on Chaos: Guerrillas, Stockbrokers, Politicians, and Mexico's Road to Prosperity.* Boston: Little, Brown.

Pagnini, Deanna L., and S. Philip Morgan. 1990. "Intermarriage and Social Distance Among U.S. Immigrants at the Turn of the Century." *American Journal of Sociology* 96(2): 405–32.

Park, Robert Ezra. 1926. "Our Racial Frontier in The Pacific." *Survey Graphic* 9(May): 192–96.

Park, Robert Ezra, and Ernest W. Burgess. 1921. *Introduction to the Science of Sociology.* Chicago: University of Chicago Press.

Passel, Jeffrey S. 1987. "Measurement of Ethnic Origin in the Decennial Census." Paper presented at the Annual Meeting of the American Association for the Advancement of Science, Chicago (February 14–18).

———. 1994. "Immigrants and Taxes: A Reappraisal of Huddle's 'The Cost of Immigrants.'" Report. Washington, D.C.: The Urban Institute.

———. 1999. "The Number of Undocumented Immigrants in the United States: A Review and New Estimates." In *Illegal Immigration in America: A*

Reference Handbook, edited by D. W. Haines and K. E. Rosenblum. Westport, Conn.: Greenwood Press.

Passel, Jeffrey S., and Rebecca L. Clark. 1998. "Immigrants in New York: Their Legal Status, Incomes, and Taxes." Report. Washington, D.C.: The Urban Institute.

Passel, Jeffrey S., and Barry Edmonston. 1994. "Immigration and Race: Recent Trends in Immigration to the United States." In *Immigration and Ethnicity: The Integration of America's Newest Arrivals*, edited by J. S. Passel and B. Edmonston. Washington, D.C.: Urban Institute Press.

Passel, Jeffrey S., and Karen A. Woodrow. 1987. "Change in the Undocumented Alien Population in the United States, 1979–1983." *International Migration Review* 21(4): 1304–34.

Patillo-McCoy, Mary. 1999. *Black Picket Fences: Privilege and Peril Among the Black Middle Class*. Chicago: University of Chicago Press.

Patterson, Orlando. 1998a. *The Ordeal of Integration*. Washington, D.C.: Civitas.

———. 1998b. *Rituals of Blood*. Washington, D.C.: Civitas.

Penner, Rudolph G., Isabel V. Sawhill, and Timothy Taylor. 2000. *Updating America's Social Contract*. New York: W. W. Norton.

Perlmann, Joel, and Roger Waldinger. 1999. "Immigrants Past and Present: A Reconsideration." In *The Handbook of International Migration*, edited by Charles Hirschman, Josh DeWind, and Philip Kasinitz. New York: Russell Sage Foundation.

Piore, Michael J. 1979. *Birds of Passage: Migrant Labor and Industrial Societies*. New York: Cambridge University Press.

Ponce, Elsa. 1996. "Lawfully Resident Aliens Who Receive SSI Payments." Report. Washington: Office of Program Benefit Payments, Social Security Administration.

Portes, Alejandro. 1987. "The Social Origins of the Cuban Enclave Economy of Miami." *Sociological Perspectives* 30: 340–72.

———. 2001. "Theories of Development for a New Century: Migration, Transnationalism, and the Informal Economy." Paper presented at the Annual Meeting of the American Sociological Association, Anaheim, Calif. (August 16–20).

Portes, Alejandro, and Robert L. Bach. 1985. *Latin Journey: Cuban and Mexican Immigrants in the United States*. Berkeley: University of California Press.

Portes, Alejandro, and Leif Jensen. 1989. "The Enclave and the Entrants: Patterns of Ethnic Enterprise in Miami Before and After Mariel." *American Sociological Review* 54(6): 929–49.

Portes, Alejandro, and Dag Macleod. 1996. "What Shall I Call Myself? Hispanic Identity Formation in the Second Generation." *Ethnic and Racial Studies* 19(3): 523–47.

Portes, Alejandro, and Rubén G. Rumbaut. 1990. *Immigrant America: A Portrait*. Berkeley: University of California Press.

———. 2001. *Legacies: The Story of the Immigrant Second Generation*. Berkeley: University of California Press.

Portes, Alejandro, and Richard Schauffler. 1994. "Language and the Second Generation: Bilingualism Yesterday and Today." *International Migration Review* 28(4): 640–61.

Portes, Alejandro, and Alex Stepick. 1993. *City on the Edge: The Transformation of Miami.* Berkeley: University of California Press.

Portes, Alejandro, and Min Zhou. 1993. "The New Second Generation: Segmented Assimilation and Its Variants." *The Annals of the American Academy of Political and Social Science* 530: 74–96.

———. 1996. "Self-Employment and the Earnings of Immigrants." *American Sociological Review* 61(2): 219–30.

Qian, Zhenchao. 1997. "Breaking the Racial Barriers: Variations in Interracial Marriage Between 1980 and 1990." *Demography* 34(2): 263–76.

Qian, Zhenchao, Sampson Lee Blair, and Stacey Ruf. 2001. "Asian American Interracial and Interethnic Marriages: Differences by Education and Nativity." *International Migration Review* 35(2): 557–86.

Raijman, Rebeca, and Marta Tienda. 1999. "Immigrants' Socioeconomic Progress Post-1965: Forging Mobility or Survival?" In *The Handbook of International Migration: The American Experience,* edited by Charles Hirschman, Josh DeWind, and Philip Kasinitz. New York: Russell Sage Foundation.

Rank, Mark. 1994. *Living on the Edge: The Realities of Welfare in America.* New York: Columbia University Press.

Rector, Robert. 1996. "A Retirement Home for Immigrants." *Wall Street Journal,* February 20.

Reed, Deborah. 2001. "Immigration and Males' Earnings Inequality in the Regions of the United States." *Demography* 38(3): 363–73.

Reimers, David M. 1983. "An Unintended Reform: The 1965 Immigration Act and Third World Migration to the United States." *Journal of American Ethnic History* 3(fall): 9–28.

———. 1985. *Still the Golden Door: The Third World Comes to America.* New York: Columbia University Press.

———. 1992. *Still the Golden Door: The Third World Comes to America* 2nd ed. New York: Columbia University Press.

———. 1998. *Unwelcome Strangers: American Identity and the Turn Against Immigration.* New York: Columbia University Press.

Reischauer, Robert. 1989. "Immigration and the Underclass." In *The Ghetto Underclass: Social Science Perspectives (Annals of the American Academy of Political and Social Science 501),* edited by W. J. Wilson. Newbury Park, Calif.: Sage Publications.

Repak, Terry A. 1994. "Labor Market Incorporation of Central American Immigrants in Washington, D.C." *Social Problems* 41(1): 114–28.

———. 1995. *Waiting on Washington: Central American Workers in the Nation's Capital.* Philadelphia: Temple University Press.

Reskin, Barbara F., and Irene Padavic. 1994. *Women and Men at Work.* Thousand Oaks, Calif.: Pine Forge Press.

Reskin, Barbara F., and Patricia A. Roos. 1990. "Job Queues, Gender Queues: Explaining Women's Inroads into Male Occupations: Summary, Implications, and Prospects." In *Job Queues, Gender Queues: Explaining Women's Inroads into Male Occupations,* by Barbara F. Reskin and Patricia Roos. Philadelphia: Temple University Press.

Reyes, Belinda I., Hans P. Johnson, and Richard Van Swearingen. 2002. "Holding the Line? The Effect of the Recent Border Build-up on Unauthorized Immigration." San Francisco: Public Policy Institute of California.

Roberts, Bryan R. 1995. "Socially Expected Durations and the Economic Adjustment of Immigrants." In *The Economic Sociology of Immigration*, edited by Alejandro Portes. New York: Russell Sage Foundation.

Roberts, Bryan R., Reanne Bean, and Fernando Lozano-Ascencio. 1999. "Transnational Migrant Communities and Mexican Migration to the U.S." *Ethnic and Racial Studies* 22: 238–66.

Roberts, Bryan R., and Augustin Escobar Latapi. 1997. "Mexican Social and Economic Policy and Emigration." In *At the Crossroads: Mexico and U.S. Immigration Policy*, edited by Frank D. Bean, R. O. de la Garza, B. R. Roberts, and S. Weintraub. New York: Rowman & Littlefield.

Robinson, J. Gregory. 2002. "Coverage of Population in Census 2000: Results from Demographic Analysis." Paper presented at the meetings of the American Association for the Advancement of Science, Boston (February 18).

Rodríguez, Clara E. 2000. *Changing Race: Latinos, the Census, and the History of Ethnicity in the United States*. New York: New York University Press.

Rodriguez, Gregory. 1999. *From Newcomers to New Americans: The Successful Integration of Immigrants into American Society*. Washington, D.C.: National Immigration Forum.

———. 2001. "Forging a New Vision of America's Melting Pot." *The New York Times Week in Review*, February 11, p. 1.

Roediger, David R. 2002. *Colored White: Transcending the Racial Past*. Berkeley: University of California Press.

Root, Maria P. 1992. *Racially Mixed People in America*. Newbury Park, Calif.: Sage Publications.

———. 1996. *The Multiracial Experience: Racial Borders as the New Frontier*. Thousand Oaks, Calif.: Sage Publications.

Rose, Peter I. 1997. *Tempest-Tost: Race, Immigration, and the Dilemmas of Diversity*. New York: Columbia University Press.

Rosenberg, Tina. 2002. "The Free Trade Fix." *The New York Times Magazine*, August 18, p. 28.

Rosenfeld, Michael J. 2002. "Measures of Assimilation in the Marriage Market: Mexican Americans." *Journal of Marriage and the Family*. 64(1): 152–62.

Rumbaut, Rubén G. 1995. "The New Immigration." *Contemporary Sociology* 24(4): 307–11.

———. 1999. "Immigration Research in the United States: Social Origins and Future Orientations." *American Behavioral Scientist* 42(9): 1285–1301.

Saenz, Rogelio, Sean Shong Hwang, and Benigno E. Aguirre. 1994. "In Search of Asian War Brides." *Demography* 31(3): 549–59.

Saenz, Rogelio, Sean-Shong Hwang, Benigno E. Aguirre, and Robert N. Anderson. 1995. "Persistence and Change in Asian Identity Among Children of Intermarried Couples." *Sociological Perspectives* 38(2): 175–94.

Sakamoto, Arthur, Huei-Hsai Wu, and Jessie M. Tzeng. 2000. "The Declining Significance of Race Among American Men During the Latter Half of the Twentieth Century." *Demography* 37(1): 41–51.

Salgado de Snyder, Nelly, Cynthia M. Lopez, and Amado M. Padilla. 1982. "Ethnic Identity and Cultural Awareness Among the Offspring of Mexican Interethnic Marriages." *Journal of Early Adolescence* 2(3): 277–82.

Salt, John. 1981. "International Labor Migration in Western Europe: A Geographical Review." In *Global Trends in Migration: Theory and Research on International Population Movements,* edited by M. M. Kritz, C. B. Keely, and S. M. Tomasi. New York: Center for Migration Studies.

Samora, Julian, and William N. Deane. 1956. "Language Usage as a Possible Index of Acculturation." *Sociology and Social Research* (May–June): 307–11.

Sánchez, George J. 1997. "Face the Nation: Race, Immigration, and the Rise of Nativism in Late Twentieth Century America." *International Migration Review* 31(4): 1009–30.

Sanders, Jimy M., and Victor Nee. 1987. "Limits of Ethnic Solidarity in the Enclave Economy." *American Sociological Review* 52(6): 745–73.

———. 1996. "Immigrant Self-Employment: The Family as Social Capital and the Value of Human Capital." *American Sociological Review* 61(4): 231–49.

Sanjek, Roger. 1994. "Intermarriage and the Future of the Races." In *Race,* edited by S. Gregory and Roger Sanjek. New Brunswick, N.J.: Rutgers University Press.

———. 1998. *The Future of Us All: Race and Neighborhood Politics.* Ithaca, N.Y.: Cornell University Press.

Sassen, Saskia. 1988. *The Mobility of Labor and Capital: A Study in International Investment and Labor Flow.* New York: Cambridge University Press.

———. 1989. "New York City's Informal Economy." In *The Informal Sector: Theoretical and Methodological Issues,* edited by Alejandro Portes, M. Castells, and L. Benton. Baltimore: Johns Hopkins University Press.

———. 1990. "Economic Restructuring and the American City." *Annual Review of Sociology* 16: 465–90.

———. 1991. *The Global City: New York, London, and Tokyo.* Princeton, N.J.: Princeton University Press.

———. 1994. *Cities in a World Economy.* Thousand Oaks, Calif.: Pine Forge Press.

———. 1995. "Immigration and Local Labor Markets." In *The Economic Sociology of Immigration,* edited by Alejandro Portes. New York: Russell Sage Foundation.

———. 2000. "Urban Economics and Fading Distances." Lecture presented to the Project "De Ondergang Van Nederland?" (March 30).

Schoen, Robert, and James R. Kluegel. 1988. "The Widening Gap in Black and White Marriage Rates: the Impact of Population Composition and Differential Marriage Propensities." *American Sociological Review* 53: 893–907.

Schoeni, Robert. 1998. "Labor Market Outcomes of Immigrant Women in the United States: 1970–1990." *International Migration Review* 32: 57–78.

Schoeni, Robert, and Rebecca Blank. 2000. "What Has Welfare Reform Accomplished? Impacts on Welfare Participation, Employment, Income, Poverty, and Family Structure." Working Paper 7627. Cambridge: National Bureau of Economic Research.

Scholes, Robert J. 1999. "The 'Mail-Order Bride' Industry and Its Impact on

U.S. Immigration." Immigration and Naturalization Service. Available on-line at: *www.ins.usdoj.gov/graphics/aboutins/repsstudies/mobappa.htm.*

Schuman, Howard, Charlotte Steeh, and Lawrence Bobo. 1985. *Racial Attitudes in America: Trends and Interpretations.* Cambridge, Mass.: Harvard University Press.

Schumann, John H. 1986. "Research on the Acculturation Model for Second Language Acquisition." *Journal of Multilingual and Multicultural Development* 7: 379–92.

Select Commission on Immigration and Refugee Policy. 1981. "U.S. Immigration Policy and the National Interest." Washington: U.S. Government Printing Office.

Simon, Julian L. 1987. *Effort, Opportunity and Wealth.* Oxford: Basil Blackwell.

———. 1989. *The Economic Consequences of Immigration.* Cambridge: Basil Blackwell.

Skrentny, John D. 2001. *Color Lines: Affirmative Action, Immigration, and Civil Rights Options for America.* Chicago: University of Chicago Press.

Smelser, Neil, William Julius Wilson, and Faith Mitchell. 2001. *America Becoming: Racial Patterns and Their Consequences.* Washington, D.C.: National Academy Press.

Smith, James P. 2001. "Race and Ethnicity in the Labor Market: Trends over the Short and Long Term." In *America Becoming: Racial Trends and Their Consequences,* edited by Neil J. Smelser, William Julius Wilson, and Faith Mitchell. Vol. 2. Washington, D.C.: National Academy Press.

Smith, James P., and Barry Edmonston. 1997. *The New Americans: Economic, Demographic, and Fiscal Effects of Immigration.* Washington, D.C.: National Academy Press.

Smith, Peter H. 1997. "NAFTA and Mexican Migration." In *At the Crossroads: Mexico Immigration and U.S. Policy,* edited by Frank D. Bean, R. O. de la Garza, B. R. Roberts, and S. Weintraub. Lanham, Md.: Rowman & Littlefield.

Sorensen, Elaine, Frank D. Bean, and Leighton Ku. 1992. *Immigrant Categories and the U.S. Job Market: Do They Make a Difference?* Washington, D.C.: Urban Institute Press.

Spener, David. 1995. "Entrepreneurship and Small-Scale Enterprise in the Texas Border Region: A Sociocultural Perspective." Ph.D. diss., University of Texas, Austin.

Spener, David, and Frank D. Bean. 1999. "Self-employment Concentration and Earnings among Mexican Immigrants in the United States." *Social Forces* 77(3): 1021–47.

Spickard, Paul R. 1989. *Mixed Blood: Intermarriage and Ethnic Identity In Twentieth-Century America.* Madison: University of Wisconsin Press.

Stark, Oded. 1991. "Migration Incentives, Migration Types: The Role of Relative Deprivation." *Economic Journal* 101(408): 1163–78.

Stephan, Cookie White, and Walter G. Stephan. 1989. "After Intermarriage: Ethnic Identity Among Mixed-Heritage Japanese-Americans and Hispanics." *Journal of Marriage and the Family* 51(2): 507–19.

Stepick, Alex. 1989. "Miami's Two Informal Sectors." In *The Informal Economy:*

Studies in Advanced and Less Developed Countries, edited by Alejandro Portes, M. Castells, and L. A. Benton. Baltimore: Johns Hopkins University.

Stevens, Gillian. 1985. "Nativity, Intermarriage, and Mother-Tongue Shift." *American Sociological Review* 50(1): 74–83.

———. 1992. "The Social and Demographic Context of Language Use in the United States." *American Sociological Review* 57(2): 171–85.

———. 1994. "Immigration, Emigration, Language Acquisition, and the English Language Proficiency of Immigrants in the U.S." In *Immigration and Ethnicity: The Integration of America's Newest Immigrants*, edited by Jeffrey Passel and Barry Edmonston. Washington, D.C.: Urban Institute Press.

———. 1999. "A Century of U.S. Censuses and the Language Characteristics of Immigrants." *Demography* 36(3): 387–97.

———. 2000. "Nativity, National Origins, and Intermarriage." Paper presented at the Annual Meeting of the Population Association of America, Los Angeles (April 20–22).

Stevens, Gillian, and Nancy Garrett. 1996. "Migrants and the Linguistic Ecology of New Jersey." In *Keys to Successful Immigration*, edited by Thomas J. Espenshade. Washington, D.C.: Urban Institute Press.

Stevens, Gillian, and Susan Gonzo. 1998. "The 1998 Survey of Incoming UIUC Freshmen: Race/Ethnicity and Language." Urbana: Office of the Provost, University of Illinois, Urbana–Champaign.

Stevens, Gillian, and Diane Muehl. 2001. "Linguistic Diversity Among Elderly Americans." Paper presented at the Annual Meeting of the MidWest Sociological Association, St. Louis, Mo. (March 27–28).

Stevens, Gillian, and Robert Schoen. 1988. "Linguistic Intermarriage in the United States." *Journal of Marriage and the Family* 50(1): 267–79.

Stevens, Gillian, and Gray Swicegood. 1987. "The Linguistic Context of Ethnic Endogamy." *American Sociological Review* 52(1): 73–82.

Stevens, Gillian, and Michael K. Tyler. 2002. "Ethnic and Racial Intermarriage in the United States: Old and New Regimes." In *American Diversity: A Demographic Challenge for the Twenty-First Century*, edited by N. A. Denton and S. E. Tolnay. Albany: State University of New York Press.

Stewart, James B., and Thomas J. Hyclak. 1986. "The Effects of Immigrants, Women, and Teenagers on the Relative Earnings of Black Males." *Review of Black Political Economy* 15(1): 93–101.

Stolzenberg, Ross M. 1990. "Ethnicity, Geography, and Occupational Achievement of Hispanic Men in the United States." *American Sociological Review* 55(1): 143–54.

Stromswold, Karin. 2001. "The Heritability of Language: A Review and Meta-Analysis of Twin, Adoption, and Linkage Studies." *Language* 77(4): 647–723.

Suárez-Orozco, Marcelo, ed. 1998 *Crossings: Mexican Immigration in Interdisciplinary Perspectives*. Cambridge, Mass.: Harvard University Press.

Suárez-Orozco, Marcelo, and Mariela Páez, eds. 2002. *Latinos: Remaking America*. Berkeley: University of California Press.

Sullivan, Kevin, and Mary Jordan. 2001. "Siblings Spur New Look at Immigration." *The Washington Post*, August 29, p. A1.

Suro, Roberto. 1998. *Strangers Among Us: How Latino Immigration Is Transforming America*. New York: Alfred A. Knopf.

Suttles, Gerald D. 1968. *The Social Order of the Slum: Ethnicity and Territory in the Inner City*. Chicago: University of Chicago Press.

Taylor, J. Edward. 1987. "Undocumented Mexico-U.S. Migration and the Returns to Households in Rural Mexico." *American Journal of Agricultural Economics* 69(3): 616–38.

———. 1992. "Remittances and Inequality Reconsidered: Direct, Indirect, and Intertemporal Effects." *Journal of Policy Modeling* 14(2): 187–208.

———. 1994. "Mexico-to-U.S. Migration in the Context of Economic Globalization: A Village CGE Perspective." Paper prepared for the Annual Meeting of the American Association for the Advancement of Science, San Francisco (February 22).

Taylor, J. Edward, Joaquin Arango, Graeme Hugo, Ali Kouaouci, Douglas S. Massey, and Adela Pellegrino. 1997. "International Migration and National Development." *Population Index* 62(2): 181–212.

Taylor, J. Edward, Philip L. Martin, and Michael Fix. 1997. *Poverty amid Prosperity: Immigration and the Changing Face of Rural California*. Washington, D.C.: Urban Institute Press.

Taylor, Lowell J., Frank D. Bean, James B. Rebitzer, Susan Gonzalez-Baker, and Lindsay B. Lowell. 1988. "Mexican Immigrants and the Wages and Unemployment Experience of Native Workers." Publication PRIP-UI-1. Washington, D.C.: Program for Research on Immigration Policy, the Urban Institute.

Taylor, Paul. 1970. *Mexican Labor in the United States*. Vol. I and II. New York: Arno Press.

Teitelbaum, Michael S., and Myron Weiner. 1995. *World Migration and U.S. Policy*. New York: W. W. Norton.

Terdy, D., and David Spener. 1990. *English Language Literacy and Other Requirements of the Amnesty Program*. Washington, D.C.: ERIC National Clearinghouse on Literacy Education.

Thernstrom, Stephan, and Abigail Thernstrom. 1997. *America in Black and White: One Nation, Indivisible*. New York: Simon & Schuster.

Thomas, William I., and Florian Znaniecki. 1927. *The Polish Peasant in Europe and America*. Vol. 2. New York: Alfred A. Knopf.

Tienda, Marta, and Leif Jensen. 1986. "Immigration and Public Assistance Participation: Dispelling the Myth of Dependency." *Social Science Research* 15(4): 372–400.

Tocqueville, Alexis de. 1945 [1835]. *Democracy in America*. New York: Alfred A. Knopf.

Todaro, Michael P., and Lydia Maruszko. 1987. "Illegal Migration and U.S. Immigration Reform: A Conceptual Framework." *Population and Development Review* 13(1): 101–14.

Tolbert, Charles M., Patrick M. Horan, and E. M. Beck. 1980. "The Structure of Economic Segmentation: A Dual Economy Approach." *American Journal of Sociology* 85(5): 1095–1116.

Topel, Robert H. 1994. "Regional Labor Markets and the Determinants of Wage Inequality." *American Economic Review* 84(2): 17–22.

Trejo, Stephen J. 1992. "Immigrant Welfare Recipiency: Recent Trends and Future Implications." *Contemporary Policy Issues* 10(2): 44–53.

———. 1996. *Obstacles to the Labor Market Progress of California's Mexican-Origin Workers*. Berkeley: Chicano/Latino Policy Project.

———. 1997. "Why Do Mexican Americans Earn Low Wages?" *Journal of Political Economy* 105(6): 1235–68.

Tuan, Mia. 1998. *Forever Foreigners or Honorary Whites? The Asian Ethnic Experience Today*. New Brunswick, N.J.: Rutgers University Press.

Tucker, M. Belinda, and Claudia Mitchell-Kernan. 1990. "New Trends in Black American Interracial Marriage: the Social Structural Context." *Journal of Marriage and the Family* 52(2): 209–18.

U.S. Bureau of Labor Statistics. 2001. "Employment Estimates." Available online at: *stats.bls.gov/bls/employment.htm*.

U.S. Commission on Immigration Reform. 1994. *U.S. Immigration Policy: Restoring Credibility*. Washington: U.S. Government Printing Office.

———. 1997. "Becoming an American: Immigration and Immigrant Policy." Report to Congress, Executive Summary. Washington: U.S. Government Printing Office.

U.S. Department of Commerce. U.S. Bureau of the Census. 1913. *Thirteenth Census of the United States Taken in the Year 1910*. Washington: U.S. Government Printing Office.

———. 1933. *Fifteenth Census of the United States: 1930*. Vol. 2, *Population*. General Report. Statistics by Subject. Washington: U.S. Government Printing Office.

———. 1982. *1980 Census of Population and Housing*. "Public Use Microdata Samples." Machine-readable data files, 1 percent sample. Washington: U.S. Government Printing Office.

———. 1992a. *Census of Population and Housing, 1990: Summary Tape File 3 on CD-ROM*. Washington: U.S. Bureau of the Census.

———. 1992b. *1990 Census of Population and Housing*. Public Use Microdata Samples." Machine-readable data files, 1 percent sample. Washington: U.S. Government Printing Office.

———. 1993. *1990 Census of Population. Social and Economic Characteristics. United States. 1990 CP-2-1*. Washington: U.S. Government Printing Office.

———. 1995. Census of Population and Housing, 1990 [United States]: Public Use Microdata Sample: 1-percent sample [Computer file]. Washington: U.S. Bureau of the Census.

———. 1995–2002. Current Population Survey: Annual Demographic Files [computer files]. Washington: U.S. Government Printing Office.

———. 2001a. "United States Census 2000." Available on-line at: *www.census.gov/popest/estimates.php*.

———. 2001b. Statistical Abstract of the United States, 2000. Available on-line for this and earlier years at: *www.census.gov.prod/www/stat*.

———. 2002a. Census 2000 Supplementary Survey (C2SS) [computer file]. Washington: U.S. Bureau of the Census.

———. 2002b. Census 2000. Demographic Profiles. Washington: U.S. Bureau of the Census.

———. 2002c. "Foreign-Born Population of the United States. Current Population Survey, March 2000. Detailed Tables." Washington: Population Division and the Ethnic and Hispanic Statistics Branch.

U.S. Department of Defense. 2001. "Active Duty Military Strengths by Regional Area and by Country." Vol. 8. September 30. Available on-line at: *www.defenselink.mil/ pubs/almanac/almanac/people/serve.html.*

U.S. Department of Justice. 1992. "Immigration Reform and Control Act: Report on the Legalized Alien Population." Washington: U.S. Government Printing Office.

U.S. Department of Labor. 1971. "Monthly Labor Review." Vol. 94.

———. 1981. "Monthly Labor Review." Vol. 104.

———. 1991. "Monthly Labor Review." Vol. 114.

———. 2001. "Monthly Labor Review." Vol. 124.

———. 2002. "Monthly Labor Review." Vol. 125.

U.S. General Accounting Office. 1995. "Recent Growth in the Rolls Raises Fundamental Program Concerns." Testimony before the Subcommittee on Human Resources, Committee of Ways and Means, House of Representatives. Washington: U.S. General Accounting Office.

U.S. House of Representatives, Committee on Ways and Means. 2000. *1990 Green Book: Background Material and Data on Programs Within the Jurisdiction of the Committee on Ways and Means.* Washington: U.S. Government Printing Office.

U.S. Immigration and Naturalization Service. 1975. *Historical Statistics of the United States, Part I.* Washington: U.S. Government Printing Office.

———. 1984. *1983 INS Yearbook.* Washington: U.S. Government Printing Office.

———. 1994. *1993 INS Yearbook.* Washington: U.S. Government Printing Office.

———. 1995. *1995 INS Yearbook.* Washington: U.S. Government Printing Office.

———. 1998. *1997 INS Yearbook.* Washington: U.S. Government Printing Office.

———. 1999. *1997 INS Yearbook.* Washington: U.S. Government Printing Office.

———. 2000a. *1999 INS Yearbook.* Washington: U.S. Government Printing Office.

———. 2000b. *Statistical Yearbook of the Immigration and Naturalization Service, 1998.* Washington: U.S. Government Printing Office.

———. 2001. *Statistical Yearbook of the Immigration and Naturalization Service, 1999.* Washington: U.S. Government Printing Office.

———. 2002a. *2000 INS Yearbook.* Washington: U.S. Government Printing Office.

———. 2002b. "Immigration and Naturalization Legislation from the Statistical Yearbook." Vol. 2. Available on-line at: *www.ins.usdoj.gov/graphics/ aboutins/statistics/legishist.*

———. 2002c. "Statistical Yearbook of the Immigration and Naturalization Service, 1999." Vol. 2. Available on-line at: *www.ins.usdoj.gov/graphics/ aboutins/statistics/IMM99list.htm.*

Usdansky, Margaret L., and Thomas J. Espenshade. 2001. "The Evolution of U.S. Policy Toward Employment-Based Immigrants and Temporary Workers: The H-1B Debate in Historical Perspective." In *The International Migration of the Highly Skilled: Demand, Supply, and Development Consequences in Sending and Receiving Countries,* edited by W. A. Cornelius, Thomas J. Espenshade, and I. Salehyan. La Jolla: Center for Comparative Immigration Studies, University of California, San Diego.

Valdivieso, Rafael, and Cary Dains. 1986. "U.S. Hispanics: Challenging Issues for the 1990s." *Population Trends and Public Policy* 17(December): 1–16.

Van Hook, Jennifer, and Frank D. Bean. 1998a. "Estimating Unauthorized Mexican Migration to the United States: Issues and Results." In *Migration Between Mexico and the United States, Binational Study*, vol. 2. Mexico City and Washington: Mexican Ministry of Foreign Affairs and U.S. Commission on Immigration Reform.

———. 1998b. "Welfare Reform and Supplemental Security Income Receipt Among Immigrants in the United States." In *Immigration, Citizenship, and the Welfare State in Germany and the United States*, edited by H. Kurthen, J. Fijalkowski, and G. G. Wagner. Stamford, Conn.: Jai Press.

Van Hook, Jennifer, Frank D. Bean, and Jennifer E. Glick. 1995. "The Development and Assessment of Census-Based Measures of AFDC and SSI Recipiency." Working paper. Austin: Texas Population Research Center, University of Texas.

———. 1996. "The Development and Assessment of Census-Based Measures of AFDC and SSI Recipiency." *Journal of Economic and Social Measurement* 22(1): 1–23.

Van Hook, Jennifer, Jennifer E. Glick, and Frank D. Bean. 1999. "Public Assistance Receipt Among Immigrants and Natives: How the Unit of Analysis Affects Research Findings." *Demography* 36(1): 111–20.

Vasquez, Mario. 1981. "Immigrant Workers in the Apparel Industry in Southern California." In *Mexican Immigrant Workers in the U.S.*, edited by A. Rios-Bustamante. Chicano Research Studies Center Anthology no. 2. Los Angeles: University of California Press.

Ventura, Stephanie J., S. C. Curtin, and T. J. Mathews. "Variations in Teenage Birth Rates, 1991–98: National and State Trends." *National Vital Statistics Reports* 48(6): 1–13.

Vialet, Joyce C. 1993. "Refugee Admissions and Resettlement Policy." Congressional Research Service Issue Brief, Washington, D.C.

Villar, María de Lourdes. 1994. "Hindrances to the Development of an Ethnic Economy Among Mexican Migrants." *Human Organization* 53(3): 263–68.

Waldinger, Roger. 1986. *Through the Eye of the Needle: Immigrants and Enterprise in New York's Garment Trades*. New York: New York University Press.

———. 1989. "Immigration and Urban Change." *Annual Review of Sociology* 15: 211–32.

———. 1996. *Still the Promised City? African-Americans and New Immigrants in Postindustrial New York*. Cambridge, Mass.: Harvard University.

———. 1997. "Black/Immigrant Competition Re-Assessed: New Evidence from Los Angeles." *Sociological Perspectives* 40(2): 365–86.

———. 2001. *Strangers at the Gates: New Immigrants in Urban America*. Berkeley: University of California Press.

Waldinger, Roger, and Jennifer Lee. 2001. "New Immigrants in Urban America." in *Strangers at the Gates: New Immigrants in Urban America*, edited by Roger Waldinger. Berkeley: University of California Press.

Waldinger, Roger, David McEvoy, and Howard Aldrich. 1990. "Spatial Dimensions of Opportunity Structures." In *Ethnic Entrepreneurs: Immigrant Business in Industrial Societies*, edited by Roger D. Waldinger, Howard Aldrich, and R. Ward. Newbury Park, Calif.: Sage Publications.

Wallerstein, Immanuel. 1983. *Historical Capitalism*. New York: Verso.

Warren, John Robert. 1996. "Educational Inequality Among White and Mexican-Origin Adolescents in the American Southwest: 1990." *Sociology of Education* 69(2): 142–58.

Warren, Robert. 1990. "Annual Estimates of Nonimmigrant Overstays in the United States: 1985–1988." In *Undocumented Migration to the United States: IRCA and the Experience of the 1980s*, edited by Frank D. Bean, Barry Edmonston, and Jeffrey S. Passel. Washington, D.C.: Urban Institute Press.

———. 1992. "Estimates of the Unauthorized Immigrant Population Residing in the United States, by Country of Origin and State of Residence: October 1992." Report. Washington: U.S. Immigration and Naturalization Service, Statistics Division.

———. 1994. "Estimates of the Unauthorized Immigrant Population Residing in the United States, by Country of Origin and State of Residence: October 1992." Office of Policy Planning. Washington: U.S. Immigration and Naturalization Service.

———. 1997. *Estimates of the Undocumented Immigrant Population Residing in the United States: October 1996*. Washington: U.S. Immigration and Naturalization Service.

Warren, Robert, and Jeffrey S. Passel. 1987. "A Count of the Uncountable: Estimates of Undocumented Aliens Counted in the 1980 United States Census." *Demography* 24(3): 375–94.

Waters, Mary C. 1990. *Ethnic Options: Choosing Identities in America*. Berkeley: University of California Press.

———. 1999. *Black Identities: West Indian Immigrant Dreams and American Realities*. New York and Cambridge, Mass.: Russell Sage Foundation and Harvard University Press.

———. 2000. "Immigration, Intermarriage, and the Challenges of Measuring Racial/Ethnic Identities." *American Journal of Public Health* 90(1): 1735–37.

Weil, Alan, and Kenneth Finegold. 2002. *Welfare Reform: The Next Act*. Washington, D.C.: Urban Institute Press.

Weintraub, Sidney. 1997a. "Nafta at Three: A Progress Report." Washington, D.C.: Center for Strategic and International Studies.

———. 1997b. "U.S. Foreign Policy and Mexican Immigration." In *At the Crossroads: Mexico Immigration and U.S. Policy*, edited by Frank D. Bean, R. O. de la Garza, B. R. Roberts, and S. Weintraub. Lanham, Md.: Rowman & Littlefield.

Welch, Finis, ed. 2001. *The Causes and Consequences of Increasing Inequality*. Vol. 2. Chicago: University of Chicago Press.

White, Michael J., and Gayle Kaufman. 1997. "Language Usage, Social Capital, and School Completion Among Immigrants and Native-Born Ethnic Groups." *Social Science Quarterly* 78(2): 385–98.

White, Michael J., and Sharon Sassler. 2000. "Judging Not Only by Color: Ethnicity, Nativity, and Neighborhood Attainment." *Social Science Quarterly* 81(4): 997–1013.

Williams, Kim. 2001. "Boxed In: The United States Multiracial Movement." Ph.D. diss., Cornell University.

Wilson, Kenneth L., and Alejandro Portes. 1980. "Immigrant Enclaves: An Analysis of the Labor Market Experiences of Cubans in Miami." *American Journal of Sociology* 86(2): 295–319.

Wilson, William Julius. 1980. *The Declining Significance of Race.* 2nd ed. Chicago: University of Chicago Press.

———. 1987. *The Truly Disadvantaged: The Inner City, the Underclass, and Public Policy.* Chicago: University of Chicago Press.

———. 1996. *When Work Disappears: The World of the New Urban Poor.* New York: Alfred A. Knopf.

Wise, Donald E. 1974. "The Effect of the Bracero on Agricultural Production in California." *Economic Inquiry* 12(4): 267–77.

Woodrow, Karen A., Jeffrey S. Passel, and Robert Warren. 1987. "Preliminary Estimates of Undocumented Immigration to the United States, 1980–1986: Analysis of the June 1986 Current Population Survey." Paper presented at the Annual Meeting of the American Statistical Association, San Francisco (August 12).

Wright, Lawrence. 1994. "One Drop of Blood." *The New Yorker*, July 25, pp. 46–54.

Wrigley, Julia. 1997. "Immigrant Women as Child Care Providers." In *Immigrant Entrepreneurs and Immigrant Absorption in the United States and Israel*, edited by I. H. Light and R. Isralowitz. Aldershot, U.K., and Brookfield, Vt.: Ashgate.

Xie, Yu, and Kimberly Goyette. 1997. "The Racial Identification of Biracial Children with One Asian Parent: Evidence from the 1990 Census." *Social Forces* 76(2): 547–70.

Yang, Philip Q. 1995. *Post-1965 Immigration to the United States: Structural Determinants.* Westport, Conn.: Praeger.

Yinger, J. Milton. 1994. *Ethnicity: Source of Strength? Source of Conflict?* Albany, N.Y.: State University of New York Press.

Zhou, Min. 1999. "Segmented Assimilation: Issues, Controversies, and Recent Research on the New Second Generation." In *The Handbook of International Migration*, edited by Charles Hirschman, Josh DeWind, and Philip Kasinitz. New York: Russell Sage Foundation.

Zhou, Min, and Carl L. Bankston. 1998. *Growing Up American: How Vietnamese Children Adapt to Life in the United States.* New York: Russell Sage Foundation.

Zhou, Min, and John R. Logan. 1989. "Returns on Human Capital in Ethnic Enclaves: New York City's Chinatown." *American Sociological Review* 54(5): 809–20.

Zimmermann, Wendy, and Karen C. Tumlin. 1999. "Patchwork Policies: State Assistance for Immigrants Under Welfare Reform." Report. Washington, D.C.: The Urban Institute.

Zitner, Aaron. 2001. "Immigrant Tally Doubles in Census." *Los Angeles Times*, March 10, p. 1.

Zolberg, Aristide R. 1992. "Response to Crisis: Refugee Policy in the United States and Canada." In *Immigration, Language, and Ethnicity: Canada and the United States*, edited by B. R. Chiswick. Washington, D.C.: AEI Press.

———. 1999. "Matters of State: Theorizing Immigration Policy." In *The Handbook of International Migration*, edited by Charles Hirschman, Josh DeWind, and Philip Kasinitz. New York: Russell Sage Foundation.

═ Index ═

Numbers in **boldface** refer to figures and tables.